MY NEW WORLD

by Ernest Dimnet 1869-

AUTHOR OF

THE ART OF THINKING

AND

MY OLD WORLD

SIMON AND SCHUSTER

NEW YORK · 1937

CONTENTS

v

PART THREE

AMERICA

vii

Part One

PARIS

I

READERS of a previous volume, *My Old World*, may remember how a twist of French politics in 1902 suddenly reacted on my life. I had been teaching seven years at Lille University. I was happy there with friends, books, a fine collection of works of art close at hand, and with a wealth of provincial leisure which allowed for frequent trips to Paris or London. I was launched on my literary career, both in France and in England. In short, I was contented, only fighting the foolish wishes which human restlessness will produce. Moreover, I am averse from changes. I get exaggeratedly attached even to inanimate things which somehow appeal to me almost as much as animals do. I cannot take final leave of an old watch, an old bicycle, even an old stump of pencil which have served me faithfully. I pay them furtive visits as I do to the streets I love. So I expected the wrench which accompanied my separation from Lille.

But I also felt the confidence which comes to most men of thirty when they are moderately successful, and if Lille was my sentimental, Paris was my spiritual home. For years I had visited it frequently, every few weeks. I had many friends there; I knew that my future must be smoother with the chances which a great city obviously offered, and probably there had been lurking in my dreams the hope that some unexpected circumstance might force upon me the separation which I could not have arranged for myself.

Besides, I was proud in advance of College Stanislas to which I was going to be attached. Two of the idols of my youth, Lacordaire, the illustrious orator, and Gratry, the famous philosopher, had been connected with it, and, as reading and travelling gradually acquainted me with the world, I had come to the realization that no Catholic school in Europe was so deservedly renowned. In the early years of the twentieth century few, if any, French writers equalled Anatole France or Edmond Rostand in *éclat*. Not only they but seven other members of the French Academy were former pupils of Stanislas. The democratic movement known as *Le Sillon* had also originated there, and although Rome was soon after to deal summarily with it, it appeared at the time as an extraordinarily successful return to the brotherly spirit of Christianity.

I can never forget the morning of October first, 1903, one of those perfect Autumn forenoons which seem to put Time to sleep. I had arrived the evening before. I spent most of the morning on a warm bench in the college "park," an exquisite garden. The students were not to return for two more days and the stillness of the buildings and courtyards answered what I felt in myself, the repose which comes after a rather difficult change has been successfully made. I never remember that forenoon without imagining that beneath its apparent sleepiness lay the secret of happiness which we everlastingly wish to formulate but which dodges us like quicksilver every time we want to put our finger upon it.

The windows of M. Pautonnier, the headmaster, opened on the place where I sat. I could see him slowly pacing his rooms, breviary in hand, and every now and then he smiled at me over his book. Towards ten o'clock he made signs that he was going to join me, and soon after he was guiding me through the maze of rambling courtyards and snow-white, almost African-looking buildings which are the characteristic of the College. There was no beauty anywhere except in the park we had just left and in the historic Pavillon Belgiojoso where I was soon to live and to which I shall revert. But as we went up a dark stairway leading to the chapel M. Pautonnier turned on a light and, to my astonishment, facing a glass case in which lay recumbent a garishly painted statue of Saint Charles Borromeo, I saw a replica—not a copy—of the sublime *Christ Entombed* by Holbein which I had admired several times in the Basle Museum. I expressed my surprise that this masterpiece should be left in the dark on a drafty staircase. "The Marists," the headmaster explained, "they were holy men and great educators, but they had no taste."

A few more steps and we were in front of the chapel door. It could not be opened. A white ribbon with two scarlet seals joined the two valves and gave the impression of an impassable barrier. "The Government's seals," M. Pautonnier said. "We shall not be able to use the chapel till we have bought back the property which the legislators of our country have stolen from the Marist Fathers." I knew what he meant, of course. I had written a number of articles about the anti-religious campaign and against the Confiscation Act which seemed to be finally summed up in this white ribbon with two red wax blotches. A Prime Minister, M. Waldeck-Rousseau, had promised authorization to such religious orders as would apply for it. His successor, the notorious Combes, refusing authorization to all, coolly confiscated their property. I had been a champion of the republican *régime* till this dastardly action showed me what the atheistic French Masonry parading as Democracy could do. From that day on I was full of misgivings and ceased to believe in the virtue of political *régimes*. Montesquieu is only too right in saying that Democracies should be built on virtue, but George Washingtons are scarce.

As our visit drew to an end, walking out of the Gym which would do credit even to an American college pampered by rival angels, we found ourselves in front of a high and long wall draped with thick manes of ivy. A tiny door in this wall aroused my curiosity. "I want you to go in there by yourself," the headmaster said, "you are sure to like what you will see." In fact, on the other side of the little door was one of those improbable nooks which, even after half a lifetime of exploration, you still discover every now and then in Paris. Between hundreds of pots

of chrysanthemums, which a slow-moving gardener was arrang-
ing in straight lines as for a military review, and a few dreamy
trees, stood a country-house, an absolute country-house, which
seemed to have been left only a moment before by its eighteenth-
century owner. "The infirmary for contagious cases," the gardener told me, but it was seldom occupied except by the nurses.
There was a narrow court in front, and from it a little remnant
of a street, paved and curbed and complete, seemed to be boldly
starting on its way across Montparnasse, all glare and noise,
but was brought up sharp by a sullen wall: places like dreams
should not be wandering into the vulgar world. I loved that relic
and often revisited it later. It gave me the impression of the past
much more than even medieval buildings five or six centuries
older, but where the flow of life has never been arrested as it
was here.

Two days later the students returned and my new life began
in earnest. There was a complete division at Stanislas between
the Faculty and the staff in charge of the administration. The
latter were mostly priests who had within the last three or four
months replaced the banished Marists. They had maintained the
traditions of their predecessors. The Marists were a religious
order of Alsatian origin who had decided ideas about education:
they believed in freedom, but they also believed in thoroughness,
and both tendencies appeared clearly to me from the first.

Though the College was emphatically a Catholic school, no
religious exercise apart from Sunday mass was compulsory.
Many boys chose to go to chapel every morning, but they were
not expected to do so. The same with the yearly retreats habitual
in religious institutions. A boy, and not the teacher, said the
usual prayer to the Holy Spirit before and after classes. The consequence was that religion was taken extremely seriously by the
students and I never saw a trace of flippancy in any of them.
Elsewhere—quite decidedly in the school in which I had been
educated—religious instruction was left to not very brilliant

prefects. Here the Marists, and M. Pautonnier even more, insisted on the five chaplains being not only first-rate specialists, but in possession of the same academic degrees as the other teachers. It took me several years to realize that the prize most coveted by the boys was given for sacred studies. Non-Catholic students were naturally not expected to compete, but one year a young Monod (of the well-known Protestant dynasty) who took all the other prizes insisted on also getting that one, and he carried it away in triumph.

Thoroughness appeared in the importance given to study. Dismissal for laziness, which is the test, was not infrequent. The Marists had invented a system, still maintained, whereby every mark given in class was converted into "points" which really were the College currency. Studious boys were affluent, lazy ones were penurious. With a given number of points you could buy your Sunday outing, a monthly play-day or a day or two extra-vacation at Christmas or Easter. So was virtue rewarded while remissness looked on. Towards 1910 I found this system violently assailed in an English book written by some lady who declared it immoral, contrary to honour and likely to develop acquisitiveness. This lady was unmarried and had probably had little to do with children. Like all theorists on education who have not been educators themselves she had a vague conception of ideal schoolboys and wrote in accordance with it. I, who saw this system in use during twenty years, never found it at fault. It seemed to me a good preparation for real life. The boys did not judge it differently: they were happy when they were flush of "points," a bit blue when they were broke, but their disappointment was not unwholesome. It could only have appeared so to people imbued with the notion that schoolboys should constantly lie on beds of roses. Our students would have protested against the disappearance of the "points," as English boys resent theories which would deprive them of the schoolmaster's cane.

In the same way Stanislas boys used to make endless fun of the bare marble tables on which a Napoleonic tradition, only subsisting in Paris schools, made them eat. But when I described

to them the luxurious dining-halls of American schools those
scions of refined families made disgusted faces and shrugged
their young shoulders. They knew that before sports had been
introduced, or re-introduced into French schools, their fathers
and grandfathers had been made manly by rough refectories and
uncomfortable dormitories preparing them for barracks hardly
more austere. And no doubt their fathers and grandfathers also
believed in Spartan indifference to petty comforts. Most boys
were the sons of alumni. General Gouraud once told me that
he and his brother were the fourth generation at the College.

Our Faculty consisted of about eighty, all laymen with the
exception of four or five priests. Before the anti-clerical spell
which made the years 1901–1905 such a trying period in France,
the professors were lent to the College by the Minister of Education on the suggestion of the headmaster. This compromise, the
only one of its kind I ever heard of, worked perfectly. Professors
felt entirely free, and the administration of the College never had
to part with any of them for abusing their freedom. During many
years M. Paul Desjardins—the well-known initiator of the
"Spiritual Decades" at Pontigny—taught the fifth form. He was
the noblest kind of Tolstoist, but not a practising Catholic. His
influence on the students was as great as it still is on the wisdom-
seekers who attend the "Decades," yet it was never hinted that
he diverted any boy from his belief. In 1902 an obscure deputy
denounced to the Chamber the Stanislas arrangement as a dangerous concession to clericalism and it was voted out. One third
of the professors preferred forfeiting their claim to a Government pension by staying on; the others had to be replaced either
by volunteers from the *lycées* who were already sure of their
pension, or—in anticipation of what the late Miss Thomas did
with such success at Bryn Mawr—by young *agrégés* just out of
the Ecole Normale Supérieure.

Abbé Pautonnier managed to bring together a faculty that
was in no wise inferior to the former one. The names of Doumic,
Dimier, the Tharauds, Baruzi, Jacques Maritain, Lasserre,
Jacques Rivière, Baudin, Thérive and, on the scientific side, of

Humbert, Biehler and Camman would do credit to any University.

Three or four hundred out of our fifteen hundred students were being prepared for Government Schools like the Ecole Polytechnique, Saint-Cyr (the French West Point) or the Naval College. This accounts for the fact that so many Stanislas alumni belonged to the army, and that no less than seven hundred were killed during the first year of the Great War. Candidates to those schools naturally devoted most of their time to mathematics. But, in spite of that fact, it can be said that the College was pre-eminently literary. This is so true that nobody there seemed to remember, until I discovered it, that one of the greatest astronomers of the nineteenth century, Leverrier, had once been a member of the faculty. The trustees of the College were not retired rich merchants somehow interested in education. It was almost amusing to see that their list was limited to Ferdinand Brunetière, then the greatest French critic, Paul Bourget, the greatest novelist, and Marquis de Ségur and Marquis de Vogüé, both of them literary marquises and members of the French Academy. These men took their duties seriously and were frequently seen at the College. Brunetière was a strange apparition with his attenuated body, parchment face, dead eyes and a dying cigarette everlastingly hanging from his lip, but an indomitable will-power imparted to his cadaverous face a weird life which made one shiver. Brunetière's criticisms of the lectures of those of us whose classes he attended were unforgettable.

Ségur and Vogüé were first-rate business-men, as the soberer class of aristocrats not infrequently are. The year after my arrival bills of sale were posted up on the College doors by the Government: the time had come for paying the robbers whatever ransom they demanded. I was head of the English department and, at the time, I employed a British assistant, or reader, a non-Catholic, whose sense of fair play, added to the usual English tendency to doubt unpleasant realities till they become crushing facts, had so far prevented him from believing that a religious persecution was going on. I was returning from a stroll with him when we found the official white posters nailed on our main door. The young man's amazement and sudden indignation were an almost amusing contrast to his former scepticism. Four million francs had to be found within a few days to make our own property once more our own, but I knew that M. de Ségur and M. de Vogüé had long before obtained definite promises from friends of the College: in twenty-four hours the money was put up. I have always felt inclined to think that the reputation of intellectual people for lack of practicality is a figment of people, far on the wrong side of intellectuality, who look for comfort in what certainly is an invidious fallacy. Voltaire and Victor Hugo must have left their bankers dazzled and wondering more than once.

Most of my colleagues answered to the definition of a French professor as a man who has written, is writing, or will soon write a book. Few are the English, or especially the American masters of whom the same can be said, because the phrase, in scholastic advertisements, stipulating that "masters are expected to take part in the life of the school" really means that they will have little or no time for themselves. We only taught an hour and a half or two hours a day, after which we did what we pleased. The time indeed was not far back when a *lycée* professor was not supposed to know his students by name. So the tradition of the teacher supremely interested in literature and interested in little else was kept up at Stanislas.

This attitude deserves the criticisms to which lopsidedness is always open. The lack of balance between ideas and realities, between the intellect and the will-power so often noticeable in the French is due to this. I believe I have been annoyed by it more than anybody else, for living part of each year abroad I have gradually become accustomed to regard ideas as the foundation of action instead of as an end in themselves. But, on the other hand, what strikes foreign observers as "French brilliance" is largely due to that cult of the intellect as independent of anything practical. It is a fine thing in the life of the world that there should exist places where a man is sure to bring a glow on the faces of schoolboys by merely alluding to the interior development of privileged beings, the poets, by regarding inspiration as the supreme human experience, and by preferring what the half-forgotten word "glory" still connotes to mere bread-and-butter advantages.

Our boys were used to the ideal of men who, being writers, habitually bore in mind literary perfection. When an essay of theirs got 58 or 60 they were overjoyed at the exceptional piece of luck, but they were not led to imagine that their achievement could not be bettered—as they would have been in schools where it rains ninety-fives so that the very ordinary best of a boy comes to be regarded by him as perfection.

In the same way I never read with the students anything but literature. The knowledge of the English language was not proposed to them as an end but as a means of getting in touch with masterpieces. The notion that any intellectual result will be secured by the possession of a language obtained through a chatty book chosen because it does not go beyond the possibilities of everyday parlance is a complete fallacy. Polyglot worldlings obtain no more culture from the two or three languages in which they can air platitudes than is possessed by polyglot waiters at a restaurant in Venice. Words are only words.

I used to prepare some twenty students for the stiff entrance examinations of the Naval College. People were surprised sometimes that I read Thackeray's *Vanity Fair* with these future seamen. I answered that my dodge was simple enough. The book is irresistible. I always found that the boys read it through in their free times long before the Christmas holiday. By that time their vocabulary was ample, for the English of Thackeray somehow slips into the mind and stays there. (Much less the English of Dickens and not at all the exquisite language of Goldsmith.) All I had to do was, just before the examination, to dictate to the boys a list of the naval terms which we could find in two or three chapters of Marryat and a few more of Conrad's. One

evening, walking through the College with Hilaire Belloc, I told
him of my success with *Vanity Fair*. He seemed a bit shocked.
"I never thought of *Vanity Fair* as a school-book," he said. "It
is not," I replied, "I never read *school*-books with my classes.
But observe that *Vanity Fair* is in all the school-libraries of
England." "I never read it," Belloc went on. "I know," I said,
"your novelist is Homer and you seem to turn him to pretty
good account, too." Belloc laughed. That same evening I found
to my surprise that he did not have to be guided through the
intricate passage-ways of the College. "Why! I was at school
here when I was sixteen," he said, "I was one of that very Naval
class you were speaking of." Belloc frequently surprises one.

I had also an hour a week with students of eighteen or nineteen preparing for the Ecole Polytechnique. The poor lads were
crammed full of mathematics and I pitied them sincerely. I
made up my mind to keep them entirely from anything suggesting examinations or even practicality. I would dictate to them
every Saturday one of the shorter poems of Browning or Kipling,
both of them poets who while pretending to use only the vocabulary of prose, manage all the time to find their way to the most
intimate depths of the soul. How those boys did love them! Yet
they are not always easy, those lyrical narratives with their every-
day words made magnetic by elusive rhythms and the equivalent
of which cannot be found without patient effort. Sometimes we
would be at it a long time before being finally rewarded. This
mental work went on while the little girls in an adjoining boarding-school practiced their scales just on the other side of the
partition. During long minutes the young fingers would go
listlessly up and down the soulless gamut, but, all of a sudden,
a passage to the minor key seemed to open a mysterious door
onto infinity. So with us as we hit at last on the syllables which
the English poet would have preferred had he written in French.
I sometimes meet the officers or engineers, now men of forty,
who sat with me through those thoughtful winter evenings in the
warm class-room. They have not forgotten them any more than
I have.

Over-intellectual as too much literature must inevitably make our boys, hampered as they were, though seemingly guided, by principles of criticism which they could not criticize, and unduly respectful of genius which had not been associated with character, they were not, for all that, highbrows. They were ahead of most other French schools in sports, especially fencing, and I remember the surprise of my friend, Dr. Thayer, of Saint Mark's School, when he saw, being trained in our Gym for a race, such a superb young athlete as neither of us thought Paris could produce. And even little fellows were manly. Once I saw in the park a group of four or five excitedly discussing something. "What is the matter?"—"*Monsieur, on ne peut plus se battre!* (fighting has just been forbidden!)"—"Nonsense! who said that?"—"The Censor!"—"Count on the future! such a cruel ruling is sure to be short-lived."

They were sincere, too. One year, in a class of juniors which I had taken in charge to try a few pedagogic experiments, I asked a question: "What is the most intelligent nation in Europe?" —"The French!" the whole class answered by acclamation. —"Nobly answered! No hesitation! Splendid! Now suppose that this class represents the French nation: look around and find what would be the proportion of really intelligent people in it." All faces turned around, eagerly taking stock of the amount of intelligence displayed in the room. They soon reappeared, cross and disgusted. "One in ten!" one boy said, "three or four in the thirty of us! Nothing! Which is the most intelligent nation in Europe, then?"—"The most modest," I answered.— "There isn't any."—"Only too true," I said, "let's try to be the one."

Another peculiarity was that, in spite of too much literature, Stanislas boys knew contemporary history and political geography with a perception of concrete details which would have naturally belonged to the sons of political English families but surprised me in my students, even in those who were planning a naval career. Whenever I had to touch on an international question in my letters to the London *Saturday Review* I would

start those boys on the issue and found many a time that their
suggestions were useful. I felt great respect for the three or four
of my colleagues who taught them how to read history into the
map, modest men, these teachers, but who seemed to know the
whole planet.

What I have said about education at College Stanislas is the
result of many years' experience which, naturally, I could not
have anticipated when I first arrived in Paris. All I knew was
that the College was famous and it was an honour to belong
to it. After the first shock of change was over I discovered I was
not as happy as I had imagined I should be. My Lille friendships and associations returned in full force upon me, and there
was little to take their place. The many people I knew in Paris,
from the Mérodes to Angellier, were still in the country. Most
of my fellow-professors were married men and only appeared
at the College to lecture. Twenty years later there were still a
dozen whose faces had become familiar but whose names I did
not know. They looked busy, happy, self-contented. It was only
after six months that, during the Easter vacation, six of us happening to be at the same time in Rome, we had a little social
gathering at the Café San Carlo in the Corso. Dimier was there
and I marvelled at his extraordinary knowledge of Italian art.
But we soon dispersed and nothing came of that contact when
we were back in Paris.

Even those of my colleagues who, like me, preferred living in
College, were not easily transformed into friends. I had been
used to Northern characteristics which I might occasionally
mock but which habit had taught me to like. My new colleagues
came from all over France and I had to get accustomed to their
local, as well as to their individual, peculiarities. There were
Midi men who might be either ebullient or, on the contrary,
more self-contained than any Fleming ever was. And there were
Bretons, *extremi hominum*, who did not look or act like anybody
from any other province I knew, and were subject to Irish-like

fits of melancholy. There were cold and brilliant Lorrainers of
the type made popular by M. Poincaré. There were five or six
Alsatians too, and I think I liked them the best. I admired their
religion, their common sense, their humour, their irrepressible
attachment to France, and I enjoyed their curious hybridism as
Alsaciens de Paris. Nobody seemed to own Paris as they did.

Big cities are the worst places to be homesick in. One is un-
forgivable for being bored in a town full of books, of works
of art, of the monuments of the past, and where beauty seems
to beckon you from every corner. But it only makes you feel
worse to be unforgivable. The Luxembourg Garden is not five
minutes' walk from College Stanislas. We used to have lunch
at the old-fashioned hour of half-past eleven. Shortly after twelve
we could be in the Luxembourg, and at that hour, with no children raising clouds of dust and hardly a dozen stragglers in
the avenues, one actually had the place to oneself. The Luxembourg is no ordinary city park. Poets in all languages have said
that it has no peer anywhere, and its power over the imagination
baffles expression. Antiquated parallels between English parks
and *jardins à la française* are only misleading. There is no effort
here to suggest nature, no matter how disciplined, nor do we
feel like extolling the art of the landscapist who designed it.
What one is conscious of in that park is harmony. The avenues,
terraces, flights of steps and parterres seem to be dancing a
grand ballet into which anybody with a soul is invited. It is
difficult to resist the promise of happiness which emanates from
it all.

Yet I did. I understand people who refuse to visit fortunate
regions where everything speaks of beauty and joy unless they
feel sentimentally attuned to them. In October when I began to
pay it a daily visit, the Luxembourg is at its most beautiful. For
the gardeners who serve it, after toying through the summer
with all sorts of delicate shades of colour, suddenly, in August,
seem to become intoxicated with Delacroix' passion for high-
strung lyrical reds and the grand parterre runs riot with scarlet
plants. Often this feast of rich colours lasts late into October

and even its decline has a grandeur to which only a Ravel's music could do justice. Yet, many times, sitting there, conscious of all this, and conscious too that everything in me refused it, I wished myself miles away.

I am ashamed to confess also that, during the three or four years preceding my fortieth, I was not so interested in my work as I had been before, and became again later. I feel certain that if the tradition of simple but effective methods were restored so that debates about educational systems might not disturb the minds of inexperienced teachers, the young instructor, the man of twenty-five to thirty, would be found to be the best. He possesses more knowledge than is necessary, he has enthusiasm, and, instead of feeling above his occupation, he is conscious of being matured by it and of gaining as much as his pupils do. Add that if his belief in his own mission is strong enough to radiate from him he appeals to the young more than he will ever do afterwards, when instead of being Professor So-and-So he hardens into the unmagnetic position of professor of this or that. I had a method—in which I still believe—I was a good disciplinarian, I hated to bore anybody, and I was touched by the infinite trustfulness of my students, so that they never were conscious of being neglected; but when they now remind me laughingly that I was frequently late for lectures, the words have for me a sting which they do not suspect, and I feel like apologizing to the boys long buried in these men of forty-five.

I fought my ennui by the usual methods. I took trips to Trélon, Lille and London, I went to Bruges for All Saints' Day and intoxicated myself with chimes. But my heart remained empty and I regretted Lille where, however, I would not have liked to return for good, till, early in December, Paris unexpectedly seemed to fill again with people whom I had known long enough to be glad of their return and invitations poured. For Parisians are hospitable, and it is no fault of theirs if strangers, especially foreign visitors who say they are not, will not give them a chance, or intimidate them by expectations which many French families are not in a position to satisfy.

I soon felt that I had not been mistaken in believing that Paris could be my real home. It is true that the first indefinable whiff or strange beauty emanating from the town's multitudinous visages hardly ever returned after I settled down, but peaceful habit is also a charm, and if I had to be uprooted from Paris now the wrench would be worse than any I experienced in my younger days.

Paris is a gigantic book which few people will read, although it is opened for all. The display of beauty, of quaintness, of endlessly varied human scenes, from the French Academy to the *Foire à la Ferraille*, cannot be fully appreciated in a lifetime. The chief appeal to me has always been the human one. I do not like my friends to say—in a phrase too worn-out not to be objectionable—that "I like people." For I have always enjoyed solitude. As a boy I loved our Trélon forest and preferred lonely places, and now I am always grateful when I can be by myself on an ocean voyage or crossing the wide American continent. Yet, I must admit that keen interest in men and women, in what they are, in what they think and feel, is natural to me. Even in the Louvre I am as conscious of the living faces brightened up by the pictures as I am of the pictures themselves. I listen to what people say at art-shows and innumerable disappointments have not killed my curiosity. Strangers write asking permission to call. Busy as I have become, and in spite of experiences which ought not to make me over-sanguine, I still regard these visits as an adventure. I never stand passive or listless in a group, whether it be a gathering of literary men or a knot of workers discussing their affairs. I invariably expect people to be understanding, and I always hope to find them happy. There is nothing I enjoy so much as the give and take of the best European conversation, the chance one has in a party of six or seven to hear something worth while. Every time I have that experience and think of the hundreds of thousands who can never hope for it, because so-called civilization only allows them a narrow outlook on the world, I feel that none of us has a right to intellectual happiness unless he makes some effort to initiate less fortunate people into it.

During the first six or seven years of my Paris life, I renounced my bookish past and, while living intellectually, I felt as if it were enough just to live. I wrote, it is true, hundreds of articles for the reviews, but I wrote them as if they had been mere letters dealing with what I heard or saw. I felt strongly disinclined to write books. The headmaster of Stanislas who kept a friendly eye on my development would sometimes expostulate with me, thinking Paris proved a little too much for my resistance. "By this time you should have at least three or four volumes to your name," he would say. And I would reply: "What's in a book? What is a book? I live constantly with people who write books. Are they different for writing them? And are not their books mere pretences, as they mostly consist of reprinted articles exactly similar to my own? Better be what one really is than appear to be something else."

So I went on enjoying the best that Paris offered me, and enjoying it deliciously. For the man of thirty-five is free from the phantasm which harasses the man of sixty; he does not watch the clock, he does not think he has to hurry if he wants to finish this or that, and his ambitions have not yet entered into a league with his conscience to make him husband every tyrannical minute. I read what I pleased, lots of it; I went to plays, to art expositions, to concerts, to the Chamber of Deputies, to every Convention where I was invited; I travelled to most parts of Europe; I paid week-end visits to dear old towns not too far from Paris and enjoyed their rooky cathedrals, their quiet museums and their platane promenades; I loved the countryside of the Ile-de-France, so provincial yet so refined by its rich past, so interesting by the contrast between its graceful landscapes and the sturdy ruggedness of its village churches. An intelligent friend accompanied me: one summer evening we discovered an enchanted spot, an apparently deserted garden where three roses, by an old bench, seemed to burn like lamps in the waning light. But, above all, I was social, immensely appreciative of good conversation yet not over-eclectic in my choices and discarding nothing that could lend me information or give me pleasure worth the name.

Casual visitors could not have suspected that College Stanislas was an active centre of information, a veritable mart of news, for it had the semi-monastic look habitual to French schools and it stood in one of the quietest neighborhoods of Paris. Five or six large convents occupy most of this section and, before the boulevard Raspail pushed its way through it, its most busy thoroughfare was the rue Vavin which is only a village high street. Of the convents we knew as little as if they had been inaccessible *chaouias* in mysterious Morocco. There was one, not sixty yards away, the name of which I do not know even to-day and the gate of which I saw open for the first time less than two years ago. There, unsuspected by everybody, lies a deep garden, surrounded by *charmilles*, which would seem likely enough in a provincial capital like Dijon or Bourges but is improbable in Paris. Even nearer, and, in fact, just over the way, what had been the Petit Séminaire was now a retreat-house of the Sulpitians, and that too was mysterious. Almost every day I met, trotting back to it, a little old priest whose head, apparently too heavy for his body, kept him walking in a hurried frightened way. After two or three years somebody said to me that this was M. de Foville. He had had a scientific career before taking orders, and now was famous for an uncompromising sincerity of which amusing instances were quoted. Another Sulpitian, whom he was visiting on his deathbed, said to him: "I had no idea that death could be made so welcome."—"Don't say that," Foville answered, "you've read it in a book." The old gentleman himself

died shortly after I was told of his identity, and *he* bequeathed
to his *confrères* a dying speech which certainly never could be
read in a book. The Sulpitian student who was attending him,
seeing his vitality ebbing away one Thursday evening, said to
him: "Would it not be a kindness of Providence, Sir, if you were
to die on Friday, the same day as our Saviour?"—"Monsieur,"
the old man answered, "si ce n'est pas vendredi ce sera samedi
(Saturday will be just as good as Friday.)"

The quietness of this Notre-Dame-des-Champs quarter attracted writers and artists. I saw many times Paul Fort, the
"prince of poets," lunching at the *Closerie des Lilas* with his
pretty girl of a daughter. Almost every day too Huysmans would
be leaving the parish church when I arrived there: his flayed-
looking face suggested a sublime Flemish horror in one of the
less frequented Bruges galleries and seemed out of place in Paris.
In comparison, Mézieres and Boissier shuffling along the rue
Bara were insignificant celebrities.

The true characteristic of the quarter appeared when you
looked at its position on the map. Nearby, the Latin quarter
is a bee-hive of activity in comparison with it; so is the St.
Sulpice neighbourhood where professional men abound, and,
on the western side, the Faubourg Saint-Germain conceals its
hauteur behind studiously unpretending outbuildings. From
these three quarters came our students, and from them their
fathers had also come, and as our alumni always seemed exceptionally faithful to their *alma mater* the least echoes of the
literary or political worlds were perceived in the stillness of
our courtyards.

After a year I was moved from the uninteresting flat which I
had been given at first to another, full of colour and character,
in the Pavillon Belgiojoso. This Pavillon was the architectural
gem of the College. Even twelve years after leaving it, I have
to feast my eyes every now and then on its perfect proportions.

It is a classical building, a cross between the smaller kind of château and the more elegant Paris mansion, the central idea of which was evidently a large niche with a statue facing the entrance portico and concealing the staircase. The wainscoted salon, rather ill-treated by the Marists, and a few oval rooms are perfect examples of eighteenth-century elegance. This little masterpiece is only one of many which the infatuation of a rich *seigneur* or financier produced for the caprice of a courtesan and which were appropriately called *folies*. The lady in this case was none other than Madame du Barry who, no doubt, dictated her wishes to the architect, for this mansion strikingly resembles the exquisite château where she spent her summers at Louveciennes.

After the Revolution this Pavillon and its park were repeatedly sold and bought, always for a song, by a succession of proprietors till one more remarkable than the others gave it the name it still bears. This was the famous Princess Christina Belgiojoso who appears in the *Encyclopaedia Britannica* under the illustrious name of Trivulzi. She was a Milanese who, like all the Italian intelligentzia of the early nineteenth century, could not endure the Austrian yoke which had weighed on her ancestors, was caught in a conspiracy and was banished from her country. She went to Paris where, in a few years, her beauty and intellectual brilliance gave her an even more prominent position than that which she had occupied in her own city.

Distinguished men crowded her salon and the seductive oval rooms. Several felt her fascination beyond mere intellectual admiration. Alfred de Musset, shortly after his separation from George Sand, was one of her suitors. He was rejected, felt as provoked as a disappointed humming-bird and, poet-like, vented his irritation in a curious little piece entitled *On a Dead Woman*. He intended this to be a murderous epigram, but, as he wrote it, the fascination of the lady and the self-pity of his own mood produced lyricalness, so that poor Musset curses the fair one much too harmoniously, and, as it were, to the accompaniment of a guitar.

These stanzas begin:

> *Elle était belle si la Nuit*
> *Qui dort en la sombre chapelle*
> *Où Michel-Ange a fait son lit*
> *Immobile peut être belle.*

And end, to a grand but disdainful rhythm:

> *Elle est morte et n'a point vécu,*
> *Elle faisait semblant de vivre;*
> *De ses mains est tombé le livre*
> *Dans lequel elle n'a rien lu.*

One afternoon, strolling by the Seine, I chanced on a four-volume apology of Christianity written in facile French by Princess Belgiojoso, perhaps in the very room which now was my study. It seemed to me that this lady had read in the book of life a good deal more than peevish Musset would admit.

One of the windows of my study opened onto a wide balcony from which I could survey the whole quarter and see the modest house where Sainte-Beuve wrote most of his *Lundis*. From there too I could hear the deep rumour which the life of Paris exhales day and night. When I was at a loss for the subject of my weekly letter to the London *Saturday Review* I would step out onto that balcony, listen to the murmur rising from the three quarters where I knew scores of people, and I seldom stood there more than two or three minutes before a few words remembered from some recent conversation provided me with my subject. It only seemed natural when I made a selection from those letters to entitle it: *From a Paris Balcony*.

A smaller window, so high that I never shut it at all, gave on one of those little farmhouses which the mercilessness of urbanism will sometimes overlook. Cackling and crowing were heard all the time through that little window. Round the corner the song of a caged blackbird always stopping his *marseillaise* three syllables before the end bespoke the presence of a cobbler. In fact, four or five cottages—since then bought over by the College and now destroyed—stood there, exactly like village cottages in

bean or potato-growing gardens. Children abounded. It was a
ronde of them that I heard one summer day singing:

Un jour l'amour nous blesse

to such a mocking rhythm that these children seemed to express
the pathetic experience of old age. As for the clucking chickens,
they gave me material for the only English short story I ever
published, *The Revenge of Chanticleer,* printed in *The Atlantic
Monthly* a few years after I began to contribute to American
magazines.

I shall always be grateful to College Stanislas for giving me
what I had consistently craved but especially needed in that
period of early maturity, viz., enough contacts to keep me wide
awake, enough freedom to enjoy them, and enough discipline
not to be carried away by them. Angellier, on several occasions,
said to me: "What a good cove Stanislas is for you to be an-
chored in!" The metaphor was right. I could feel the ocean of
Paris life offering its innumerable chances to me, but the rules
of community-life, the long silent hours commented upon by
the bell, the very admixture of worldly elegance and pensiveness
of my Pavillon enabled me to take the best that Parisian life
provided without being overwhelmed by it.

II

I had had, before leaving Lille, a correspondence with Mr.
J. E. Bodley, the author of a book on France which was at the
time as widely noticed as Lord Bryce's *American Commonwealth*. Mr. Bodley had been secretary to Sir Charles Dilke. So
had Sir Henry Austin Lee who, when I arrived in Paris, was
Commercial Attaché at the British Embassy. Mr. Bodley gave
me a letter to him and, when November started city life once
more, I went to the Embassy and presented my letter.

Sir Henry Austin Lee was a tall, handsome, dignified man of
fifty-six. He had had a brilliant career, capturing an Oxford
fellowship at twenty-two, being secretary to no less a person than
Beaconsfield at no less an event than the Congress of Berlin in
1878, and, since 1892, being the real pillar of the Embassy, as
Commercial Attaché till 1906, then—till 1917—as Councillor.
Five or six ambassadors came and went, but he stayed twenty-
five years and made a great place for himself in Paris.

He was an extremely modest man who could have held an
audience spellbound in French as well as in his own language,
but preferred listening. Publishers were after him more than
once. He had known intimately five or six men of capital importance in the history of modern England, and his recollections
of the Berlin Congress alone would have made an invaluable
book, but it was difficult to draw him out. Not that he had more
than his share of English reserve: nobody could be more genial
than he was. When his face passed from its naturally thoughtful
to a smiling expression it became delightfully childlike. And he
enjoyed funny stories: one of a man who heard a queer noise
at the door of his hotel room, opened it, and was confronted by
a lion apparently as surprised as himself; another of a practical
joke staged by Oxford undergraduates pretending to be on a
special embassy from Kabul, and received with great ceremony
by the authorities at Southampton. It was a joy to see Sir Henry
laughing heartily when he said, "So-and-So was the interpreter."
But when you tried to egg him on to details of the international

affairs in which he had been an actor, he relapsed into thoughtfulness, or shrugged his shoulders apologetically. Consciousness
of his own importance annoyed him.

He used to speak of English schools and English scholarship
deprecatingly. "What on earth can be the use of Greek?" he
would ask. More than once I wondered if he had not been unfortunate in his tutors and bore them a grudge for time wasted.
But, one evening in his study, he showed me his Oxford notes
on the Greek plays, and the scholarship displayed in them was
stupendous. The moment he saw that my surprise was making
room for admiration the copy-books disappeared in the drawer
and I never saw them again.

At our first interview he showed me nothing but kindness,
asking many questions about my English contributions, and
inviting me to luncheon the following Sunday which I remember
was November 13th, 1903.

Lady Austin Lee was an American by birth, but she was entirely Europeanized and her French was so fluent and faultless
that it was difficult to realize she was not a Parisian. She was a
Catholic convert. Her interest in religious and charitable works
was well known and made her indifferent to the many gifts—a
superb singing voice among others—for which she was famous.
She was uncompromising in her principles which she asserted
with great courage, but this decision in expressing what was
nearest to her never lost her a friend. She and her husband were
untiring in their kindness and I can never be grateful enough
to them.

I met many interesting people, both French and English, at
their house in the Avenue du Trocadéro. A few appear clearly in
my memory, as usual for subconscious reasons which I should
be at a great loss to explain, for other people whom I ought to
have remembered quite as well are only vague shadows in my
recollection. And even of those whom I remember, only a general
impression, helped by one or two details, generally insignificant,
has subsisted. I see Lady Bertie, the ambassadress, all grace and
fan; Lady Herbert of Lee, whose books I knew, was a perfect

example of English elegance, but her name chiefly recalls the
long black gloves in which she ate, as many women of her age
and class did; Lord Halifax, whom I was to see elsewhere many
times, only left with me in that first interview the impression of
infinitely trustful pure blue eyes.

One Sunday Sir Charles Dilke appeared at luncheon. I knew
he had been that unique thing, an English Republican, and had
been rewarded not only by immense abuse but by the most unjust indifference to his extraordinary ability. Yet nobody looked
less like a martyr or seemed so indifferent to what people might
think of him. He was all naturalness and nonchalance, but out
of his listlessness seemed to fly sparks of his brilliant radicalism.
Sir Henry looked at him all the time with an admixture of amusement and admiration, perhaps with a shade of "what next?"
which interested me as much as Dilke's quiet but high-powered
vitality, or his preferences for French personages whom I mostly
disliked. For English politicians invariably show astonishing
indulgence to ours.

I had another occasion to notice this when Sir Henry Austin
Lee introduced me to Lord Bryce. Like everybody else interested
in America I had consulted many times *The American Commonwealth*, which is not a work of genius but is certainly a mine of
intelligent information, and I was curious to see its author. Sir
Henry had told me: "You will find Bryce a guileless, really *un
peu naif* person." In fact, nobody could be less sophisticated.
It was delightful to find that this great Scotchman, who had
served Britain in the most important posts, had retained the
full burr of Glasgow. He was, at the time, travelling all over
Europe to collect data for his book on Democracy. He had attended several sittings of our Chamber of Deputies and could
not express strongly enough his admiration for French eloquence. "The rank and file in your Chamber," he said, "talk as
well as our front-benchers." I said to him, in words which, on
a later occasion, I heard Lord Dunsany use in speaking of the

Irish: "Yes, we can talk, we all can talk, but tra il dire e il fare
c'è di mezzo il mare."

A few days later Lord Bryce came to see me at the College and
autographed my *American Commonwealth*. He seemed agitated
and began to ask me questions about our deputies. He had evidently heard things about them which outweighed the impression
made by their eloquence. Finally he said with a great effort: "Do
you think Leygues is corrupt? *Could* Leygues be corrupt?" I
do not know why he was so particularly interested in M. Leygues
who was one of the best Ministers of the Navy France ever had,
but I reassured him about his integrity by telling him that he
had recently come into an inheritance of over twenty million
francs.

At the house of Sir Henry and Lady Austin Lee I also met
several great journalists: Mr. Wickham Steed who knew more
finance than a banker (no irony here); Mr. Saunders, the last
correspondent of the London *Times* who looked and acted like
an ambassador, living in a superb mansion and not having to
hunt for information because information dutifully came to
him; he had charming children whom I liked; finally the famous
Dillon. Dillon was, at the time, contributing, like myself, European letters to the *North American Review,* but I should never
dare to say that we were colleagues. I was a mere intellectual
trained to systematize, in order to clarify them, the more obvious
phenomena of European politics; Dillon was a powerful individual with a vast scientific culture, and an intimate knowledge
of not only what was going on in three or four capitals but of
people who actually made politics. He looked the part too. While
I studied his capacious head and his tense expression, taking
note of the various reactions he produced on the other guests, he
sat indifferent not only to me but to everybody else, entirely
attentive to what engrossed and impassioned him. He made me
feel once more how remote from action I was born and must
remain, and how narrowly literary I should be were it not for

my devouring interest in the human elements of the world's
tragi-comedy.

The Austin Lees were naturally in contact with, and entertained, French aristocrats bearing historical names. Some were
interesting by the qualities they possessed, others by their lack of
them, but they all deserved careful observation, for the history of
France could be read in their characteristics. As the specimens
I saw rose in the estimation of the editors of Court Almanacks
they were generally found to approximate a purely human,
rather than a class, ideal. It has been my lot unexpectedly to
know two royal princes: one whom I met in England was the
brother of the King of Saxony, Prince Max, now a priest; the
other was a descendant of Saint Louis, Prince Sixte de Bourbon,
who every now and then appeared at my door, talked half an
hour and went away. Both men were so evidently above what we
call aristocracy that they might have been out of it. It took some
effort not to regard Prince Sixte as just a friend, so near one
his searching interest in mankind seemed to make him. Prince
Max surprised me by another trait which probably belongs to
royalty and means a whole apanage in itself: he was never bored.
The two men were evidently artists of a superior kind, never
at the mercy of mere contingencies and far less hampered by
hereditary categories than many people inclined to regard them
as living prejudices.

But of all the titled gentlemen who appeared at the Austin
Lees' none came so near, or became so dear to me, as the Marquis
de Saint-Paul. I was thirty-seven and he was nearly sixty-five
when we first met, and friendship seldom unites men separated
by such a length of time, but it did in this case. During the
twelve years he still had to live, Saint-Paul was a considerable
element in my happiness. His face—the face of a serious, kindly
Francis the First—often appears in my thoughts, not far from
that of my intellectual master, the poet Auguste Angellier.
When Summer brings a perfect day I invariably re-live happy

weeks at Saint-Paul's château near Orléans, La Bretauche, a delightful Abbaye de Thélème where restlessness was as impossible as passivity.

Charles de Saint-Paul was a distant relative of Lady Austin Lee's through his American grandmother, née Livingston, who had brought him up and whose memory was sacred to him. A few years ago, lecturing at Russell College, I discovered prim little Troy whose eighteenth-century houses, quite as elegant as those of Albany, tell a different story from that suggested by the factories in its lower quarters. It was at the door of one of those mansions that, one evening in the Spring of 1793, a horseman drew up to deliver the message that Louis the Sixteenth had been executed. Miss Livingston was then a girl of fifteen. Her emotion was impressed on her future grandson, and I still felt it every time he alluded to that incident. He would note, as I have often done myself, that a century is not so very long a period after all.

Saint-Paul owed his grandmother not only the remarkable command of the English language which his strong French accent and his unmistakable general Frenchness made rather surprising, but several ingredients in his make-up seldom to be found in men of his social class. He had a decidedly American preference for the present and an interest in the future which he sometimes carried to excess. Some city-planner wanted to transfer the Bourse to the Jardin du Palais-Royal which only needed a glass roof to be ready for its new destination. The Palais-Royal is full of lovable ghosts which the sight of a broker would put to flight forever, and as a lover of that dreamful place I protested against such a sacrilegious conception. But Saint-Paul defended it. "I like life better than even the most poetic death," he said. "Paris is full of useless graveyards."

He was also liberal in his politics, and was not a little amused by the uncompromising monarchical principles of the many American ladies whom marriage had turned into French countesses. His sincerity in this respect was the more remarkable

because of a peculiarity which many others would have carefully
concealed but of which he made no secret. His mother, a Princess
of Valori, was of ancient lineage, but his nobility on his father's
side only dated back to Louis the Fifteenth. He would explain,
with delightful sincerity, how his ancestor, the famous financier,
Le Rey de Chaumont, had been given his title shortly after buying the magnificent château of the same name on the Loire.
What would have seemed a corner difficult to negotiate to people
caring more for appearances than for realities he treated as a
purely historical affair. He might have pointed out that if few
English titles date further back than Henry the Eighth and the
secularization of the monasteries, few French titles can claim a
remoter antiquity than the period of the last Bourbons. But it
did not even occur to him to do such a thing: his sincerity not
only made him an absolute gentleman but a philosopher. Although his reading did not go beyond the current reviews, the
best modern poets and the more readable historians, his reaction to all he read was as critical and energetic as that of a
professional. Nothing was second-hand in his judgments.

He had a charming way of acknowledging a mistake. When
Abbé Duchesne put up his candidacy to the French Academy
Saint-Paul heard at his Club that this unknown Abbé was the
director of some school in Rome which "only numbered seven
or eight pupils." I explained that the so-called pupils were all
scholars engaged in independent research, and that the great
historian who superintended their work at the Palazzo Farnese
was entirely qualified to enter the French Academy. Saint-Paul
laughed silently over his pipe and said: "I find I have said an
uncommonly silly thing." Explanations he did not give and
would not have given even if he had not suspected that I could
infer them myself from his mention of the Club.

His emotions as well as his thoughts were always expressed
with remarkable economy. He was devoted to a small French
bulldog, Tige, a fascinating little creature with whom I played

games the rules of which we both understood perfectly. Poor little Tige only lived six years. The day after his death, Saint-Paul sitting alone in the sadly quiet salon merely said to me: "Gros petit chagrin, Monsieur l'Abbé." **

Saint-Paul was devoted to his friends whom he never analyzed critically. He loved the people in the Orléans region, "my own people" he called them, and, as long as he remained active, he went down every Saturday to give them free consultations. Every four years they faithfully returned him to the General Council or Legislature of the province. But, one general election, Saint-Paul ran for the Chamber of Deputies and was beaten. "Think of the intelligence of those poor wine-growers," he would say, "they see the difference between what I can be in the General Council and what I should have to be in the Chamber! Marvellous people!" Marvellous man, who could take such a disinterested view.

Saint-Paul died, in 1915, the death of a Christian Stoic. His attitude while he received the last rites was simplicity itself, probably the same which struck the soldiers who saw him in action in 1870. "Should I recite anything?" he asked the priest in his still strong voice. There was a rumour the day he passed out that Lille had been re-taken by the French troops. This false news gave him his last joy.

To me Marquis de Saint-Paul was the living distinction between a mere titled man and a nobleman. But he was also, without knowing it, the embodiment of much that I value most in human nature. That accounts for the fact that often in my mind an apparently general conclusion about life or morals suddenly and vividly conjures up the figure of my friend.

** I wrote Tige's epitaph which may give comfort to a few animal-lovers:

> Tu naquis pour aimer, tu fus bon et soumis;
> On t'aima: tu créas du bonheur sur la terre;
> L'éternelle Bonté dans ce peu de matière
> Que tu fus se mira. Périrait-elle entière?
> Non, douce chose aimée, en quelque lieu tu vis.

Living in such a College as Stanislas it was inevitable that my chief intercourse should be with professors: my own colleagues, of course, then lycée professors, once my fellow-students; finally the teaching aristocracy at the Sorbonne and at the Collège de France. As a schoolboy I had been so interested in the latter that they appeared to me in a positive aura. I had known, at Trélon, M. Martha, whose very name seemed a symbol of elegance, and I remember being fascinated by lists of Sorbonne professors or even by their Paris addresses. I would revert to that academic register as a child might to irresistible pictures, marvelling at the delight it must be to teach Greek Epigraphy and live in a street calling itself rue Madame.

A few years after I left school I fell under Angellier's influence, and I was shocked at first to notice the offhand manner in which he spoke of those illustrious colleagues of his. Most of them he regarded as mere card-collectors whose industry made up for lack of genius. Historians—the "historic outfit" he called them—were his pet aversion. I heard him at a great academic function analyze their methods and their turn of mind with all the penetration and picturesqueness of antipathy. When he was appointed Professor of English Literature at the Ecole Normale Supérieure I thought he would enjoy such an admittedly intelligent audience, and I asked curiously about his first impressions of them. He seemed surprised and said coolly: "*Mais non, ce sont des instituteurs frisés*"—(literally: frizzled schoolteachers, but the meaning was something like "ordinariness in its Sunday best"). The same week I heard my friend, Père de Pascal, a Dominican of aristocratic lineage, whose saintly simplicity had never been able to conquer a sarcastic tendency, referring to the same young men as "uncassocked seminarians."

Both quips I found later to be unjust, but my first contacts with Sorbonne professors chiefly revealed unkempt persons whose frowziness was sadly emphasized by that of dowdy wives. In 1904 a mere accident placed me on the roster of an examining body at the Collège de France to look into the merits of several artificial languages competing for a prize. There were illustrious men on that Board including the Danish philologist Jespersen, the logician Couturat, the Italian mathematician Peano, and, towering rather too consciously above all the others, the German chemist Oswald. In the middle of this areopagus rose a high Academic French official, M. Boirac, author of a popular text-book of philosophy, who read "in the name of the Esperantist nation" a ridiculous manifesto challenging the whole Board and in advance questioning their decision if it happened not to be in favour of Esperanto. I felt humiliated and hoped that the verdict would be in favour of Ido—an obviously superior arti-ficial language—but it did not, and the Pope of Esperantists retired with great majesty, persuaded that his declaration had cowed us all into submission to his will.

I must say I never came across another Sorbonne professor who approached M. Boirac in empty pomposity, and I soon met many whom I liked and not a few who rather intimidated me either by their brilliance or, on the contrary, by the silences of their modesty. Even apparently commonplace specialists would, when started on their subjects, not only show the intelligent per-ception which perfect possession of data generally produces, but the healthy gusto in the consciousness of it which I prefer to wit. You then discover how unwise it always is to judge a man from his or his wife's appearance, or even from what he may say be-fore you have given him a chance to feel really at his best.

I am speaking of the rank and file in a faculty numbering two hundred. When it comes to its more distinguished repre-sentatives, reservations have to disappear. Bergson is all *lumière* (the French word implies the happiness as well as the comfort which are derived from light); Bédier charms by the simplicity with which he tells of his discoveries as if they had only been fortunate accidents; dear old Legouis is so personally fasci-nating that you forget his rare distinction as a specialist; Bal-densperger is the gentleman of erudition; Paul Hazard, my friend of more than thirty years, delights audiences in two hemi-spheres, but the April waywardness of his conversation, his

naturalness in converting a plaint into a humorous statement,
the amusing struggle between his doubts and his certainties give
me more pleasure than his lectures; Siegfried leaves on you the
impression that everything is clear or could easily be made
clear; Gilson's robustness passes like a cannon-ball through the
most intricate subjects: I love his mental muscle.

I met Salomon Reinach a few times, at dinner at General
Sherrill's. He was ill-favoured, ill-dressed, ill-brushed and might
have sold ill-smelling things in the Paris ghetto a few blocks
from the close of Notre-Dame where I am now writing. But the
man was alive with intellectuality, the smallest arteries in his
body tingling with curiosity and hypotheses. You could not understand how a person afflicted with such squirming mental
activity could ever go to sleep. His intellectual daredeviltry was
a by-word and was so frequently impugned that he might have
been damped by the atmosphere of criticism about him. But he
was not. He was full of the most buoyant certainty that an im-
minent archaelogical discovery, a shred of papyrus found in a
crack of some Egyptian statuette must confirm one of his pet
theories, or make something, anything clearer than it was yesterday. People said that no man's erudition could keep up with
such bounding curiosity, and their mistrust, in a few instances,
turned out to be grounded. But few men knew as much as he
did. One year, having to lecture at the Louvre on the French
Primitives, I asked Reinach a few questions which he answered
in the most illuminating way. He made me feel as if I actually
were in Clouet's studio. The next day the postman brought me,
in a battered unregistered envelope, a hundred pages of MS.
notes on the Primitives which it would have taken me three years
to collect. A brief note said that I was welcome to the whole
bundle if I cared to keep it. Such generosity—of which I naturally did not avail myself—and the wealth of information
which made it possible showed me another Reinach than the
one supposed to be real. Surely when his conjectures appeared
fanciful it was not because the scholar had been at fault, but

because the philosopher associated with him could not resist his passion for imaginative panoramas.

Writers in prose or verse I, of course, met by the hundred in Paris or London, as well as later in America. Nothing palls on the readers of Memoirs as much as the merciless lists of celebrities which most memorialists will not abbreviate. So I should be careful to avoid that pitfall even if I were not conscious of the great fact that only one Frenchman, Auguste Angellier— watched every week and, at intervals, every day during almost twenty years—appeared to me of superhuman stature. I do not feel like adding to what I said about this powerful individual in *My Old World*. Writers, even the best known of them, never struck me as superior human specimens, except possibly two or three minor poets, caught when their faces showed the wistfulness of even disappointed spiritual efforts. The straining after effect, the desire to outshine others, the angry silences frequent in Paris literary salons used to depress me and still make me uncomfortable on the rare occasions when I am enticed into purely literary company. Even Barrès, who certainly had a soul and who strove towards greatness all his life, who, moreover, attained something like literary perfection in several of his books, was too restless under his apparent confidence and too near ill-nature in his brilliant sarcasms to give the reassuring sensation which Angellier's superiority left with everybody. I only remember one brief moment during which Barrès reacted upon me in a way which I have not been able to forget. This was a year or two before the war, at a semi-literary, semi-political dinner at the Café de Madrid. He was chairman but only arrived from the Chamber when the dessert was already on the table. He was too tired and too long past his usual meal hour to eat any dinner. He sat opposite me and we exchanged a few words as he sipped some champagne. Soon he fell into a reverie while running his dark eyes along the big tables. All the men who sat there were admirers or followers of his, but I could see that, without any of his usual bitterness, he was more conscious of

their inadequacy than of their devotion. In time he jotted a few
notes on the margin of the menu, rose and during a short ten
minutes poured out the noblest, the most Roman that was in
him. Every man there surrendered to his earnestness, evidently
feeling that he had risen where no one of us could climb. But
as I left with another guest, a stocky old admiral—Bienvenu, I
think, was his name—who had recently begun to flood the press
with patriotic articles, this gentleman stopped me on the steps,
to ask: "Barrès upstairs, where does he write? I seem to see his
name quite often, don't I?" What had struck me as an exceptional revelation of the best Barrès had been wasted on this old
salt and perhaps on others.

For some reason association recalls to me another experience,
also literary, but of an entirely different character. I have related, in *My Old World,* the impression made upon me when I
was in my early twenties, at Douai, by a lecture which M. Henry
Cochin gave on Raphaël's 'prentice years at Urbino. Henry Cochin loved art and beauty and he loved Italy. All he told us
that evening about the atelier of Timoteo Viti and the little
Court of Urbino acted upon me as beautiful pictures commented
upon by appropriate music might have done. Perhaps that talk
set for me the ideal of perfect lecturing. Some fifteen years later,
in Rome, I made the personal acquaintance of Henry Cochin,
through his brother, Denys, the brilliant political leader of the
Right. Henceforth I saw a good deal of the two brothers. During
the Long Vacation of 1918 I spent a few days at the Château
of Beauvoir as the guest of Denys and the Baroness Cochin. The
booming of the guns could be heard day and night in that quiet
country-place, but allusions to the war were reserved for the
walks which Denys Cochin and I took together. As soon as the
Baroness was present the subject was avoided, for the brilliant
son of the family, Claude, had been killed at Verdun only a few
months before.

The day I left, M. Denys Cochin, looking at the map I was
consulting before cycling back to Chevreuse and thence to St.
Germain, found that my route took me within two or three miles

of his brother's place at Etiolles. He must have telephoned Etiolles soon after I left, for, as I drew near to Corbeil, I found
Henry Cochin's grandson, a Stanislas boy, cruising also on a
bicycle near a crossroad I was pretty sure to pass, and the boy
took me prisoner to Etiolles. We spent the evening in the magnificent library which M. Cochin had filled with an incomparable
collection of ancient Italian books and documents. The conversation turned upon Petrarch to whom my interlocutor had devoted eight or ten years of continuous study. M. Cochin spoke of
the Italian poet with the same subdued fervour I had noticed,
thirty years before, in his lecture on Raphaël. I was all the audience, but as he went on he warmed to his subject, and for a
long time I knew he did what he pleased with my imagination
and sensibility. Finally he went to a drawer and returned with
the facsimile of the last six or seven lines which Petrarch, a few
hours before his death, copied from an ancient manuscript. The
handwriting was perfect but the lines went down in an unusual
manner. We looked at the page in silence. "Petrarch was a little
over seventy, wasn't he?" I asked.—"Yes, seventy-five."—"A
perfect age for dying," I said.—"Yes," he replied, "nobody
ought to crowd the stage much longer than that." I remembered
his saying this when, a few years later, he died at precisely
seventy-five. He was no powerful orator, like his brother, no exceptional writer, he was only a perfect connoisseur. But the sincerity of his love for Italy was a human rather than a literary
trait, and that is rare enough to influence whoever happens to
encounter it.

I met many English writers. The Catholic celebrities of course:
Dr. Barry, Mrs. Meynell, Chesterton, especially Belloc who, a
year or two ago, delighted my soul by taking over Bremond's
flat next to mine, paid his rent punctually for a long time without
spending a single night in his property, finally appeared with
his friend, Ware, and started keeping house on two cots, a kettle
and two French soldiers' mugs which his loyalty to barrack-life
showed to him as indispensable. After two nights he decided he
could not sleep in the place, not, as I was afraid, because the

clock of Notre-Dame chimed too loudly, nor indeed because of
any noise in particular, but because "of the expectation of noise."

I also met scores of non-Catholic writers, from Frank Harris,
a curious admixture of pensiveness and brutality, to exquisite
Whibley. I corresponded, for years, with Anne de Sélincourt,
violet-like cousin of iridescent Nathalie Colby and of Ellery
Sedgwick. I saw a great deal of Arnold Bennett between 1909
or thereabouts and his death. I cannot remember how we became
acquainted, but I recollect taking Filson Young to his house at
Moret in the Summer of 1909. An impression of commonness
which the first encounter with him generally produced had already worn off. It was caused by his shrill voice—a great contrast to his French wife's beautiful contralto—and by a perpetual
fidgeting which did not go well with his social aspirations. But
you soon ceased to notice even the voice, and people who say
that Bennett took great pains to look like a gentleman repeat a
cruelly unjust misjudgment. Bennett was a gentleman. Under his
agitation he possessed the simplicity of the gentleman as well as
of the real artist. You never saw a trace of meanness in his
attitude. It is true he was over-literary, more so than any English
writer I ever came across. A young lady we both knew and appreciated distressed all who knew her by committing suicide.
I wrote Bennett what I witnessed of the deplorable case. To my
surprise he replied "envying me the experience." The tragedy
was copy to him.

Yet, he was kind and extremely loyal to his friends. He took
great interest in my contracts and, while appreciating his own
publishers—against whom he was cushioned by a literary agent
he could not praise highly enough—he would constantly put me
on my guard against the book trade. Successful authors are apt,
as he put it, "to go over to the enemy," but he never did, contrasting to the end the poverty of most writers with the wealth
of most publishers.

We often talked shop on a higher plane than contracts. I
have always been interested in the methods of novelists and
dramatists, and I would ask him questions about his invention

which he answered with his usual directness. He readily admitted
that there was a good deal of "must" in his production of fiction.
When he lived in the rue de Grenelle—in the court behind the
famous fountain—he would get up early and go to the Luxembourg garden where he walked for hours asking himself cheerfully but doggedly: "And what do they do to-day? They surely
must be doing something." Towards ten o'clock he returned
home, drank strong tea, and till lunch-time wrote indefatigably
what *they* did. André Maurois tells me he has much the same
method, but with a passion for perfection which, in the case of
Climats, was only satisfied after seven re-writings.

I never found Arnold Bennett vain as most people represent
him. He spoke of Dostoevsky—whose *Brothers Karamazov* he
constantly re-read—as of a model he never could attain. Once
he told me he had never been able to conceive how he ever
wrote anything as good as *The Old Wives' Tale.* I know vain
writers, I almost said merely that I know writers: they seldom
say anything of this sort. Probably what people called vanity in
Bennett was only the sensitive man's recoil from a slight or even
from lack of appreciation.

There was another bond, besides literature, between Bennett
and myself. He loved artists and I have, all my life, been attracted by them. Most literary men are. There is between the
writer and the painter the resemblance that each is more interested in what is going on in his own mind than in the so-called
real world (unreal to him) which is everything to "practical"
people. A book, like a painting, is the exteriorization of a dream:
you read a man's soul in his canvas as in his poem. But the artist
is an object of wonderment to the writer while the writer can
only be an occasional adviser to the artist. The latter is more
intuitive, nearer to his inspiration, and the philosophy which
he formulates in terms of his own invention seldom owes anything to books. So the artist seems to be all the time what the
literary man is only during occasional phases, viz., a conscious

child or a reconstructed Primitive. Hence his attractiveness. Bennett felt it strongly, and I hope I shall respond to the same appeal all my life. I have told elsewhere how early I began to be aware of it. When I arrived in Paris I felt quite as much interest in ateliers as in salons.

A cousin of mine, Raoul Baligant, was an artist and had his studio a few blocks away from College Stanislas in the rue de la Grande Chaumière. He was in the academic tradition, was not ashamed of it, and professed himself an admirer of Bouguereau who lived almost next door and sometimes showed a rather pathetic visage at the front gate of a mysterious garden. "The man draws better than anybody alive," Raoul would say, "his colouring is the envy of every honest painter, why should we not be satisfied with that?" There was a good deal of truth in that view. A first-rate craftsman must be, at times, an artist and, every now and then, the fact has to be recognized. When the admirers of Gerard Manley Hopkins pooh-pooh Tennyson, there is a chance for Wordsworth, and flashes begin to appear even in Pope's *Heroids*. Simultaneously we find that the most extreme modern French musicians display an unexpected respect for Gounod. Paradox and fashion both play havoc with reason in the realm of art as in every other, but the old Salerno doctors were right in their quiet certainty that nothing violent can endure.

I knew Cottet well and liked him very much. Many a time I would hesitate, after lunch, between a stroll in the Luxembourg or a visit to the artist in the studio out of which a living tree thrust its head through the roof. Frequently I decided to go up the Avenue to him and never regretted it. Cottet too had been a modern, violently abused for painting dark when people were enjoined to believe in brightness; he gradually became the chief of a triumphant school—his Spanish exhibits at the Salon of 1905 outshone everybody else's—later again he survived himself as the representative of a movement which appeared to be spent simply because it had been successful. He never minded what people said against him and little what they might say for him.

When I had the joy to discover a real artist in Jules Joëts, before anybody else seemed to dare to proclaim him one, I recommended him to Cottet for a prize. "Yes," Cottet said, "I believe you are right, but tell the young man he paints too dark." I laughed, whereupon innocent Cottet asked why I laughed. He never remembered that people once accused him of the same fault, and when I recalled the fact to him he took no interest. Painting was the beginning and the end for him.

We met occasionally in the peacock studio where Jacques Blanche distils his rather acrid wit. Blanche is a man of the world—which Cottet never dreamed of being; he is also a writer, and a time came when the most exclusive reviews sought his collaboration. Cottet taking up the *Revue de Paris* showed delighted surprise at seeing his friend's name on the cover. Blanche resented the surprise more than he liked the approval, and lectured Cottet on the danger of being a one-groove man, living in an oil-smelling studio. The old artist felt the truth of the rebuke and stroked his beard with proper embarrassment. A few minutes later we went up the miller's ladder at the top of which Blanche himself does his oil-smelling work. He showed us two or three flower-pieces and one larger canvas. Then Cottet appeared as the master while Blanche, though barely his junior, became if not a pupil at least a brother artist who gladly bowed to mastery. I have not forgotten the perfect tone, a little subdued, in which he acknowledged every criticism with a *"Très bien, Cottet"* or *"Bien, on le corrigera, Cottet."*

The first time I went to Spain, Cottet gave me a letter to the uncle of Zuloaga. I greatly admired the Spanish school and, Salon after Salon, I anticipated the pungent sensation which the exhibits of Sorolla, Sert or Zuloaga were sure to give me. There was in the Luxembourg Gallery a picture of Zuloaga's called "My Cousins." This canvas represented two extremely Castilian-looking girls, one leading a fine dog in leash, the other carrying a bouquet in her right hand and a red book in her left hand. When I reached Segovia I asked for the address of Zuloaga's uncle and prepared to hand in my letter. This uncle, also called Zuloaga, was a stained-glass painter whose studio was in a twelfth-century church, long disused, on a deserted portion of the city-wall. I found the place one very hot afternoon. It looked so still and uninhabited in the devouring sun that I did not feel up to the effort of trying to wake it up. I sat under the ghost of a tree and waited. In about half an hour I heard a shuffling sound in the sere leaves and beheld an apparition which I knew at once. There stood one of the two Cousins, in white, as in the Luxembourg painting, and carrying the identical red book which I had thought was merely a studio property. Only the bouquet was missing. I got up, and both the young lady and I smiled so naturally that I imagined that Cottet must have announced my visit. He had done nothing of the kind, but the señorita had read on my face my familiarity with the Luxembourg painting. She had not carried the book while wearing the white dress twice, she said, since Ignacio had asked her to sit for that portrait.

Twenty-four years have gone by. The picture has long disappeared from the fickle Luxembourg, and I do not know what has become of the cousin, her book and her bouquet. She may be the mother of a large and voluble family, and I have no doubt that she has forgotten the stranger of many years ago. But I have not forgotten the welcome which those delightful people gave me. Spanish hospitality is proverbially simple: a glass of wine in the afternoon, a thimbleful of *anisette* after dinner outside a café on the Plaza, but what lavishness of that which money could never buy! And what an environment, and what stars in the cool night!

I never exchanged a word with Rodin, but I sat three or four times at the table next his at the Restaurant Trianon outside Gare Montparnasse where the sculptor landed when arriving from his Meudon studio. The square-shouldered, square-headed little man still looked like the stone-cutter of fifty years before. He

also ate like him. I saw him once begin with a dozen and a half
oysters, go on to three or four courses and after his dessert stuff
himself with biscuits which he soaked in a stiff glass of brandy.
He always ate alone and noticed nobody or nothing except his
food. I could not help remembering Macaulay's description of
Johnson "in the delightful action of gobbling" as I saw the
cordlike veins on Rodin's square forehead swelling to his effort.
Gsell, in his book of Rodiniana, ascribes to the sculptor this
pretty profound criticism of Anatole France: "Anatole may have
the sauce, but he hasn't got the rabbit." The man who said this
had achieved world-wide celebrity, but he had not deigned to
sophisticate himself out of the vocabulary used in the taverns
of his youth when his Sunday treat was the same Belgian hare
which kept his workmen friends longing through the week.

Another sculptor who had started as humbly as Rodin, and
who, without rising so high, was however respected by all artists
and worshipped by his friends, was Jean Baffier. I often visited
him in the *impasse* near Montparnasse where he worked. He
was a giant. His powerful frame when he appeared outside his
studio in his blouse seemed to fill the street. He came from a
village near Bourges and had once squared blocks in the Cathedral yard. He loved to speak of those early days. He had
retained the accent, the smock and the hurdy-gurdy of his province. Moreover, he was an encyclopedia of its folklore. All his
inspiration was derived from it, and upon it he had piled an
erudition which was surprising in a self-educated man but which
to him only seemed a natural growth. The man was not a rough
diamond, he was a pure nugget, and I enjoyed in him more than
in any other the spontaneity, the lavishness and the childlike
seriousness of the artist. He was poor and did not care, except
because lack of means prevented him from seeing in marble a
monumental mantelpiece on which he had worked all his life.
Once I took Miss Anne Morgan to him hoping that she might
see a place in America for the plaster poem which almost filled
up the studio. But that kind of dream is never realized. Baffier,

whom I had never seen self-conscious, was made nervous by the unexpected chance, and Miss Morgan, who had thought she was going to see a home ornament, felt dwarfed when she saw the thing towering above her. Nothing happened.

Baffier was one of those simple men who go to art from mere love of beauty, but whose art teaches them philosophy. The philosophy was remarkably like Ruskin's. I also knew two painters whose minds were naturally metaphysical, who rationalized every æsthetic impulse they were conscious of, and who could not help building a whole complete system on their æsthetics. One was Maurice Denis, met by mere chance in the Perugia gallery, in the Spring of 1904 when he was cycling home on the rocky roads of pre-Mussolinian Italy. It was delightful to see him soar up on the least provocation, even in the explanation of a mere detail of chiaroscuro. Later, during the war, I saw a great deal of him in the Priory he fitted for himself at Saint-Germain, and I heard him speak most of what puzzles to-day the readers of his difficult books. I confess that my mind would often wander, for there was no common vocabulary between his creativeness and my criticism, but I knew ways of getting him back to the portfolio we had been diverted from or to the cartoons for his Geneva church-windows.

The other painter-philosopher was Caro-Delvaille, the husband of the well-known French lecturer who, long before she could speak the English she has gradually mastered, delighted American audiences by that miraculous something which we unanalytically call charm. Caro-Delvaille had early made a reputation by delicately sensuous studies. He made the mistake of emigrating to America where he had to adopt a different style and where he finally secured a new fame by murals of profound inspiration. When I first met him he was entirely engrossed by the psychology of Spanish or Buddhist monks whom no artist since El Greco or Zurbaran seems to have so thoroughly understood, and he was on the brim of an even deeper religious inspiration. I am surprised to see that so few of those pictures, still in America, have been bought by the museums. Caro-Delvaille

was an astonishing person who, one minute, would dance a
basque *baile,* and the next would be discussing the most abstruse
idealism with Dr. Carrel. His mind was in his soul, and his soul
was a springing fountain of fine emotion ready to be translated
into theories. He too has left a book on the interior life which
even technicians will not find easy, but which restores to those
who heard the man and felt entranced by the rapidity of his
flights something of what they felt in his presence. He has been
dead ten years, yet I often see him alive in the room where I am
now writing. The mystery of his melancholy fate and the mys-
teriousness of the true artist's intellectuality are almost one to
me.

III

Literature and art have filled many a life and I owe them full and peaceful hours, but in the first years of my Stanislas period, say, between 1903 and 1910, they were merely my recreation. My real interest was elsewhere.

I have told in *My Old World* how, even as a student at the Cambrai Seminary, I became aware of certain facts—their being facts was what struck me the most—which had to be reconciled with the body of doctrine going by the name of theology. Later on, at Lille University, my intercourse with intelligent Catholic professors in the School of Science as well as constant reading of English reviews showing the same respect for facts which, in spite of my Latin education, seemed natural to me, made a few notes of interrogation extremely urgent to my consciousness. The answer to those meant the reconciliation of my faith with the facts.

In other words, I was in quest of an Apologetics suitable, not for the men of the generation before mine, but for people who had attained the reading and questioning age simultaneously with me. In school and at the Seminary my questions had been given the classical answers. The usual admonition was not to be too inquisitive, not to attach too much importance to one's own judgment or to conclusions which were probably rash or insufficiently grounded, but, on the contrary, to give in to the authority of the Church. Sometimes, however, my questions were given individual attention, and were answered singly by the Apologetics of the day. This was still, almost universally, Concordism. The facts which exercised me were either not facts at all or they were perfectly reconcilable with an intelligent interpretation of the Bible or an up-to-date theology. Concordists made a great display of comprehension and generous Liberalism, and practiced their innocent legerdemains with not a little self-satisfaction.

But, analyzed by restlessness or by thoroughness, neither the leave-it-to-the-Church admonition nor the Concordist discussions

46

were satisfactory. For, in the first place, it was not always apparent to what extent the authority of the Church was guaranteeing a solution. At the time of the Galileo affair, for instance, practically all Christendom took it for granted that geocentrism was essential to the Christian belief, and Bellarmine who thought differently remained isolated. To-day apologists are unanimous in their declaration, copied from Bellarmine's, that the Church's business is to tell us how to go to heaven, but not how the heavens go.

In the second place, Concordism has turned out to be an opportunistic method easily satisfied with appearances and at bottom indifferent to the questions which cause anxiety to sensitive people. It is the apologetics of those who do not really need apologetics.

Towards the end of the nineteenth century a totally different method of meeting so-called scientific or critical difficulties appeared, first in Protestant circles, gradually in Anglican, and finally in Catholic publications. It was based on the simple but radical affirmation that religion is totally separate from science and consequently no conflict between them is conceivable. Concordism, far from solving difficulties, was declared to go out of its way to create them. Faith was faith, it was no demonstration. Belief certainly required some justification, but the justification must be expected to be vital rather than narrowly intellectual. You *lived* your religion, that was enough. If anybody challenged you to defend it, you were fully justified in simply answering that it satisfied you, as you may state that you feel well without going into the physiological explanation of your well-being. If your questioner should become unpleasantly urgent it was easy to tell him that evidently he lacked sympathy with religion, had no talent for it, and was to be prayed for rather than argued with. Religious people were brushing aside the long irritating debates with the representatives of Enlightenment in which so-called orthodoxy was not so infallibly victorious as it was apt to think itself. They reappeared as the

descendants of Paul's converts to whom the Mystery of Jesus was
happiness, life and salvation, and against whom argument would
have been not only useless but in extremely bad taste. And behind the humility of such simple folk the observers of this
transformation felt the overcoming presence of the mystical
poetry of Augustine, Aquinas and Pascal whom even the greatest
sophisticates hardly dare to patronize.

My preferences went to this new attitude the moment I became
aware of it. This was done through my English reading. No
sooner did I read the essay—on "Theology and Devotion"—
which revealed Father George Tyrrell to the world as a writer of
startling originality and heroic sincerity, than I realized the
similarity of its thesis with the central idea in the *Grammar of
Assent*: Tyrrell's "devotion" corresponded to Newman's "real",
while his "theology" was evidently what Newman calls
"notional." Religion, or the real, matters more than its notional
rationalization, unfortunately referred to by both critics and
champions as theology. This distinction gave me the key to the
admixture of freedom and loyalty which had puzzled me more
than once in contemporary Anglican scholars. It also clarified a
sentence of Dr. William Barry's which my scholastic logic had
wondered at when we first met at Dorchester, near Oxford. Barry
said, as a thing which went without saying: "When I step into a
church I leave all criticism at the door." He meant that the real
in him did not care about the adventitious notional.

While I was going back to the history of the Church trying to
satisfy myself that the distinction which I found so serviceable
must have appealed many times in the past to people inclined to
think of religion as belonging to the soul more than to the intellect, I discovered that the French, Italian and German Catholics
who preferred the new apologetics were beginning to be called
Modernists. Somehow the word had already acquired a none too
complimentary fringe. In fact, Modernism was never defined by
friend or foe in a satisfactory manner. Even the encyclical
written against it by Pope Pius the Tenth described it somewhat

allusively. Shortly after the publication of this celebrated document I visited some English friends whose daughter had recently joined the Poor Clares. We went to see the young novice and found her naturally in the seventh heaven. I had a conversation with the Mother Prioress whose transparency of soul I have not forgotten. Pretty soon this Reverend Mother asked me: "Oh! by the way, what is Modernism?"—"Why!" I said, "you have read the Encyclical; you know that Modernism is the sum total of all heresies."—"I know," the Prioress insisted a little sharply, "but *what* is it?"

It took me some time to find that, after all, the Pope's encyclical was right in not trying to define Modernism in clear-cut formulas. Modernism was a mental attitude, a Wish, much more than a body of statements. Only this tendency was regarded by people favourable to it as an effort to save all that was essential in the traditional doctrine, whereas its adversaries scorned it as a hypocritical plan to undermine dogmas. I never saw any machiavellism in men like Tyrrell or Loisy, but both of them ceased to be Modernists when they became rebellious. The typical Modernist to me remains Frederic von Hügel. I always shied from meeting this great friend of Tyrrell and Loisy because I suspected in him—wrongly, I now think—a preference for spirited horses one could have the pleasure of reining in, but, more than any other thinker of this period, he was sincere in his apparently conflicting loyalties and he was submissive enough never to break bounds. Also he enjoyed the incomparable advantage of being a layman, and, fundamentally, Modernism is a layman's attitude.

Until I arrived in Paris in 1903, I was not much interested in the theological debates going on there. It is true that my former schoolmate, Joseph Bricout, the editor of the *Revue du Clergé Français*, kept me posted on their developments. It is also true that in the summer of 1901 I called on Loisy in his Bellevue hermitage and was deeply impressed by the order which seemed to prevail in his thoughts as it did in his conventual-looking chambers. His library, entirely consisting of texts and lexicons, was impressive. But Loisy was too technical for me. So was Duchesne whom I frequently saw later on, as he came to Stanislas every day when he was in Paris. I never liked him. I did not like his tendency to combine the advantages of boldness with the profits of orthodoxy. I did not like his wit which I thought semi-professional and suspected of being a convenient screen. Too technical also was Turmel on whom I called in 1899 at the Rennes institution where he served as chaplain. Yet I still remember how thoughtful he appeared as he walked out of the chapel in his surplice to meet me, and how evident his self-collectedness was in his whole appearance. I was at work, at the time, on Newman's *Essay on Development*. Without changing his surplice-manner Turmel told me that he was sorry but he constantly found that famous book at variance with the "facts." Though he was not forty then his erudition was already stupendous, and what he called facts were patristic utterances which he could marshal in powerful array.

After I settled in Paris I used to attend, with Bremond, Loisy's lectures on the New Testament, at the *Ecole des Hautes Etudes*. My initiation into biblical criticism was sufficient for me to appreciate the astonishing mastery over the texts displayed in those lectures. The three Synoptists barely amount to three thousand verses and, at first sight, it would seem as if nothing were easier than to become familiar with such short writings, dealing as they do with the same events. The truth of the matter is that very few scholars succeed in finding their way through them. Even people who know them by heart cannot pass from one to the other readily, as confusion is a perpetual danger. Loisy played with his three texts as I have seen Widor playing with the three keyboards of his Saint-Sulpice organ. But my admiration of such prowess did not blind me to the radicalism which Loisy took no pains to conceal. His mind, unlike the mind of my English authors, was all logic and its conclusions were rigid. I only know one other such logician, Charles Maurras, and it is remarkable that there is no essential difference between the two men's views concerning the Gospel and the Church, except that Loisy prefers the Gospel which Maurras abominates.

Loisy's prodigious scholarship did not make me theologically one of his disciples. My intellectual sympathy was with the more philosophically inclined Catholic writers: men like Blondel, Laberthonnière or Le Roy in France; Tyrrell in England; or Fogazzaro in Italy. I often saw Laberthonnière, without ever being able to call him really a friend. He was a reserved little man, too near his own thoughts ever to be near other men's. Even his occasional quiet gaiety was not enough to put one quite *en rapport* with him. One felt in him also the obstinacy of the gentle. To tell the truth, I enjoyed his books more than his conversation. However, he appealed irresistibly to me during the latter part of his life when a decision from Rome compelled the superiors who were justly proud of him—he was an Oratorian—to forbid publication of anything he might write. He was only just over fifty when this decision was made public and he had twenty more years to live. He acted heroically. He never printed another line; he never said a word in protest, even at Lemire's friendly table where we often met; he preserved his smiling gentleness. Only he prematurely began to age, from year to year looking more like a fading pastel or an enfeebled tree. Deafness added to his weakened appearance, and I wondered many times how a man who had been so active and influential could fill the long months in the high-perched little flat where he lived his now mute life. It was no small surprise when, recently, M. Louis Canet, of the Ministry of Foreign Affairs, began the publication of the works produced during those years of absolute silence, with two volumes on Descartes, which might be the work of a happy specialist.

Fogazzaro came to Paris shortly after his *Il Santo* was translated into French as well as in twenty other languages. He was the guest of my friend Saleilles, a professor at the Law School,

so that I saw a great deal of him. He was lionized to death and I
pitied him. One afternoon he had been explaining to a large
circle his method for composing his romances—curiously like
Zola's, though no two men could be more different—and he was
sitting down to a few minutes' rest when a voice was heard at
the end of the room piping the question: "Sir, when you write
those novels are you thinking of actual, living people?" The
enquirer, an interesting-looking person with a shock of white
hair, was none other than the famous economist, Leroy-Beaulieu,
so that poor Fogazzaro had to begin all over again, "Well, I
take little note-books," etc. This great Italian was wonderfully
sensitive. Towards the end of that exhausting afternoon a small
string orchestra appeared, consisting mostly of harps. This
poetic band charmed Fogazzaro who promptly revived, every
now and then repeating like a happy child: *"Oh, que ces jeunes
filles me font de plaisir!"*

Tyrrell appeared in Paris for the first time in 1905. He was
coming chiefly to see our mutual friend Bremond, but Bremond
was not equipped to receive anybody. He was constantly changing lodgings and did not take the trouble to furnish, beyond
absolute necessities, the queer little flats which he only rented
for a few weeks. He had been used too long to the luxury of
monastic poverty, and this son of a *notaire* who had accumulated
four garretsful of provençal furniture not only did not care
for appearances but was, all his life, unconscious of them, a bo-
hemian without knowing it. He had a library in his Pau house
which I never saw, but in his ephemeral Paris lodgings this man,
who read everything, never kept more than twenty or twenty-five
volumes, most of them outside his particular field of study. He
did his work in the public libraries—where however I never once
saw him—or in his friends' houses. For years he came to see me
every Sunday morning. He would talk for a few minutes in the
rich amusing vein under which it pleased him to hide the fundamental seriousness and the smouldering passion which run
through his books, but as he spoke he edged towards the re-

volving bookcase where I kept the novelties sent to me by Paris or London publishers, and he looked through them without ceasing to speak to me. I shall always regard him as the accomplished reader, the man who never opens a book without demanding of it something definite, and who remembers the decisive two or three words in a page no sooner glanced at than it is turned over. This worshipper of literary beauty went through books as an hotel-porter goes through the time-table and yet missed nothing.

Dossiers were equally absent from the rickety tables on which he wrote. He did not believe in index-cards which he derided as *les petits papiers*. He prepared his many books from old-fashioned unwieldy copybooks which he seldom allowed anybody to see, but through which his nimble though thick fingers found their way with infallible accuracy. When, in 1924, he finally settled at 16 rue Chanoinesse, in the apartment adjoining mine which he kept till his death, he took to talking his books all day long to an extraordinary variety of visitors, from candidates to the French Academy anxious to win his vote to poor provincial priests for whom his reverence was touching. English-speaking visitors were numerous. He would speak to them in careful bookish English to which his syllabic pronunciation imparted a strange evenness more arresting than puzzling. Whenever these English visitors were particularly worth while Bremond knocked on my door and required a little assistance which it was amusing to give.

When Tyrrell landed on that first visit, Bremond lived in two or three bare rooms in the rue Cassini, and his household consisted of one good-natured, very primitive country-maid whom fine talking ravished and who would stand in the room listening, without a pretence of not doing so, and smiling with delight at the beautiful things she did not understand. So, Tyrrell went to the Hotel des Mines, on the Boulevard Saint-Michel. On another occasion he stayed at the Hotel de la Minerve, in the rue de la Chaise, an old-fashioned place.

Tyrrell must have had enemies, but they must also have been people who never were in contact with him. It was impossible to see him without liking him and liking him instantaneously. Not that he was good-looking, for he was the reverse to such an extent that I should consider it treason and a misrepresentation to describe his features. Nor was he apparently sociable, either. He lived so intently with his own thoughts that if you ceased to address him during a few minutes you found, on returning to him, that he was staring into space with, not infrequently, his lips moving in some inaudible conversation. Once, walking with him on the Boulevard Montparnasse I had to leave him in front of the church of Notre-Dame-des-Champs. I watched him as he moved off in his coachman's coat. He was not six steps away before I noticed a stiffening of his body and a change in his gait showing that he was plunging into a world entirely different from that in which our conversation had just been concluded. Readers of his books, familiar with the concentration of his every sentence, will not wonder at that capacity for abstraction which I have seen in nobody else to the same degree.

However, it must be admitted that people who have that gift for withdrawing into themselves are not generally prepossessing. What made of Tyrrell a man whom you could not approach without loving was a capacity for human sympathy which you felt at once. It was made of an appealing pliability which seems hardly reconcilable with mental superiority. You knew that this writer of epoch-making books would be with you whether you chose to be intellectual, or humorous, or even sentimental. The painfully irregular features vanished as you took cognizance of the unique quality of the eyes, so unlike anything one generally sees in a very brainy person that what they suggested was the appeal of a beautiful child or that of a wounded creature. Tyrrell was all appeal even for people who admired him the most, and yet his manly dignity was unmistakable.

At this time his theological troubles had not seriously begun, although he had already followed Bremond in his exit from the

Society of Jesus. Modernists were more talked about than really threatened. The liberalism of Leo the Thirteenth had lingered on in Rome after his death. My friend, Canon Looten, and I went to Rome at Easter, in 1904, and called on a number of dignitaries. Cardinal Satolli was the only one who spoke to us about Loisy in a tone which boded a storm. *"La testa! la testa!"* he repeated, shaking his head and adding that "even if grace should change the heart of that man, his notions would still remain the same." We found Cardinal Merry del Val not only, as people said, all aristocratic seduction, but more liberal than he was represented. He emphasized the necessity of a revision of the Vulgate, and I was glad to find that Newman's ideas on the subject were familiar to him.

The consequence was that I went on peacefully with the preparation of my book *La Pensée Catholique dans l'Angleterre Contemporaine.* Early in 1905 I took the manuscript for approval—the subject being theological—to the office of Cardinal Amette, then Archbishop of Paris. The manuscript was read by the curé of Saint-Etienne-du-Mont, Abbé Lesêtre, himself a well-known writer. His report was so favourable that when I took it to Monseigneur Odelin, the Vicar-General, the latter said amiably: "Oh! but with such a report the usual *permis d'imprimer* is not sufficient," and he substituted the more formal *"Imprimatur."* And so, the book was published under the Archbishop's *Imprimatur* in the summer of 1905. My publisher was Lecoffre, a delightful old gentleman whose father and grandfather had printed books of a similar character since early in the nineteenth century.

Shortly after the appearance of my book the atmosphere changed and the strong reaction known as Integralism set in. It would be unjust to deny that a reaction was necessary, but it would be silly not to say—now that more liberal influences prevail in Rome—that some opportunists made Integralism a paying affair. The Vice-Rector of Stanislas was not a little shocked to hear an obscure priest—sent from Rome to disband the small religious order known as the Brothers of Saint Vincent de Paul—bragging to him: "Look at me! I am only a little monk, but the French bishops quake at my approach." They might well do so.

In that same year, 1907, Modernism was solemnly condemned in two famous documents, the encyclical *Pascendi* and a syllabus containing sixty-five propositions declared erroneous. In August I was travelling in Italy when a newspaper lying on a café table, and, shortly after, a letter from Countess Paravicini de Revel, informed me that my book had just been placed on the Index. Similarly noted was M. Edouard Le Roy's book *Qu'est-ce qu'un Dogme?* The day was the perfection of an Italian day; the Lake of Como outside my window proclaimed the presence of the invisible enchantress who certainly lives on its banks; I did not feel theologically-minded the least bit. So the news seemed to me a sort of incongruous joke. However, I had to get to business. I returned to Paris, saw Cardinal Amette who had heard of the possibility of an unfavourable verdict of the Roman congregation and had done all he could to avert it, less to save his office from the annoyance of having its imprimatur overridden than out of kindness to me. A letter which he wrote me helped to comfort my poor old aunt (the Titine of *My Old World*), whose imagination already showed her mediæval auto-da-fés. I shall always be grateful to him, as well as to the headmaster of Stanislas, Abbé Pautonnier, who took the longish trip to Trélon purposely to explain to my aunt what the appearance of a book on the Index really means. She revived as he told her that the Index does not record condemnations, although the word is often loosely used in that connection, but is merely a list of publications which the faithful are not to read without an authorization by no means difficult to obtain. He quoted a number of titles which rather surprised dear Titine. And when he finally said that Alexandre Dumas' *The Three Musketeers* was on the Index, but would probably be taken off, she laughed outright and became serene.

Two or three years ago, on the occasion of a new edition of the Index, the American press noticed with amusement a certain number of titles. One of them was *La Pensée Catholique dans l'Angleterre Contemporaine.* Visibly most columnists thought this a good joke, for they will think of my collar when they read what I write. No less visibly were they vague about the true significance of the Index. I must say that ever since Countess Werner de Mérode explained to me, when I was sixteen, very much the same things which M. Pautonnier said to Titine, I have regarded the institution of the Index as too valuable to be treated lightly. Anybody who has watched the reading of the young knows how absurd it is not to put them on their guard against publications which they are not equipped to criticize. The Jews were right in reserving the *Canticle of Canticles* for men above thirty. But there is another advantage in having an official list of books thus reserved: it makes for the freedom of the writer. A man may refrain from expressing himself openly from fear of offending pious ears, but he is reassured if he knows that his book can be protected against rash curiosity by an official warning that this kind of production is not for everybody.

Tyrrell took the encyclical and the syllabus very hard, harder even than the measures decided against him personally. For, paradoxical as it may sound to people who only know his story from the outside, he was deeply attached to the Church. His frequent temptation, after 1907, to go back to the Anglican community he had left in boyhood came from his desire to be, in Renan's words, in a place where people keep close together in order to feel warm. The letters he wrote to me, entirely free from repining, were full of discouragement. He foresaw the setting in of Pastoralism. The many theological students in the Roman Seminaries whose interest in my *La Pensée Catholique* had made the success of the book would be replaced by students who would only care for boy-scoutism, agricultural associations or at best missionary work in the suburbs of big cities. There was no

chance, Tyrrell thought, for the great theological overhauling
which Modernism had tried to bring about. The effort had been
crushed to death before even being quite conscious of itself.

I took a different view. The Church had been wise in slacken-
ing a movement which aimed at remodelling the whole intellectuality of Christendom within a few years. The Church was not
the association of the happy few, it was the vast body of the
faithful whose slowly developing notions react on the official
teaching which its questions largely condition. And the slowness of this development can hardly be conceived. Walk into the
hall where a debate on the existence of God is going on. Two
centuries after Leibniz ninety-nine in a hundred of the people
seated there have no idea even of the most secular philosophy.
They ask you questions: "Do you believe in a personal God?"
and while you proceed with the necessary explanations concerning personality another question suddenly makes it clear to
you that what the audience wants to know is simply: "Do you
believe that the Lord God walked in the garden in the cool of the
day?" The word "personal" on which the discussion is centred
has no meaning. How long will it take to give it its all-important
significance in the minds of the multitude? Even the "real" and
the "notional" of such a human doctrine as Newmanism take
years to be approximately conceived. The great Italian word:
Pazienza! must also be the motto of the Church.

But there was another aspect of the development which seemed
to me unquestionable and which I felt ought to satisfy even the
most impatient modernistic expectations. History had stepped
into the teaching of the seminaries and with it the concept of
development which clarifies and vivifies everything. Was not
that enough? Minds which had long been used to the notion that
everything connected with religion was static would henceforth
think, on the contrary, that dynamism was the rule. That was as
much fraught with consequences as visualizing the history of
man on this speck of Earth in connection with the boundlessness
of Time and the immensity of Space. It meant the substitution of

reality for appearances as misleading as the waning of the moon
is to an African primitive.

All this Tyrrell knew, as well as I did, and conceived infinitely
more clearly. But he pointed out the evident eclipse of intellectual curiosity, as Scoutism and Moralism and even, in much
higher spheres, the Benedictinism dear to Bremond became more
and more popular. Tyrrell has only been dead a quarter of a
century and Moralism, i.e., the more Hebraic aspects of Christianity, has brought over to religious practise millions of young
people whose parents were kept away from it by superficial unbelief. After being so long a doctrine of old people, Catholicism
in France, or even in totalitarian Italy, has lately become the
vivifying belief of the young. It is true that they do not care a
straw for philosophy, need only the apologetics of the "Study
Circles," and I recently heard a highly cultivated Cardinal com-
plaining of the surprising theological ignorance of young priests
who come over to the seminary from the law schools or from
technical institutes of European reputation. But it seems to me
that it is that very indifference to controversy, that notional stillness, which gives its full force to the real which formulas would
only inadequately translate. The sloughing off of antiquated
notions is taking place during this wintry immobility. Certain
mental forms become so remote that they no longer count. Listen
to a young mother teaching sacred history to her children, and
the fact will be brought home to you. A vital transformation has
been produced without any interference of formulas. In the
same way Catholics born under Pius the Ninth, will die without
getting quite used to the present relation of Italy and the Papacy.
But the Turin boy-scout who will be elected Pope in 1985 will
have great difficulty in realizing his grandfather's view concerning the same question. Similarly, the contemporaries of Bossuet
might be shocked by his teaching on the subject of the eternal
fate of children dying unbaptized, but they believed what the
illustrious Bishop said. Our contemporaries merely read of it as
of an intellectual curiosity: they show no reaction. It is so true
that the so-called silent period of which Tyrrell only saw the be-

ginning was not theologically barren. Indeed, it did not prevent the famous Jesuit professor, Cardinal Billot, from propounding a view of the Incarnation which nobody else would have dared to make public in Rome.

George Tyrrell died on July 15, 1909. Bremond who had arranged to spend August with him at the Scilly Islands wanted me to join them on one of those rocky mounds the sombre outline of which always impresses me when I see it from the ship on my return voyages from America. I had other plans and Tyrrell, who had been fighting Bright's disease, suddenly got worse and died. The flowers were still fresh on his grave in Storrington churchyard when I arrived. Bremond had left, after delivering, over his friend's coffin, the most touching oration he ever wrote. Miss Petre, the friend and biographer of Tyrrell, gave me as a souvenir the four volumes of his breviary. She also allowed me to stay for long hours, during several days, in the two narrow rooms where Tyrrell's things lay, exactly as he had used them such a short while before.

Somehow the same peace which prevails over the wealds around Storrington and over its churchyard has gradually crept over Tyrrell's memory. Of the few men, his intellectual opponents, who still survive none ever uses a bitter word in speaking of him who was brave to temerity but was as gentle as a child.

La Pensée Catholique was not a mere book to me. It was the summary of an examination of conscience, the kind of religious inventory which Saint Paul definitely recommends. Such an examination requires courage: one seems to be looking down the crater of Etna against the advice of the guides. Many times I felt—in the words of Coventry Patmore—

> rash with theories of the right
> Which stretched the tether of my Creed
> But did not break it.

However, honesty and perseverance in the search for truth will produce peace. Ever since that inventory was made I have felt happy and secure in my religion. Catholicism attracts many non-Catholics by the solidity of its rationalization and the rigidity of its discipline. Catholics, too, are aware of what they owe to the firm structure of their Church. But there is something they value instinctively, and that is the wealth and variety of the religious life they can enjoy within the pale. Here, intellectual constructions, divergences between theologians, or the hypotheses of the higher critics count for little. I was struck in childhood by the remark made by the author of the *Imitation* that it is better to please the Trinity than to descant profoundly about the Trinity. Later on I was equally impressed by a picturesque sentence of Bremond's about the humble market-woman who, tiptoeing to the chapel of the Blessed Sacrament, is as much at home in Notre-Dame as the learned ecclesiastics she passes pointing out to a visitor the beauties of the cathedral. The strength of Catholicism lies in its dogma; the interior life of Catholics develops in their devotion, and all languages repeat in a thousand forms that where love begins freedom also begins.

I have never felt like going again over the ground I travelled during the fifteen years preceding the publication of *La Pensée Catholique*. I have no interest at present in religious controversy, and even apologetics is a little argumentative for the state of mind in which I have long been. Once, in America, I was near debating Mr. Clarence Darrow on the concept of God, but that debate would not have been a real debate, at all events not on my side. I would have limited myself to showing that the God of Plato, of Saint Augustine, of Aquinas, of Descartes and Leibniz has nothing in common with the tribal god whom Mr. Darrow, a powerful orator, or such a well-equipped man as Mr. Max Eastman, still assault with Ingersoll's old-fashioned weapons. They have no trouble in being victorious, but their god is not my God.

My real interest is in religious psychology. For more than thirty years I have endeavoured to see the extent and nature of what Christians, during the years 35–100, regarded as their essential belief, how they prayed, how they lived and died. People who think that this effort need not be very great, as the New Testament gives us all the data we require, will overlook an all-important point: we cannot read, really read, the New Testament without first forgetting a great deal which obscures our vision while we read. Forgetting in this case, means getting rid of the innumerable accretions which eighteen centuries have laid between us and the reality. It also means learning an immense amount mostly useful in helping us to forget. The task is stupendous and would be discouraging if even modest results were not so valuable to mind and soul.

I have never written and I may never write—no matter how inclined I feel to tackle the subject—about the early Christian mentality. In thirty years I have not written a word that can be called theological. A few chapters in *What We Live By* which misinformed people might regard as theology are purely philosophical. Before there was any rumour that *La Pensée Catholique* might be placed on the Index I had turned into the broad literary avenue. This was done largely on the advice of my senior, Dr. William Barry, who, in his turn, had taken his cue from Erasmus. Barry felt that merely to create the atmosphere in which the truth will best be apprehended, or to secure an audience favourable to it, is doing no mean service to those who try to administer the truth straight and *ex cathedra*. There are people who will not see the accuracy of this statement, and who hear with terror that a priest can be in the literary field and yet preserve his character. It may be the fault of a certain way of pronouncing the word literature. But it is chiefly the fault of thoughtlessness. Such people endlessly hear the New Testament read in church without noticing that even Christ used literary forms. Some day, however, they discover that, long before Monsignor Benson or Canon Sheehan wrote, Cardinal Newman and Cardinal Wiseman published romances which seem to have been pretty convincing parables. Their surprise is comical. It is also pitiful. There are innumerable ways of preaching what one believes. Some people merely look their conviction, others sing it, others again prefer forcing it on the mind through logic: each method is right where it is rightly used.

I wrote articles of all kinds and all lengths for the English and American reviews, and I still wrote often in French. The two volumes which followed *La Pensée Catholique*—*Figures de Moines* and *Les Sœurs Brontë*—were in French. I enjoyed writing them. There is singular pleasure in toying with the central idea of a book, or of an essay, and watching it in different lights till its possible expression begins to show a definite contour and one knows it is time to begin writing. Then another kind of pleasure awaits the writer who has been conscientious in his preparation: the general outline on which he is working unexpectedly becomes alive and dictates to him things he had not even glimpsed while his book was in its inchoate condition.

I used to write in a leisurely way. Nowadays, being my own employer and apparently doing what I please, I am a pretty hard task-master to myself. This comes from the necessity to face a world which for a long time only knew my name, but now has crept into my life and demands advice or sympathy which after all I have no right to refuse. It also comes from the phantasm besetting a writer as his time grows shorter: the chimes of Notre-Dame seem to dole out minutes instead of hours to me. During the twenty years of my connection with College Stanislas, my life was regulated by the community bell. I was rung out to work but I was also rung in to freedom. The consciousness that I had done what I was bound to do gave me the pleasant sensation that I was not expected to do more. I experienced what Charles Lamb tells us he used to feel when, his work at India House being left behind, he could begin to live with himself and for himself. I played often with my friends, and my private work was only another kind of play. I have always written for my

reader—often as if I saw him seated close beside me—and I
have regarded that way of writing as a mere form of politeness.
Of the dangerous phantom called the public I have generally
been unconscious, and a delicious sense of freedom has been the
consequence.

Money was not much of a consideration either. My articles
being more than decently paid for, I could not help regarding
them, along with teaching, as my livelihood. But I never thought
of a book as a thing intended to bring in money. *La Pensée
Catholique*—which was out of print less than two years after
publication—produced exactly three hundred and fifty francs,
and I had no idea that I was ill-treated. I had published a book,
that was all. I was what publishers must have regarded as a
splendid author, a fine associate or what not. I had an inkling of
this when Perrin who published *Figures de Moines*—to all in-
tents and purposes a successful book noticed by a first-rate press
—paid me my first instalment. Perrin, like several other French
publishers, and at least one British one, did not send in a statement or report of any kind. You just called at his office, not without a feeling that you were intruding, and you asked about your
book with a Chinese politeness which you hoped your interlocutor might understand. He sometimes did. Perrin did. He
fussed with his ledgers a while, then opened a safe in front of
which he stood for quite five minutes and finally returned with
three coins: two twenty-franc gold pieces and a two-franc silver
piece which he pushed towards me with a complex *"Voilà! voilà!
ah! voilà!"* which I did not quite make out at first. I suddenly
realized that these forty-two francs were all I was to expect.
Before me stood the little publisher with his pinched avaricious
face, his dyspeptic long nose and a funny frightened look. I knew
that he and his brother lived in a château outside Paris which
authors' books had bought for them. I also reflected that, in the
morning of that very same day, I had made six or seven times
forty-two francs by scribbling a few pages in English. I laughed
outright. The little man seemed more reassured than puzzled but,
in a second, his face changed again to a violent expression: "Ah!

you are reasonable! But other writers are not. Some are awful! M. Barrès! . . . oh! M. Barrès is the worst of them all. He comes in here and asks questions, shocking questions, my dear Sir, as if we kept two sets of books in this house where everything is as transparent as daylight. That man, Sir, that man would put you on a table and rip you up for money." A few years later I related this scene to Barrès: he laughed his cruel quiet laughter.

Les Sœurs Brontë was paid for in a lump sum, five hundred francs. So was the first English book I published, a literary biography of Paul Bourget: Constable paid me a shabby twenty pounds. But I did not mind. I enjoyed writing both books: the Brontë study because I liked the three sisters, imagined my Trélon helped me to understand their North, and felt pleasure in quietly demolishing absurd legends about them; the Bourget biography because it gave me a chance to weigh a reputation which had rather intimidated me and, on the other hand, to defend a talent which the younger school was, as usual, beginning to attack savagely. I gave Bourget a pretty high niche, but among novelists of not quite the first order, and this he resented. The Brontë book won me some reputation for English scholarship, in America as well as in Paris and London, and I still occasionally find college professors who are as grateful to me for writing it as I am grateful to them for remembering it.

However, I was not a little surprised when, in the summer of 1912, the Executive in the house of Chatto and Windus, Mr. Percy Spalding, who was soon to become a dear friend, wrote me a surprisingly deferential letter, asking if he might come to Paris to make arrangements for a book—the volume which was published under the title *France Herself Again*. Mr. Spalding was a delightful person with the most gracious manner, a twinkle in his eye, a psychological acumen which he could, in a second, harness in the service of business, and the raciest vocabulary I ever heard an Englishman of the upper middle class use in speaking. Listening to him I felt as if he had been talking all his life with Bunyan or Daniel Defoe. After we had talked about the book, the idea of which immediately appealed to me, Mr. Spalding asked what sort of contract I preferred. Remembering my other publishing ventures, and mustering all my resources against this rare and improbable publisher, I quickly said I wanted a lump sum and this sum could not be inferior to three hundred pounds (which I thought was an absolutely Shylockian demand). Mr. Spalding smiled delighted assent and left me almost ashamed to have imposed such a figure on such a delightful person. I only felt better when Arnold Bennett pooh-poohed my qualms and said in his treble: "You never even thought of the American rights, eh? did you, Innocence? they alone are worth three hundred pounds." I had no idea of the existence of American rights, and Bennett was everlastingly recommending to me his London agent who, he said, would be father and mother to me.

I immediately started the preparation of my book for which I soon discovered that, without knowing it, I already had valuable notes. Towards the end of 1913 I began to write it, and I worked at it, under great pressure and amid great difficulties, during the next eight months. It was finished on the twenty-second of July, 1914, a bare ten days before the war broke out. But this is the place to tell how I had been affected by political developments in France and in Europe during this first phase of my life in Paris, and how my reactions account for the spirit of *France Herself Again*.

My political tendencies early became, as readers of *My Old World* may remember, liberal and democratic. I belonged to my generation. I believed in the republican form of government, in the rights of the proletariat, and in the internationalism which these preferences generally entail. It was natural that I should consort with people similarly minded. I had done so at Lille, somewhat to the disgust of those in authority in my university, and I followed the same inclination in Paris. Even before settling

there I was seldom in the capital without visiting the well-known
Henri Lorin.

Lorin was a gentleman of considerable means, of active and
nimble intelligence and of extraordinary kindness. He had had
a strict scientific training but to that he never alluded, and
many people were surprised when they were told about it. His
chief interest was in politics and his delight was to see and
talk endlessly with intelligent people similarly interested. He
knew hundreds, of all kinds, from M. Millerand, the penitent
socialist who became a conservative President of the French
Republic, to a brilliant Hungarian aristocrat, Monsignor Vaÿ
de Vaÿa. The latter he had met in boyhood—still dressed at
fifteen in girls' clothes to humour a Betsy-Trotwood-like
family. Later Vaÿ de Vaÿa became a diplomatist as well as the
most shining social light in Paris, and now he was a Roman
prelate whose robes recalled his former familiarity with feminine apparel but could not conceal vestiges of brilliant worldli-
ness. That host of friends Lorin loved and handled with affectionate mastery, a unique adept at drawing people out, and so
prompt at repartee that he never looked like the professional
host. Some people, observing his diversified life, imagined he
must be superficial, but he was not. He was the kind of man who
knows how to save from each busy day two or three meditative
hours, and the quality of his mind appeared in what he occasionally wrote. I always think of him when some American business
man, apparently unliterary, surprises his friends by producing a
few pages of well-knit, well-chosen English. As for Lorin's
kindness, it was only fully revealed at his death, early in the
Great War, by the hundreds of people he had obliged, but one
felt it when, every now and then, he insisted on dining tête-à-tête
with a friend. You knew, on such occasions, that you were not
one on a list. This discreetly devout man was an apostle in his
own way.

Lorin was married. His wife, as Marquise de Las Marismas,
had been, in her youth, one of the beauties at the court of Napo-

leon the Third and appears in Winterhalter's historical picture.
But she presided neither over his salon nor his table. I saw Lorin
dozens of times dictate to the maître d'hôtel capital menus which
he invented on the spur of the moment, and Madame Lorin was
indifferent to democracy or social reforms. She never listened
to a word that was said at her husband's table. From time to time
she would ask him whether such and such a thing had been sent
to such and such a poor person, or she would admonish some
young foreign guest: "So-and-so, do please mind your accent."
She herself was half Scotch and half Italian and never quite
acquired a French voice.

Once in a while another lady who also lived in the house appeared at the table. This was Tante Annette, Lorin's aunt, an
exquisite little old lady whose never-fading grace transformed
the table as a rare bouquet sometimes does. She never grew old,
never grew modern either, and never ceased to charm us. Many
times I saw a group of men pressing around her when there were
in the room pretty women who, in her absence, would have been
eagerly surrounded. When she and Madame Lorin died Lorin
ceased to invite women altogether.

Every Sunday Lorin had twelve of us, always the same, at
luncheon. Of those, Goyau, now in the French Academy,
de Vogüé, Pinon, Moysset, Paul Hazard, Masson, Arren, Lau-
rentie and de Vaugelas had made, or were making, a reputation.
(The last four were killed early in the war.) The conversation
was incredibly brilliant, never more than one voice being heard
at a time and everybody contributing of his best. Another man,
whom I dearly loved, Legendre, now director of the French
Academy in Madrid, never spoke a syllable, but sometimes he
would go through such an amusingly clever pantomime that his
silences attracted constant attention. Once I reproached the
whole tableful with being rather cool to Abbé Lemire in an
emergency when he had needed his friends. "Not one of you!"
I said, "not one!" Legendre raised one finger in mute protest and
went on with his dinner. The last time I met him it was on a

steamer going to Morocco. He smiled his pleasure at seeing me
but hardly spoke.

Lorin was the most eminent Christian Socialist in France, and
the founder of the yearly conventions known as *Les Semaines
Sociales* where his name is still frequently invoked. Like all
Christian Socialists he had built his doctrine on the encyclicals
of Leo the Thirteenth and was frequently received by the Pope.
When M. Millerand required a corpus of social doctrine which,
busy lawyer and politician that he was, he could not evolve by
himself, Lorin provided him with the system he has ever since
defended.

Lorin was also a believer in the possibility of that complete
reconciliation between the Church and the Republic which, paradoxically, we now see accomplished, in spite of the activity and
comparative success of the French Royalists. Nobody could meet
anti-clerical politicians on neutral ground as he did. His experience, like mine, was that there are few people one can despise
and even fewer one can hate. But all his life Lorin remained a
confirmed democrat whereas I outgrew my youthful enthusiasms
and the certainties which I had carried away from Cambrai
Seminary, and now believe that democracies ought occasionally
to go into receivership.

This was not done in a day, for I thought there was a good
deal of prejudice in the opposition of the older clergy and of
the bourgeoisie to the Republican régime, and my reaction to the
incomprehension which frequently disgusted me, for a long time
made me over-indulgent. I condoned the anti-clericalism of the
Republic as the almost inevitable consequence of a fight in
which the clergy had not always been the underdog and had
frequently exceeded the bounds of its own domain. This was
not an instance of a harmless minority gradually rising to eminence as was the case with the Catholics of America, but, on the
contrary, the defeat of an exaggeratedly powerful body which,
during many centuries, had owned two thirds of French land. On
the whole, the Republic and the Church of France stood in the

same relation as Henry the Eighth and the English monasteries: only the Republic was much more moderate than Bluff Harry was ever known to be.

I was also willing to give the Republic time to right itself. Certainly the Panama and the Grévy-Wilson scandals had thrown an unwelcome light over a régime which proverbially should be built on virtue, but it was the fault of an imperfect constitution. Who had framed the Republican constitution absurdly as it was, viz., with an irresponsible Chamber centralizing all powers over against a President deprived of any authority? A Royalist assembly which planned this makeshift in order to restore the Monarchy whenever it pleased. The Republicans could not be blamed for what had been caused by Royalist perfidy. So I was at one, on two vital points, with the optimism of Lorin's democrat friends.

What shocked me out of it was, in the first place, the cowardly hypocrisy of Combes' action against the religious orders. Combes' predecessor, Waldeck-Rousseau, had passed an Association Law whereby the many modern religious orders which had been founded without official authorization were not to enjoy the privileges of association unless they submitted their statutes and a list of their members to the Minister of Interior. This was fair and reasonable, so most orders sent in the required information. Only, when Combes, an ex-cleric, took office he compelled *all* the orders to send in the same data along with a detailed inventory of their property. Once in possession of this information he refused authorization to all the orders founded since the French Revolution, confiscated their property and disbanded their members. This dastardly action recalled a well-known revolutionary scene. A number of men summarily sentenced to death were to be killed by cannon-shot. They were huddled together on a parade ground and a salvo was shot. The commissaries present suspected that some of the men lying on the ground were not really dead and cried out: "Let all survivors stand up, the Republic pardons them." No sooner were those few men up than another salvo mowed them down. Some people in my circle were able to find reasons for this execution, I never could. For the first time I had to admit that behind the democratic façade of our Republic lurked a secret and much stronger agency: the atheistic French Masonry which has but little in common with the lodges of Great Britain and the United States but corresponds only too closely to the Mexican Masonry. I loathed the revelation. It showed me that I had been fooled while innocently imagining myself a Liberal.

It also became clear pretty soon that our Democracy could not reform itself, or, if it had been able to do so, would not have even tried. People who, like myself, have been much in contact with politicians know that politicians are only interested in themselves, not in reforms. A smilingly contemptuous book published in 1910 by Bertrand de Jouvenel, himself one of the ruling party, said as much in its title, *La République des Camarades* (The Logrollers' Club), which at once became a by-word. It is a painful fact that democratic reforms have been slower in France than almost anywhere else. French women do not vote. Parisian workmen stand huddled in buses while their London brethren travel in armchairs. Dozens of similar instances could be adduced. Words have done duty for deeds. The average elector still says "the Government" in very much the tone in which his ancestors of 1780 said "the King." He has not yet realized that there may be Cabinets in France but never any Governments, seeing that the real ruler is an amorphous aggregate of six hundred deputies. Every time a man has appeared, seemingly strong enough to effect constitutional reforms—a Clemenceau, a Poincaré or a Doumergue—he has invariably been thrown out by obscure deputies thinking their petty privileges in jeopardy. Hence my growing distrust of Democracy as we saw, and still see it, in France, pure, unadulterated, and often impotent.

Most of us, friends of Lorin's, were great internationalists and consequently pacifists. I was one, not merely on general principles, like anybody in his senses, but because I simply could not conceive the possibility of a European war. I was an infant in 1870 and so the memories of that humiliation did not count. Sentimentally attached as I was to Lorraine, the land of my father's father, I felt strongly that it was for that province to show what it wanted. If it kept up its French language and did not change its French customs, the modification on the map would mean nothing. If it became Germanized, well and good, let it please itself. I had a shock in 1898 when entering Metz and noticing how French the natives had remained, I also noticed how constant and powerful the German influx had evidently been in a quarter of a century. I was also deeply hurt when I heard a foreign friend with whom I was going to Germany, say quite naturally as we got out of the station at Strasbourg: "Now we are in Germany." I promptly turned to a gentleman who was being met by his wife and daughter and asked him if we were in Germany. His French was perfect, so was his answer, and so was his ironical smile as I delivered up my companion to him.

Peace was such a certainty that even Fashoda did not alarm me. All the annoyance it caused was limited to silly anti-British songs. The same with the Triple Alliance which only struck me as a meaningless effort of diplomacy to keep its old game going. The same with the Russian alliance, visibly an Oriental dodge to obtain money. Even the beginnings of the Entente Cordiale did not succeed in making me ask myself why Great Britain should go out of her isolation. Delcassé was evidently playing a bold game, but it could not lead to war because war was inconceivable to the modern mind.

The sudden appearance of the Kaiser at Tangier, in 1905, and the tone of the speech in which he assured the Sultan of his protection, were rudely awakening flashes. In a moment my whole outlook was changed. War? Why war was there, written in glaring letters. The Moroccan question was only a side issue. What we saw was German force asserting itself in a manner which showed that it could not indefinitely be kept in check. Shortly after, Germany demandèd the resignation of Delcassé and, to my utter humiliation, this great minister was thrown overboard.

Yet the nation as a whole did not react. The shock of the defeat in 1870 had left it nervous and doubtful. The effort to dominate the nervousness had not made it realistic and manly, it had only made it sceptical and cynical. The philosopher of the period was Anatole France with his everlasting: "What does it matter?" I had no doubt that Anatole France was only, at bottom, an astonishingly gifted *græculus,* the perfection of a man who is not a real man. I was not very much surprised when, in April 1914, four short months before the war, I saw his signature on a poster declaring war an impossibility. It was disheartening to see such a wonderfully equipped man showing such blindness. It was humiliating too. I associated a great deal with English and American newspaper correspondents. Their attitude hurt and irritated me. Many of them were Francophiles, but what they loved in us French was precisely what I disliked in Anatole France, viz., wit at all costs and a marvellous indifference to realities. When I would expostulate in sentences beginning: now, suppose your own country . . . they merely shrugged their shoulders and I knew that they meant: ah, but ours is a serious, not an amusing, country like France.

Even people who must have known better, the men in the governments which came in after the Tangier incident, acted as if they neither knew nor realized. There never was a more patriotic, a more intransigeant Frenchman than Clemenceau. Yet, in 1909, half way between Tangier and the Great War, so much of the radical spirit still clung to him that, in spite of the urgent needs of the French army, he unconscionably reduced the war budget by one fourth. Surely there never was a nation not only so pacific, but so immersed in pacificism, so trammelled and hampered by pacifism, as the French nation of that period. Every now and then I still meet abroad a fossil whose mind cannot get rid of the old equation: Frenchman=militarist, and

I remember what I felt as year followed year without any marked improvement in the common sense of my compatriots, absurdly unaware of the danger at their door.

Finally a reaction set in, produced, as usual in France, much more by literature than by life. The Socialists had been steadily rising, and their number in the Chamber grew large enough to cause alarm. While people imagined that the literary expression of Socialism was *Das Kapital,* Georges Sorel suddenly published his famous *Reflections upon Violence.* The doctrine embodied in this book was simple. The essential tenet of Socialism was not the material progress of the working classes through the nationalization of wealth, it was the *Class War.* By teaching men to be ready to give up their lives in the war of class against class, socialism restored to them the virtues produced by self-oblivion. It was an introduction to heroism, a spiritual value, nothing else. The effect produced by this view was considerable in literary circles.

Simultaneously, Maurice Barrès who had started as a technician of Egotism was going through a reaction against his own doctrine, which promptly made him the leader of a band of thinkers antagonistic to Anatole France. The latter insisted on thinking of the immensity of Time and Space and the insignificance of earthly affairs in comparison. Barrès replied that the Universe is not practically interesting to Man. Man's own microcosm is the only universe he really knows, the only one he lives in. What is seen from Sirius is not what man sees. An Ethic was implied in this philosophy: we had to live, and live our best *hic et nunc.* Barrès being a great writer and a magnetic individual was read by millions and followed by thousands.

All these phenomena I noted during the years following the Tangier revelation, and I became more and more convinced that many who paraded the Anatole France spirit were only trying to conceal their cowardice in face of the reality, viz., the fact that, sooner or later, Germany would put French energy to the test.

Meanwhile the British were also going through an evolution. The history of the years following the beginnings of the Entente is well known. The British wavered in their politics. Sometimes they realized that a nation whose Emperor gave it as its motto: "Our future is on the water" must inevitably come into conflict with Britannia, queen of the seas. Sometimes the absurd "German cousin" fallacy would recover its force and we witnessed the Haldane period. In 1912 Arthur Balfour, the most absolutely English admixture of idealism and realism, saw the situation clearly and simplified it in an article published by a German review, *Nord und Süd*. The gist of it was this: "If Germany goes on building ships, a war between it and Great Britain will be unavoidable." I am often surprised that people who ought to have noticed this article, not only in America but even in England, were not aware of it. This accounts for the fact that such men as Mr. Lloyd George, Mr. Ramsay MacDonald, or even Sir John Simon have never grasped the fact that the Great War was fundamentally a trial of force between the so-called cousins in Great Britain and in Germany. They foolishly insist on seeing it as a repetition of 1870, one more duel between France and Germany. However, the real, if invisible, leaders of the foreign politics of England had no illusions. They knew that, as the German Dernburg was soon to say, France must be "the soldier of England," and they began to take more interest in a moral evolution of the French which might make them, from the ultra-pacifist nation they had become, a people once more capable of producing an army. How that conviction managed to ooze into the mind of a publisher even remarkably wide awake, I do not know, but Mr. Spalding's visit to me and his ideas concerning a possible book showing the evolution of France were obviously a manifestation of British interest in the steeling of the French.

As I said above, the preparation of *France Herself Again* took me more than a year, and its writing seven or eight months during which I was busy to dizziness. I was so intent on the composition of the book that I missed the significance of the Sarajevo

incident. I was strolling up the boulevard Raspail, that perfect
summer Sunday, as the newsboys cried out the extras announcing
the historic murder along with the results of the Grand Prix.
I bought *La Liberté*, inwardly commented, "Another Austrian
tragedy! poor old man!" and hurried back to the College and
to my manuscript.

I finished the book on July 22nd, sent it to London, and immediately left for Switzerland where I had discovered a restful
nook beside a humble little lake just off the Lake of Zurich. I
was exhausted by the effort to write a big book without cutting
down my teaching hours and, during a few days, I did not look
at a single newspaper, only asking about the Caillaux case—
then going on at the Paris assizes—when I happened to meet a
Parisian banker who was staying at my hotel. On the morning of
July 30th this gentleman replied to my usual question: "Madame
Caillaux be d——! we are going to have war!" He handed me
a German newspaper in which, in fact, I read about the *Kriegs-
zustand*. I spent the day waiting for more news and trying to
exchange bank bills for gold which was already vanishing. Next
morning I took a slow-moving train to Paris. Next to me sat an
elderly German, a *Landsturm* officer, who did not try to conceal
the tears falling on the telegram which had just mobilized him.
We shook hands when he got out at some junction. It was late in
the afternoon when we crossed the French frontier. From two
or three railway stations I heard the unforgettable sound of the
mobilization bells. Next morning, the train crawling on with
long delays at improbable stations, we began to pass troop-trains
going East. I have not forgotten a handsome young soldier who
with his arm affectionately round the neck of his horse, a beautiful mare, said to me in gentle chaffing, *"Ah! c'est pas par là
qu'il faut aller* (You're going the wrong way.)" A little farther,
at Chaumont station, I saw Jean Saleilles, a dear serious boy of
twenty-three, the son of my friend Professor Saleilles. There he
stood motionless in his new uniform. He was killed in one of
the early battles. A few steps away another officer, much older,

was dragging his canteen along the platform. I never saw such a sad face.

Just before dark we reached Paris and the Gare de l'Est. The faraway corner of the yard where I was landed was deserted by all employees. I found a pushcart, piled my valises upon it and wheeled it to the outside door. Paris was before me, unrecognizable. The boulevard de Strasbourg was crowded with an immense but silent multitude. There was not a taxi, not a tramcar left. The stillness of that broad avenue impressed me more than the most formidable sounds. People who have not seen that awestricken beginning of the war cannot know what war is when suddenly universal danger restores the *peuplade* to its consciousness, and the tribe feels like one person under the gloom and doom.

Part Two

THE WAR

THE next morning I started early on my business which was to get back to Trélon as soon as possible. I had no doubt that the neutrality of Belgium would be violated. Nor had any of my compatriots in the North, whatever the rest of Europe might be thinking. Many of us had read General Maitrot's book and felt sure, as this officer was, that Germany's first objective would be the Trouée des Ardennes, right in the middle of which Trélon is situated. My native town was separated from the German frontier only by the narrow width of Eastern Belgium, and all the time I was imagining an armoured car of the enemy easily covering the distance in three or four hours and its occupants preventing my poor old aunt from seeking security in the interior.

I was under no military obligations, but my first step was to go to the War Office where I entered my name as a possible interpreter. England was sitting on the fence, and it was an extraordinary disappointment to me that King George did not make that answer to President Poincaré's appeal which would undoubtedly have prevented a general war, but nobody had any doubt that Britain must come in as soon as Belgium's neutrality was violated. Whenever she did I could be employed as some sort of liaison agent.

From the War Office I went to the Gare du Nord and enquired about trains to Trélon. The answer was discouraging: only troop-trains were running and nobody could buy a ticket for at least four or five days, unless they got a special permit. From whom? The answers were conflicting. I went back to the War Of-

fice. The Minister of War, Messimy, stood on the door-steps of
the main building talking with three or four civilians. He himself was in mufti. He seemed full of his own importance, this
once anti-militarist officer, and the airs he gave himself made a
bad impression upon me. Inside I was told that I could not get
a permit without a special authorization from the Préfecture de
Police. There I found that my connection with the British and
American press would be of great use to me, but some official
endorsement was necessary. So I went to the British Embassy,
and Sir Henry Austin Lee gave me testimonials. While we were
discussing the events in his office—he was entirely optimistic
and prophesied a crushing defeat for the Germans—I noticed,
idly leaning out of a window on the other side of the courtyard,
an elderly officer in khaki whose plain but strong features recalled pictures seen in the newspapers. This officer was Kitchener,
who slowly swung his powerful frame from right to left as if he
were expecting somebody, but was in reality only killing time.
This naturalness I could not help contrasting with Messimy's
attitudinizing, but on the other hand I could not help reflecting
that, strong as he might be, Kitchener was only the head of such
a small army that it did not dare to call itself more than an
expeditionary force. That was the first paradox I noticed in a
war which was to show many.

I jumped on my bicycle once more and prepared to go back
to the Préfecture de Police. On my way I went down the rue de
Lille and passed the German Embassy. Germany had not declared war as yet, although it did so a few hours later, and the
Ambassador, Baron von Schoen, not an unpopular figure in
Paris, had not left. Seven policemen were protecting the entrance
to his mansion, but their presence seemed unnecessary: the street,
quiet at all times, was deserted.

Not so the adjacent streets and the boulevard Saint-Germain,
strewn with small knots of people exchanging impressions in a
low voice. There was no excitement. I was struck by the recurrence of two short sentences heard all the time from men between
the ages of twenty-four and forty-eight: *"Je pars aujourd'hui*

(I am off to-day)," or "*C'est que je pars demain* (Yes, but I am off to-morrow)," spoken in a matter-of-fact tone very different from the *Nach Paris* enthusiasm which at the same minute kept Berlin yelling. All my life, narratives of past mobilizations had made me familiar with the thrilling significance of that homely word *partir*, but it was the first time I realized how truly sublime its very simplicity could be. An unprovoked, unexpected war created a state of affairs in which you had to go to places from which you might never return, that was all. The spy-fever, inevitable in the beginning of all wars, was already rife and workmen were busy tearing down the fronts of the many Maggi dairies wrongly supposed to belong to a German company. The crowds looked on with indifference.

Remembering that war means dearth, I stopped at a big grocery in the rue de Rennes and bought a heavy bag of edibles which I tied to my wheel. When I paid the cashier I noticed that a revolver lay ready on his desk. Opposite this shop was my bank, and there too a pistol was within reach of the teller. These guns surprised me a few seconds, then they seemed natural. Everything seemed natural, apparently because great emergencies simplify what the habitual routine of daily life charges with useless accretions. I had not gone fifty yards from the bank before I met another cyclist who beckoned to stop me and jumped off. This was my friend of a good many years, Georges Ducrocq, a good poet, a great traveller, and an extremely handsome fellow whom a bodily deficiency (he had the kind of weak left arm which annoyed the German Kaiser so much) did not keep from such strenuous exertion as mountain-climbing. "I am enlisting," Ducrocq said, "foreign legion first, as our people won't have me; however, they will have to have me. Good-bye!" He was perfectly calm, but I had never seen him so happy. At the College, where I left my commissariat stuff, I met one of my colleagues, Kaeppelin, the brilliant young historian of the East India Company, the most French-looking of Parisian Alsatians. There was more than usual a curious, a rather frightening complexity in his smile: he was a great patriot. *"Je pars demain,"* he said. I never saw him again but once. He was killed in 1915.

My endeavors to obtain a permit were vain. Three times, after being sent from pillar to post, I turned up at the Préfecture de Police which seemed to be the eelpot in the maze. That last time as I was listening to the sickening repetitions of the official, a disgust came over me and, with that, an idea. "I have a bicycle," I said, "I'll just ride home." The man was so relieved that he did not even think of telling me that a *laissez-passer*, a sort of passport, would be necessary. I returned to the College and looked for Antoine, the servant who had lent me the bicycle, to negotiate with him the purchase of the wheel. Poor Antoine had just been mobilized and was as pale as a sheet. Strangely enough he proved to be a brave soldier when he had to be, and did well at the front through the four years.

At three o'clock of the afternoon of August fifth, having burnt many papers which I did not want to leave unprotected in my rooms, I took to the road. A heavy storm kept me for an hour in the gateway of the inevitable and odious Préfecture de Police, after which I pushed up the rue d'Allemagne, a long thoroughfare now called by some other name. After clearing the city gate I dismounted to look back on Paris. I had never seen that section of the ramparts and, built as it was on steeply rising ground, it struck me as unfamiliar, outlandish, African and rather sinister. Gradually the suburbs showed more open spaces and more gardens, till suddenly, at Drancy, I found a wheat-field on the other side of a cheap row of villas. I looked for the post-office and sent Titine a telegram announcing my arrival within forty-eight hours. Pretty soon, after passing Le Bourget, I became conscious of real country on both sides of the road, as well as of rather oppressive solitude. Before me the road stretched away under its four rows of tall trees. The sky was blue, after the storm, with huge balloon-like bright clouds sailing over the tree-tops. Paris was not twelve kilometers behind, yet there was no traffic on the road, no sign of life in the fields. Another cyclist, four or five hundred yards ahead of me, was the only human figure beside my own. After a while the man looked round, turned round, and rode up to ask me was this the right road to Crépy-en-Valois. He was poor and queer, with lifeless eyes and a colourless face. He sped on, his bicycle not being heavily laden like mine, but five or six times within the next two hours he turned back again to ask me in a frightened insistent tone was this the road to Crépy-en-Valois. I preferred my feeling of solitude to this man's visits.

About half-past six I was brought up sharp at a railway crossing by two reserve soldiers in uniform who asked for my *laissez-passer*. I could not produce any. All I happened to have about me was an old election card and the letter from Sir Henry Austin Lee. The men did not look at the card but, although they knew no English, they put their heads together and puzzled for several minutes over Sir Henry's letter. Finally they gave it up as a bad job, and seeing on the top of one of my parcels two or three evening papers which they instantly longed to read, they said: "Oh! just come to the *Pomme d'Or* with us; our sergeant will be glad to talk with you."

We were soon at the inn, and the news of the arrival of a stranger in possession of fresh newspapers spreading like wildfire, in a few minutes I was seated at the dinner-table with the sergeant who was a man of about forty-five, and the village school-teacher, an eager, intelligent, very short-sighted little man devouring my newspapers, full of false news though they were. The sergeant interested me. He was a clerk in some office, but his burning patriotism, the expression of which a taciturn disposition kept smouldering, transformed him for me into a very different person: here was one of the men of 1792 about whom I had read so much in my schooldays. I more than respected that sergeant, and every time I am impressed by some manifestation of character his dignified bearing and stern countenance reappear in my memory.

His men were all employed in the stock-yards at La Villette. They discussed the war in the matter-of-fact sober manner which had struck me so much in Paris, with silent spells charged with resentment whenever the German aggression was mentioned. They had been mobilized too recently to have forgotten their slaughter-house work. Their conversation was full of disquieting technicalities. I learned that a *plata*, a *malgache* were oxen endowed with qualities or faults as different as their nationalities. All the time I was afraid of having to hear some allusion to rough dealing with the poor creatures, but animal psychology remained the topic. Next morning the schoolmaster, who was also town-hall secretary, wrote me a *laissez-passer* and I pushed on my way north.

It took me two days to cover the remaining one hundred and thirty kilometers, for the west wind alternately swept the sky beautifully clean or crowded it with squally clouds, and I had frequently to look for shelter. At Soissons the shower lasted long enough for me to write my usual weekly letter to the London *Saturday Review*, in a café full of busy officers. For nothing was so remarkable as the contrast between the loneliness of the road and the bustle of the towns. I had imagined that as I drew nearer to the Belgian frontier I must meet with marching troops and commissariat convoys, but I was mistaken. All I saw was, shortly after passing Laon, a mob of about a hundred horses conducted by two men in their every-day clothes and only militarized by the mobilization brassard on their sleeves. The horses were farm-horses marching with heart-rending patience to where thirst or exhaustion would soon end a career which might have been peaceful, if not happy, in the beetroot fields. The two men, both of them peasants, seemed sullen and resigned. A week before, hundreds of peasants like themselves must have made the country alive with July activity. Where were they now? The newspapers were packed with more or less dramatic details, but there was already, over the whole section of territory between the Parisian region and the North-eastern frontier, that veil of impenetrable secrecy which, during four years, no reporter ever lifted and no imagination satisfactorily removed. Two million men during that long period were as shadowy to the rest of us as the souls in Purgatory.

At five o'clock of a perfect summer afternoon, on August eighth, I stopped at a friendly rectory to exchange my tie for a clerical collar and put on, over my suit, a long coat which the curé lent me. A few minutes afterwards I dismounted at the foot of our front-garden steps and entered my aunt's ivy-clad house.

I had thought of our reunion with some anxiety, for dear Titine, in her old age, had grown more timid than ever, but she had remained imaginative and I was afraid the declaration of war might have upset her. But I found her, on the contrary, calmer than I had seen her for years. The minor worries with which she used to keep her nervousness active had vanished before the infinitely more powerful note of interrogation which Germany, two days before, had written across the sky, but this brand-new anxiety she had not had time yet to assimilate. She was cutting to the right lengths gladioli which our Honorine handed to her. She kissed me joyfully but with the least shade of absent-mindedness as if I had interrupted some pleasant meditation. What train had I come down by? Where had I borrowed this ugly bicycle? No, no telegram had come from Drancy or anywhere; no letters either; she had supposed I was still in Switzerland. Was my book being printed? Pretty soon, however, she came to the subject of the war. She was optimistic. I did not remember the war of 1870, did I? Well, wars looked at first as if they would never end, but all of a sudden, unexpectedly, you saw their end quite near. Armistice, peace-preliminaries, a universal relief, and then a marvellous boom of everything. This old darling who had manufactured for herself so many chimerical cares only needed to have danger at her very door to become calm and composed; only the least dash of dreaminess replaced the old agitation. Titine remained like that through as many months of the war as she was to live, and my one anxiety about her was lest sudden realization might come. But it never came.

Our little Trélon also basked, apparently undisturbed, in the happy sunshine. All the men were gone. "So-and-So's man," two or three doors away from us, had been mobilized (*était party*) two hours after the bells rang! a man of forty-seven! mobilized the first day! This was going to be a quick war. And undoubtedly victorious. The Russians were innumerable and, Belgium's neutrality having been violated, the decision of England was expected hourly. Had troops been seen in the vicinity? No? Well, troops this time were moved with incredible secrecy. Everything was different from 1870.

People in our town believed and said about the same things. But it seemed to me they either spoke in a dream or forced themselves into an attitude of happy make-believe, for almost all the time they also gave me the impression of trying to make themselves so diminutive in their homes that they might be invisible. Mentally they were quite brave and I often admired them. What acted on their nerves was, in the stillness of the summer, the silence over Belgium next door, and the consciousness of the enemy's proximity. The very vagueness of such impressions makes them harder to resist. The capture of Mulhouse by the brilliant and popular General D'Amade was welcomed with delight but did not succeed in creating enthusiasm.

What surprised me and kept my fellow-citizens wondering in those early days was the absence of French troops in a section which we all regarded as in great jeopardy. Day after day we expected the arrival of some regiment with its flag out and its band playing, but nothing came. A young cousin of mine was finishing his military service in a Lille regiment when the war broke out, and as soon as Belgium's neutrality was violated I imagined he and his regiment would be shipped off to Liége without a moment's delay. As a matter of fact, that regiment never got into Belgium at all. It was moved eastward by slow progress on our side of the frontier but, as late as August 20th, it was still at Aubenton, some twenty-five miles from us, and farther away from the Belgian border than we were. It was only months later that I realized the dilemma in which Belgium was placed at first. She wanted help, only too obviously, but she disliked even the semblance of pre-war arrangements with the French Staff.

However, on August eleventh, we were startled by the appearance in our street of African *goumiers*. There they were! on their camels! with their wives and funny babies riding behind them! The contrast of the Sahara, or even the circus associations they conjured up, with their modern armament was bewildering and I looked at them aghast. I have always thought that the story of that Algerian caravan would be interesting reading, but I never heard a word of their adventures.

Two days later rumour asserted that the British were at Avesnes, our county-town ten miles away. I rode there in great excitement to proffer my services. It was true. Four British officers, after losing their way in search of Avesnes, had finally found it, but they were gone already. It was a Sunday, and the little town of the seventeenth-century de Forest family was alive with soldiers on leave going in and out. I found Count Frédéric de Mérode, who was a sergeant in the regiment, standing at the door of the High School temporarily transformed into barracks, checking off the men's permits. We talked. I was very much attached to that young man and hated to think that, within three or four days, he might be under fire. He showed the indifference belonging to his class. Some of the men, too recently returned to military life to have resumed its habits, and conscious of Frédéric's social standing, called him Monsieur which does not correspond in the least to the "Sir" of American privates.

Next day was market-day at Trélon. Towards eleven o'clock, the streets being crowded with buggies, stalls and pushcarts, I heard the sound of an angry mob proceeding from the Court-Tournant—a cross-roads where my parents lived for a few years in my infancy. I went down to the *grille* and saw a hundred or

so market-people besieging the first house on the little square.
They were shaking their fists at a window out of which my
childish curiosity used to feast on a variety of things, from
old Marianne on her donkey going out to milk the cows, to the
glorious sunsets over the *gendarmerie*. Standing in that window
was a young woman in the last stage of hysteria, hissing insults at
the crowd. "Yes, yes, beaten you shall be," she vociferated,
"beaten hollow by the German soldiers. My brother is in that
army. He'll lick you too! he will!" The mob answered back
furiously and certainly would have torn the woman to pieces if
they could have got hold of her. I rushed to the scene and tried
to quiet the people. A young man, calmer than the rest, told me
that the woman was a Luxembourg housemaid well-known for
excitability and who was probably inventing that brother. As he
spoke, I saw two gendarmes looking impassibly at the affair
from behind the *grille* of their barracks. I went to them and upbraided them pretty severely. "What are you for?" I asked,
"either that idiot ought to be protected, or she ought to be locked
up. In either case you should be over there acting."—"We have
no orders," one of them answered coolly. But just then a troop
of cavalry was seen moving down our street. At its head rode
an elderly major, a sad-looking thoughtful man. I explained to
him briefly what was going on; at a sign, his men began circling
around the little square, and in a few moments it was cleared
while the heroine disappeared from her window.

I remembered the gendarmes' excuse when, a year or two after
the war, General Gouraud told me of an incident he remembered
of his first week at the front. He was inspecting the front lines,
and came to an outpost in a bushy place where a French sentry
was serenely looking at a few Germans, three or four hundred
yards away, cutting down saplings for a trench. Gouraud, very
much surprised, turned to the sentry and inquired why he did
not shoot. "*Mon général, je n'ai pas d'ordres* (I have no *orders*.)"
I noticed that Gouraud himself did not volunteer to use the
sentry's rifle and did not consider his own suggestion as an
order.

On August twelfth our butter-woman delivering the weekly provision told my aunt that, very early that morning, milking her cows in a quiet meadow by the forest, she had heard the boom of artillery faintly but distinctly. This piece of news which was to become so trivial moved me strangely that day. The thing called war was becoming real. In the afternoon riding to Wallers through the wheat-fields I was puzzled by the whirr of birds flying past me but which I never could see. I dismounted to look around. The afternoon was warm and quiet, incredibly happy in fact. Tall thistles showed their heads above the wheat-spikes. Little birds were balancing on some of them. I waited till one, then another, flew away. Their wings did make a soft whirr but more prolonged than the sound I continued to hear. Suddenly I realized. I, too, was hearing the guns. Day after day they were to grow more perceptible.

The next day a woman went past our house, stiff and erect, but holding a handkerchief to her eyes. According to the cruel custom of war she had been summoned to the town-hall to hear that her step-son, whom she loved more than her own, had been killed in Lorraine. She was the first. Many more—a hundred and three—were to follow, but in most cases, the German occupation preventing their being directly notified, they only heard through a Swiss bureau, months after the event.

On the nineteenth, what I had so longed to see finally appeared: a whole army corps with its guns and cavalry. They marched past, through the day, many a company passing our house. They let loose the flow of enthusiasm I had not so far witnessed and produced the phenomenon I had read about but never thought I could study, viz., the transformation of well-trained, disciplined French girls into that primitive, baffling and rather disquieting type, the war girl. Titine kept her old maid incessantly making fresh coffee which she herself served to hundreds of soldiers on our steps. The gratitude of the poor Midi lads expressed itself in outlandish-sounding phrases. In the street the girls were pressing humble gifts or flowers on the soldiers,

beseeching them with doe-like eyes and mute supplication to
accept their little offerings.

In the evening, at benediction, I found five soldiers kneeling
in the chancel where only clergy were usually to be seen. They
were priests, two of them ambulance orderlies, the other three
infantrymen. The Dean and I talked with them after benediction.
One of the orderlies, a bit grandiloquent as Midi people sometimes are, said: "In a few days we may be getting back wounded
men from under fire." Whereupon one of the priest soldiers replied rather impatiently: "*We* shall be doing that firing." Next
morning, about six o'clock, our street was so full of horizon-
blue uniforms that they produced a misty effect. We had put up
a major, a taciturn little man full of quiet determination. As he
thanked me before leaving he looked up the street alive with blue
figures and merely said: "How like last Autumn's manœuvres!
but this time there are bullets in the cartridges."

On the twenty-second the Dean asked me to take some money
—gold—to his curate, mobilized a fortnight before, whose ambulance had been reported at Robechies, a few miles beyond
the Belgian border. I rode there in the afternoon. I was stopped
four or five times on the way by customs officers or rural constables who demanded my passport. People saw spies everywhere, and one customs officer had a strong impression that my
paper was a forgery. He kept looking at it and then at me, as
if he could not reconcile my face with my name. He let me pass
into Belgium with evident reluctance. I could not find the curate,
but I had a conversation with his captain who was extremely
optimistic. As we talked, the burr of an airplane was heard
and in a few moments the machine was above us. "Yes," the captain explained, "we have a small flying squad at Seloignes." "*I*
know Seloignes," I said, "it is in the East, over there, whereas
this plane is coming straight from the North. And can't you
see the iron crosses under its wings?" In fact, this was a German
plane flying so low and so slowly that we could see its every part
distinctly. When I reached the French frontier again, I found

the revenue officer very much perturbed and his wife in tears. They too had seen the iron crosses. At Trélon I hesitated whether or not I should tell my friends about that airplane.

August twenty-third was a Sunday. On that day our people's outlook on the war appeared considerably modified. They had learned, without losing their composure, the violation of Belgium, the capture of Liége, Louvain and Brussels, the passing of the Meuse and even the capture of Dinant, only forty miles away. For mere newspaper reports do not affect people when other reports seem to contradict them, and the Lorraine news was good. But news, whether good or bad, became insignificant when war operations suddenly appeared to be close at hand. By nine o'clock of that Sunday the rumbling of gunfire became continuous like low thunder the steadiness of which makes one dread a more violent clap. At noon the crack of individual reports was perceptible with, every now and then, such loud explosions that they shook all the windows. Simultaneously the first Belgian fugitives poured into our little town. Well-off people in good cars at first. They gave news. Charleroi was on fire and Thuin—a small town which many of us knew well—was occupied. Why they did not stay in their homes? Had we not heard of the Dinant massacres? ** Could anybody in his senses face such possibilities?

** NOTE:—On August 16th and 17th, 1914, no fewer than six hundred and seventy-four men and women, citizens of the charming summer-resort of Dinant, as well as several children, were shot by the Germans against a wall which I pass almost every year and never can see without a feeling of horror. There are still alive in the pretty little city several thousand people who witnessed the gruesome scene. The German soldiers broke into the houses and dragged out whomever they found there. Immediately after, the terrified prisoners were driven to the wall and shot down without even an appearance of judgment. The Germans admit the facts but account for them by the repeated assertion that civilians shot at them, a statement which all Dinant people indignantly contradict. I have always been surprised that some American searcher, less likely than his European confrères to bring into such an investigation a partisan spirit, should not

The roads in Belgium were crowded with processions of people in flight and we could not but see them in the course of the day.

have collected the evidence which can still be easily gathered both from Dinant citizens and from German veterans. A reference to this massacre in the last edition of the *Encyclopedia Britannica* is so casual that the reader wonders if the writer of the Dinant article believed in the actuality of the facts he relates. People in England and in America have been made so sceptical by conflicting propagandas that they have adopted an "it-may-be-so-but-it-also-may-not" attitude which is the greatest achievement of the propagandist. One is rather surprised to find the same even in serious books by real historians. In the early editions of *The Epic of America* Mr. James Truslow Adams wrote (page 370) : "The French executed two war nurses under almost the identical circumstances of the German execution of Nurse Cavell, but we were not told." This is a typical statement revealing the state of mind I was alluding to above. The natural reaction of a French reader who never heard of this shooting of two German nurses was to ask: "But where could the French get hold of two German nurses to shoot?" I wrote to Mr. Adams asking for his authorities. Let me say at once that the correspondence which followed was entirely to the credit of Mr. Adams. He had found the two German nurses' story on page 32 of *Propaganda Technique in the World War* by Professor H. D. Lasswell, of Chicago, and he had not questioned it till a letter, written shortly before mine, by former Ambassador Jusserand, raised doubts in his mind. He had then written Professor Lasswell asking him about his sources. Professor Lasswell had replied regretting "that Mr. Adams' letter had not reached him a fortnight sooner as he had just returned to the University from Germany and his evidence for his statement was there." This letter was dated December 7th, 1932. I wrote immediately to Professor Lasswell asking him to give me the address of *any* German information bureau as the shooting of the German nurses, if it had really taken place, must be well-known in Germany. My letter did not reach Professor Lasswell. After waiting a few months I wrote to him again and received the following answer (dated June 2nd, 1933) which I communicated at once to Mr. James Truslow Adams: "The story, as related in my *Propaganda Technique in the World War*, is practically a verbatim quotation from Mr. Karl von Wiegand, a German-American. He was head of one of Mr. Hearst's news-gathering organizations, the Universal Service, who was on close terms with the Germans. He referred to Oberst Nicolai." Mr. Adams did not think that evidence of this kind, ultimately based on the *obiter dictum* of an Oberst about whom nobody ever heard, was sufficient to satisfy the requirements of history, and he acted as a real scholar was sure to act.

In fact, after Vespers, as hundreds of Trélon people returned
from a specially venerated shrine in our own street, and while
the thunder of the cannonade sounded nearer and nearer, those
humble Belgians appeared. Many were on foot and had trudged
since very early morning, carrying bundles or pushing baby
carriages in which children lay surrounded by all sorts of parcels. One man was reeling from fatigue and nearly fainted when
the *notaire,* whose house faced ours, brought him a garden-chair
into which he collapsed. Other families rode with their neigh-
bours in rough harvest-waggons. A tragic-looking priest, coun-
try-bred, no doubt, was walking, very erect and stark, beside
two tired horses. Five or six praying nuns and two elderly women
were seated in the cart, mute with fright. You could see that the
growling of artillery was racking their nerves and had done so
for hours. No pen could describe the heart-rending spectacles
we saw. A paralyzed old woman in a wheel-barrow, and a railway-crossing keeper with his wife and three children carrying
their chickens in baskets are vivid in my memory. Terror and

He not only deleted the allusion to the German nurses from the new editions of *The Epic of America* but he added a note without which the
suppression might have been unnoticed. Unfortunately he could not send
an *erratum* to the hundreds of thousands who had previously read his
book, and I still meet Americans who, believing that the French shot two
defenceless German women, feel like condoning such things as the Dinant
massacre, because "in war everything is horrible." So it is, but there are
degrees in horror and it behoves history to establish such degrees. The
moment an historian seeks to give the contrary impression he falls to the
rank of propagandist. I hope I have not more than the inevitable amount
of racial prejudices. Many people who are violently in favour of, or antagonistic to, some foreign nation substitute emotions for reasons and can
have no intellectual standing. I am only telling what I saw, and I saw
with my own eyes the effects of *Schrecklichkeit.* The terrorized Belgians
who, in August, 1914, made such a ghastly entrance into my native town
were the victims of a system of frightfulness which Germany openly defended at the time and practiced ruthlessly. I know scores of other instances less striking than the Dinant slaughter but equally shocking. To
deny is not to delete them.

despair were words I understood for the first time in my life. Our people did all they could in a timid way to help.

Strangely enough, they seemed to have no suspicion that, within three days, they themselves would be presenting the same lamentable spectacle to villagers twenty or thirty kilometers south of us. They heard the Belgians repeating: "They shoot everybody," but they felt too much pity to catch the contagion of fright. Somehow the belief that the Germans "would be stopped at our frontier" had taken hold of them and kept up in them a nervous optimism. The doctor next door to us believed the same thing and stated his firm intention not to leave.

"*Et s'il n'en reste qu'un, je serai celui-là,*" he quoted. The Dean, whom I saw ten minutes later, repeated the same thing. Unimaginative men, both of them, who I knew would not long be quoting heroic poetry.

About six o'clock I called on a friend, the wife of a lawyer mobilized at Maubeuge, and the mother of a little girl of eight whom I liked. This lady had been to see her husband in the afternoon, and driving back home on roads where she had encountered no Belgians, she was brimful of optimism and in a state of elation in impossible contrast with the scenes I had witnessed during the past two hours. She was a Belgian by birth but her marriage had made her extremely French. The wonderful fortifications of Maubeuge and the morale of the men in her husband's outfit had acted on her impressionable nature and she felt sure that a tremendous victory was in sight, at the frontier, naturally. I, on the contrary, had felt no doubt, since the Germans unopposed had crossed the Meuse on intact bridges, that the frontier would also be crossed as easily as if it were the Equator. I listened with impatient patience to the lady's outpour of enthusiasm, and then said in a tone which seemed to act at once: "You're a regular Joan of Arc. But, mark my words, the Germans will be here at the latest Thursday morning. Trains still run on our line, but to-morrow may be the last day. You're going, please, to pack up as many things as you need for at least three months

and, to-morrow morning, you and the child will take the ten
o'clock to Paris. I shall be here early to see that you are ready,
and I shall inform your husband." She was sobered at once. On
my way back I stopped at the house of another lady—Titine's
best friend—and repeated the same admonition. But here I was
met by blank smiles and gracious nods, meaning "no" while
saying "yes." The lady remembered 1870, which really was
a picnic, and she was unequal to the resolve to leave her fine
big house. The next day I found her profuse in excuses and repeating that silly thing about the frontier. That next day the
gendarmes' families were secretly moved away before dawn, and
the news of their disappearance was not bruited. Not a word was
said either about our railway-station being locked and empty.
More Belgian fugitives passed through the town all the morning,
then suddenly stopped and French troops appeared in their
place. Already, on my way back from early church, I had met
on the square three zouaves full of the news of Charleroi. Their
morale was not good and showed itself in cynical sarcasm. These
men realized perfectly that the French tactics supposed to be the
official doctrine, viz., the superiority of infantry with a high
morale over even heavy artillery had been tried and found
wanting: you might charge with all possible heroism, big guns
mowed you down long before you crossed no-man's land.

In a short time five German planes appeared, flying insolently
low and peering down at the roads. Within two hours the roads
were crowded with troops. French regiment after regiment passed
through, and during the whole night I heard their tramping and
the pawing of their horses. There was something blood-curdling
in the sight of that endless retreat, yet it also encouraged me.
For the units were not mixed up in the least and the men were
splendid. "*Il ne faut pas avoir peur.*" "No fear! no fear!" they
repeated.

But people acted in a way recalling to me the councils of
swallows twittering to one another on the telegraph-wires the
morning of the great departure. They had deserted their houses
and consulted in the street in quiet voices which the effort to

reach a resolve, while keeping nervousness under control, made almost matter of fact. Less than fifty in a population of three thousand finally made up their minds to stay, and their decision came so evidently from a vague certainty that "it would be all right" that several of them, the next day, mistook the German vanguard for a British column of cavalry.

At two p.m. of August 25th, my aunt's Honorine left in a buggy with a lady, our neighbour. An hour later Titine drove away in Madame de Berghes' car. I rode off at five on my bicycle. A few minutes before, reports came that several Trélon soldiers going back to their regiment at Avesnes had killed a uhlan on the road, whereas, in the forest north of us, a French rearguard was being attacked by German cavalry. Both rumours turned out to be true. Even before I left, our forest was full of uhlans who were to march into Trélon at dawn next morning. Nobody reported their approach.

Titine, Honorine and I met at Hirson station which offered a strange sight. Hundreds of fugitives, silent but determined, were there, boarding car after car as the train was being made up, and never thinking of paying any fare. The clerk showed surprise when I asked for three tickets to Paris. Nobody would check my bicycle, so I just put it myself into the van. Everybody did what they pleased, but the crowd having only one object, which was to get away, this unanimity resulted in a certain amount of order.

The trip to Paris which usually does not require more than three hours was slow and capricious. At dawn, next morning, we were astonished to find ourselves standing in Compiègne station which is not on our line. The station-master on the platform near us was having a heated conversation with our guard. I caught enough of what they said to infer that the station-master, acting on orders which did not sound too definite, wanted to shunt off our train in the direction of Rouen where it would not interfere with military transportation. I jumped out and showed my three tickets, saying that I had no intention of being shunted off to Rouen. A good-looking young officer joined our group and also said that his orders were to be in Paris before noon and he was not going to Rouen either. To my surprise, the station-master hesitated a moment, turned towards our guard, and said in a tone of indifference: "Well, then, to Paris!" By seven o'clock we were at the Gare du Nord.

Titine, who ought to have been exhausted by a sleepless night, barely showed signs of weariness. She had been enjoying the greenness and sunniness of the fine forests one can see from the train between Compiègne and Paris and the beauty of nature always vitalized her. Paris also looked its best, for the agitation it had shown three weeks before had subsided, and the streets outside the big station only displayed the morning exhilaration which strikes all visitors in summer. We must have looked like a happy little group as we were eating breakfast on a café terrace.

It was only four years later that I learned what was going on at the same minute in Trélon. Every house in our street, except the one next us, had been deserted by the inhabitants. A column of German cavalry rode up first in the cool morning but did not stop. Exactly on the minute when we were reaching Paris infantry appeared and the men were given two hours' rest. They at once proceeded methodically to enter the houses. A panel in the lower part of the doors would be staved in, often at one blow of the rifle's butt-end and, in a few seconds, the door would be wide open. I had written in chalk, in German, where our key was deposited. I had also written in large letters a sort of placard saying, in my poor German too: "Treat peacefully a peaceful family's home." Seven or eight soldiers made a meal off the provisions I had left in a conspicuous place, then drank all the cherry brandy and sloe gin which my aunt used to make, Autumn after Autumn, and feeling inclined to jocosity, they dressed up in my clericals and danced in them in our front-garden. Finally they made a mound of them and of a score of books in the dining-room and smashed on the top of it all the eggs they found in the pantry. The whole thing was found squirming with vermin a few days later when Honorine's brother returned from a futile attempt at getting away. (Some fifteen hundred were thus beaten off the crowded roads sometimes by French, oftener by German, troops who overtook them in their flight.) No houses were burnt. Nothing violently disorderly took place, although in villages near Trélon *Schrecklichkeit* was the motto and several men were shot without any reason, while incendiarism was frequent. A German officer, a gentleman, billeted with our friend, M. Léon Macaigne, was shocked even at the mild excesses narrated above, and could not believe his own eyes when he was shown the watches in Lambert the watchmaker's window strewn on the road outside the shop to be crushed under foot. Léon, remembering the well-known book of the Alsatian artist Hansi, showing on one page the Germans of 1870 carrying away valuable clocks and, on another page, the Teutons of the fifth century slinking away with sun-dials, remarked philosophically to him: "Well, this time your men seem to have watches of their own." Later on, other German officers were billeted with him who would not tolerate even a smile supposed to imply irony, and he went to prison for an incredibly slight offence.

Titine only stayed a week in Paris, in my rooms at College Stanislas first, then in Marquis de Saint-Paul's apartment.

The contrast between Stanislas on that morning of August twenty-sixth and the tragic Trélon I had left the day before was startling. An ambulance had been made ready in some of the collegiate buildings, but there was only one wounded soldier there, Georges Saupicque, the sculptor, an alumnus of ours, and his wound did not confine him to his bed. The place, happy looking in the warm sunshine, was as quiet as I remembered it on my first arrival twelve years earlier. Paris seemed as remote from the front as if it had been Toulouse or Nice, and a smiling optimism prevailed. Charleroi, as represented by the newspapers, had been entirely unnoticed, and the retreat of the

French army was either unknown or interpreted as a mere manœuvre. My first conversation was with Georges Saupicque whose
morale was excellent and who enjoyed giving me graphic details
about the skirmishes in which he had been engaged. My presence
evidently surprised and, to a certain extent, dismayed him. I
told him of the scenes I had witnessed, and explained my conviction that not only the whole of Eastern Belgium but even
the northern section of France must be by this time occupied by
the enemy. "I should be surprised," I said, "if Lille were not
already taken." (In fact, it was occupied that very day, without
any resistance, but the Germans left it at once and had to bom-
bard it to march in again, in October.) An hour after that
conversation, I met our good head-master, M. Pautonnier, who
said reproachfully, "You hurt Saupicque's feelings by what
you said about Lille being taken. Why should Lille be taken?"
I explained again at full length that the German army in Belgium
had left behind it all the natural obstacles, and the Allied troops
opposing it were evidently outnumbered. M. Pautonnier remained unconvinced and offended, and there is no doubt that if
the word defeatist had then been invented he would have applied
it to me. I merely said that we should not have to wait very long
before the facts must show which of us was right.

The next morning I went out early and bought newspapers.
The historic "Somme to Vosges" communiqué appeared in all
of them. I found M. Pautonnier in the park and showed him the
statement. He read it over and over, winking and blinking in a
queer way as he did so. *"De la Somme aux Vosges?"* he wondered several times, "what does *he* mean? There was no mention
yesterday of anybody being anywhere near the Somme."—"Except what I told you," I said. "Now, on which side of the Somme
is Lille, please?"

I remembered this little incident seven or eight years later,
when the newspapers gave publicity to something supposed to
have happened in the French Academy. The Academicians were,
as usual, working on their Dictionary and the word "Defeatist"
was under discussion. As member after member suggested defi-

nitions Marshal Joffre was reported to have said with sublime
simplicity: "Such a word cannot be French." Only a week or
two before I had had the good fortune to meet Joffre at dinner
at a friend's house and I had been impressed by his evident
aversion to anything grandiloquent. So I felt doubtful of the
authenticity of this remark and mentioned my scepticism to
my friend and neighbour, Abbé Henri Bremond, himself a
member of the Academy. Bremond shrugged his shoulders and
gave me the real facts. Joffre, in the chair next to his own, had
been dozing in great comfort when the little debate woke him up.
"What word?" he whispered to Bremond.—"Defeatist."—"Ah!"
Joffre said good-naturedly, "that was the name people gave,
during the war, to those who thought differently from themselves." "(*On appelait comme cela, pendant la guerre, les gens
qui n'étaient pas de votre avis.*)"

In the afternoon of that August 27th a *Taube*—as the German
planes were then euphemistically called—terrified many Parisians by dropping a bomb which hit one of the towers of Notre-
Dame and damaged the big bell. Titine did not mind the least
bit, but Honorine, equally disinclined to stay upstairs in M. de
Saint-Paul's apartment when bombs were being dropped, or to
associate with mice and rats if she went down to the cellar, began
to beg for a move. She made capital of the fact that the next
day more German planes came; a house—next door to which
some friends of Titine's were living—was badly battered; the
French Government decided to emigrate to Bordeaux; and the
exodus of the Parisian population began. During more than
a week the railway stations commanding the safer routes were
besieged. After a few days' hesitation Titine decided to go to
Nevers where we had faraway relatives and where some Trélon
refugees were already settled.

I went to the Gare de Lyon to buy her tickets. Right in the
middle of the Place de la Concorde, and looking listlessly at
the Obelisk, I met the curé of Liessies—a village four miles out
of Trélon—with his squire, M. Cavrois. The latter was in a

mackintosh—under which he wore no coat—and in his slippers. This costume showed the haste with which both men had left our North. They were anxious to return home at once, even if they had to walk back, and, in fact, succeeded after many adventures which I only heard four years later. I entered the Gare de Lyon by the main steps in front, and I was delighted to find it not only less crowded than I imagined but even almost deserted. The courtyard on the left where a sign said "Tickets" would have been empty had it not been for one solitary soldier pacing up and down the space in front of the office. This sentry seemed surprised to see me walking up. When I got quite near he smiled and seemed even more surprised. "You want a ticket," he said.—"Yes," I replied, "and I am delighted to see that there are only those few people in the office."—"*Attendez!*" the man said, as he led me to the parapet commanding the street outside. Fifteen feet below us this street was one mass of people standing in a long line six abreast. The soldier smiled as he saw my astonishment. "Look over there," he said. I looked where he pointed and realized that the *queue* wound round and round three or four streets. "That's where you ought to begin," the sentry went on, "and you would be lucky if you arrived where we now stand in fifteen or sixteen hours. That's the average." My face registering the disappointment I felt, the soldier said: "You don't remember the mole-catcher in the Bois de la Deûle, at Lille, do you? but I remember you very well and you shall have your ticket in five minutes." More than once during the war I prayed for that anonymous friend with whom I did remember exchanging remarks about the weather on a few occasions.

As soon as Titine was safe at Nevers—you strike this town when you put your finger on the very centre of the map of France —I decided to go to London where my book *France Herself Again* waited, already printed, for an urgently needed Preface and Epilogue. For I had not looked at the proofs yet, I only vaguely recalled the manuscript, and I was afraid that the war might have put the whole book out of focus.

On September third I left for London by way of Dieppe. Up to that date my personal impression of the war had been and could not but be different from that of the hundreds of thousands who felt sure of victory one day but left Paris in panic the next day. What I knew was that the Germans had concentrated five times as many troops in Belgium as the Allies had found to oppose them, and it was no comfort to reflect that the enemy had only been able to do so by treating a solemn document as a scrap of paper. Even illiterate Trélon people had been sure that the neutrality of Belgium would be violated, and I wondered why the General Staff had calculated differently. When I was asked to prophesy abont the future, I refused to do so, except with a vast accompaniment of *ifs*, and *ifs* were not supposed to be patriotic. Only one thing made me secretly optimistic, and this was the certainty that the French Army might be retreating, but it had not at any moment been routed. Joffre's *communiqués* were reassuring by their daily avowal that more ground was being given up to the enemy. Visibly the generalissimo managed to accomplish an extraordinary feat of self-control. Thirty-odd million Frenchmen were, day after day, hoping that he would make a stand, and he actually resisted such a formidable wave of desire. He could look at the map as his manœuvre was developing and act as if it were the physical map of Europe and not the political map of France. Meanwhile we heard of a no less difficult achievement which seemed to leave Joffre's serenity equally unruffled: day after day he got rid of inadequate officers, many of them generals, whom he replaced on the spot by inferiors whom he regarded as superior. There had been none of that in 1870 and Joffre was no Lebœuf.

No sooner had the Dieppe train pulled out of Saint-Lazare than a delicious wave of optimism filled my parched soul. For, all along the Seine, for miles and miles, I could see from the car-window magnificent troops the existence of which I had not suspected. Men and horses looked fresh and rested. There was no sign of hurry or confusion. The yearly September manœuvres had seldom taken place in such an atmosphere of orderliness, even of happiness. More and more troops were visible as we moved away from Paris, and I reflected hopefully that there must be, hidden away from such easy inspection, even more than what I saw. Surely these superb reserves were going to be used. When I boarded the Newhaven steamer I felt like another man, and the sight of a boat sunk close by the very pier by an astonishingly bold German submarine gave me more surprised excitement than concern. Here was something which the Paris newspapers had not said a word about, and yet I discovered it as I had discovered that Normandy was full of troops. My own eyes gave me all the information I wanted and the information was reassuring.

As soon as I was in London I got in touch with Belloc, who had recently signed a contract with *Land and Water* for weekly military articles which all England was eagerly reading, and I told him of what I saw. "Of course," he said, "the inevitable manœuvre is for the French to make the German lines of communication thinner by making them longer, and then outflank the enemy's right wing. All that you saw shows that the manœuvre is being carefully prepared." What Belloc—whose confidence in Joffre never flagged—was telling me then was simply an anticipated narrative of the battle of the Marne. Three days later extras, shouted all over London, gave it almost word for word, as he had outlined it in our conversation. It was a glorious morning. I might live a thousand years, I shall never forget the heavenly transition from gloom to hope which those London newsboys created in a few moments in my soul.

But this exhilaration only lasted three or four days. In less than a week it became evident that a short campaign was out of the question. The Germans dug themselves in, and instead of decisive battles followed by spectacular movements, we read, day after day, of minute incidents affecting infinitesimal sections of a line extending from the North Sea to the Swiss frontier. A longing for a change of outlook, a vague expectation of some-

thing imagined to be in the air, an impalpable ennui, soon succeeded the blaze of illusory hopes produced by the battle of the
Marne. The atmosphere of the so-called Great War was one of in-
sufferable tedium, and the recollection of it is like that of long
dull days remembered from childhood.

Yet London seemed happy enough with Business as Usual,
the clubs hospitable and comfortable as they had always been,
the offices of the *Saturday Review* and of Chesterton's *New
Witness* exactly as I had seen them a few months before. Lean
bands of recruits were being drilled here and there in the parks
to the shrill sound of a whistle, but there was nothing encouraging in the sight of those volunteers mostly shabby and physically
below the average. The Call to Arms of Kitchener had not met
with any enthusiastic response, and only my most pro-French
acquaintances dared to hint that conscription would soon be
a necessity. All historic associations led the British to believe
that their wars were to be fought at sea, with somebody else's
soldiers fighting on land. And, after a few days, I realized that
the English nation as a whole had not even begun to regard this
war as its war. My friend, William Wray Skilbeck, editor of
The Nineteenth Century, showed me an irate letter from a German correspondent which made the opposition between Germany
and Britain pretty clear, but few people must have received such
letters. The fallacy that France and Germany were face to face
in one more duel, with Britain somehow helping the French,
had not yet been dispelled. The press disappointed me. Hardly
any newspaper dared to explain that it was not the French that
the British were supporting but the Belgians, while not one
Englishman in twenty really felt that the defence of Belgium
was nothing else than the defence of the United Kingdom. My
English friends resented this mental supineness even more than
I did. They found no words strong enough to express their contempt for politicians like Ramsay MacDonald or even Lloyd
George. But I met every day society people who alluded, more
or less tactfully, to the service their country was doing to mine.
Others would ask comically selfish questions without realizing

their selfishness. I remember a comfortable, jolly-looking old
lady who wanted to be reassured in every way. Surely no German
planes would dare to come over London as they were going over
Paris, would they? And surely Paris would not be giving in to
foolish notions which would change its atmosphere. It would
stay gay as usual, would it not? And one could have a good time
there as in the past, couldn't one? I answered in the most sooth-
ing manner, but the very intelligent lady in whose drawing-room
this conversation was taking place was suffering tortures, and
begged me not to imagine that this old "fool" represented anybody except herself. This no doubt was true, but apart from the
most intelligent circles—the men I met in Chesterton's office or
at the house of that charming person, Mr. Harry Cust—I was
frequently irritated by a smile which meant as clearly as any
words: Aren't you lucky that this time we are on your side?
The whole misunderstanding arose from the absurd "German
cousins" fallacy ** and from the confusion, in most English
minds, of the Empire of Germany (viz., historic Austria) with the
German Empire (viz., Prussia expanded to its imperial position
after 1870). Nobody seemed to have heard anything of Bis-
marck's overtures to France, in 1878, for an alliance the object
of which could only be the prospective division of the British
Empire. Belloc and Chesterton, who were trying to enlighten
their readers about these all-important points, had not succeeded
in doing so. Kipling himself, in spite of his popularity, mostly
spoke to the winds. Sometimes I would wonder if I had not over-
estimated the political sense of the British. But every time I felt
tempted to conclude that I had done so, an unexpected contact,
sometimes with plain people, showed me that the capacity of
the English for grasping realities was not merely a thing to be

** NOTE:—The reference in England to the "German cousins" is entirely modern. It never appears before the nineteenth century (Freeman,
Kingsley) and has never spread beyond the snobbish bourgeois milieus
who copied Queen Victoria's partiality for her husband's fatherland.
Americans of British origin never brag about that so-called cousinship.
Even an Englishman who does so will feel like knocking you down if
you remark that, in fact, there is something German about him.

discussed in text-books, and that, sooner or later, they must read on the map what is so clearly written upon it viz, that France and Britain are bound together, whether they like it or not, by similar interests.

II

I devoted a good deal of time to the preparation for immediate publication of my book *France Herself Again*. I was surprised to find, on reading the proofs, that the possibility, even the probability of a war underlay many pages of it. Professor Harry Elmer Barnes once accused me of having written it, not only in expectation, but even in something like hope of a war. Nothing could be farther from the truth. As I said before, I had no doubt, after the Kaiser's speech at Tangier, in 1905, that the new Germany would soon want to make an international trial of her strength, but I had too many reasons to dread that such a trial might be successful to desire its materialization. The only thing that caused me to rejoice was the certainty that my countrymen, at first shocked and dazed by the threat, had gradually steeled themselves against it. If France were attacked, she would defend herself, that was all. Only the moral effects of such an attitude had promptly become visible, and that showed progress. My book said nothing more warlike than that, and I had to write a longish preface and epilogue in order to make it clear that it did say even that.

My friend, Percy Spalding, of Chatto and Windus, and his associates took an extraordinary interest in the book. They seemed to regard it as a possible tonic for its prospective English readers, and no commercial consideration ever appeared in what they said about it. I like to remember many details showing that its publication was seen in that light. The book was treated as a favourite child. The title-page was designed with loving care by one of the junior partners, Mr. Frank Swinnerton. Mr. Swinnerton was not, as yet, the author of *Nocturne*, but no good judge had any doubt that his literary future must be brilliant. The qualities which are to-day universally recognized in him, his preference for art that does not air his wealth of human experience, his simplicity of outlook and the sincerity (another name for conscious force) that accompanies it, were already unmistakable in his mental equipment. Yet, no young man endowed with such gifts ever was so surprisingly modest. I used to put him on his guard against a positive cult for our mutual friend, Arnold Bennett, which I was afraid might hinder his development. In vain: he would remain a perfect violet in Saint Martin's Lane. I was and still am deeply grateful to him for the interest he took in my book.

France Herself Again was extremely well received not only in England but in America—where Putnam published it. Propaganda had not dared as yet to support the astonishing contention that all nations were equally responsible for the war. That France had been unjustly attacked was not disputed by anybody. Sympathy with her was not criticized. My book, showing that during the past nine years she had recovered enough of her traditional energy to meet an invasion, was not misconstrued even by German sympathizers who were to say, later, that you show an aggressive spirit if you are preparing for defence. However, some readers stared. France to them had too long been Paris, and of Paris they only knew the cabarets at Montmartre. The very morning when the battle of the Marne began, a foolish American, named Murphy, said to a few friends of mine, at the Savoy Hotel in the Strand, that "there was no chance for France as the French were all cowards and degenerates." An indignant woman, also American, dealt him the punishment he deserved and, the next morning, he must have read the newspapers with a deepening blush on his obtuse brow,—but there were undoubtedly many like him. My book came in good time. What it was to do for me in America I did not then for one moment suspect.

I stayed five or six weeks in England. Everybody's life was so disorganized by the European cyclone that I took it for granted that my College Stanislas, already partly militarized when I left, could not re-open at the usual time. I never wrote to the headmaster. I even made plans to go back to Trélon from behind the lines. My friend, Henry van Dyke, was American Minister to Holland and I asked him to get me a German safe-conduct. He very sensibly and kindly replied that I would go back to the

occupied region over his dead body. About the middle of October
I returned to Paris and to my rooms at the College. To my surprise I found that, although the ambulance was full, the headmaster had succeeded in saving room for five or six hundred
students. The Faculty, much reduced by the mobilization, was
however sufficient and the routine which was to last four long
slow years already seemed natural to everybody. I did not do
any teaching during that autumn term. I whiled away the time by
translating into English—under the title *The March to Tim-
buctoo*—Joffre's report on his well-known expedition along the
Niger river. I did that translation with more literary interest
than I had expected. Joffre, contrary to most French officers
who write with ease and fluency, suffers from an incredible
scantiness of vocabulary. But his vision is so infallible and his
thinking is so lucid that, in spite of that dearth of words, he
gives an impression of fulness such as might be produced by a
meditative Trappist monk who had remained silent too long.
His occasional reference to some Tuaregs as *religieux pasteurs*
(monastic shepherds) every time lent poetry to his Cæsarlike
narrative and was more evocative than elaborate descriptions
might have been.

Needless to say that not a single day found us unconscious of
the tremendous drama in which we were only infinitesimal
supernumeraries. During the first year alone seven hundred of
our alumni were killed. Most of them were officers and it was
a matter of course, at first, that officers should show more bravery
than prudence. Many of those young men were dear to me, or
their brilliance had led me to expect great things of them: to see
them cut off was heart-breaking. One charming young fellow,
Martin-Decaen by name, often relives in my memory. I remember his youthful enthusiasm over Karsavina, his delight in horses
and horsemanship while he served his three years in a cavalry
regiment, and the unexpected gravity which descended upon him
when he decided to exchange his uniform for a cassock and en-

tered the seminary at Issy. Yet he was only one. Scores of others
possessed, like him, the undefinable charm of young manhood
unconscious of its attraction and the more seductive for its indifference to effect. Killed, killed. Mortally wounded. Reported
missing. The phrases acquired a horrible familiarity by repetition which never succeeded in blunting their cruel edge.

I taught mostly boys between the ages of seventeen and nineteen. The latter were constantly drafted, schoolboys to-day, can-
non-fodder the next day. The younger fellows would often enlist
as soon as they felt ready for physical examination. The French
are infinitely less communicative than people who will see them
as "Latins" imagine. Many times I was surprised by the sudden
resolve of slender lads who, while apparently enjoying Tennyson
with me, were planning a letter which their mother would read
with tears. Three or four months at some depot, two months in a
military school, then the front and the baptism of fire. Sometimes
those few months would transform them out of recognition. I had
often been irritated by the self-satisfied affectation of one young
fellow belonging to a famous equestrian family and apparently
full of pride in that tradition. On his first leave he reappeared delightfully natural. A few weeks of the Homeric directness at the
front had done what years of moral training had not been able to
accomplish. Another boy, the son of French parents but born
and brought up in Egypt, showed an Oriental indolence and a
coddling tendency which fully deserved the appellation of sissy.
That young fellow surprised us all by enlisting before he was
eighteen. When he reappeared, eight months later, as a young
aspirant with already a fine citation to his credit, he still preserved some of his Persian kitten appearance but he smiled the
smile of a man. Interested as I have always been in the phenomenon called bravery I asked him my usual question about
his reaction to the approach of the zero hour. "I get deadly pale,"
he said, but shrugged his shoulders. This may be the place to
recall a similar conversation with a cousin of mine, a taciturn
young fellow with an undercurrent of grim humour inherited
from his father. I saw him in 1916 when he had already been in

all sorts of hot places. *"Es-tu brave, Amédée?"* I asked. "No, cousin," he answered simply, "nobody is brave." After a moment's silence he dropped his chin to a cadaverous wryness and said: "Some of the fellows look like this before going over the top." He laughed a quiet frightening laughter and looked astonishingly like his father. He was very badly wounded a few months later, but refused to be side-tracked and went into a tank regiment which only ignorance could look upon as safer than infantry.

Our own bravery was not badly taxed, but it was all the same put to a mild test by the nightly bombardments which began very early and never stopped till the Big Bertha started its tiresome work in the spring of 1918. At first the German planes only dropped six to ten-inch bombs which were not very alarming though they could destroy the whole top-floor of any house, and most of us refused to take shelter. After a few months the Germans replaced the bombs by torpedoes and these no nerves could stand: the most formidable claps of thunder do not swear as a torpedo can. In a few minutes all the collegiate buildings would be empty while the cellars quickly filled with soldiers, nurses and boys. The wounded in the ambulance—often eighty to a hundred—were taken down first, and it was no light job. Our bigger students took charge of it. Some men could not be moved out of their beds, and although a special outfit stayed with them, they hated to be left behind: bravery in fighting must be frequent enough, composure while being assaulted by death in a bleak hospital ward is another thing. The boys soon became used to those nightly alarms: they would march to shelter quickly but in perfect order, sometimes saying the most amusing things as they went. But it was pitiful to see little fellows under ten years of age carrying puzzles or checker-boards on their way down to the cellar. Many looked pale with the fatigue of fighting sleepiness off when, towards one or two o'clock, the reassuring bells of Notre-Dame-des-Champs, nearby, and the firemen's *berloque* sent them back to bed. What the Germans wanted, of course, was to wear out the nerve of Parisians. Pretty often the *berloque* was no sooner heard than a second alarm was sounded and the whole process of dormitory to cellar had to be repeated. Next morning the classes were not good for much.

During the last months of the war the anti-aircraft defence became, if not efficient, at least wonderfully spectacular, for hundreds of batteries on the fortifications answered the bombing. Their deep-mouthed barking was heartening, but what kept us looking out of windows when we should have been seated on old boxes in the cellar was the marvellous fireworks effect of shells exploding three thousand feet above and filling the sky with a belt of sulphurous flamelets. Every now and then a shower of fragments would descend from where those explosions constantly succeeded one another, and their tinkling, as they fell on the neighbouring roofs, sounded harmonious because we knew it to be friendly.

The Vice-President of the College, Abbé Martin, had been mobilized the second day of the war, and he saw the whole four mortal years through. He was a thickset but athletic man upon whom military duty had left an unexpected imprint. The students noticed with amusement that even after scolding them and still a bit irritated, he would invariably move off, his left foot out first, as he had been taught to do in his regiment twenty-five years earlier. He acquired a legendary reputation for bravery, his last citation beginning with "Once more," showing that his chiefs almost despaired of giving him his due. Every four months he would get four days' leave which he generally spent with us. He took a professional interest in what he heard about our night-bombardments and was rather disappointed that he never saw any. Finally, in May 1918, his curiosity was satisfied. The blaze in the heavens gave him extraordinary pleasure. "Aren't you defended!" he would say admiringly. But all the time habit made him conscious of the ominous burr of the German machines invisible above us. We were watching the scene from the College park. My natural impulse was to stay on the well-rolled gravel-walks, but Martin every other minute would draw me away from them onto the dewy lawn. He seemed to do this instinctively. After a time I protested and he said: "Ah, but one ought to be prudent. Good soft ground here; no danger of being killed." Killed, killed. That word which, in childhood, I dreaded to hear was on people's lips and in their ears all the time.

The Luxembourg Garden near us was frequently hit. Dug-outs were built there for the gardeners. One afternoon I was watching some men at work on a new one made of cement-blocks when I became aware of a conversation in English going on close by me. After a minute or two my eyes met those of the gentleman —a tall distinguished person—who was speaking, and this gentleman, realizing by my expression that I understood what was being said, addressed me with a "Don't you think so?" which started us talking. I happened to disagree and we were soon in an animated little debate. "My husband is quite right," a voice soon said behind my interlocutor. He moved and disclosed a woman of rare beauty standing on his right. "Mrs. Clews, my wife," he said. I was to hear this lady repeating this same remark, "My husband is quite right," many times in the future. And I always liked the way in which she said it. We strolled back to the grille of the park, talking and disagreeing in the most friendly way. At the gate the gentleman said: "Do come and see us. We live just over the way, and we are always in at tea-time." We exchanged cards. This gentleman was Henry Clews the sculptor, a fine artist, and the future author of *Mumbo Jumbo*. His wife had been one of the Whelen girls, famous Philadelphia beauties. I waited eight or ten days before ringing their bell one afternoon at tea-time. "I'll bet you have been investigating us," Henry Clews said, with a complex smile of his own. But I had not. It would not have been playing the game after Providence had arranged this encounter in such an unconventional way. We became great friends. We still meet whenever we have a chance, and I regret more than ever—now that the Clews eat the lotus in a fairy-like place near Cannes—that Paris was not built on one of those Mediterranean bays near them where hours fall so

lightly on your consciousness that you do not feel them. I have
always admired the Clews for not leaving Paris till the last shell
was shot.

My chief care, apart from the routine of teaching and writing,
were the wounded. Every afternoon I would go through a ward
of the College ambulance: there lay French or African, and
during the last eighteen months, English soldiers who were glad
of a little company. On Sundays I used to accompany to the
Val-de-Grâce an American woman who kept up her charitable
work to the very end. How eager the poor fellows were for those
visits! A whole ward was devoted to men threatened with blindness, or already beyond the hope of ever seeing again. They were
intensely pathetic, of course, especially when one knew their
case to be hopeless, and yet they would continue to be sanguine
about their recovery. It required months sometimes to bring
them to a realization of their plight. A few took it so hard that
even now I hate to remember their despair. But as a rule they
were patient. One of them wrote a beautifully resigned sonnet
which I have quoted in one of my books. In time they almost
invariably regained cheerfulness—thereby verifying a well-
known law. They realized that half an inch might have meant
the loss of their life instead of merely the loss of their sight.
I remember hearing three of them emphatic in their thankful-
ness. They could easily find wives, they said. Not so a man who
had lost an arm or a leg. And they congratulated one another.

This capacity for thinking oneself privileged seems to be universal in the blind. In 1917 a young fellow of eighteen entered
College Stanislas to follow a course of mine on *Enoch Arden*.
He had the poem printed in Braille and found his way up and
down it absolutely like the other students. One day, after the
lecture, he remained behind to ask me a few supplementary
explanations. I congratulated him on his astonishing facility in
reading and making notes. A distinct expression of superiority,
which delighted me, came over his face as he volubly expressed
his disdainful pity for the "new blind" who never could amount

to much. He almost strutted out of the room, finding his way to
the door without the least hesitation. About the same time, the
blind scholar, Pierre Villey, world-famous authority on the
Greek and Latin sources of Montaigne, published in the *Revue
des Deux Mondes* an article which, in the authoritative style of
an excellent writer, betrayed the same providential complacence:
the blind were in mental conditions far superior to those of the
seeing.

Another ward nearby, at the Val-de-Grâce, was reserved for
"wounds of the face," a terrible euphemism which the soldiers
retranslated into the more frank *gueules cassées*. I dreaded to
walk into that room. One man whose tongue darted out of an
impossible wire-supported destruction received his wife's visit
every Sunday. She was the kind of pretty doll to whom heroism
would never appeal. One day I read that clearly on her face as
we went out together. Her husband stood at the door watching
her graceful retreating figure. Hideous war!

In that same ward too I had my only contact—apart from the
many facts I heard later in the North of France—with a well-
ascertained war atrocity. One of those men with a shattered
face told me how, badly wounded in the hip, he lay by the
roadside when three German soldiers came along and stopped
to look at him. They went on and consulted a little, after which
one of them came back and shot him through the jaws. He told
his story without a flicker of hatred.

Also in that same ward, but badly disfigured, I saw several
times one Lerouge who interested me particularly because he
was one of the nine hundred who, when Maubeuge surrendered
—a little too soon—managed to dodge the Germans and successfully reached Dunkerque under the command of a major whose
name the historians of this Anabasis will no doubt keep alive.
This man came from near Lille, and we used to talk about his
native Lambersart. One Sunday he said to me that his sister had
just visited him, and told me about her an extraordinary story
showing well that the old Rector of my seminary was right when
he said that *tout arrive*. This young woman one morning made

up her mind to attempt the impossible feat of crossing the lines. She left Lille—thickly garrisoned with Germans—at the Porte de Roubaix, and nobody said a word to her. She walked calmly on till she found herself several miles out of the town. Not a shot was heard from either side. She reached the German front trenches, and German soldiers looked curiously at her over the parapet, but not one challenged her. A few more steps and she found other trenches manned, this time, by English soldiers. She had accomplished the impossible, as it might have been in a dream. Her difficulty began in Paris when she tried to locate her brother who had been transferred from his original regiment. Lerouge told me this extraordinary story without excitement and even without showing much surprise. The war caused the most improbable things to appear natural.

My old friend, Abbé Lemire, lived a few blocks away from the Val-de-Grâce, in a deserted street where I was often entirely alone. I frequently called on him after my visit to the hospital. I loved his seventeenth-century house—once part of the English College—his dreamy garden and his pets. At the beginning of the war he was still in difficulties with the authorities of our native diocese because of his re-election to the Chamber of Deputies in spite of the Archbishop's decision that he was not to run. Lemire, with a Fleming's obstinacy and a passion for politics which I often deprecated in talking with him, was a deeply religious man as well as one of the greatest philanthropists of the nineteenth century. Being denied the authorization to say mass, but not under an interdict, he would, every morning, go to Saint-Etienne-du-Mont, assist at mass kneeling on the cold stones, and receive communion at the altar rail with the poor people of his quarter. A strange admixture of pride and humility, characteristic of him, caused him to find a sort of happiness in this abnormal situation, but his friends resented it and I, for one, felt it deeply. At the beginning of the war this rare doer of deeds welcomed to Hazebrouck—the town of which he was mayor during thirty years—thousands of Belgian refugees whom he assisted in every way. The Belgian Queen, hearing of this, went out of her way to thank him personally in his Haze-brouck house. He happened to be in Paris, but the press gave wide publicity to this visit of Queen Elizabeth.

I thought I saw my chance to help a dear and revered friend. The Austin Lees knew well the Belgian Foreign Minister, Baron Beyens. I asked them to introduce me, and I persuaded the Baron to interest the Queen in Lemire's ecclesiastical status. Pope Benedict, recently elected, was a man of great sensibility and fairness. I felt sure that if the Queen would write to him on behalf of my friend some solution must be found. My step was successful, and with less delay than I thought would be necessary Lemire was summoned to Rome and had a long interview with Benedict the Fifteenth. As Lemire went out, the Pope said audibly to a secretary: "This man has been unjustly treated; he has suffered persecution." Within a week Lemire could say mass is a pretty private chapel which his friends decorated for him, and an odious cloud was lifted off one of the most guileless existences I have ever known.

Every three months, during the intervals of my college work, I would visit my dear old aunt at Nevers. It was a twelve hours' trip, on incredibly slow trains generally packed with soldiers. Everybody spoke to everybody else and my memory is full of narratives heard from unknown companions and showing how flat our daily life is in comparison with those astonishing four years.

Nevers, with its cathedral and its ducal palace rising out of picturesque old streets, is the typical French provincial town. Nobody can pass it by. It was too far from the front and not military enough to attract the enemy's attention. No German airplane ever visited it, and such of its inhabitants as did not have mobilized relatives never quite realized the war. In the Autumn of 1914 when Titine arrived there this lack of comprehension was shocking. My aunt rented a furnished apartment from a retired schoolmaster who was not grasping enough to overcharge, but who gave one the impression that he was sorry not to be. He and his wife would point out how reasonable their arrangements with us were. The old lady was a mincing spinster-like sexagenarian who had had one peak in her life, many years before, when her husband had given her a fortnight at some sea-side resort. "Ah! but when we were at the seaside in 1884 we paid so much," she would sigh when it occurred to her that Titine did not pay quite enough for the good time she was having.

Later on, this unimaginative old thing helped me to understand the much more excusable English or American people whose reasonings I have had to interrupt many times with the gentle reminder: "Ah! but there was a war." She was kind, too, in her way, and probably only talked in her miserly strain because she had been led to think it was good form or moral to do so.

Life in Nevers was the reverse of agitated. The natives had retained the feeling, handed down from the days of their medi-æval independence, that they were living in a capital. They also had a queer belief in the excellence of their climate and insisted that their magnolias were in bloom full five days before those in Paris. Titine, looking out of her window, used to laugh at their habit of putting up sunshades on the least provocation of even a yellow February sun. She, in her Northern heart, blamed them for indulging in those walks. But noticing the neatness of Nevers housekeeping she would remark audibly to herself: "They have some method, these silly sunshade people, they must have a method!"

There were a few other *emigrés* in the quarter where she lived. They would meet in the little city-park on warm afternoons, or in front of the Porte de Paris—a seventeenth-century Arch of Triumph—where the communiqué was posted up round four o'clock every day. There were frequently as many as two or three hundred people assembled there in eager expectation of what was considered inevitable, viz., the drive through the enemy's lines. "Nothing to report on the Eastern front," repeated in a hundred forms did not discourage their hopes. The next day found them in the same place, full of the same certainty.

Titine herself seemed to be in that complex state of mind which I used to notice in her about supernatural manifestations, for instance. Her imagination believed what her mind rejected. I felt that many times when she said pessimistic things with a happy smile, or with a slight effort at superficial sadness. All her life her mentality had shown the same admixture of Yea and Nay living in unexpected harmony. One afternoon, returning from my ride, I told her a story to which I could personally testify. A priest on a bicycle was riding past the *ferme-modèle* when two of the young delinquents apprenticed there shouted some insult and promptly vanished behind a haystack. The priest dismounted, selected the newest of a few shovels lying where the boys were working, and shouted back: "Saucy boys will find their shovel eight hundred yards away from here, near the next milestone. Here it goes!" Whereupon he rode away with the shovel. Titine loved that story. "How clever!" she repeated, "No cruelty, and yet those naughty boys so cleverly taken in! What long faces they must have pulled as the clergyman rode away with their tool high up in the air!"—"I hoped you would approve of him," I said, "I was he."—"You weren't! How could you do such a foolish thing without thinking of the danger of retaliation? Those horrid boys will murder you! they surely will, and I shall be miserable every time you go out!" But she was not. Her fundamental optimism could be detected in a variety of ways.

Our Trélon home was a great deal in my mind. Yet, during more than four years no letter came from there, no photograph, nothing likely to provide information. A veil of secrecy which the passing months made thicker and thicker hung over those familiar places. The mystery of the front, the epic of those chalky trenches, inaccessible to all but the mud-plastered soldiers who were seen every now and then outside railway stations, so

laden and caparisoned with things that they looked like walking
towers, weighed on every imagination. I remember a moving
article of Maurice Barrès' written, it seems to me, in 1916, when,
after a long delay, he was allowed to see the front-trenches and
their mysterious occupants. "There they are!" he wrote, as a
naturalist might exclaim after a long hunt for rare birds. To that
mystery was added for us, *emigrés,* the even more absolute inaccessibility of the invaded country. For the French and German
statements every day would say something of what happened
along the six hundred kilometers of the line, but of the region
beyond that line nothing was said, nothing was known. Our
homes were there, but who lived in them? What was happening
to them? The seasons came and went over the landscape of pasture and forest, but soldiers in unfamiliar uniforms still made
our glades and lanes strange with a raucous language. Fifteen
hundred of our compatriots had stayed there or found their way
back. How were they faring? What were they doing or thinking?
They were as shadowy as if they lived in Elysian Fields never
yet described by any poet-explorer. In time I became conscious
of a curious mental attitude of my aunt's as she went on, through
the long months, endlessly thinking the same things: we knew
nothing about our friends, but *they* knew. Whatever might
happen to them, they knew. The uncertainty which oppressed us
did not weigh upon them. In time Titine came to imagine them,
in consequence, as happy, happy in an inexplicable way which
might coexist with purgatorial discomfort. She would not give
full utterance to what she felt, but I read it on her aging face, and
her very reticence imparted to her some of that happy mysteri-
ousness which she imagined in our friends beyond the Known.
That she disliked having such complex thoughts I have no doubt.
She would frequently hint at the queerness of old age. One day
I was watching her as she looked at herself seated in her chair.
She laid down the mirror with a "silly little old face! (*petite
vieille sotte figure*)," in which there was more philosophy than
regret.

Pretty frequently letters written by prisoners in German

camps would come to us or to people we knew. No news. Only
vague allusions often in such cryptic language that they were
unintelligible. There was in Geneva a Bureau of Information to
which you could apply for news of this or that person. It would
take four or five months to hear that So-and-So "was in good
health." The formula was printed. Finally, during the early part
of 1916, a few Trélon people who had obtained permission to
be repatriated into what they curiously called La France Libre,
actually wrote that they had just arrived in Switzerland, and
shortly after appeared in Paris. How eagerly I interviewed the
first two or three! But how unsatisfactory the information they
gave! The Germans—they never said the Boches as, by that time,
everybody else did—had accustomed them to discretion, and the
Gazette des Ardennes had warped their judgment, to such a
degree that they hardly dared to speak. They sat, happy and
comfortable before more food than they had had for two years,
but, apart from a voluble interest which they showed in their
slow journey through Germany and Switzerland, they seemed
almost neutral. So-and-So was dead. Yes, M. Falleur was still
mayor. He had hidden in the woods through a whole summer but
suddenly he had reappeared. Shops? No, there were no shops,
but there was an American centre of *Ravitaillement*. Freedom?
Well, you had to be indoors by five o'clock, even in summer,
with your shutters closed. And you couldn't walk farther than a
kilometer from the town-hall. Otherwise, oh yes, otherwise you
went to jail in an old outbuilding at the glass works, or in the
Carmelite convent. The green gendarmes always got you. All
this was stated in a colourless voice, without repining and without much interest. Titine listened without much interest either
until she heard that a friend of hers, Mademoiselle Lixon, had
been in jail a month and harshly treated for giving a piece of
bread to an English soldier who somehow had dodged the
enemy's police for more than a year. Titine had been accustomed
to rise from her bench when German prisoners marched past the
park at the end of the afternoon—she never could witness with
indifference any sort of affliction—after hearing that story she

stopped doing it. About our house, we heard that during the first
year it was occupied by an officer who was a gentleman and used
it as if it had been his own. Then two non-commissioned officers,
rowdy fellows, had taken possession. It was now a Colonel's
office, and several hundred men visited it every day. I shuddered
at the thought of queues of German soldiers trampling Titine's
front garden, a dainty little plot she loved, but she was indifferent. Her interest was in the English hospital which I visited
every day: she would ask so eagerly about the French soldiers
who were tended there that I could not tell her all I heard or saw.
The day this bit of information about our house came my own
powers of endurance were pretty cruelly taxed. In the morning
a Parisian soldier, a boy of twenty-three, small but extremely
manly, asked me to mail three letters which he quickly and
firmly wrote in my presence—to his mother, his fiancée and a
friend. He thanked me in a strong voice, in a brief military way.
He saw that I had difficulty in believing that he was in danger
of his life. "Gangrene," he said, "don't you notice that I already
smell like a dead body? Oh! I shall be dead to-night." He was.

In the afternoon of the same day I visited a Breton soldier
who had been quickly losing ground during the past few days.
His father and mother sat beside him, grief-stricken beyond
description. Yet, the conversation of these three concerned the
impossibility for the elders to stay away from their farm at this
period of the harvesting. "If I don't die to-day," the boy said, as
if he were facing a self-evident necessity, "they *will* have to leave
by the evening train." He survived three days. A princess of
Battenberg who had tended him and I were the only two behind
his coffin.

In the Autumn of 1916, the Trélon neighbour whom Titine had
followed to Nevers decided on moving to Saint-Germain. There
too my aunt again followed her. Saint-Germain being only
twelve miles out of Paris I could ride there at least twice a week.
This move was providential, for my beloved old dear, the play-
mate of my childhood, the anxious vigil-light of my grown-up
years, died on January sixth, 1917. She would have been seventy-

three the next day. Her body lay in the poetic cemetery of Saint-Germain till June, 1920, when I had it transferred to our Trélon churchyard.

As usual, the British, after taking longer than anybody else to realize the war, realized it more fully than anybody else. They positively settled down to it. I remember how shocked I was on hearing that they had rented for five years the building in which they had established their Nevers hospital. Most French people had counted on the war lasting three or four months at most, and they resented the calmness with which their Allies envisaged a much longer trial of endurance. This attitude was more or less vaguely interpreted as a resolve not to hurry with urgent preparations. The slowness with which the British Government had come to a decision to enforce conscription was not understood in a country where conscription is as much a matter of course as school-attendance. Many people regarded the delay as shilly-shallying.

German propaganda which was as active in France as it was elsewhere saw its chance to breed discontent. It soon pointed out that the British lines of communication occupied far more men than the Front itself: Tea and Jam were the main concern of what the German Emperor had called "the contemptible little army." You could tell where the French line stopped and the British line began by noticing the sudden change from Spartan to comfortable living. In time a deadly slogan, no doubt manufactured in some special German laboratory, began to be circulated: "King George will fight to the last Frenchman." I saw the effect of this poisoned arrow on many occasions.

The British defended themselves with the smiling nimbleness they can show whenever activity becomes necessary. I was only a *littérateur* giving some of my time to journalism, and my success as a writer was far from being then what is was to become later. Yet I was surprised to find myself surrounded by a barrage of friendly efforts destined to keep intact my well-known

English sympathies. Distinguished newspaper men, quite apart from those I met in the house of my very good friend, George Adam, the London *Times* correspondent, visited me frequently. A former member of Parliament, the Hon. Claude Hayes, was a constant caller and an almost daily correspondent. No man of such limited magnetism ever tried to throw out such a volume of conviction. I have kept a huge dossier of his letters, models of their kind. Delightful officers called too: their naturalness was more irresistible than the deepest diplomacy. I have also a recollection of two Irish M.P.'s calling on some errand which I cannot now recollect, but I well remember that they were the two most exquisitely-mannered men I had seen in my whole life, anglicized Kelts who had blended the characteristics in their two nationalities, as hot and cold might be in an iced cordial of high grade.

Once, in 1915, General Morgan whose keen perception of things I greatly admired said casually to me: "I wonder how long you can wait for us. I often think of Cæsar's remark about your ancestors, the Gauls: they begin things as men but they end them as women."—"Morgan," I replied, "you British can die wonderfully, but you do not suffer well; we can." He laughed, for, in spite of this passage of arms, he was and still is a great Francophile.

There was much friction between the Allies during the war, but as George Adam showed, in a dispassionate lecture which I admired, friction is felt less and less as mutual understanding increases. There was only one thing which my English friends did not seem able to conquer, viz., their jealousy of the welcome which the French gave to the American soldiers. "Your new love," they would say, rather bitterly, to me. I had to explain that, in spite of the ocean between them, the French and the Americans are inevitably conscious of many similarities. This was no easy task, for my English interlocutors would often jump to the conclusion that similarity of disposition entails a community of interests, a fallacy which subsequent history was to dispel only too soon.

I paid several visits to England during the war, although multitudinous demands on shrunken resources made it impossible for me to be as often in London as I had formerly been. I wrote regularly for *The Saturday Review* and for Chesterton's *The Eye-Witness*, also, every now and then, for Skilbeck's *The Nineteenth Century*. You did not see in London the many *poilus* who made Paris both touching and picturesque, but London showed more the grip of the war than Paris did. One evening I was dining with Skilbeck at his club, the Oxford and Cambridge, and we had a flagon of Spanish wine and a bottle of claret on our table. Suddenly I noticed a flutter of surprised annoyance at all the tables, while Skilbeck hastily seized our two bottles and spirited them away under his chair. "The Police," he whispered. In fact the door stood ajar and a characteristic face was peeping in. It was a false alarm; the detective was only after an excess of light streaming from our dining-room, but I felt that London was more pinched than we were. Voluntary service among men past the military age was also more frequent. Skilbeck acted as a constable and I found this was no sinecure.

I met Marshal French at luncheon at Mrs. Alec Tweedie's. French had none of the mental agility which I had a chance later to admire in Foch. I have no doubt that his deliberation often caused people to call him slow-witted. He had just arrived from Paris where he had gone to see the anti-aircraft defences, especially at Mont Valérien. He was astonished to have been met at the entrance of the Fort by a negro major, whose intelligence and social ease had entirely dazzled him. "Pure black!" he would repeat, "and in command of the whole thing, and three or four French captains under him!"

In 1917 I was invited to give a course of lectures at the University of London. At Bedford College, Regent's Park, where three of those lectures were delivered, I met a young French instructress called Mademoiselle Têtenoire. During one of our conversations I told her that her way of speaking our language puzzled me: it was not Parisian but, in spite of long practice, I could not connect it with any French accent in any part of

France. "Why!" the young lady said, "I have never been in
France. My people are French, but they were settled in Petro-
grad long before I was born, and my four brothers are officers
in the Russian army." This was illuminating, but it also accounted for something else. The girl already spoke English with
remarkable fluency although she had only been six weeks in
London. She was not a Russian, yet she showed the well-known
Russian facility for acquiring a foreign language. This proved
to me what I had long suspected, viz., that the Slavs learn languages quickly merely because of the belief current among
them that languages are the easiest thing to learn. The contrary
effect is produced in countries where the same study is supposed
to meet with insuperable difficulties. This phantasm hinders
the working of the brain.

At Whitsun of 1917 the British Government invited me to
visit their front. This was a great surprise and a great honour,
for even members of the British Embassy to Paris who were
anxious to receive the like invitation did not succeed in getting
it.

I went by train to Abbeville—on the Paris-to-Boulogne line
—where I was met by an English officer. After that I was always
transported by army cars. The guests of the British Government
were entertained at the historic château of Azincourt (the Agin-
court of the Hundred Years' War), about fifteen miles from the
front. No place could look as still and happy in the vast wheat-
plain. Millions of the poppies which decorate so many war-
poems fluttered in the warm breeze. Five or six officers, chiefly
occupied in entertaining guests of all nationalities, gave their
visitors the same generous hospitality, careful not to infringe on
personal freedom, which is characteristic of a house-party
everywhere in England. With one exception these officers were
young, and their conversation as well as the pictures they had
added to the sober family portraits hung by the habitual occupants, showed it. English newspaper men, not knowing that
this *Police-Gazette*-like decoration was the choice of their own

compatriots, would not have failed to remark: how French! I said nothing, of course. Dinner came. I was the only civilian present that first night.

The next morning the senior officer, a man of about fifty, took me in charge and asked me where I would like to go. Vimy Ridge had been re-captured by the British only a short time before and I asked might I be taken there. Some telephoning was necessary to ascertain that this was possible and we started. The morning was unbelievably poetic and caressing. The farm-dotted countryside did not seem any nearer to the present war than it did to the battles of the fourteenth century. It took us at least half an hour to arrive within sound of the dull cannonade familiar to my Parisian ears. Then suddenly the scene changed as we rapidly crossed three very different zones. One consisted of villages still partly inhabited but which shells evidently visited at intervals: people stayed here at the peril of their lives chiefly to trade with the British soldiers while teaching them the strange "napu" language which the privates imagined must be French. The next belt was one of entirely deserted hamlets which solitude, even more than destruction, made sinister like murder-haunted inns. Shortly after leaving this zone you came to the front proper. This was not visible at once from the road we were following. We left the car in a small wood, the officer gave me a gas-mask which I slung over my shoulder and we emerged onto the famous plateau of Lorette.

The view from this comparatively high spot over a scarcely rolling country was immense, but no buildings except the towers of Saint Eloi's Abbey, five or six miles to our right, were visible. Although artillery boomed round us we could see no traces of military activity anywhere, no trenches, no fortified ridge, nothing. Especially not a human figure, not a horse: the happy sun was the sole owner of all we saw, with flowerets in every shell-hole and the sky full of lyrical larks. My companion was a careful old warrior. He proceeded slowly, looking for something which turned out to be a disused trench where we now walked. As we trudged along he asked me did I know

Hilaire Belloc, who was up at the château two days before. Couldn't I tell him that it was hateful to the military to read what he published every week on the operations? No civilian ought to be allowed to say a word about strategy. They never knew, they could not know. Very irritating, civilians were. I did not defend Belloc. Living in an over-intellectual country as I do I have always enjoyed good old Saxon anti-intellectualism, and I let my companion indulge his grudge against a civilian who imagined he could write up the war because he had a brain.

I was listening to the officer when a vivid impression of the streets of London suddenly woke up in my mind. Simultaneously I became conscious of the cause of that vision which was none other than a faint perception of Egyptian tobacco-smoke wafted by the breeze down our trench. Turning a curve we found ourselves in a subterranean chamber, an O.P., from which two Scotch soldiers, peeping with field-glasses over a tiny parapet, were watching the operation of an invisible battery somewhere below us. The range insisted on being too short, and one of the men every now and then would telephone in an impatient tone: "Back, back! Back, I tell you! Far back!" The London smell of Oriental tobacco made a zone of peace around him. In time the range was found and we could see shells exploding two or three miles ahead of us. A huge volume of sulphurous fumes and dust would rise and subside. Then the belated sound of the shot would reach us. No effect was visible from where we were. Had it not been for the villainous smoke this would have looked more like some gigantic ninepins game than like war. No response whatever came from the German side, nothing dramatic happened. What my mind registered all the time was the vastness of the view, the perfection of the summer day, and the strangeness of this being war.

A few hundred yards farther, our zigzagging trench stopped and we issued onto something which had once been a road leading to the village of Souchez. The road was a thickness of pounded brick between banks which ought to have been starry with daisies, but now only showed the bleakness of a vacant lot near a chemicals factory. The village was what I had seen hundreds of times in newspaper pictures, but had never realized: confusion and horror. Complete destruction would have been less depressing. I saw, during the following days, and again the year after, in the Verdun region, many villages the traces of which resembled mere cigarette ashes on a large scale. There was a sadness over them, but they did not give one the shock of actual desolation as Souchez did. Madness suddenly become infuriated seemed to have been at work on what was left of the church and of the ripped-up houses. Practical jokes abounded. The first I saw was a baby-carriage preposterously hanging from a chimney. Here and there a sturdy lilac-bush or apple-tree would rise out of impossible ruins. Close by the church a semicircle of newborn white pansies appealed for pity like an orphan compelled to beg in the streets. Teams and groups of soldiers went up and down what must have been once the village high street, but they were silent, unexpectedly and incredibly so as if they too were, in spite of long habit, oppressed by the horror around them, or choked by the impalpable brickdust filling the air. My officer stopped a sergeant to ask the question I was to hear every morning from my daily-changing guides: "Is he shooting?" *He* meant the Hun naturally, but the phrase sounded to me almost funny. "No, Sir," the sergeant answered, "but yesterday was awful."

We crossed over to Vimy Ridge. It was held by a Canadian battalion and the men were bathing in a large pond at the foot of the hill. They were vociferous in their enjoyment of the sport and, though so near the malediction over the spot I had just seen, they seemed like happy schoolboys. We found the major in command, a lawyer from Edmonton whose card I long treasured and whose name I wish I could remember. I think it was Dawson. There was nothing military about him, yet he was eminently a chief, with a sense of his responsibility written on a grave and intelligent brow. I at once felt deep respect for that man. "Do you really want to go over the ridge?" he asked in almost incredulous surprise. He gave me a khaki coat and we began to

climb the hill, leaving my English officer in a shell-hole. The hill
was nothing but shell-holes, and the major told me that the
pounding of the slopes had been so repeated and violent that
before the present shell-holes there must have been three or four
generations of others no sooner opened up than they were filled
in, then opened up again.

We reached the top and followed the ridge slowly. The view
was even vaster here than from the Lorette plateau, but apart
from the vague expanse there was nothing to see. A few faint
traces below us seemed to indicate trenches. "You are a brave
man," the major said to me as we stood still looking around.
I did not know what he meant. "Why!" he said again after a
time, "I never saw such a brave man as you are." The truth
dawned on me and I asked: "Do the Germans see us?" "Well,"
the major said, "they are just behind the willows you see down
there." The green line was not more than half a mile away. I
thought of snipers with infallible rifles secure on tripods and
my self-ignoring bravery deserted me at once. I was glad a moment later when the major jumped into a shell-hole inviting me
to follow him. There were the poor remains of a dead German on
the very lip of that hole, and shrapnel bullets lay all round.
The château seemed a delicious place when we got back.

During four more days I was taken, in the same way, to various parts of the line. My guides changed every day. I liked them
all, even a very young subaltern whom a slight wound had left
more nervous than he should have been, and who acted queerly
as soon as we got near the front trenches. We would leave early
and drive briskly through the bright morning. Day after day I
marvelled at the peace and beauty of that part of Artois. Even
the signs of war we saw were more picturesque than saddening.
I remember strains of bagpipes wafted from a by-road where
some Highlanders were encamped. Also a few score of German
prisoners working on a road and resting a while on their shovels
to watch us: they were northern Germans, very foreign-looking,

with cold pale eyes. Gradually the roads would show rougher
and rougher usage till we entered the zone of destruction and its
impossibilities. Arras was a grand picture of ruins with only the
fronts of the houses left standing on its two magnificent squares,
and half its superb cathedral lying in confusion over the royal
stairway in front of it. The road went right through what was
left of the railway-station, a strange sight. The streets seemed as
deserted as those of Baalbek. After roaming about for an hour I
discovered five or six tommies with an officer engaged in rather
unfriendly conversation with an old woman whose picard patois
it was lucky for him he did not quite understand. How that poor
old thing was allowed to stay on I could not comprehend. When
I asked her about bombardments, and she said they were frequent, she also added that "a person in business could not take
any notice of such things," and bridled a little as if I were in-
terfering.

That same day we left Arras by the Porte de Cambrai and followed the broken main road several miles. Every milestone said
"Cambrai so many kilometers," and the name of the old town
where I was at school moved me deeply. In time the stones also
said Boursies and I used to know people there. We left the car
and walked. With every rise of the slowly dipping road I thought
I should see the three towers, all exactly of the same height,
standing in a perfectly straight line, and separated by exactly
the same distances, which had often fascinated me as we strolled
back to school in our walks of many winters ago. But every time
I was disappointed. The three towers never appeared, and suddenly I saw that the banks of a little stream, the Cojeul, had been
"organized" and we could not go a step further.

That place with a tall calvary by the roadside, two or three
officers riding past and a company or two variously busy, is
photographed on my memory forever. The men looked grave,
even careworn. The English newspaper men who made fun of the
"sublimity" of French *ordres du jour*, and contrasted them with
the attitude of the tommies charging to the cry of "Front seats,
sixpence!" probably told the truth. Men cannot charge unless

they feel excited. But what I always found in the vicinity of front trenches was extreme seriousness, with a touch of anxiety which did not prevent the men from attending to their work. That morning the question "has he been shooting?" was answered by a private in a flustered manner. "No, Sir! he has not to-day. But the battalion's smith was killed day before yesterday." Two or three other soldiers nodded sympathetically, repeating "day before yesterday, where that hut is standing." We might have been in a faraway Cornish village where an accident was being discussed by villagers unused to dramas. A man in a platoon which came along at that moment whispered to me with a noticeable Irish accent that this was a very dangerous place.

I realized in that melancholy spot what modern warfare seems to be nineteen days out of twenty: something like nervous work in a quarry where a loose block may crush you to death any minute. No more romance there than in an accidental factory death. As for bravery, it must vary from the indifference to death of a very few, or the sanguine certitude that death cannot be for oneself of others, to more or less resignation accompanying degrees of fear difficult to determine. All I have to say is that people who imagine that soldiers are gay in the presence of death are foolishly misled and dangerously misleading.

In the morning of my last day at the château, quite a party of new arrivals were taken with me to an apparently peaceful section. There were four of five Dutch or Scandinavian newspaper men of middle age, and a young and very nice American, a Mr. Flaherty, with whom I felt at once in strong sympathy. Our guide, a captain, had no sooner asked his ritual question about the shooting and been assured that everything was quiet, than HE (the Hun) sent a few brisk volleys, each shot getting nearer and nearer to our little group as if the shells had been suddenly gifted with malicious intelligence. Our captain shouted to us to scatter about, but the last seventy-seven fell quite near before we had time to obey the order and a spray of dust and small pebbles spurted over us. One of the elderly gentlemen began to blubber, while another said to the captain something about their "having wives." I felt no panic, but a longing, an irrepressible longing to be elsewhere came over me. Yet I joined Flaherty in a hearty laugh at the old fellow with a wife. Fifteen years later, lecturing in Chicago, I recognized Mr. Flaherty in a still astonishingly young-looking gentleman who came up to me at the end of my talk. I found he had been disseminating a rumour that I was an extremely brave man. I know I was nothing of the kind. *He* was the brave man unless, like myself, he wished himself elsewhere with all his might, but I doubt if he did.

Late in the afternoon as we drove back along a road positively honey-combed with large shell-holes, the captain, our guide, told us that he had seen those holes in the making less than a fortnight before. He was driving himself when the shelling began, devilishly accurate. He spoke without any boastfulness of "those great big shells" falling at regular intervals right in front of him. Finally he could not stand the nervousness of it any longer and ran to a homestead on the right—which we soon saw, still intact—fifty yards away from the road. As ill-luck would have it there was in the farmyard a growling mastiff whom the shelling was making even more wicked than he must naturally be, and the captain was afraid of strange dogs. The shelling was getting worse. The captain took his revolver and prepared to shoot the dog. No! he couldn't do that, nor could he brave the glaring white teeth either. In a minute he was back in his car, pushing his way behind the shells, but glad to have escaped from the dog. Such is bravery.

We reached the château later than usual that afternoon, and dinner was announced as soon as we got out of the car. In the salon I found five or six American gentlemen, talking. They were scientists who were visiting the whole length of the front in quest of discoveries in acoustics elicited by war necessities. They had already recorded several hundred items. I soon became conscious of the fact that the conversation of these gentlemen did not concern their work, but ran on a subject which, familiar as it is to American men, is never, *au grand jamais,* treated by them as this company treated it. Believe it or not, those American husbands, illuminated by Experience and liberated by Distance, were criticizing the American Woman, criticizing their absent innocent American Penelopes. They went on for quite a while, mocking and bitter, while I wondered if I could believe what my incredulous ears reluctantly transmitted to my mind. Suddenly, the pot-bellied little man who was shaking the cocktails put a stop to the scandalous talk. "*I* have a French wife," he said with quiet complacence.

By this time Americans were frequently seen in France. Many of them had long wished to be on this side of the ocean; many of us had longed to see them arrive. The anxious uncertainty of two years and a half had finally come to an end.

One American, at the beginning of the war, acted in a way which France will never forget. This was Ambassador Myron Herrick who, even when the Government emigrated to Bordeaux, insisted upon staying on in Paris. His action may not have been logical—embassies were naturally to follow the Cabinet—but it was the outcome of a sentiment as superior to mere logic as disobedience to military orders sometimes is to mechanical carrying out of instructions. If the enemy were to enter Paris, Herrick wanted to be there, as his colleague Whitlock, under similar circumstances, had been in Brussels. The appeal of danger was stronger for him than that of technical necessities. His bravery at a time when the Paris populace was getting panicky reassured thousands.

What happened in America itself was not so satisfactory, and worried the many Americans living in France. It was natural that the United States should be anxious not to be involved in a quickly-developing conflict. There may have been something comical in the slogan "We are too proud to fight," but not in that which re-elected President Wilson: "He kept us out of the war." Certainly the business of a ruler is to keep his country out of a war to which it is not a party. But Americans in Paris resented their friends at home writing to them that, in accordance with the President's directions, they were "trying to be neutral in mind as well as in action." How could Americans be neutral in mind about such a thing as the violation of Belgium's international rights which the United States was guaranteeing? For a long time the attitude of the American Government recalled that of a man looking away from what he does not like to see. Its frequent attempts at protesting against what Germany was doing without offending the Germans were not convincing. People in Allied countries became more and more inclined to think that the thought of the German vote in America was influencing American statesmanship, and the phrase "President Wilson will send in a note" became a funny by-word applied to any *coups d'épée dans l'eau*. Francophile Americans grew as restless and gradually as indignant as Francophile Englishmen were in August, 1914, while Mr. Lloyd George kept the British Cabinet sitting on the fence. They were frequently sarcastic. At one time, President Wilson having sent his usual compliments to the Kaiser on his birthday, an American woman friend of mine, Louise Morgan Sill, wrote the following epigram which delighted Theodore Roosevelt:

> "When, in the everlasting contest led
> By good and evil, evil wins ahead,
> Let us be neutral down to any level
> And send congratulations to the devil."

But sarcasms were not enough for the millions of friends of France in America. Gifts of all sorts had, from the first, been sent over to the Red Cross. Gradually men also came. I met a number of these volunteers after the war. They demonstrated the fact that French and American nationalities could easily be interchangeable. Many of these young American officers in French uniforms were only separated from their French comrades by nuances of accent. Their background had been transformed in two or three years by the simplicity and magnitude of the issues for which they were endangering their lives.

The submarine campaign of Germany could not be intensified

as it was from month to month without simultaneously intensifying the resentment of Americans. I remember the effect produced by the indignant cable which Professor James Mark Baldwin flashed to the President after the torpedoing of a boat on which his daughter was crossing the Channel. Mr. Baldwin was a friend of mine: he was an extremely self-possessed philosopher. The sincerity of his outraged feelings made of him a political force overnight. The *Lusitania* affair only brought to its natural conclusion a development which had been perceptible for months. I am always surprised when I meet, in the United States, people who still insist that America was propagandized into declaring war and might have been kept out of the conflict to the end. This attitude presupposes two notions both of which ought to offend Americans equally. One is that the United States was tricked into a decision which it hated to take, and that makes a great country cut a ridiculous figure. The other would lead to infer an aversion from even a defensive war which is not reconcilable with the American's well-known impulse to take off his coat the moment he thinks himself insulted. America was not pushed into the war, it was dragged into it. The situation at the time was perfectly clear. What is now obscuring it in retrospect is the puzzling complication of European politics along with an opposition to the Versailles Treaty—and to the Covenant forcibly bound with it by President Wilson—which is instinctive in most Americans but is reasoned out by very few. The fundamental attitude here indicated could probably be expressed in some sentence like the following: "I am sorry I ever got mixed up in any business as difficult to understand as this is." Such disinclination to a necessary intellectual effort should be condoned by Europeans whose only reason for invariably skipping important Chinese news is that the names of antagonistic Chinese leaders discourage attention. Seen from Wyoming European politics is a Chinese puzzle.

America's entry into the war lifted up French morale in a wonderful manner. My friend and I would show to the wounded at the Val-de-Grâce a map of the United States traced over one of Europe. Many soldiers who had no idea of the vastness of the United States could not resist the revelation of strength produced by this map, and, no matter how they happened to feel physically, they brightened up as soon as they realized the possibilities which America's decision involved.

Soon Paris filled with Americans. I met many, owing to my connection with New York and Boston reviews as well as with the Yale Library whose Paris correspondent I had been for some years. The first of these who came to see me was a young Middle Westerner of the name of Duiguid who was to be killed in one of the earliest engagements. He was an earnest young fellow with the usual touch of American humour. He wanted things to be expedited and showed disgust at any slowness. He used to carry a little map of the front clipped out of some newspaper and would brush it with an impatient finger saying: "The British! with their little bit of a line!" I had to explain that Britain took care of other fronts in the East, but he remained sceptical. "Slow pokes," he would insist, "the war is here and not in Arabia."

Mr. W. A. Neilson, at that time professor at Harvard and later President of Smith College, was exchange professor at the Sorbonne in 1916–1917. The war depressed him, as well it might, and he did not show then that capacity for the terse effortless expression of a whole chaplet of thoughts which I have often admired in him since, but his originality appeared in other ways. Like my other very dear friend, Bliss Perry, he was one of the first American professors whom admiration for German erudition did not blind to the quality of French scholarship, and he then decided to show his appreciation in a practical way: for many years there has been at the Sorbonne a strong party of Smith girls. Even new-comers from that college seem sooner at home in Paris than other visitors.

After Mr. Neilson came Bishop Perry of Providence, now Presiding Bishop of the Episcopalian Church. He was a cousin of Lady Austin Lee's—whose maid, unable to distinguish between bishops, called him Monseigneur—and I saw him constantly at her house. Bishop Perry is such a modest man that it takes long familiarity with him to discover the hidden strength and the remarkable statesmanship which have secured for him his eminent position. When away from his cares he becomes the most genial of men. We have great times together when he and Mrs. Perry reappear in Paris.

A man whose early loss I shall always deplore, Frederick Trevor Hill, a good lawyer and a good writer, joined the Paris headstaff of the American army early in 1917. He was a most conscientious officer. He never let me know where he was stationed when he was not in Paris: his letters never gave the least military clue. In fact I never even discovered what his real duties were. Friendships with many officers on the French staff made him a great Francophile—which he had not always been—but he remained an American and always spoke and acted as one who was fighting the battles of America. I approved of that attitude. If it had been universal many minor misunderstandings between America and France might have been avoided.

We frequently met and I became acquainted with several of his American friends. Once he announced to me the arrival of a financier, recently mobilized, who, he said, was the "livest wire" he had ever known—a phrase new to me at the time. I was to meet this gentleman at a great dinner of big wigs. He might be a little profane, but I must not mind that. Wars meant oaths and you could swear innocently. Besides, the brilliance of this officer would so dazzle me that I should not notice what Friar Jean des Entommeures might have called the ornaments of his expression. In fact I sat near this general and I thought he was the gentlest soldier I had ever met. He rather surprised me by drinking champagne after his soup, and coffee and milk on the top of that, but his brilliance remained on a low voltage. Finally I decided to turn him on full light. "General Dawes," I said, "Mr. Hill tells me that you have a little habit which I beg of you not to repress on my account." The habit was at once richly indulged and the keen intelligence gave itself free play. General Dawes and I have remained intermittent but faithful friends. Shortly after the appearance of my book on *The Art of Thinking* the General wrote to me that this book had enabled him to pass on to a lady very near to him indirect advice which he had never dared to offer before.

American women flocked to Paris, perhaps in even greater numbers than their men. They started all sorts of useful associations which more or less unexpected occasions elicited. I all but witnessed a remarkable instance of American practicality. Many French working-women who were needed in munitions factories could not respond to the offer because of their children. It soon appeared that the only way to free the mothers was to create more places where the children could be kept in their absence. Two American ladies were present at a discussion of possibilities which occupied the whole afternoon of a group of French-women. The French habit of insisting on foreseeing every contingency put off decisions to a future meeting. As the two American ladies went out one asked the other, "How much have you got? I have so much. The two of us can pay to have Madame So-and-So's children placed at the *pouponnière* at once."

Shortly afterwards I was invited to visit a small Maternity Hospital opened by Americans in the rue Pierre Nicole, behind the Luxembourg. This clinic was a perfect little gem and visitors were delighted with it. A cradle was already occupied by just-born twins to whom everybody, except one gruff-looking Yankee, was duly paying homage. The nurse smiling an invitation to this gentleman to join the admiring chorus, I was amused to hear him ask "were they Amurrican, those twins?" They were, and the gentleman walked across the room and scrutinized the babies for a while. He was the kind who does not believe that Americans should be born out of America, but this variety, as a rule, does not travel, and I never came across another such specimen during the war. What I saw, what was going on in the United States at the time, and what M. Tardieu later filled a whole fat book with, were proofs of the joy with which Americans not only exerted themselves but even welcomed hardships to do their bit.

I watched the progress of the American mobilization in several families I knew. There were shirkers, of course, but for this I

always blamed the mothers more than the sons. The latter, as a
rule, showed admirably. One young Washingtonian in whom I
took particular interest, E. S. Alvord, Jr., finding things a little
too slow at home—he was too young to be called—begged his
people to let him manage them for himself. He took ship for
Bordeaux where he was planning to enlist in the Foreign Legion.
On the boat he met another young chap who dissuaded him.
"Come over with me and joint the Tenth Machine Gun Battalion!" Everything that could happen did happen during the
war. This extempore enlisting materialized and, in less than two
months, the two boys were in action at Château-Thierry where
my young friend was gassed. They were crouching side by side
in the kind of insufficient protection called an individual trench
when their first shells began to fall around. "What are you shaking for?" Junior's friend asked him. "Shake? I don't shake. *You*
do!" Junior answered, as he noticed in his companion the usual
phenomenon of tremor caused by the fear of fear, of which he
had not been conscious himself.

The day before Palm Sunday, 1918, I was returning from
Saint-Germain on my bicycle when, in the Bois de Boulogne, I
crossed another cyclist who shouted as he passed me: "A funny
time of it they're having in Paris."

I did not have to wait long to know what the man meant; on
arriving at the Auteuil Gate I found that the life of Paris seemed
to be at a standstill. The morning was heavenly, with the chestnut
trees on the avenues cheerily greening against the blue, but there
were only a few pedestrians in the streets and they looked puzzled
or annoyed, gazing at the sky as they exchanged remarks. No
vehicles of any kind were to be seen except a few straggling
taxis. Suddenly I heard a loud report immediately followed by
a strange echo, whereupon everybody stopped short and scrutinized the four quarters of the sky. Nothing was to be seen anywhere. I asked questions. For two hours shells had been dropped
every twenty minutes on Paris but those shells were mysterious.

Evidently German airplanes must be above Paris, but so high that no one yet had been able to see them. This mystery held people in a panicky suspense, and life had been interrupted for more than an hour. At the College—where the Easter examinations were in process—I found that the upper storeys had been deserted and all the schoolwork was carried on in the basement. The students showed no excitement. Only when, every twenty minutes, the explosion was heard they raised their eyebrows or laughed a little nervously.

In the afternoon a friend of mine called. He was mobilized in the Auxiliary Services, but he had been a gunner and it was with the air of an expert that he showed me a jagged bit of iron which he took out of his pocket. "You believe, like everybody else, that German planes are bombing Paris?" he said. What else could I believe? "Well," he went on, "look at this fragment. It is a gun, a gun over a hundred kilometers away, that is shooting at us. The streaks you see on this bit of iron would never appear on a bomb, they have been made by a gun." An hour later the official communiqué corroborated what this friend had told me.

The next day the exodus which I had witnessed in 1914 when the Germans were in sight of the Eiffel Tower began again. Once more the railway stations were besieged by crowds pressing to buy tickets. It being Holy Week and the Easter vacation almost at hand many people pretended they were leaving town as usual, only a little earlier. Among the eager travellers, bag in hand, happened to be Sacha Guitry, the playwright and actor. "Going too, Sacha?" a friend who saw him asked. "Yes," Guitry said, "but I am not leaving for the same reason that brings all these other people here."—"No?"—"No! *I* am scared to death."

During the next six months, with only short respites, the Big Bertha shot at us with mathematical regularity. At seven o'clock, sharp, every morning, the rude report of the first shell would be heard, and, every twenty minutes till late in the afternoon, other explosions would follow. The range was most of the time remarkably accurate, the first shell hitting the court in front of Gare de l'Est and hardly any ever falling outside the fortifica-

tions. One morning, at twenty minutes to twelve, the shell struck
the War Office which had been a frequent target, and at noon
the next shell damaged a house close by.

The range was almost invariably north to south, so that many
of the projectiles passed over College Stanislas. Their wheeze
was perceptible, and the shell became visible as it curved down
just before falling, but I never saw any. Nobody minded the
shelling very much after a few days. Although the Luxembourg
Garden was repeatedly hit, the croquet-players who, year in,
year out, are at their game on the terrace near the Senate-House,
never gave in to intimidation. There they were, in full force,
playing. Where they came from I never knew, as nine in ten
houses in the quarter were empty. Promenaders in the streets
hardly noticed the explosions though they walked, by orders,
on the sheltered side of the street. My friend, Mr. Hill, once saw
a shell falling in the Seine almost opposite the Hôtel de la
Méditerranée where his office was located. Not one of the people
who happened to be passing the bridge even stopped.

Indoors, especially if one were alone, the expectation of the
shot was a more nervous business. Over two hundred people got
killed by the Bertha, and intellectual work became difficult when
the twentieth minute drew near. Sometimes my friend, M. Bouvet,
would open his window to call me when the shot was nearly due,
and he stood with finger lifted listening till the report and its
echo were heard. "They want to kill us, those people," he would
say as he shut his window again.

A block away from the Port-Royal Maternity Hospital, where
nine lives, mothers and children, were snuffed out by one of the
shells, was the dear little restaurant Sainte-Cécile where I took
most of my meals. Once an artist seated opposite me showed
me a portfolio full of interesting sketches he had made at the
famous Café de la Rotonde almost over the way. He drew my
attention to the strange head of a Russian habitué whom he had
just added to his collection. That outlandish physiognomy was
unforgettable. I remembered it at once when the pictures of
Trotzki first appeared in the newspapers. Sainte-Cécile had a

basement which became a great attraction when the Big Bertha entered into the life of Paris: there you could eat your lunch in peace. It gradually became monopolized by young American officers who ate to the sound of a banjo and were as happy as larks.

The last few months of the long, long war seemed as brief as weeks with swift spectacular changes. Ludendorff felt he must not lose a minute before the Americans were over in full force. I had no suspicion that he was working at his plans in a château ten miles from Trélon belonging to my friends the René Legrands. Early in May Ludendorff suddenly broke through the lines of the Fifth British Army. We had not yet recovered from the shock of this surprise when something equally surprising and even more shocking happened: the long range of apparently impregnable cliffs known as the Chemin des Dames was unexpectedly stormed and held by the Germans who gained twelve or thirteen miles without encountering any resistance, because no attack on such a point had been anticipated. Foch was not disturbed by these accidents which, from his own standpoint, only produced salients less likely to annoy him than to give him a chance. But civilians, even thoughtful ones, felt their faith in victory shaken. I remember how cynical M. Denys Cochin began to sound. Even such a cool-headed political writer as M. Auguste Gauvain, of the *Journal des Débats,* could not refrain from dropping hints about peace which I, for one, deeply resented, for though wrongly disbelieving in the possibility for the Allies to break through the Hindenburg line, I felt sure that the Germans must ask for peace.

Very early in the morning of July 15th, 1918, I got up and went to my study-window to watch the dawn, a thing I never do. Nature was expecting the sunrise in a world of coolness and placidity. There was not a murmur from the North East where the cannonade was usually heard. A bird, entranced by the magic of the hour, gave two or three long and sweet whistles which I was to hear again a few years later in the green desert of Sonora, in Mexico, but which I had never imagined a European bird could produce. Shortly afterwards the sun appeared. Simultaneously the rumbling from the front began and I was preparing to regain my room when I noticed that this was not the usual cannonade. A formidable artillery preparation, probably from the German side, was in process. It was four o'clock. The Germans had taken the habit of shelling the positions in front of their own during four hours before attacking them: eight o'clock, therefore, would be their zero hour.

I was cycling once more to Saint-Germain that morning. Towards nine o'clock I noticed, from the Bois de Boulogne, that the cannonade not only had not stopped but had acquired a triple intensity. I dismounted in a solitary lane and listened. Why this extraordinary violence? Suddenly the truth flashed on me. We must be counter-attacking. Perhaps the day had come at last when it was our turn to break through. It had. Next morning the newspapers revealed how Mangin had fooled the enemy into attacking him at his strongest point and had launched a victorious counter-attack. What had seemed an impossibility till a few weeks before had turned out, with the new armament, to be a matter of course. The Germans were retreating, they had been forced off their second positions, and a war of movement was beginning. A few days later the British reported the same success in Belgium and, in less than a week, the hinge of the Hindenburg line at Saint-Quentin at long last gave way.

Ludendorff, in his Memoirs, says that it was not till August 11th that he knew he was beaten, because, on that day, he could not conceal from himself the fact that the morale of his army was broken. One never can read such an admission from an opponent like Ludendorff without the sympathy to which intelligence and courage have a right. But I know that from that July 15th *we* felt that the circle of iron had been broken and freedom would soon be an actuality. My imagination began to dwell on the fate of my dear little town and of the home which had been left, four years earlier, under the precarious protection of my request in uncertain German: "Treat peacefully a peaceful man's house." Retreats could be, often were, mercilessly destructive. What should I find when, in a few months, perhaps in a few weeks, I should return to our belt of orchards in the middle of the Fagne forest? There were still to be anxious moments. In September I met an artillery officer who also came from that same countryside. The Germans opposite him held their positions with as much tenacity as ever before, he said, and I noticed that they defended during a whole fortnight the little Rhonelle, an insignificant stream which anybody could jump. Still, the troops moved on at other points, moved continuously on. In October the débâcle came. Bulgaria asked for peace. Shortly afterwards, Austria-Hungary did the same, and Franchet d'Esperey could dictate an armistice which, had it not been for Lloyd George's opposition, would have enabled him to push his way on to Berlin without any possible resistance of the enemy. (There never was any chance of reaching Berlin from the western side.) Finally eleven o'clock of November 11th came, the bugles actually sounded: Stop firing! and after a minute's stillness, the greatest minute, probably, in the history of mankind, the bells of all churches became lyrical. I was in my study at the College. I opened the French window, stepped out on the balcony and tried to force acclamations out of my constricted throat. My own language seemed weak. I shouted in English like a madman.

III

The Armistice left people dazed. They found it hard to realize that this bell-ringing and bugle-blowing meant the event they had been praying for so long. In a variety of languages the four continents repeated: the war is over, over! Many soldiers had gradually hardened into professionals. Two months before the Armistice I travelled from the Pyrenees to Paris with several non-commissioned officers who did not seem different from the *soldats de métier* in Louis the Fourteenth's armies: they knew war; it was still their enemy but much as the lion is the big game hunter's enemy. Expertness gave those men an ease and confidence which, had it not been for occasional shrugs, might have passed for contentment. A number of soldiers had experienced a psychological crisis after which they had entered a complex condition which the phrase "he has made the sacrifice of his life" used to describe adequately before all sorts of accretions gave it the unreality of mere literature. The "Stop Firing!" signal once more transformed their lives. I have never known any of them to allude unmoved to "the place where he heard *le cessez le feu*."

To the civilian population the event meant: no more anxiety, no more dreading horrible news coming through indifferent town-halls! no fear of a hideous peace leaving the country amputated. But more than three million men and women scattered all over France on November Eleventh were refugees from northern France or Belgium. From the innumerable villages where these refugees lived arose an intense wave of longing for home. Home often was only a ruined spot which could be ascertained but vaguely by its distance from once familiar landmarks. Severe regulations were necessary to keep these families where they were. But even those who knew for a certainty that their homes were standing could not be allowed to migrate northwards *en masse* as they would have loved to do. Transportation was scarce, and provisioning remained for many months a problem. So permits were grudgingly given, and, through November,

I saw the Gare du Nord crowded with forlorn-looking, often ill-smelling, families seated on the bare stone pavement and waiting for an improbable chance to leave without the official permit. My loose connection with the press served me once more, and, two weeks after the Armistice, as soon as a daily train could be counted on, I set out for Trélon.

The cars were packed. I sat next to a young American officer in French uniform. Opposite us were two girls, sisters, whose luggage choked up every bit of space under the seats and in the racks. They explained that what they were carrying with them was all they would have to keep house with when they reached Laon, their home-town. They were interesting and pretty. The young American soon saw that, but could not make up his mind which of the two girls was his choice and so was profusely attentive to both. Shortly after passing Compiègne the train wheezed its curiously uncertain, pioneer's way into the red zone, and for a while the boy stood up at the window looking out for something. The something was Ribécourt which we reached in due time. "This is the place where I was under fire for the first time," he said, almost to himself. Ribécourt had been a prosperous village. Big farms and distilleries stood a short hundred yards away from us, reproachful in their destruction. I was surprised to see tears in the young officer's eyes: he was a manly little fellow, but so very young that his youthfulness suddenly moved me more than the desolation of the country-side.

Shortly afterwards we stopped in front of Noyon. This most ancient of the smaller cities of the Ile-de-France had been very dear to me. I loved its cathedral, every aërial nook of which I had visited with a friend, Maurice Gossart, who had been at the Ecole des Chartes and was a professional archæologist. Its streets had a soul. Its people were the first whose natural distinction had repaid my childish interest in strangers. Now the sight of it was terrible. The cathedral showed irreparable gashes. The graceful hills dominating it were charred and bare with the skeletons of a few remaining trees cursing the massacres they had witnessed, for those slopes had very recently seen some of the worst fighting on record. Heavy silence weighed on it all, and everything seemed remote and shrinking.

From that point on our progress became very slow, with manœuvring, whistling and long despairing stoppages at unexpected places. Three weeks earlier this was still a scene of battle, and every bridge had been put up so hastily that the crossing of each train caused anxiety.

Finally, late in the short November afternoon, we reached Laon Station, so full of gaps stopped somehow with chicken-wire that it looked like a bird's cage. The train disgorged its soldiers and its remigrants with their paraphernalia. Many stayed a long time, bewildered, on the platform. The first to get out were the two sisters. Before it grew quite dark I could see them with their faithful escort half-way up the three-hundred-steps stairway leading to the Upper Town. The young officer, carrying two of their bundles on his shoulders with another hanging in front of him and two suitcases pulling at his wrists, looked as shapeless and enormous as the poilus on leave so often did. I liked that boy.

I had been told that there would be no lack of military lorries travelling north which could help me to cover the sixty miles between Laon and Trélon. I walked three or four hundred yards along the boggy road to an important crossroads where trucks driven by soldiers did pass every few minutes. I challenged every one of them. Did they go in the direction of Hirson? No! not Hirson! Montcornet, Charleville, Rethel, Fismes, but not Hirson, were the replies shouted back in the wind. Most often the destination was Montcornet, and a dislike I had conceived as a boy for the name of that little town quickly became intensified by the disappointment attached to its homely syllables.

In about half an hour the night closed in and sadness descended with the soft darkness. I was the only civilian abroad. Frequently small outfits of soldiers lighted by a sergeant's torch marched past, but their quick disappearance was not cheering. Behind me a long, low, dilapidated building in which a few

soldiers were reading or writing by candle-light showed the
sign of the Salvation Army. If the worst came to the worst I could
perhaps spend the night in that place. Rockets began to flare in
the sky, the same rockets which, during four years, made the
night hideous along the six hundred kilometers of front-lines.
But now they were not hideous, there was something sanguine in
their endless effort to rise. It was by the light of one of them
that a stern-looking, red-bearded lieutenant, probably a priest,
saw me and went out of his way to say: "If you find no transportation, go up to the Archpriest's house. He'll put you up.
Extremely nice man!" I waited another hour or so till lorries became very scarce and still not one went north. Finally I gave it
up and decided to go up the zigzag to where the rockets every
now and then drew vividly the fanciful outline of the most lace-
like of French cathedrals. I did not exactly feel like trespassing
on the hospitality of an Archpriest who might never have heard
my name.

It was pitch dark between rockets and the climbing road was
dangerously boggy. As I turned one of its curves I saw ahead of
me the flash from somebody's torch. This was an officer, a very
old major, a man of over seventy, who had probably re-enlisted
for the war. "Is the Hôtel de la Hure still open?" I asked.—
"More than ever, my dear Sir, as you will soon see," was the
answer, but I knew at once that this old gentleman was a wag.
"Nice road, this!" he went on, "in a minute you will come to a
particularly interesting spot which you might have missed without my light." The interesting spot was soon reached. The major
raked with his light two enormous shell-holes which would undoubtedly have offered me unwelcome shelter for the rest of the
night. "Eh?" the old gentleman said, "What do you think of
this?" Shortly afterwards we came to the street where the once
familiar Laon hotels, la Hure, la Bannière, and l'Ecu used to
stand cheek by jowl. There they were still, but roofless and
windowless. "You see at present that la Hure is very much open,"
the major said, "I'll take you to the Deanery, less draughty."

I shall never forget the charming evening I spent with the Dean, a most scholarly and courteous gentleman, scarcely older than myself. He was surrounded by books and ancient furniture which had been kept in safety through the war at Valenciennes, and had only just returned to where they used to be. One of my French books was on the revolving bookcase by his desk.

By seven o'clock the next morning I was out on the Cathedral Square looking once more for cars. Five or six tractors and two jitneys stood there in a row, being groomed by their drivers. "Anybody going in the direction of Vervins?" I queried. A voice from between the wheels of one of the jitneys replied. Not going to Vervins but going to Marle—would that do?—only in a devious way, as roads which were good yesterday might not be good to-day, bridges were insecure and postal delivery inevitably went on crooked lines. The speechifier appeared. He was a Parisian soldier, slow but rich in utterance and evidently priding himself on a ceremoniousness which he knew was exceptional. His circumlocutory speech was full of allusions to boorish fellows, people who never could respond adequately to an urbane invitation and who were, on no account, to be imitated.

After a long delay at the post-office which was a converted public-house, to which, however, a few bottles had already returned, we had to go for an additional supply of gasoline *chez les Américains* on the other side of the hill. Two cans having been lent in an offhand manner by gentlemen who seemed to think Texas just around the corner, my driver disappeared inside. He reappeared after about twenty minutes, stroking his moustache with the back of his hand, and apologized for involuntary delay, but added that only a clodhopper could refuse such a polite invitation as he had just been given, in fact was given every morning by *les Américains*. Real gentlemen, those boys were, he concluded as he fumbled with his gear.

It is eighteen kilometers from Laon to Marle, but we drove fifty before getting there. For postal delivery goes on devious ways and the roads were terrible. Every now and then the car would give a back-breaking jolt and the driver had barely time

to choke back an oath which he however managed to convert
into a most polite apology. We met troops too, silent, sullen
troops disgusted with the roads, and every village was a mass
of destruction, every bridge a problem. "The Germans are
swine," my driver said, "but they know how to retreat." There
were still German signs everywhere. In a few minutes we reached
a suburban-looking place, also completely destroyed, and the
driver pronounced, again in his connoisseur's voice: "French
work, this: notice, only one shell to each house. First-rate shooting." Every six or seven kilometers we stopped at improbable
post-offices in precariously standing buildings and my soldier
delivered the mail. I thought the delivery took longer than it
should have done till, in one place, a swarthy, Corsican-looking
old lady, the mother of the post-mistress, beckoned me to come
in and I found my driver discussing what undoubtedly was his
fourth breakfast. The post-mistress herself, a pretty Parisian,
was amusedly watching him while furbishing brass articles she
had just exhumed from under the kitchen-pavement. "How can
you refuse ladies?" the driver said as we passed between the
planks which did duty for an absent door. His politeness compelled him to accept two more breakfasts from two more post-
masters, one of whom was a jolly butcher who obliged me
also to join in. When finally we reached little Marle on its
little hill trying as usual to copy Laon on its big hill, my driver,
looking at his watch, apologized for not seeing me to the American car he felt sure I could catch, because, he said, he had to
be back at Laon in time for luncheon and it was later than he
thought. He seemed a bit worried at the prospect of seeming
rude if he kept his Laon friends waiting for him.

   Close by Marle church stood what I knew at once must be
"the American car."
   "Are you going to Vervins?"
   "Yee-ah."
   "Going any further north?"

"Yee-ah, I am going to Chimay."

"You are, bless your heart! May I get in?"

"This is your car, Sir. We take this trip every day, leave by schedule and get home by schedule."

"Do you go anywhere near an inn called *Le Cheval Blanc*, three miles before you get to the Belgian frontier?"

"Pass it twice a day, Sir. Badly damaged place. Are you from the States?"

In a minute we were off, and the roads which had been very much deserted became crowded with home-goers of all kinds as we got out of the red zone. Every now and then one or two passers-by would beg for a lift only to be replaced by others a few kilometers further on. Most of those people talked excitedly of what had happened to them since 1914, and I heard astonishing tales of adventure. In time we reached Haudroy where, less than three weeks before, the German plenipotentiaries came in contact with the French outposts—a scene I had vividly imagined—and I passed, intact but deserted, a farm to which some friends took me years ago for pancakes and new cider. The name of Trélon unexpectedly appearing on a sign-post brought a big lump to my throat. The American student noticed it and stopped talking. With each kilometer the landscape became more familiar. It seemed wet and sad, unspeakably saddened by the memory of things which I had not seen but could read in its altered sameness. Processions of coarse, insolent telegraph-poles started from crossroads where there had never been any, and pushed their straight brutal way in endless lines to the very horizon. New roads too, indifferent to the delicate beauty of the pasture land. I was glad I had not seen them built.

At the Cheval-Blanc, badly damaged as my young American had said, I took leave of the latter who gave me an appointment for the next noon, opposite Fourmies church, and I turned my steps towards home. It was only a mile and a half away through the orchards. Pretty soon I reached a green hillock from which I knew I could command a view over Trélon, and I went up to the top of it. Our church-steeple appeared, grey-coloured and gaunt, with all its slates gone. Around it the familiar roofs. Everything seemed smaller than I had remembered it; everything too seemed full of memories of which I knew nothing, but which said audibly: "Oh, you shall hear, you will soon hear!" I was deeply moved. A little boy who was picking hips on bushes near-by noticed it and stared at me a long while, finally saying in our patois: "*Vo stez scran* (you're tired, aren't you?)"

I came to the first houses and the impression: how small! and how dirty! was intensified. Hardly one pane of glass was left unbroken and many windows were boarded up. People too began to appear, one or two whom I knew. One was an old woman who asked me had I heard about her grandson and sobbed. I soon heard that a hundred and three of the men mobilized in Trélon had been killed. At last I was in front of our house. I stood a while on the other side of the street, gazing at it. All vestiges of the front garden which we had left full of late roses and early dahlias had disappeared from the terrace. The mantle of ivy draping the house to the very chimney-tops had grown enormously thick. All the shutters were up. I stopped a moment at the door which had long lost its knob and showed a rough board where used to be the panel staved in by a German rifle-end four years ago. Finally I pushed the door open and went in.

The dining-room would have been pitch dark had it not been for a curious little light quivering on a table. It showed a thin, frightened-looking old man warming his hands at a kitchen stove. I saw at once that not a thing in that room belonged to me. Disproportionate looking-glasses hung everywhere, very ugly. The Germans had commandeered the largest café in the town to turn it into a casino, and the *cafetier* with his hideous furniture had been moved into our house. There he sat. He hated the change, and as soon as he knew me in the semi-darkness he began to lament and reproach. The German colonel who had his office in the salon had left the whole place in a state of unspeakable filth. I should see the mess in the back garden. The explosion of November 7th had smashed every window, but that was nothing; the roof was in very bad repair and the dampness set-

tling in the walls of such an old house might make them collapse
any minute. "Your ivy, too, is a pest," he concluded, quite
wrought up and in the tone of an ill-used tenant.

Those complaints did me good. I had not expected that my
first conversation in the old place would make it difficult for me
not to burst out laughing, but it did. I apologized to the old
gentleman, as I asked permission to go over the premises and
said there was nothing I was so anxious to do as to find and pay
workmen to repair what had to be repaired. In my room, upstairs, I found the not very tidy luggage of an army-doctor
billeted there. A few things of mine were about, and half of
my books still stood in great disarray on their shelves. My heart
warmed when I saw my school Horace, an eighteenth-century
family heirloom, opened on the mantelpiece. Probably the army
doctor had been looking at it and I did not dare to take it away
with me. Four years is a long separation. I felt like an intruder,
and even like a deserter. After all, the house was standing, and
Trélon, in comparison with hundreds of places I had seen in the
red zone, had been wonderfully lucky. What did little losses matter? I hardly listened when the old codger told me that he knew
where some of my furniture was (in an extremely unpleasant
German hospital out of town), and I went out without once
looking again at the dear little place which five generations had
loved and tried to make happy.

It was getting dark. On my way to the Dean's I watched the
variety of lights visible through the slits of shutters. The most
frequent was the war-lamp simultaneously invented by many
people in the invaded country. It consisted of a sardine tin full
of some fat on which a bit of rag floated between two thin blades.
It gave more light than might have been expected, and the people
had become so accustomed to it that, a year after the Armistice,
I still saw a few specimens in use. As I looked at it in house after
house I also looked at the people—most of them known to me—
who sat or busied themselves around its little flame. I looked at
them eagerly, greedily. They were the same who during four

years had so often been in my thoughts and about whom I had
wondered till they had become almost preternatural to me, living ghosts who were familiar with what I could scarcely imagine
and derived from this an eerie superiority.

As I was peeping in at a window in the baker's house I heard
a voice calling me and a tall slender figure appeared close by.

"Hello, Doctor! are you here too?" I asked.

"Arrived yesterday. I have just discovered this where I buried
it in my coach-house. My wife will be glad."

The Doctor was twirling in his fingers a handsome brooch
glittering in the dark and a duller thing which was a pearl-pin.
I remembered that I too had buried our silver and a few old
pewter and brass things under a plot of chervil (where the
German searcher's rod barely missed hitting them half a dozen
times).

"You are lucky, Doctor."

"Yes, but twenty-five thousand francs' worth of bearer's bonds,
which I had buried in the same place, have turned to absolute
dust and the government will never refund that money on my
honourable word. Madame Méhaut expects you. You'll find a
bed. I am staying there myself and we shall talk."

"Do you find your old patients?"

"Only too many. The place is full of vile grippe, and it is forty
miles to a grain of quinine. But everybody is as merry as a
grig."

The phrase was not accurate. After a flash of happiness which
a brief interview with the kind hostess mentioned by the doctor
gave me, I went from one friend's house to another along the
infamously dirty streets and my impression was not that people
were cheerful. They were over-excited, and their excitement
turned sometimes into mad delight but oftener into irritated ret-
rospection. At the Dean's, where I arrived about six o'clock,
there was no light, the servant having unfortunately spilt the
pint of oil doled out every week by the French Commissariat.
Four or five people were engaged in animated conversation, their
faces dimly lighted by the fire. I noticed at once that the Dean

had lost a great deal of flesh (not less than fifty-five pounds), and that everybody—even my wealthy friend Léon Macaigne— was poorly dressed. He wore a forester's rough cape. I also inferred from a queer shortening of the faces that all these people had had false teeth the last time I saw them. I was given a warm but obviously incidental welcome. No questions were asked of me. The loud chorus of angry reminiscences interspersed with crowing laughter which my arrival had interrupted was resumed at once.

Two visions seemed to fill my friends' imaginations and to afford them inexhaustible delight. One was the whirling past of the German plenipotentiaries' motor-car with its tall white flags at the four corners. Peace at last! The Germans, so long merciless and tyrannical, craving for peace! The other was the sudden indiscipline of the German army as it felt the wind from the revolution at home and realized that the end had come. The men sang Bolshevik songs in the streets and braved their officers. Then the retreat began and oh! the confusion, and the hurry, and the disappearance of all that had been specifically German, the units fighting for the right of way. Finally French cavalry, in a uniform which had never been seen before, appeared at the gates of the Mérodes' park and after a rapid engagement the last German soldiers fled by the Chimay road. The soul-absorbing image was that of the final disappearance of an intolerable race.

Yet I noticed that hardly anything was said of individual Germans. Not infrequently one or another was mentioned by name without any of the detestation attached to the collectivity: it was the spirit of Germany that was loathed and abhorred. The memory against which these men revolted was that of another people coolly taking possession of everything. "We are home here, you are not," was a German piece of impudence which they repeated with rage. The slow systematic robbery of their property was not what embittered them, it was the matter-of-fact natural way in which it was done. Suddenly the Dean rose, stiffened and called out in a mocking German voice: *"Per-qui-si-ti-on* (searching)." "This house was searched more than forty times,

Sir," he went on indignantly; "once that brute in a green uniform stayed fifteen hours, sounding every ten square inches in the garden and destroying everything."

"The strawberries in my garden were *counted*," said Léon Macaigne, "counted lest I should eat one. I was in jail once for refusing to accompany the German services on the church-organ, but I was threatened with imprisonment time and time again."

"Was the prison very uncomfortable?"

"You first go and visit the cells at the glassworks. Ten feet long, five feet wide, and no windows, only tiny sky-lights."

"Your schoolmate, Pluchart, returned from captivity last week," the Dean resumed, "he was four years in a miserable commando in Germany, without being allowed to write to his sister, merely for commenting on a hymn in words which displeased a German officer who was listening to his sermon. As for your friend Delbecque, he was shot in 1914 and buried so casually that his cassock stuck out of the stone-heap above him."

I heard more as I went from house to house. To my boundless astonishment everybody said that the Germans, whose towns are so clean, were prodigiously dirty, and the filth which shocked me in the streets did not shock them. War was war.

At dinner at Madame Méhaut's I heard a quieter note than at the Dean's. This dear old friend has never been bitter, and the happiness of liberation still overwhelmed her. She would constantly revert to the "last day." She had seen the plenipotentiaries' car and its white flags and she expected the end. Three German officers were billeted with her. They had been preparing the blowing-up of the colossal munitions dump in our forest. They had finished their work; only a button had to be pressed to start the explosions, but of this the officers said nothing. They sat down, after looking at their car outside, and Madame Méhaut prepared to pour out their acorn coffee for them as usual. Two of them accepted the courtesy, but the third hesitated in a queer way and finally refused. An hour after their departure the first formidable explosions began and the houses near the railway station were blown down while almost every window in the town was smashed. The big door of Madame Méhaut's coach-house came unhinged and fell across the sidewalk. But this was the end. The next day three French officers were in the three Germans' rooms. Madame Méhaut saw the horizon-blue uniform for the first time, and, for the first time too she heard the name *poilu* applied to French soldiers. Most Trélon people did not know either that the Germans were called Boches, but she did. In 1917 an Alsatian soldier had slily let her into that secret which gave him enormous amusement.

I asked Madame Méhaut about the Germans she had housed during the four years.

"They were mostly Catholic chaplains whom I never liked and army doctors whom I could have liked if I had respected them. But I could not respect drunkenness and even worse which went on in my own house and even in the room next to mine. The legend of German morality is not for me. But these doctors— apart from one who reported me at the Kommandantur and had me threatened by the spy, Arthur, because he thought my lamp better than the one I gave him—were not bad. I took quite a liking to one whom I used to call *le petit cochon* and scolded as if I had been his mother."

"Would you say that three in ten of those officers were nice?"

"Three in ten? That would be saying much. Oh, no! I cannot remember more than three or four ever giving me the right of way in my own house, and my bedroom was all that was left to me and my maid. Painful, I assure you!"

"Who was Arthur?"

"The interpreter. A horrid little sneak. Born, educated and employed in Paris and yet an absolute Prussian who delighted in torturing people. He'll be selling shoes in his Paris shop soon again, I'll wager."

"Did you ever see the Kaiser?"

"He was several weeks at the château and then several weeks more in his train which was kept moving all the time for fear of the English aviators. He came to church across the road every

Sunday, and I caught sight of him two or three times. Little
man. Not impressive. You will see his palatial dug-out outside
the station. He dreaded those English planes which we loved to
hear because they sometimes dropped French newspapers."

"The time must have seemed horribly slow to you, even slower
than to us?"

"Not at all. Everybody will tell you that Christmas seemed to
come on the heels of Easter. Remember that nothing happened
to us. We could not walk out of the town; we received no letters and read no newspapers except that traitor's rag, *La Gazette
des Ardennes*; we could neither walk out nor even look out after
five o'clock, even in summer, and you know that sameness is
what gives the illusion of quickly passing time whereas ten days
of an eventful trip seem as long as a month."

We talked till late in the night, my mind gradually filling in
the gaps which four years of unsatisfied curiosity had left in
my picture of invaded Trélon. What I heard that evening was
supplemented during many more talks with other compatriots
of mine. The impression they have left on me is that the war,
from the flight before the enemy to the delight of the Armistice,
provided more adventure and developed more sense of the immense possibilities of life than a hundred years of average existences might have done. While waiting for cars outside Laon
station I heard a man telling an extraordinary story to a little
group of people seated on a crumbling garden-wall. That man
and his brother were mobilized in the same regiment. During
the retreat, after Charleroi, the brother was terribly wounded
and the two men parted thinking they would never meet again. In
1917 the narrator, a skilled mechanic, was demobilized and sent
to a munitions factory at Rouen. A few weeks later he found his
brother recovered and working in the factory next door.

Next morning I left early. In our windowless church I saw
General Humbert, in horizon blue, assisting at mass. No soldier

could look more superbly military, no believer could show more
faith. I walked to Fourmies through the meadows to which cows
taken away by the Germans were already returning. Opposite
Fourmies church, as agreed with my American student, I waited
for the Marle car. I was a bit anxious, for the Laon station-
master had told me that the one daily train left "some time
between 3 and 5" and I did not wish to be stranded.

Somebody else was waiting for the car, a French officer, a
captain, who was rather impatiently pacing up and down the
sidewalk. He was a dark-looking man, probably a southerner,
with black eyes, a black moustache and the most soldierly way
of carrying himself. After a few minutes he asked whether I
was thinking of taking the American car, because I might be
waiting in vain: this car was *not* for civilians. I said I had an
appointment with the driver. "*Not* for civilians," the officer
repeated in a final, decidedly too final, way.

Just then the car appeared round the corner. The same American student was driving it and I asked him, in French, whether
his car was not for civilians. "*C'est pour les militaires et c'est
aussi pour les civils,*" was the very correct but very English-
sounding reply. The smart little officer shrugged his shoulders,
surprised at being contradicted, and bowed me into the car; but
seeing the *médaille militaire* on his coat next to the legion of
honour, and seeing in retrospect what the last four years must
have meant for him, I insisted on his getting in first. We were,
during a few minutes, on terms of rather cold civility, but the
captain thawed out when I offered him some lunch from my
valise. We talked. He was the typical soldier, brief and direct
in utterance, remembering clearly and expressing himself vividly. He had been lucky. The whole four mortal years of it, the
whole seven months of Verdun, and not a scratch. He was a private in 1914, but he had learned a lot about strategy as he went
up in the army, and he would never lose his interest in the
military art. He had already a good library dealing with it, and
he would buy more books. The dark face brightened up as he
talked. He was an extremely intelligent and nice-looking little

officer. He took out a cigarette-case. "I am a priest, myself," he said nonchalantly, as he blew away the smoke of the match. He could not have astonished me more if he had said that he was the Pope in disguise. "Yes," he went on casually, "diocese of Mende. I am going to see my brother who has a parish in the mountains. He was a captain too, but he didn't have my luck. He walks on a wooden leg."

I think sometimes of that priest-officer, now once more a cassocked curé in his native Cévennes. Did he ever shake off his military appearance? and does he go on reading histories of the war which he can check off here and there from his own experience? His parishioners on the bare plateaus, first-rate soldiers themselves,—as the humble monuments in their hamlets show—must be proud of him. But friends of his are now colonels, or even generals, and he is a mountain clergyman motorcycling sometimes to his lame brother's when the solitude of his own rectory becomes too oppressive. One summer I cycled through the hilly region where he lives hoping that perhaps I might recognize his dapper figure. He never appeared, of course.

At Marle I changed cars, creating a certain sensation by my command of the English language as I took leave of my young American. The new car was crowded and we sat on sections of a ladder lying across the lorry. At Chambry, in the red zone, queer-sounding calls were heard from a row of ruined cottages. Two American Negro soldiers leapt out and ran after us with surprising nimbleness, for they were fully armed and in their best uniforms, having just been passed in review by "général francess." They said this in fairly intelligible French as they clung to a bicycle tied to the tail-gate of the lorry, and showed the white teeth in their dark faces. I helped them in, speaking to them, naturally in English, as I did so. When they were safely in and I sat down again I noticed a flutter of admiration among my fellow-passengers. I was wondering at this when I heard a lady whispering to another as she looked at me: "Probably a missionary; speaks also those African languages." I was going to point out that English was not bambara, but suddenly reflecting that the prestige of the Church might be at stake I refrained from saying anything in depreciation of my imaginary linguistic universality.

The next few months were hardly less feverish than the four years of the war, for it soon appeared that the Treaty must be as difficult to frame as victory had been to accomplish. Allies are only people who wait for an occasion to fight, and I was not surprised to hear Admiral Sims saying to me once that his admiration for Napoleon greatly diminished when he realized that the Emperor had only Allies to beat. As soon as the Paris negotiations began we heard of nothing but divergences and subterranean manœuvres. In time there was the scandal of both the Italian delegation and President Wilson quitting the Conference. Visibly men were unequal to the magnitude of such a task as the re-building of Europe. I was invited on several occasions to dine at the Hôtel Majestic and my impression, every time I saw those illustrious statesmen in the humble action of eating, recalled Shakespeare's lines about the smallness of Cæsar. Much as I have always liked English informality I got tired of Lord Balfour's endless teasing of Sir Robert Cecil. The latter did not show much fight and the scene seemed childish.

So, although it is irritating to hear people criticizing the Treaty who, when they are given a map and a blue pencil with which to correct what was done in 1919, stay mum and look foolish, I can understand serious persons entertaining doubts of the Versailles achievement. If there is one thing about which I should like to see English and American people clear it is the absolute impossibility to solve, even partly solve, all the European problems. The most cursory inspection of the map, helped by even a superficial knowledge of history, leaves no doubt that a satisfactory redistribution of influence among the great powers is a dream. So Versailles could only be a tentative effort to do justice where, at the time, justice seemed to be the most imperative.

However, there are a few mistakes which no thoughtful student of history or careful newspaper reader ought ever to make:

1st. It is historically absurd, in spite of huge propaganda, to say that Germany *consented* to ask for an armistice because she believed that President Wilson's Fourteen Points were to be the basis of the future treaty. Germany did not consent to anything, she collapsed, both in Berlin and at the front, as my Trélon compatriots saw with their own eyes and have many times repeated to me. It is not derogatory to what we owe in justice to the most astonishing resistance ever offered to a coalition by any country to say so. The German nerve broke down when the limits of human endurance were reached, that was all.

2nd. People who connect the end of the war with President Wilson's Fourteen Points ought never to be the same people who blame the Treaty for restoring such nations as Poland or Bohemia. For this restoration loomed large in the Fourteen Points. Yet, they often are the same. Parlour statesmen who also want to be parlour economists can hardly be expected to be logical. It has always seemed to me that historic justice is worth one or two economic depressions, and I would rather live on short rations than not see Poland revived as it is.

Moreover I doubt if the rehandling of the map was, as so many people imagine, the cause of the great economic crisis. Was not there a tremendous boom after the Great War as after all other wars? The main cause of the depression was the depletion of several national fortunes by the cost of the war. Billions went into thin air as shell after shell burst into atoms. Until human labour, assisted by thrift which at present is not much in fashion, has re-created the riches destroyed in that way, the commerce of the world must inevitably suffer. A striking proof of this is the fact that the British Empire, politically increased and immensely strengthened after the war, has however been one of the worst victims of the depression. What visitors imagine they see in happy London ought not to deceive them.

Conversely, it may not be as certain as German megalomania imagines that German prosperity would return if Germany succeeded in dominating Central Europe as she has traditionally wished to do. Nor would it if Germany were given back her colonies. Great Britain which has colonies enough has also difficulties enough, while Sweden which has no colonies is prosperous.

3rd. Italy's irritation which was one of the chief causes of the European unrest was not a consequence of the Treaty. It was a consequence of the rash promises made by Great Britain to Italy in 1915 and never redeemed afterwards. Mr. Harold Nicolson has written an illuminating book on the question.

4th. That the Versailles Treaty was more of a *Diktat* than most other treaties is historically inaccurate. Only some nations resent treaties following defeat more than others. In 1917 Germany compelled Russia to sign, at Brest-Litowsk, a treaty which was much more of a *Diktat* than the Versailles Treaty. Propaganda having been silent about it not one Englishman or American in a hundred knows that by this treaty twenty-two million people were detached from Russia, an enormous loss.

5th. The most common mistake made about the Versailles Treaty is to regard it as preëminently a French *Diktat*. The reasons are because Versailles is a French town, and because Clemenceau, who certainly was an indomitable fighter, is also supposed to have been, during the Paris negotiations, a sort of dictator. In reality he was nothing of the sort. He was caustic as he had been all his life, and reports of his sarcasms gave him a sham superiority, but causticity has never been known to result in influence. The fact is that Clemenceau's old partiality for England asserted itself throughout the negotiations so that the dominant influence belonged to a man who had more instinct for power than real capacity to hold it, Mr. Lloyd George. When Mr. Anthony Eden laughs at seeing Mr. Lloyd George assailing the Versailles Treaty for which he, more than anybody else, is responsible, the whole world ought to laugh with him, for it is one of the most comical spectacles that history ever provided for human amusement.

What the chief note in French public opinion was during the peace negotiations I remember well: it was summed up in the phrase endlessly repeated at the time: no more wars! Foreign critics have often alluded, during the first ten or twelve years following the Treaty, to a French hegemony. They should have discerned in what they superficially called by that name merely a coalition of fears. France, in 1919, was a restored country exactly like Belgium, Poland, Serbia or Tcheko-Slovakia, and it was natural that she should flock with them. Throughout that period the representative of French influence abroad was M. Briand, and the British or American observers who saw this gentleman in action at Washington in 1921 must have thought him a strangely weak Imperialist. He was not different in his dealings with Germany where he repeatedly sided with Stresemann against the chiefs of his own country's army. This Socialist remained an anti-Nationalist all his life.

Belief in the League of Nations—another name for Internationalism—was universal in France. In spite of stunning shocks it is still dominant with the French. This nation is apt to retain, long after it should shake it off, a naïve confidence in other peoples. The French are, in this respect, quite as guileless as the Americans. Hence their belief in the resolutions of conference after conference, in the protection of such a vague thing as the Kellogg Pact (which I have never seen a single American take seriously), or in a mirage like the Locarno agreement. Words, words, for which they exchanged the only sure defence they possessed, viz., the occupation of the Rhine. The consequences of this confidence in imaginary security they will have plenty of time to rue. It is not different from the inexplicable certainty their grandfathers retained, after Prussia beat Bavaria in 1864 and Austria in 1866, that their own turn to be crushed would not come. Their excuse lies in the fact that the whole world wished them to adopt this suicidal attitude, but it is the one excuse which the world itself invariably derides.

While the negotiations preparatory to the Treaty went on, Paris teemed with American troops. A visit to Paris was the natural crowning of the young Americans' unexpected visit to France. During several months the Boulevard Raspail was alive with American students in uniform but attending the Sorbonne. I constantly met groups of "doughboys" in the Luxembourg Garden or in the vicinity of Notre-Dame or of Sainte Chapelle. Many of them would look wistfully at those monuments hoping that somebody might volunteer the historic commentary they needed. I was many times the providential passer-by who could say the expected words. When I had leisure enough I would take regular parties around. Sometimes *they* would take me, for, had it not been for them, I should not have seen the inside of the Luxembourg Palace any more than I have ever seen the Conciergerie and Marie-Antoinette's dungeon. I liked those simple boys. I enjoyed their interest in what they saw, their pride in their native state, their astonishing Americanism, even when they were of German origin—which they seemed frequently to be. I was amused by their wonderings, by their frank and innocent craving for "American girls," sometimes by their funny little aversions. I laughed to see them frowning when agents of their own military police (M.P.'s they called them) appeared in the offing. I have never regretted the time I gave those honest young fellows.

I went twice again to Trélon before my aunt's Honorine could, around Easter of 1919, resume housekeeping there, and crude boards were at last replaced by such a luxury as oil-paper windows. It gradually became easier to reach the old place, but still there was a difficult train-connection to be made at Maubeuge and, on both occasions, I missed it. The first time, although Maubeuge is only sixteen miles from Trélon, I did not know of any hotel I might go to, in fact did not know the name of a single hotel in the town. I was on my way to the station-master's office to enquire when a faint memory stopped me at his door. Why! Robert Louis Stevenson spent a night here and spoke of it in *An Inland Voyage*. He spent a night at some hotel, an hotel he liked. Suddenly I clearly saw the name of the hotel on the long-forgotten page: Hotel de la Poste. "Yes," the station-master said, "the Hotel de la Poste is still here, at the top of the Big Stairs, full of English visitors probably." So it was, nice English people who, in the rear of the British Army, were already seeing sights.

When I left, the next morning, I asked the proprietor if he knew that a famous Scotch writer had been in his place and spoke well of it. He might have the passage copied and posted up near his entrance. This would delight his English guests. Well, I was going back to Paris; as soon as I could I would copy that bit of Stevenson myself and send it to him.

I am sorry to say that I forgot all about the Hotel de la Poste. In a few weeks I was there again, having missed my connection once more. The proprietor looked at me inquiringly and, as I thought, reproachfully. I apologized, feeling very much ashamed. No sooner was I in my Paris rooms again than I wrote on an index-card: "Maubeuge, Hotel de la Poste" to be sure not to forget again. Pretty soon I found the volume of Stevenson I needed and very quickly the Maubeuge entry. I was shocked to find it ran:

"Maubeuge is a fortified town with a very good inn: Hotel du Grand-Cerf."

The Easter holiday gave me two weeks at Trélon. I had great times listening to peoples' adventures and seeing them repairing their homes and getting back to their former selves. The signs of war were gradually disappearing, and the Spring would have been like old Springs if our forest had not been so atrociously disfigured and cowslips had not been smiling so sadly at its wounds. Every day, towards evening, formidable explosions came from where the Germans had left their munitions-dumps only partly exploded (it took five years to blow them up, and an English company employing French workmen got rich doing it). The sound of these anachronic explosions was hateful. However, life was beginning again.

It was shortly after my return to Paris from that Easter visit that, one late afternoon, I found at the door of my rooms one of the college servants with a clerical caller who was waiting for me. This was the head-master of a Catholic school in the diocese of Cambrai, a M. Delattre whom I did not remember having met. He talked interestingly on various subjects connected with our native North, but pretty soon I realized that this gentleman had come on a special errand which he hesitated to state, and I asked him what this was. "True," was the reply, "I am here on a mission: Lille University, where you taught several years, is one of the worst victims of the war, and the Archbishop hopes that you will consent to go to America and interest kind people there in its behalf. What shall I say?"

I felt that this was one of the great minutes in my life. In an instant I saw what the difficulties of the task would be, for the slogan "Think of America at last" was beginning to be current in the United States: my candidacy to the chair of English Literature at the Catholic University of Paris was in a fair way to be successful at the time and I did not like to desert it; finally I felt my duty to College Stanislas which had always been more than kind to me. Yet I *knew* not only that I had to say yes, but that my life was going to be changed by that monosyllable. I said to M. Delattre that everything would have been immeasurably easier four months before, but he might assure the Archbishop of my devotion to my former University. In a few weeks I would be in America.

Part Three

AMERICA

I

WHAT was America to me in that Spring of 1919? The answer to this question takes me back to my very earliest years.

I remember distinctly that when I was at school, a little boy of eight or ten years old, the word America connoted to me South America. Americans were Peruvians or Brazilians. Yet I seldom caught myself looking at the map of South America as I did at the elegant inverted shape of North America. The great lakes, the squares representing vast territories not yet promoted to the dignity of states attracted me more than even the majestic Amazon. Only, the people scattered over that continent were not Americans, they were Indians. I had read bits of Chateaubriand and a few volumes of Fenimore Cooper or Mayne-Reid, and somehow my imagination reflected the admiration of my eighteenth-century progenitors for *les sauvages de l'Amérique,* the "good savages," the taciturn philosophers in the forest primeval. This impression was so strong that when I read *Uncle Tom's Cabin,* this book, with its negroes and its Yankees, did not succeed in displacing my Indians. Miss Ophelia was an Englishwoman, that was all. So, too, was Mrs. Harriet Beecher Stowe whose ladylike effigy appeared on the fly-leaf of my copy of her book.

At school I learned about La Fayette and the influence of the American Revolution on our own, but this superficial knowledge was too algebraic to affect my store of imaginations: they remained Indian, and when I became an assiduous reader of Washington Irving's *The Sketch-Book* what I loved in it was the mystery and boundlessness of the North American continent. A jibe of Dickens's at the worthlessness of American securities puzzled me for a minute but not enough to set me enquiring. Of American millionaires I knew nothing; the part was still acted by the English "milord."

Between this strange ignorance of the United States and an almost affectionate approval of it there is a gap in my memory and there may have been one in my consciousness. The one solitary object connecting the two stages is a human figure. One of the students in the Seminary, next door to my school at Cambrai, was an American lad of twenty-two or three, tall, square, red-faced and generally beefy, but benign-looking and to me, at the time, the typical kindly giant. I saw him two or three times in the cathedral or at the country-house but I never spoke with him. He seemed to be a silent happy chap.

The next thing I remember is the passionate interest in Democracy which filled most of us in our twenties. I read that astonishingly intelligent aristocrat, Tocqueville, after reading Lacordaire and Montalembert, and America became a living thing. Shortly afterwards I learned of the existence of Archbishop Ireland, a man whom no orthodoxy could hold in suspicion and who seemed to enjoy in undisturbed peace the ideal for which Lamennais, Lacordaire and the others had fought none too successfully. I read Bishop Spalding. Finally, my future excellent friend, Abbé Félix Klein, created a sudden sensation with his distinction between passive virtues which were European—the very virtues eternally preached to me— and active virtues—the ones I did not have to pray for because I thought them too natural to be called virtues—which were declared to be American. I was violently "American," for this distinction between active and passive virtues might be as unphilosophical as theologians promptly said it was, but it corresponded to a system of morals based on what I called "legitimate activity" which, when I was sixteen or seventeen, I used to propound to rather dubious school-friends, and I was charmed to have a whole continent behind me. I vaguely remember reading Paul Bourget's *Outre-Mer* and Abel Hermant's *Les Trans-atlantiques* which gave one a queer impression of the American girl's very active virtues, but as I measured these French novelists by the great masters of English fiction I did not take them seriously. So, America remained to me the powerful new country whose development proved how right my fundamental theories obviously were and all was well. Abbé Klein had only been rationalizing what did not need to be rationalized, and he had paid the penalty.

During my six years at Lille University I came in contact with several Americans. There was, boarding in a convent where I was a frequent visitor, a Mrs. Ackermann from California, whose faraway husband was a physician paradoxically engaged in digging a canal. She spoke of him with astonishing respect as The Doctor. The Doctor was so busy digging his canal that he frequently forgot to send cheques, and both Mrs. Ackermann and Mother Superior—who was the kindest woman I ever knew —often waited wistfully for the double ring of the postman.

There were also several theological students whom the Archbishop of San Francisco had moved from Louvain to our university. They lived in the rue des Stations, in a big mansion which had known better days and looked despondent enough at the end of its neglected garden. The American boys did not look as cheerful either as American boys would under congenial circumstances. Probably the cooking in that dilapidated old place was melancholy too. Also, French universities expected an absurd amount of study. However, one of the students, Mr. Grant, was a brilliant rival of the present Rector, my dear friend, Mgr. Lesne. I found him, in 1919, pastor of Burlingame, just outside San Francisco, which Burlingame being a jolly place seemed to be a clerical situation only to be mentioned with a knowing smile by San Franciscans—and I surprised everybody by calling him, as of old, Mr. instead of Father Grant. I introduced these young Americans to my friend Madame Jaspar, who had a cup of tea ready for them whenever

they felt like dropping in, and they spoke English with Madame
Jaspar's companion, Miss Cazaly, an Englishwoman who corrected their accent to suit her own, enjoyed their humour, and
mothered them to her heart's content, for nobody could be
kinder.

One summer day the Professor of Church History, Abbé Salembier, told me that the Rector of the University, Mgr. Baunard, had instructed him to meet at the station the Archbishop
of San Francisco who was going out of his way to visit his
students. I read on Salembier's face that the Rector did not
realize what a big person an Archbishop of San Francisco had
become by the beginning of the twentieth century. So, after a
little hesitation, I called on the Rector to find out. Mgr. Baunard
was a prolific and quite celebrated writer of old-fashioned
Catholic biographies which not over-critical readers devoured,
for the author was a gifted man and, having no suspicion that
he was old-fashioned, wrote happily and interestingly. I found
him, as I expected, busy writing. "What is it?" he said, without
laying down his pen or looking up at his visitor.

I explained that I thought an Archbishop of San Francisco
a very great personage who might be accustomed to much ceremony and perhaps would be offended if he noticed the absence
of it.

"Yes," the Rector said plaintively, "but how can one do one's
work? Last week there was an Oriental Archbishop, with a
beard, and I lost a lot of time."

I explained again, using all the tact I could muster, and
emphasizing that there was nothing oriental about San Francisco. Finally the old prelate said feebly:

"Do the best you can, dear Abbé, you and M. Salembier, explaining to the Archbishop that my publishers are very insistent
just now. I shall be so grateful to you both."

We met the Archbishop and tried to look like a little crowd,
profuse in salaams and ring-kissing. But I no sooner saw the
striking figure of Archbishop Riordan than I felt the presence
of a personality very much used to being treated as one. The

eyes were searching and masterful. "Where am I going?" he asked. "With us, Your Grace," the students regretfully admitted.

I shivered, thinking of the palatial indigency these words conjured up. At the end of the Academic year old Baunard's book came out, but the Californian students were ordered back to Louvain. Many times since then has my sense of the fitness of things been satisfied even at the expense of my national feelings. I will always defend the wisdom of my grandmother's apophthegm: *de rien il n'en revient rien,* as it would be immoral if something ever came out of nothing.

In Paris I met astonishingly few Americans, although the American colony had for several years outnumbered and almost displaced the British colony so brilliant and influential thirty years earlier. Even in Lady Austin Lee's drawing-room Americans were not many, and they were anglicized or Frenchified out of their national characteristics. None of them could be said to belong, or cared to belong, to what was called with an indefinable but perceptible smacking of the tongue "the Colony." The term was evidently used in contradistinction to the "Paris Americans," mostly Bostonians, living in Paris on their own and anxious not to be regimented.

The war changed this situation considerably, for many American men and women who had been mere birds of Paradise until then at once showed the irrepressible tendency to help, natural to their nation, and the gratitude of France naturalized them. I never heard of any actually applying for legal naturalization, for while the French in America sooner or later take out citizenship papers, Americans in France hardly ever dream of renouncing their nationality. But sentimental adoption, I know it from personal experience, is superior to the doubtful privilege of casting, every four years, an ineffectual vote, and hundreds of real friends of France, born in the United States, feel it and show they are sure of it. Many of them have retained from their four years' experience during the Great War a longing to serve which no amount of antagonistic cynicism can reduce to a covert

way of improving chances to climb. There are still Americans
who are attracted to Paris by queer motives exposed in Mr. Hem-
ingway's novels, and the type endlessly writing silly letters to
the *Paris Herald* is not extinct; but nobody doubts that the froth
and frivolity of "Expatriates" is more an appearance produced
by too much money, or by the national gregariousness, than the
manifestation of fundamental inferiorities.

To tell the truth I had only the vaguest notion of America or
of American psychology when, in the summer of 1904, I found
myself the Paris correspondent of an important American review. A distinguished London journalist, Mr. Sydney Brooks,
had been, for some reason, interested in the articles I wrote for
the English weeklies, and when Mr. (now Sir) George Leveson
Gower asked him if he knew of some Paris writer who could contribute quarterly letters from France to *The North American Review*, Mr. Brooks gave my name. Mr. Leveson Gower was the
representative in Europe of Colonel George Harvey who had
recently bought over *The North American Review*. He came to
Paris to see me, I liked his proposals and thus began, through two
Englishmen, my literary connection with America. Mr. Leveson
Gower asked me to dine at the old Ambassadeurs, in the
Champs-Elysées, with a young American novelist of whom he
thought highly. This was Booth Tarkington whom I liked at
first sight and whose conversation kept us interested through the
warm summer evening. Boldi, the famous violinist, played for
the very few of us in that charming restaurant: he stood outside,
among blossoming shrubs, and sent in his Hungarian strains
through the window, but I thought Tarkington as great an artist
in words as Boldi was in sounds.

I remember how strange it felt, at first, to write those quarterly articles for *The North American Review*. I have never been
able to write on subjects of any interest without somehow visualizing the people likely to read what I write. As I knew many English and had no difficulty in guessing their reaction, this was done
naturally when I wrote for the London weeklies. Hardly knowing

any Americans I could not do the same thing when writing for
a New York, which might have been a Calcutta, public. My
effort to imagine that audience was met by a blank similar to
that facing one when he has to speak over the radio. I read many
American books and made a study of Bryce's *The American
Commonwealth* without succeeding in exorcizing that baffling
sensation.

The next summer Mrs. George Harvey appeared in Paris with
one of the Harper ladies. I saw a good deal of them, liked
them, and studied them much more carefully than they suspected. For they were my first real New Yorkers, fresh from
distant mysterious America, and the only specimens I might
see for a long time. I still have notes written after dinners at the
Meurice or rambles in the old quarters with them. Nobody
could be kinder than dear Alma Harvey, but under her quiet
Vermont manner there was a well-distributed alertness which
made conversation with her easy and pleasant. Though she had
the slight hesitancy of speech frequent in Americans, there was
no hesitancy in her judgments: I listened keenly to what she
had to say about France which she knew well, even more keenly
about American personages who had been mere names to me
but whom her directness transformed into flesh and bones. "You
must come over and see our country," she would say persua-
sively. I liked the substitution of "our country," which is affectionate, for "America" which is only geographical. I have
noted it thousands of times since without losing the slight
lavender scent emanating from the simple words.

Mrs. Harvey returned in 1907 with her daughter, Dorothy,
and her great friend, Louise Morgan Sill, whose verses I had
read every now and then in the *Review*. Shortly afterwards
Colonel Harvey, accompanied by a small retinue of Harper
men, joined these ladies in Paris. I was still unused to the innumerable military titles which do duty in America for the
everlasting Doktor of Germany, and wondered how much of
the Colonel there would be in the powerful politician who
owned *The North American Review*.

Colonel Harvey was a man under fifty, tall, thin, erect, eminently Yankee in appearance as well as in speech. He seldom spoke more than a few words at a time, and they sounded as if they were released without effort but with unspeakable regret. Much of the Colonel's conversation was carried on in shakes or nods of the head which often were imperceptible to me but which his companions never seemed to miss. I did not realize at the time how influential this tall silent man was in the politics of his country, but I have always been impressed by intelligent silences and George Harvey's were full of eloquence. I thought at first that the men on his staff were more subservient than Englishmen in the same positions would have been. Little by little I saw that their chief's taciturnity had never lost its hold upon them. They admired more than they feared him, although nobody doubted that anger might suddenly flare up out of that apparent placidity, even if it never had until then. On the whole the Colonel was a rather formidable person.

Gradually one noticed that he was lovable too, as is not infrequently the case with intimidating people. The bespectacled eyes saw what you did not suppose they could see, and their alertness when it was not sarcastic was the reverse. Colonel Harvey was kind. Few men that I have known had the same talent for suggesting the thing that would give you pleasure and doing it with grace. When you showed gratitude the eyes behind the spectacles would look at you, slightly enlarged by pleasure at your satisfaction. The day before he sailed, at the end of a pleasant evening, Colonel Harvey said: "You write for people you don't know. Next year you must come over and look at us: we are worth the trouble. And I want you to be my guest."

This invitation was entirely unexpected, and while giving me extraordinary pleasure left me wondering and uncertain. America, twenty-eight years ago, was much farther away than it is now. People only went over there for business of an exceptional character, or to write a book. Even to-day Sorbonne professors when invited over seem to take a plunge when they say yes. All the intellectual preparation of a French scholar bends him towards Mediterranean travel. During the summer preceding my trip I met, digging in the old book-boxes on the quais, Louis Dimier, the historian of art. We had our usual little scrap about the *Action Française* movement of which he was, at the time, one of the most brilliant exponents, after which he upbraided me severely for what he called my desertion of Europe. "*On ne va pas là!*" he repeated, emphasizing each one of the crushing monosyllables.

My aunt had a different but equally antagonistic view. She was, or thought she was, old, and she did not wish to be separated from me by too vast a distance. "Three weeks!" she would sigh, "I might be sick, I might die and be buried before you were back." It took several months to reassure her. Her imagination was finally impressed by the possibility I held up to her of calling, in Detroit, on a missionary, Père Laffineur, she had known in her youth, and whose presence and long life on the banks of those faraway Lakes somehow calmed her apprehensions. At Easter of 1908 it was decided that I should spend three weeks of the Long Vacation at Trélon as usual, and the remaining five or six weeks would be devoted to my American trip.

All this novelty and hesitation left something wavering in my imagination. A visit to this country of which I knew so little did not conjure up any but the vaguest images. There was only one thing about which my desires seemed to be definite. For years I had seen announcements in the newspapers of this or that work of art being sold to American collectors. I had visited all the chief galleries of Europe except those of Russia, and I kept fat note-books recording those visits. Gradually I came to a realization that American museums must by now be quite as important as those of Europe, and it would be unpardonable not to see marvellous works henceforth inaccessible on our side. An exposition of Whistler's paintings and etchings also gave me a desire to become acquainted with contemporary American art. I asked questions of Mr. Walter Gay as well as of Mr. (later Sir) Purdon Clark who was soon to be appointed Director of the New York Metropolitan Museum, and I read a few books on American art. In time I came to the decision that I should not—as so many European discoverers of America did —write a book on the United States at the end of my four weeks, but I would write on American Art an article which somehow nobody else had written so far. In that way my literary conscience compromised with the strong feeling I had conceived from the first that in my American visit, America, being entirely novel to me, would do all the work and I would merely offer myself to the freshness of its attraction.

On August 19, 1908, I sailed from Cherbourg on the White Star S.S. *Teutonic*. Honest, old-fashioned boat with excellent British service, and the usual British food. I was surprised by the ease with which untravelled English people, absolute landlubbers, found their way through a big ship the ins and outs of which remained mysterious to me to the last. We called at Queenstown, and funny old Irishmen who sold spiral canes and funny Irishwomen who sold lace and called everybody "darlin'" gave me for nothing a priceless demonstration of racial differences. I liked those Kelts who, in a minute, seemed to electrify the whole deck.

The trip was quick—barely the seven days—and uneventful. We saw a whale. Somehow the report of this trivial incident found its way into the very newspaper to which my aunt subscribed and was distorted into Stoppage of a Liner by a Whale getting caught in the Propeller. I made no acquaintances although the ship was packed. The purser, who had kindly moved me to a superb stateroom, gave me the radio news—there was no bulletin—and, whether he had a chance or not, managed to poke constant fun at America and the Americans. He regarded me as a sort of Englishman.

Early in the afternoon of the 26th we saw the long low coast of Long Island. There was a cold drizzle and the heights which sometimes make that first appearance of the land a bit romantic were invisible. But I looked with all my might at the long grey line. This was America, and no country had ever before given me such a sensation of remoteness and improbability. The word America kept buzzing in my ears. The pilot climbed on board, as he generally does, without saying a word to anybody, threw down a bundle of newspapers and made straight for the wheel. His silence and the apparent infallibility of his action made a strong impression upon me. The Americans who visited Europe were not the real thing, this sombre-looking man was. After he went up to the bridge I kept looking at his little craft dancing on the waves.

When we entered the harbour I witnessed a scene which I have never seen again. Americans, as a rule, think more of the dock and its annoyances than of home when the boat slackens up and preparations are made for debarking. The crowd on the *Teutonic* were different: they saluted the skyline of New York with almost hysterical joy, some of them with tears. "Our country! our country!" they repeated. The purser looked at this scene with a sarcastic smile. "How un-English!" he said to me while I felt exceedingly foreign and the word alien assumed its full significance. Another man seemed even bluer than I was. This was Bugle, the slightly-built little fellow who had clarioned us to luncheon and dinner through the week. This may have been his first arrival in New York; at all events, he was looking at the big buildings as if they were altogether too much for a small chap who did not get tipped any too generously.

We landed in a heavy downpour, and I walked down under a dripping umbrella to the tenebrous immensity of the dock. Two or three Harper gentlemen who were waiting for me, smiling, at the foot of the gangway, at once made things a little more cheerful. They apologized for the weather, and delivered me to Colonel Harvey's secretary who delivered me to the scrutiny—unbelievably conscientious, I thought—of the customs. Soon afterwards we were seated in a two-horse fly which took us to the ferry through wet streets mercilessly recalling the East India Docks quarter of London. I forget what the driver charged, but I remember that I paid him in gold and wondered if everything was going to be on the same formidable scale.

I had no idea that the railway-station where I thought we were was a ferry-boat, and I was watching my first American crowd—very English-looking—when the whole imaginary station suddenly broke loose and paddled out to the Jersey side. It was a great surprise.

I had another surprise in the train. While looking intently at the quickly moving scene, and deciding that a porch and no garden were the first characteristics of American houses, I kept hearing convent-bells and wondering where the invisible convents might be. Finally I asked my companion. "The train," he said, "the train-bell; trains here use a bell." He was an Englishman, very chary of words, and although less articulate in criticisms than my friend, the purser, was no less conscious of differences which, after fifteen years, he still resented. His brief explanations did not sound quite like verdicts, but they were regretful admissions that things in America should be as they were.

By tea-time we reached the station at Deal Beach where I was met by Colonel Harvey in person. He hardly spoke, but he held my hand for a while to express exceptional welcome, and he smiled as an infinitesimal motion of his head referred to the weather more raging than ever. In a few minutes we were at his house. Mrs. Harvey and her daughter were there, very welcoming; there were blazing fires in all the rooms, tea was already on the table, and Westminster chimes introducing five o'clock proclaimed the general Englishness of the hour. Suddenly I felt at home, as if the three thousand miles of ocean were a dream. As soon as he had had his tea, Colonel Harvey stretched himself full length on a long bench in front of the fire and began to read a theological book which he held horizontally over his face. This was one of his silent methods for banishing formality and letting you know that you were as free as you ever felt at any English country-house. I was grateful to him for this.

Shortly after tea the wind shifted, in a few moments the sun reappeared in a white and blue sky, and it was an active August sun over a New Jersey place. This was summer after all. Mrs. Harvey took me out into the garden. It was a large garden of fully three acres, chokeful of flowers. Innumerable insects, feeling the return of their god, were already buzzing and whizzing. The admixture of heat and coolness was delicious. Mrs. Harvey showed me things, naming the many flowers I did not know. Her hesitant manner had something appealing about it, and I always liked it, but during that first hour it was made more charming by her evident desire to make me feel at home. As we turned out of one walk into another she stopped before a little white and yellow bush and looked up from its multitudinous flowers with a happy questioning face. I recognized our familiar camomile and she said: "This may be the only camomile-plant in America: I brought it over from your own country. You can have some camomile-tea if you wish."

We met Mr. Wyckoff, the gardener, and Mrs. Harvey walked with him into the greenhouse to give some orders. I went on strolling along the wet walks. A big butterfly, much larger than any I had ever seen in Europe, flitted past me with an audible flapping of its wings. I stopped to watch it. As I did so, the words: "America! This is America" repeated themselves in my consciousness with a clarity full of significance, and I knew that this was one of the great moments of my life. I was in a new world, so new and unexpected in its strange novelty that the soul awaking to its after-death existence may not experience a stronger impression of otherness. I am glad I can still revive it at times.

At dinner I found that guests had come down from New York: Mr. Miller, editor of the *Times*, Mr. David Munro, editor of *The North American Review*, and Mr. William Inglis, also a journalist. The Presidential Election was drawing near and kept everybody excited, yet dinner was peaceful, with good-

humoured conversation. I only noted what seemed to me surprising indifference to Europe. In my room I felt that I did not
have to sort my impressions, as I generally have to, before
noting them down: they were simple and deep, they needed no
recording and I did not endeavour to put them in writing. I
opened my window and looked out at the indistinct lines of the
garden and trees: the night was velvety, soft and incredibly
calm, but what struck me most was how vocal an American
night could be. Space was full of sounds. In their rich confusion
I gradually recognized the timid tinkling of the cricket and the
throaty call of the tree-frog, but a strange noise as of somebody
brushing clothes in the distance long kept me wondering till I
decided it must come from some insect, a purely American one.
I read my Vespers, and went to bed full of the strangeness of
it all.

The next day began early. Neither in France nor in England
had I been accustomed to breakfast at half past seven. The
Colonel was seated alone in front of the teapot when I appeared, and I was surprised to see him in a military red coat.
He made a faint attempt at being cordial but could not be, for
he was grumpy in the morning—a characteristic of which I had
never heard in France and which had to be explained to me. He
was eating slowly and at the same time reading, swiftly clipping
bits off the newspapers here and there and throwing the useless
big sheets in a heap beside him. I took up *The World* and almost immediately my eyes fell on the name of his wife. "Have
you seen this reference to Mrs. Harvey?" I asked, just as the
lady herself, accompanied by Mr. Munro, was coming into the
room. "Oh!" the Colonel said, in his most Vermont-sounding
twang, "you mean that article on the nagging woman?" He
laughed the silent laughter of Leather Stocking and his grumpi-
ness seemed exorcized at once. In his cold Yankee way he was
a perfect husband but he loved to tease.

Breakfast was as full of politics as dinner had been free from it. Every man at the table was working for Taft, but nobody was enthusiastic about the man or optimistic about his election. The Colonel was a democrat, indeed a Jeffersonian—he shocked me by a violently schismatic expression of his preference for States Rights—and was championing Taft only out of antipathy to Roosevelt. You never could tell exactly whether his political passions or his political convictions were chronologically the first, but his capacity for contempt was uppermost. He helped me better than any other man to understand Dean Swift in whom I took particular interest at the time. Surely both men were glad to have ideas so that other men might disagree and thus give them a chance to indulge hatreds of a superior kind. There are in *Harvey's Weekly* many effusions which the most celebrated pamphleteers have never exceeded in passionate logic.

As he sat at that table surrounded by distinguished journalists his superiority was evident. I knew he had had no university education and was largely self-taught, but one thing was clear: the man must always have been top wherever he had been, and he had never known what the word inhibition meant. He listened indulgently to what these, his political servants, said, but he was the judge of their judgments and remained unimpressed by their emotions. He had a charming, an almost caressing way of chaffing Mr. Miller who sounded as despondent in his talk as his editorials in the *Times* were confident. Harvey had a prodigious political erudition, he knew his America as nobody else did, and his sense of the human side of an electioneering campaign was infallible. Later on I had occasion to see him discussing affairs with such a rival as Mr. William Allen White, and he preserved the same calm attitude of superiority I noticed in him that first morning. Some people, no doubt, must have been outraged by it, but the man could not help feeling superior, and unless engaged in single fight, never meant to hurt anybody by it. I had realized in Paris that he was fundamentally kind. I found in America that he could be an artist in kindness.

After the guests left to return to New York, the Colonel took me to his library in a sort of tall white tower at the end of the garden. No country has such public or private libraries as America and this was my first introduction to them. The Tower was full of scientific, philosophical and theological books in which the Colonel, though no church-goer, seemed to be particularly interested. I knew I should spend many happy hours in that treasury of books and I did. My host showed me the arrangement of his shelves and we talked till far into the forenoon. As soon as George Harvey swerved from politics his limitations appeared, and one realized once more that his literary value came of his indifference to literature. Although he visited France often he knew no French, and I soon felt that to him France was only one of the small countries of Europe annoying the American tourist by their everlastingly recurring frontiers. It was more painful soon to be sure that his ignorance of my country had been tinged with contempt by our apparently taking the defeat of 1870 lying down. For he was one of those many Americans who have only two impressions of France: decadence when the French indulge the Liberalism bequeathed to them by the Great Revolution, or militarism when they react in the contrary direction. Of our art and literature he knew nothing. I found underlined in his copy of Bagehot's *Essays* the strange epigram—referring to the country of Descartes and Pasteur— that "The French can say anything, but never have anything to say." Thomas Woodrow Wilson, who had a similar contempt for France, based on a similar ignorance of everything French, was also an admirer of Bagehot's.

Colonel Harvey's great admiration was for the British who had a worldwide Empire, spoke a language which every American understood, and acted in a way which every American felt like imitating. He was almost enthusiastic about Asquith who, after all, appears to-day as a clever politician but is certainly not one of the great English statesmen. Listening attentively I felt that the Colonel was mostly impressed by Asquith's culture and by social gifts which do not seem to abound on the hill in

Washington. But this tendency I was to find in practically all Americans.

We reverted to Taft and to the campaign. Coming from a country where the presidential candidates are never known till the week, sometimes the day before the election, it required an effort for me to understand the American atmosphere over-heated more than two months ahead of the vote. The Colonel made everything clear to me. As I left him to his weekly philippic he said: "In two or three days I'll drive you to Trenton, to the man who will certainly be our President in the very near future. His name is Wilson and he is Governor of this state." This promise could not be fulfilled, but the prophecy came true. Only, the election of President Wilson did not turn out so satisfactory to Colonel Harvey as the latter had thought it would, and a famous feud ensued.

I stayed a week at Deal rather enjoying my introduction to what the French language calls the cooking up of an election. Seeing history in the making takes the romance out of it, but it is illuminating and it is an intellectual sedative. Every time I have been mixed up with public affairs I have felt how right women are to attach importance only to their practical consequences and none at all to the way in which they are transacted: politicians differ very little from collegians.

One morning Colonel Harvey took me to New York where he had to see the editors of his various publications before they went to press. He called in each man in succession and they had a little parley which somehow suggested the confessional-box, the Colonel being very paternal and understanding. We had an amusing literary lunch at Delmonico's, after which we re-turned to Deal. As we were leaving the little station to drive home, I pointed at the tracks with my stick and told my companion that I owned some of that property. Indeed I possessed two shares of the Pennsylvania Railroad which I had bought on the principle that money made in America should be spent in America. Colonel Harvey, who was never astonished at any-thing, actually seemed on the brink of being taken aback, but he only grinned and grunted approval. I could see that this revelation gave him quite an opinion of his Paris correspondent.

After a week, I took leave of my hosts and started on the European's usual discovery of America. For the first time in my life I had been in the midst of interesting people busy doing interesting things and I had not taken a single note. I had just lived what I thought was a unique experience, unique in every sense of the word, for I felt sure it would never be repeated. Whenever I try to remember that faraway week I am only conscious of the kindness of Mr. and Mrs. Harvey, of the beauty of their place, of the exquisite September weather, and, above all, of the strangeness and remoteness of being there. As soon as the slight shock of being in a totally different country from one's own was over I plunged into the American atmosphere as into a magical spring. The delight of being inaccessible to all that spelt Europe, the delight of being anonymous, hidden in the enchanting garden of these kind friends and surrounded by the protecting vastness of their country was infinitely superior to the long-tried pleasure of adding information to knowledge. America, the America of that first visit, was not a country or a nation, it was a purely spiritual experience.

So, I did America as most people, who have four weeks to do it in, do it. I went to Washington, where I had the shocking revelation that hotel people did not shine shoes and you had to go to specialists for that; I spent an afternoon in Baltimore, most of it seated on a bench in the square at the top of Charles Street, for this square has an atmosphere, and a house on it, lighted day and night against the possible return of a lost child, had a legend; I went to Boston and Cambridge and saw Harvard deserted by all but a few stragglers and given up to the squirrels; I saw Niagara, a great thrill, promptly followed by a great weariness; I forget why I stopped a whole day in

Buffalo which I liked; finally I stayed three or four days in
Chicago which had not the look it has now acquired, but was
already full of Imperial promises. The presidential campaign
was in full swing there. My attention was attracted by a scroll
on which was written the famous "Government of the people,
by the people, for the people," which I thought a shabby dema-
gogic platitude till I was told of its illustrious parentage and
began wondering about Lincoln. I went back east by my Pennsylvania Road which gave me a lot of natural beauty to admire.
But my four weeks were not sufficient to dispel the stock of
European images fortified by European formulas which I had
brought over with me. I was constantly on the lookout for
villages, and there are in America no villages of the French,
English or Swiss variety. I wanted to see an American forest,
and I only saw ragged bits of woodland much less impressive
than what you can see within an hour's train-distance from
Paris. The gardenless farms and wall-less villas depressed me.
In short, I kept seeking in America for what was not there so
that I missed what was written large at every step. Since then I
have been irritated many times by European travellers of the
Duhamel variety who bring no sympathy to their first investigation of America, but, on second thoughts, my irritation has
always made way for humility: I, too, was that kind of traveller, once, and I was lucky to have been saved from the temptation of publishing my first superficial impressions distorted by
green-coloured glasses. I seem to remember that I was inclined
to be critical when I was a few days by myself. I resented the difference between the English I had learned in England and the
language of Americans. The torture they inflict on poor letter R
tortured me too. I was also scandalized by shortcomings in material civilization which I had not expected, the slowness of the
trains, for instance, or their curious admixture of luxury and discomfort. As soon as I was with people I thought everything perfect. I did not meet a single American, man or woman, whom I
did not like, and I did not mind anything they said. The pastor of
the Catholic church at Deal described Europe, in a sermon, as "a

musty assemblage of old nations." I relished the peaceful certitude of this statement which Colonel Harvey almost enthusias-
tically approved when I repeated it to him. I made no generalizations, no inferences or deductions. I knew I was in America
on too short a visit to be positive about anything I saw or heard.
I also imagined that I should never cross the ocean again. So,
instead of studying America, I merely enjoyed it, or enjoyed
myself in it, in exactly the lazy way which sometimes annoys me
to-day when I notice it in American tourists in Europe. My
permanent pleasure was the sense of my infinitesimal personality subsisting in an unknown and enormous continent, the joy
of being, after forty-four years, out of Europe at last, and
giving it no more thought than if the ocean had been a prodigious Lethe.

My original plan of writing a short book, or a long article,
on American art and Art in America, was not given up. I saw
a few specialists—Mr. Royal Cortissoz was particularly kind—
and I read a few books. But I did the galleries, as all the rest,
in a relaxed September spirit. Most private collections were
inaccessible at that season of the year and I caught myself
secretly rejoicing that they were. I remember the scorching day
in Boston when I was told, at the door of Mrs. Gardner's house,
that everything was closed, and I could take refuge in the coolest
part of the Common. Moreover, I soon found that American art
was given the cold shoulder in America. An exception was made
for Whistler, but solely on account of his mother's portrait, and
not because it was a good portrait but because it suggested a
good mother. Winslow Homer's things were not exhibited in
the Boston gallery; I was courteously taken to the storeroom to
see them. Inness was undiscoverable anywhere. The dealers'
shops in New York were full of third-rate French things but
showed no Innesses. The Art Institute of Chicago was, at that
time—before it became flooded by donations—a marvellously intelligent lesson in the history of art, but the Inness pictures which
now occupy an extremely attractive room were not there. I did not

care much. What kept me more interested were the spurious attributions which at the time abounded in the American museums. Mr. Purdon Clark, the director of the Metropolitan Museum, had already gone through the customs investigations proving that over two thousand pictures bearing the well-known signature of Corot had been landed at American ports. Many such badgers were bequeathed to museums by donors who expressly stipulated that not a single canvas was to be taken out of their collection, while their own portrait was to be conspicuous in it for eternity. I enjoyed the lazy kind of work which trained eyes can do in front of a picture without much collaboration from the mind; I loved the art libraries abounding in America; I made notes about artists, although I did not make any about anything else, but I never wrote the article—in fact it was not until 1922 that I published a single line about America—and I do not even know now what has become of the notes.

My last week was spent in New York, in lodgings in Gramercy Park, which I shared with Frank Craig, the English painter. Yet I went back to Deal for a day or two. Henry James had just left, on hearing that Mark Twain was arriving the next day, while Mark Twain on being informed that Henry James was a guest had found some excuse to put off his visit. I was sorry to miss Mark Twain who interested me more than Henry James, but the Harveys were so nice and their place was so poetic in the lingering summer that I could not regret anything. The day before I sailed, buying the French newspapers in the hall of the Brevoort House, I found myself face to face with Mark Twain and we talked. I thought him the most melancholy person in the world. He drawled out a long tale of woes: his daughter had just sailed, and she was not well, she had had a bad sun-burn; here he was, alone, etc., etc.

The same day an alert little man called. He was a lecture-agent who felt sure he could interest me in a tour which might easily be arranged if I would wait three or four weeks

till people returned from the country. His bright talk was full
of bright dollars. But no words can express how remote I was
at the time from any idea of lecturing in America. That agent
must have thought me an unbusinesslike unserious individual.
I did not care. I enjoyed an empty New York inhabited only
by the glorious sunshine. I loved Gramercy Park and Washington Square, both of them still intact then: the Judson, in the
shadow of the Methodist church, was more fascinating than
any lecture-hall. I wanted nothing but what I had. I came to
the last of my thirty-five days without having once been annoyed by, or perhaps even conscious of, American strenuous-
ness. My America was a powerful continent, no doubt, but
where the caressing weather and the easygoingness of the
people took the edge off the sensation of power. Whether Taft
or Roosevelt would be President was a matter of indifference to
me except as it affected my Harpers friends. After sailing, and
when a large yellow butterfly which played a long time about
the deck of the S.S. *Philadelphia* made up its mind to fly back
to Staten Island, I found that what filled my soul was not the
encyclopedia of American notions illustrated by thousands
of memory photographs which now rather overcrowds my
mind, but peaceful Deal scenes of no interest to anyone except
to me, or a happy room at the Players' Club, or nooks like a
little private churchyard outside Bristol, R. I., where a brilliant
redbird, in the infinite peace of the fields around, seemed a
symbol of immortality. I felt a pang when the long low coast
of Long Island, this time all warm sand in the sunshine, disappeared under the horizon. Many unjust critics of America
must have felt the same on leaving it, for I hardly know one
who, having visited it, can honestly say he does not want to
see the United States again.

We were a very small party on that *Philadelphia*, only seven
first-class passengers. Two young artists studying in Paris were
on board, and we became well acquainted. At Cherbourg I
watched for a long time the graceful white outline of the

steamer as she lay in the roads. When she veered round towards
Plymouth, I said a pretty melancholy good-bye to her. But my
young artists were beaming as they boarded the train. When we
passed Caen they stood at the window transfixed with pleasure
at the thought of the many beautiful things they knew in that
famous rival of Rouen. But when we drew near Paris and the
lights of Montmartre glittered above the great loop of the Seine,
the two boys became wild with joy, stamping with delight and
shouting, shouting in French: *"Voilà Paris! ah, voilà Paris!"*
I felt like an alien once more.

Stanislas College had already resumed work, and there was
not a sound in it when I entered; everything was familiar, too
familiar. I suddenly knew that, without being aware of it, I had
been in a vital and vitalizing country. Perhaps I had not been
wise in making light of the lecture-agent's offer. Two days later
I was at Trélon. It was October 6th, and the night had already
closed in when I arrived. The town-band was practising in the
town-hall: there was something ridiculous in its earnestness.
Hard by, the church looked rather imposing. Around it and
under its grey flagstones my ancestors had lain for at least three,
probably four or five, centuries. They had been happy in the
immobility of their lives, I had been assured. Probably they had
been bored too: I wished my American visit had not been a
mere dream.

Gradually layers of oblivion thickened over my brief American experience. Some memories are kept alive by the knowledge
that what they record cannot be repeated, others act in a different way: we think it wiser to let them lie dormant: this is
what I did. But gradually too I found that I knew more about
America than I had seemed anxious to learn. French and
English people sometimes betray the most astonishing ignorance resulting in the wildest notions about the United States. I
was surprised to find myself frequently correcting those ideas,

or I would be doubtful of what I heard and I would check it off by reference to good books. Pretty soon I was regarded and consequently regarded myself as a champion of unknown America and an incipient expert in things American.

Moreover, my ties with the United States grew closer: more reviews asked me for contributions and I became the Paris correspondent of the Yale University Press as well as a sort of adviser of the Yale Library. Somehow too it began to seem natural that American literary visitors to Paris should be given letters to me. When Henry van Dyke was appointed exchange professor at the Sorbonne, we became great, almost intimate, friends. I have no patience with the people—now fewer and fewer—who mistake Henry van Dyke's naïveté for conceit. Had he been physically a bigger man van Dyke would never have been accused of conceit: the size and weight of men count for much in the estimate we take of them, or they take of themselves, but of that only a few people are aware and a great deal of injustice follows.

My very dear friends, Bliss and Annie Perry, also came to Paris from Harvard in the same connection. I liked them at once and have liked them ever since. One afternoon I took them to Angellier's picturesque apartment: the conversation that followed in that impossibly crowded study is still fresh in my memory. Bliss Perry knew at once the presence of genius, while Angellier's mental exactness under imaginative appearances recognized in his American visitor the infallibility of judgment which always delighted him.

Lady visitors would come too. Margaret Deland's subdued alertness gave me intense pleasure. I also became attached to a woman who, old in years, never grew aged: kind, fantastic, secretly wise Mary Joline, who will be remembered as a benefactress of Princeton. One day, at the College, a very beautiful, rather commanding young woman was brought to my rooms. In a somewhat throaty but distinguished voice she asked me for details concerning the *Sillon* movement. It was several years before the war when society women, who wanted to break loose from mere social life, did not find the chances which the future was holding in reserve for them. This girl visibly recoiled from the danger of frittering away her pent-up energies. I liked her earnestness. She was Miss Ann Morgan whose career I have followed ·with keen sympathy. We still occasionally meet, too seldom, but busy people belong to one fraternity.

I have already told how the war brought me in contact with many more distinguished Americans. Certainly by the end of 1918 I knew the American mentality as well as I know it to-day, and my American sympathies were based on observations to which my later experiences were not going to add much. But the America I had glimpsed in that perfect month of September, 1908, seemed as remote as it had been before that visit. It had not once occurred to me that I might have another chance to cross the ocean, and so the invitation brought to me from the Archbishop of Cambrai in the Spring of 1919 came as an extraordinary surprise.

I waited a few days before speaking to M. Pautonnier, the College President, about the mission entrusted to, or more or less forced upon, me. My train of thought was not optimistic. I had been following the American press pretty closely and two tendencies were becoming every day more perceptible in it. In the first place, Americans had neglected America and it was high time that an absurd preference for Europe should be brought to an end. "America at last" was a powerful slogan. In the second place, a notion was spreading in the United States that the American soldiers had not been properly treated in France. Two shocking proofs were adduced: the French had charged the poor American doughboys even for the water they had drunk; worse than that, they had actually charged them for the very trenches in which they had fought and died for the defence of France. To say that American sentiment was deeply hurt is to put the thing mildly.

I have no doubt that even to-day, almost twenty years after

the war, the two legends still survive. I found the latter alive in
England only a few years ago. Naturally not a single American
or Englishman who fought in the war ever believed it. Anybody
who came near trenchland knew that, for miles and miles, there
were no proprietors to buy anything of. Horror and confusion
were the proprietors. What gave currency to the rumour was the
fact that American camps near Bordeaux or St. Nazaire, as well
as British camps outside Boulogne, requisitioned thousands of
acres for training of all kinds, including entrenching, and the
proprietors of those acres, often valuable land, expected repay-
ment, exactly as American farmers similarly deprived of their
land by training camps in the United States would naturally
expect it. There may have been disputes. Litigation about property commandeered by the military has always been frequent.
One morning, whiling away a few rainy hours in the public
library of Newport, R. I., I found in the sleazy files of an
eighteenth-century newspaper, *The Newport Courant*, traces of a
controversy between Rochambeau and the municipality of Newport. The French general contended he had been overcharged
for poles which he needed for his trenches. Such stories are the
very meat of propaganda.

As for anybody charging an American boy for water, I have
never had any indication that such a mean thing was ever perpe-
trated. But I know that Belgian Walloons have said many times,
with proper racial disgust, that Flemish Belgians charged
British tommies for what little water they drank. This sounds
like a proof of hideous avarice to people who no more think of
paying for the water they drink than for the air they breathe.
But visitors to the Belgian seaside places know well that everybody there pays for his water, as water has to come from the
other end of Belgium. It never occurred to the Flemish publican
to give Spa water free to an English tommy who preferred that
to beer. As the wells in some parts of Lorraine—the Woëvre,
for instance—are as suspect as those of Flanders it may have
happened that American doughboys also had to pay for im-

ported water, but, as I said above, I never met any who did not laugh when I asked him whether he had or not.

Whatever may have been the rights and wrongs of the treatment dealt to the American soldiers in France, the fact remains that Americans as a nation were getting tired of the long effort forced upon them by the war, and, like all tired people, were beginning to be irritable and reproachful. The outcome of this state of mind was that desire to get out of European affairs which has steadily been gathering force for almost twenty years. Its expression is the famous "No more entanglements!" the endless repetition of which has become wearisome to even a sympathizer who, like myself, fully admits that America is right in wishing to keep out of trouble.

This did not prevent American Francophiles from going on with a thousand and one works of relief for the French which my correspondents constantly mentioned in their letters. My conclusion could only be that the Archbishop of Cambrai would have made things much easier for me if he had suggested my going over to America earlier in the game. I fully expected people to tell me as soon as I arrived in New York: "Don't you think we have done enough for your country?" And if I should insist, they would be sure to add: "And we are still doing so much that we can do no more." To which no reply could be made, except the expression of a gratitude which I probably felt more than those of my countrymen who had not watched American generosity at close range as I had.

I finally approached our headmaster and told him that I was afraid I must leave the College shortly after the Easter vacation. M. Pautonnier seemed very much upset. "Do you realize," he asked, "that your abrupt departure will throw the whole English department out of gear?" He went on, for a while, with other flattering reproaches, then he asked: "And have you ever collected money?"

"Never."

"I have," he pursued, "you know of my Graduate scholarships: they mean endless collecting. It is a heart-breaking busi-

ness. You won't know how to approach people while they will
know how to slip away from you. Here you are, a successful
writer, going to appear as a mendicant in the country where you
are the most successful. People will not understand and, let me
tell you, they always resent what they do not understand. A
poor present is your Archbishop making you."

Every word M. Pautonnier said was echoed in my mind with
repeated admissions "Too true! only too true! Mendicant! inexperienced mendicant! Making a mess of everything!"

A similar interview with Monsignor (to-day Cardinal) Baudrillart, the Rector of the Catholic University of Paris, was
hardly more satisfactory. I was reproached with deserting my
own candidacy to the chair of English literature just when he,
the Rector, was doing all he could to promote it. The Faculty
had been unanimous in proposing me, but I ought to know that
powerful influences would work against ratification of the professors' choice by the Council of Trustees. If I did not care,
who would?

During my Easter vacation at Trélon, still full of war-scars,
I had time to think. I felt I had a duty to my Archbishop and to
Lille University which more than counterweighed the draw-
backs pointed out by Mgr. Baudrillart and Abbé Pautonnier.
Moreover, the war had bred in me, as in a multitude of Frenchmen, a desire to serve in deeds and not, as I had done throughout my life, mostly in words. My existence had been spent in my
study reading or writing what I pleased, or in the lecture-room
talking about what interested me. It was time I did something
less selfishly intellectual. Providence was giving me a unique
chance. Besides, there must be something fascinating in the
novelty of action. After all, this American trip, so different
from my first, might be a great experience. Let me prepare myself for it as thoroughly as I could.

So, I began to make plans and organize. I had long known
that what had happened to me in England was being repeated
in America. Being a literary, infinitely more than a theological,

writer, I had been invited in New York and Boston, as well as in London, to contribute chiefly to non-sectarian reviews, those which the general public reads without giving much thought to the religious denomination of the contributors. I was unconscious of my collar when I wrote, and most of my readers did not know that I was a churchman. But when the Archbishop of Cambrai asked me to help Lille University out of the morass in which the war had left it, I began to think of this institution as specifically Catholic. Lille was the only Catholic university in France that had been able to take on the burden of a Medical School. Throughout the country it was known as the Alma Mater of Catholic physicians, and the support given to it came largely from the recognition of its usefulness in training doctors more mindful of the soul than had been the fashion with practitioners since the eighteenth century. I had been deeply impressed by that fact when I was attached to the University and the consciousness of it returned in full force upon me as I began to make my plans.

So it was inevitable that I should chiefly bear in mind Catholic possibilities in America as I pondered my chances. I had only been in contact with a few American Catholics, and the only American priest I knew was Father Joseph McSorley, of the Paulist Fathers, himself a writer. But the rapid development of Catholicism in the United States during the past fifty years had led me as well as thousands of other Frenchmen to form a great idea of the American hierarchy, of their influence and of their organizing capacities. The names of Ireland, Gibbons and Spalding were constantly in my memory. On the other hand, I instinctively endowed the Bishops of the United States with the sympathy for France which was almost universal in the Americans I knew. These thoughts gradually got the better of the pessimism born of my knowledge of America's weariness of European affairs and I became almost sanguine.

I laugh at myself sometimes as I remember the morning in which I penned a circular to the Bishops of the United States destined to be signed by the Archbishop of Cambrai but em-

bodying my suggestions. They were so naïve that they almost
ceased to be ridiculous. I hoped that those busy men, afflicted
with infinitely more cares than I had, would form, in each one
of their dioceses, a small committee which I could find ready
when I arrived and with which I could work. I felt my apparent desertion of College Stanislas deeply and I wanted to return
to my duties as usual early in October. It never occurred to me
that Summer was the worst time to work in, that the eastern
States were overwhelmed with appeals of all kinds, and the
western ones too far away to be interested, while the South was
only Catholic in spots. I had never seen a Catholic Directory.
I did not know that any such publication existed.

Of course I left no stone unturned in other directions. After
long and intricate negotiations I not only obtained a personal
introduction from the Cardinal-Prefect of Studies to the American Bishops, but I succeeded in inducing the Pope himself to
write to Cardinal Gibbons recommending a collection to be
taken up in the Catholic churches of America in behalf of the
Universities of Lille and Louvain. Lille-and-Louvain sounded
better than Louvain-and-Lille, as Cæsar-and-Pompey sounds
better than Pompey-and-Cæsar which ought to be the natural
sequence, but the Louvain people were justly offended to see a
young University like Lille take precedence of their illustrious
Alma Mater. Needless to say I was in no wise responsible for
the mistake. I also obtained a letter which Marshal Foch wrote
himself in his beautiful script, and I had it photographed and
multicopied. I wrote hundreds of letters to men or women likely
to help me, and I got scores of introductions worth getting. I also
interviewed everybody in Paris who was or had been in contact
with American organizations. Paul van Dyke was helpful with
illuminating admonitions more useful than faint advice. John
Finley gave me a touching poem which he had recently written
in behalf of stricken Lille and which I used several times with
great effect. The chief representative of the Knights of Columbus

—whose name I now forget—did not actually say to me: "Young man, go west!" but he said: "Believe me, do not tarry in New York which is dead tired of appeals, but go straight to California." Monsignor (now Bishop) Kelley, of Chicago, gave no advice, but I shall always be grateful to him for the valuable information that in Chicago lived a man who liked the articles I published in *Chesterton's Weekly*, my now dear friend, Monsignor T. V. Shannon.

When all this was done I went to Lille and, between two trains, I explained my plans to the then Rector of the University, Mgr. Margerin. This prelate was as shrewd and practical as his predecessor, Mgr. Baunard, had been literary. Moreover, he was a friend of my family, had known me in long clothes and, like all people who have known one young, he did not believe I had ever grown up. As Vicar-General of Cambrai he had been very kind when my book was placed on the Index, but he visibly did not think much of a person unwise enough to write a book destined to be put on the Index, that is to say, in the way of ecclesiastical promotion. He listened to me with the charmingly ironical smile which I had always liked in him, and gave me a funny blessing as he handed me a thin bundle of bankbills. "I am afraid I shall never see these five thousand francs again and we are wofully poor," he said. "Come back as soon as you have spent them. God bless you!"

Outside the administration building my dear friend, M. Lesne, professor of history, was waiting for me. We went over the laboratories and dispensaries which the enemy had gutted to the last article. I also saw the appalling destruction of the central quarters of the city. I felt a great desire to be more useful than Mgr. Margerin thought I could be.

Just before I sailed, M. Lesne was appointed Rector of the University. His preferment delighted me and filled me with renewed courage. I wanted to help him, and his faith in his own mission was my chief support during the ten hard months I was to spend in America.

II

I sailed May 25th, 1919, on the *Chicago*, from Bordeaux. Ships were still on their guard against floating mines and, whenever they could, avoided the Channel. The boat was packed with American officers and men going home. The men were travelling tourist, but as soon as they saw a chance they would climb up to the upper deck to talk. There were a number of the most amusing "micks." But even the funniest of them loved to complain. They complained of their pay not coming in time, they complained of the military post-office, and they hated M.P.'s. They also complained of their quarters on the ship, and of being given no wine, the latter seeming to be a great grievance. Women groaned sympathetically, listening to them, but a little private investigation convinced me that the fellows were lying: they were accommodated much better than the crew and they had all the wine that was good for them. I said so to the next complainant. He laughed, and I remembered that Bickerstaff Drew, who had been a military chaplain all his life, said that soldiers lie on principle and without any motive or profit.

The officers, most of them civilians in uniform, showed no particular enthusiasm at the prospect of resuming home-life. The younger ones even less than their seniors. Europe had not been good for them: they articulately complained of the American girls "who thought they had a right to everything and nothing was good enough for them." They remembered a winter or two in the service of débutantes with rankling indignation. "French girls," one of them said, "bring you your coffee." "Yes," echoed another, "and they pay for their drinks."

There was also in the first cabin a whole party of dwarves going to America on contract. They were not the repellent kind of dwarves at all. Some of them were very well proportioned. The dean of the party, a diminutive lady of twenty-eight, was a serious woman with considerable experience of the world and so much sense that it required an effort to reconcile her wisdom

204

with her size. But somehow what she said invariably seemed to breed melancholy.

The boat was old and old-fashioned. We made no progress, the mileage on several occasions not reaching two hundred. But she was an easy-going old tub, and a delicious smell of French bread-baking pervaded every nook and corner.

Finally we reached New York towards noon of June 5th. It was a sunny but cool morning and the streets were full of animation with bunting streaming in the breeze everywhere, I have forgotten for what cause. New York, which I had not seen since my first brief visit eleven years before, somehow seemed familiar. Meeting many Americans and constantly reading American periodicals had produced that effect. But the city, with more skyscrapers and a brisker traffic of motors instead of horse-vehicles, appeared extraordinarily modern. I was also conscious of an exuberant sensation, a collective jubilation which had evidently been brought about by the successful end of the war. Before the day was over I was able to convince myself that everybody was richer, everybody felt the stimulation of prosperity. The dazed sensation accompanying the tardy relief from four years' tension, frequent in Europe, was not visible here. America had spontaneously submitted, in a fine spirit, to a great deal of restriction but the restrictions had not been forced upon her. The words "in France" had a different ring for Americans and for me. To them it meant more or less what "in Ethiopia" meant in 1935 for Italians, viz., the place in which one's army has finally come on top. They were uttered in my presence without any particular reference to me or my compatriots. Altogether New York seemed to be in a fever of health. At night I noted in my diary: "Kings, these people are," and the impression was not altered during the following ten months.

I went to the now defunct Holland House, in lower Fifth Avenue, and started business at once. I telephoned all my friends in the Harvey circle, *The North American Review* people, Mr. Miller at the *Times* office, my American publishers, the

Putnams, M. Cazenave, the successor of M. Tardieu as chairman
of the French Commission, the Clews bank on which I counted
to house my unhatched chickens, the Chancery of the diocese
of New York, M. Marcel Knecht who acted as liaison between
the Catholics of France and those of America, and I telephoned
dozens of acquaintances. Most people were more than friendly:
the natural tendency of Americans to coöperate with anybody
representing an idea worth while struck me that afternoon as it
has many times since. A friend invited me to dinner at the
Plaza: the contrast with the depleted service in our French
hotels was unmistakable. So was the superb indifference of the
guests to the luxury surrounding them. Kings they were.

Early next morning a reporter from the *Times* called. I was
grateful to Mr. Miller who had evidently sent him. Unfortunately the reporter was a ponderous, a decidedly stupid middle-
aged man. Reporters who know nothing about one and count
on you to do all the work are no rarity now, but they frequently
admit their ignorance with a frankness, sometimes a sauciness
which disarms any moderate sense of humour. That first inter-
viewer of mine possessed a well-rounded stupidity which I did
not quite realize till I saw his story in print the next morning.
Seeing my chance I had naturally tried to concentrate the interview on the mission entrusted to me. But the man had been
hypnotized by my collar. Every time I used the word mission
he inwardly noted the imaginary parish or church to which he
could not help supposing I was attached. The word appeared
thus misconstrued throughout the reporter's stodgy paragraphs.

I had breakfast with M. Knecht who is all humour and was a
great contrast to the poor newspaper man. Knecht knew his
Catholic America remarkably well and gave me invaluable
information which he charitably made as encouraging as he
could. As we talked, a secretary noted down scores of addresses
which were the basis of the tremendous pyramid of names I was
to build up in the next ten months. I left in a hopeful state. I
was to meet Knecht again at a luncheon of Catholic women who,
he said, could not fail to be interested in my undertaking.

From the Vanderbilt Hotel where M. Knecht lived I went to the diocesan Chancery. I had never met an American Bishop in America, but I had read Abbé Klein's book and I knew that American Bishops did not insist, like ours, on calling their houses palaces and were too business-like to demand much ceremony. As I walked up Madison Avenue I inwardly went over what I had eloquently said in my circular to the hierarchy, and I wondered about the members of the commission I had suggested in it. Who would they be? What would they be like? I imagined them endowed with all the efficiency I did not possess. No doubt the Cardinal Archbishop would describe them as such.

Gothic architecture can be full of warmth and *élan*, of course. It can also be pretty cold. St. Patrick's, seen from inside with its good choir and devout congregation, is as warm as any mediæval cathedral, but outwardly it is cold and even stern. I felt that as I went into the Archbishop's house and asked if I could see His Eminence. The servant seemed surprised and said she would ask Monsignor Dinneen.

Monsignor Dinneen was Cardinal Hayes' private secretary and Vice-Chancellor. I have been assured that he possessed all virtues, but he certainly did not possess the amenities so pleasant in his present successor. He was definite to roughness. He appeared, a man of barely thirty-five, in his street-clothes and in a visible hurry to finish what we had not yet begun. See His Eminence? Certainly not. This was not the hour. Come back the day after to-morrow. But what about? And who was I? I produced the rather impressive documents from the Cardinal-Prefect in Rome and from the three Bishops of the province of Cambrai. But these parchments and the red seals affixed to them did not produce the least effect. Monsignor Dinneen forgot that his question was responsible for the exhibition of these papers. "No, no!" he said impatiently, "your paper, I want to see *your* paper." I took my *Celebret* out of the humbler wallet where it had reposed. A few more police-inspector's questions about my whereabouts and the probable length of my undesirable visit to New York closed the interview. As he shut the door behind

him, the secretary turned round and said: "This city is full of
begging priests from all over the world: you must understand
that we have to be careful."

In the street, I stood still a moment: St. Patrick's looked
enormous. The pages in which Felix Klein described the welcoming appearance of American Archbishops' houses seemed
ridiculous. Suddenly I burst out laughing. I remembered what
Abbé Pautonnier had said in Paris: "You are going to appear
as a mendicant in the very country where your literary success
is the most assured." Mendicant! Of course I was a mendicant,
an apprentice mendicant at that, but Monsignor Dinneen had
not cushioned the reminder with allusions to any literary position, of which he apparently knew nothing. I had secretly felt
a pleasant consciousness that I was not really a mendicant after
all: I was a literary person trying, rather late in life, to do
something less selfish than pursuing a literary career, and likely
to be helped along by committees of charitable volunteers. Less
than twenty-four hours after landing, that illusion was being
dispelled by a remarkably sincere person who, whether I liked
it or not, had first-hand knowledge of mendicants and made
no mistake. Fifty-second Street seemed full of mendicants till
I saw a young priest walking out of St. Patrick's tailored to
admiration. No! this one was not a mendicant. Thank goodness,
he was not! (Yet he was, as I learned later, but he knew the
first rule of the business which is to awake no suspicion.)

I walked slowly on to the Colony Club where M. Knecht's
luncheon was to take place. I found some twenty women, all
Catholic and all Christian. They were all ladies, too, and some
of them showed an intimate knowledge of Paris and France
which gave me more pleasure than I should have expected. I
was surprised at the lightness of the menu—which has since
become such a familiar feature of the many Womens' Club
luncheons at which I have had the honour to be a guest—but
the party did not break up till after three. A tremendous amount
of work was dispached while we were eating. These ladies were
interested in the devastated churches of France and gave me an

impression of astonishing efficiency. But I also realized that they had been at it for almost a year, that their hands were still full, and they were looking forward to a big dinner to be given for their drive as, the moment it was over, they could fly out of New York and seek a well-deserved rest in the country. I admired those women and felt it would be an imposition to add a straw to their burden. When Knecht gave me the floor I made a man-of-the-world's nice little speech showing my gratitude for what they were doing for my country; I expressed sympathy with their weariness; but I hoped that, when they were rested, they would help a man who greatly needed help, for he did not know a thing about collecting money, and yet the cause for which he had just arrived in America was one which deserved assistance, for it meant the care of war-babies in the dispensaries of an almost ruined University.

Bless the tender-hearted American woman! These ladies who ought to have been hardened by innumerable appeals were touched. I saw their knitting-needles stop, and two of the workers, Mrs. Michael Gavin and a daughter of Senator O'-Gorman's, at once proffered assistance and gave it. But Knecht took me aside to say what I was to hear repeated by many other well-wishers: you can make a speech, but you do not know how to ask for money. He added that my British accent—more marked then than it is now—was an unfortunate thing. "You will be mistaken for some sort of an English agent," he said. The funny part of it was that I was actually supposed to be that, as I learned a few months later. But that same afternoon, as I walked into Holland House, I ran into a correspondent of the London *Times*, Perry Robinson, whose presence in America I did not suspect, and he said with great earnestness: "Whatever you do, please let me entreat you to refrain from one thing: do not throw any oil on the Irish fire!" Robinson evidently thought I might have sinister anti-British designs. Wonderful Englishness of the English! This man had only time for twenty words, and they were a concise pro-British plea. I answered that, feeling conscious as I did, of my influence on Irish people, as exempli-

fied by Mgr. Dinneen, I would certainly bear in mind his recommendation.

There was time for one more call which I thought important.
I went to the French Commission office where I had two friends:
M. Guerlac, of Cornell, and Jacques Legouis, the charming son
of the Sorbonne professor so dear to me. The Director of the
office, since the departure of M. Tardieu, was a Minister Pleni-
potentiary, M. Cazenave, who had all the suave attractiveness
of old-fashioned diplomats. But he had to tell me the truth:
the Embassy in Washington thought that the long era of French
appeals to American charity ought to be closed. The dignity of
the country was at stake. M. Cazenave would give me more
particulars if I would lunch with him the next day.

For some mysterious reason I was then passed on to a M.
Gouffy who probably attended to details. One glance at this
official was enough to show me that here sat no diplomatist, but
the reverse. A form was produced and I was cross-examined
in that nasal tone so admirably suited to cross-examinations.
Name? Age? Address? Business? Did I speak English? The
gentleman seemed to attach more importance to that than to
anything else, and sprang the question on me as if it were a
catch. I said that I wrote books in English. Yes, but did I *speak*
English? Well, I thought I did. I spelt in English letters the
name of my hotel which had not been properly written on the
printed form and I found, to my amazement, that my judge did
not know the English alphabet. He saw that I saw it, and I
knew that I was leaving no friend at that desk.

I went back three or four times to the Archbishop's house. I
never could see him. Every time it was Monsignor Dinneen who
appeared. He was sorry. His Eminence was too busy. Even now
there was a queue of New York priests waiting to speak to
him. How could he have time for outsiders he knew nothing
about? I have no doubt that the secretary was annoyed and
probably puzzled by my perseverance. Day after day I found
him a little less rude, or a little more tired of being rude, but

just as obdurate as at first. The last time I called I took a chair
—which had never yet been offered to me—and beckoned my
interlocutor to another. He sat down and I made him sit up. I
never gave anybody such a wigging. He took it admirably. When
I got up to go he said: "Of course, we know now about you;
everything will be all right; you shall see His Eminence at the
dinner to-morrow night." We shook hands.

The dinner was the huge banquet to be given at the Waldorf
in behalf of the Devastated Churches of France. I had been
invited to it by Mrs. Gavin who thought it a matter of course
that she would introduce me to Cardinal Hayes.

In the meantime I visited people and wrote to Bishops on
the Eastern board whom I was planning to visit if their secretaries would let me. Their replies were kind and courteous,
but the answers to my questions—more and more timid—concerning the committee I had suggested in my circular letter,
showed clearly that the aforesaid letter had been as unnoticed
as if it had never been received. It took me ten or twelve days
to realize that not only Bishops but all Americans of any importance were beset with requests which their very multiplicity
neutralized. A very kind friend of mine in Cambridge showed
me how briskly such petitions could be whisked into the waste-
paper basket. Mr. Otto Kahn, who gave me my first money—
2500 francs—did not conceal from me that my undertaking
was untimely. After reading some article of mine, he had sent
me, during the war, a pamphlet of his own which had led to
a correspondence. He then seemed to think that American
charity was inexhaustible, but human endurance has limits, and
Americans who, sooner than anybody else, tire of monotony,
had reached those limits.

Yet, before they could declare the slate clean, they had—M.
Cazenave told me at luncheon—to get rid of a dozen stupendous tasks. The Catholic drive for the rehabilitation of French
churches was merely a side-show. There were other drives, all
over the country, to raise the salaries of University professors;
there was the Louvain collection; there were the appeals for

the children of Central Europe, for the Y.M.C.A., for the Red
Cross; there was Miss Morgan's French work; there were other
drives for the hospitals or for the extinction of church debts.
Finally there loomed a nation-wide drive for the Episcopal
Church which would be sure to attract a lot of valuable activity.

Not a single item of this discouraging information could be
questioned, and every one was calculated to show me how slim
my chances were. I had fallen into a maelstrom of appeals in
which my stifled voice could not possibly be heard. Just then
the *Saturday Evening Post* published an article entitled "America at Last," which had been too much in the air not to produce
considerable effect.

I had been about a week in New York when the big Catholic
dinner for French churches was given at the old Waldorf-
Astoria. It was a huge affair. Six or seven hundred people were
there, and to my inexperienced eye their animation was extraordinary. I had brought my papal introductions which I hoped
to show to Cardinal Hayes, and,—on the chance that it might
be used,—Marshal Foch's letter. Somehow, before dinner began, I was discovered by a reporter carrying a copy of *France
Herself Again* which he wanted me to autograph, and I could
talk with half a dozen other intelligent pressmen. I remembered Knecht's admonition and tried to make the most of the
unexpected chance.

I was seated at a table of seven or eight, mostly clergymen.
One of them looked so French that he actually was French. I
told him I had been in New York a week. An American priest
who had picked up some French with the army in France overheard our conversation. When I gave my order to the waiter
this priest seemed surprised and said, in the loud and painfully
clear voice which people sometimes use in speaking to foreigners: "You—seem—to speak—English—al-ready—very well."
To my question what was there remarkable in that? the priest

answered: "But you've only been a week over here." I laughed, and everybody laughed, and all those men became very nice.

My conversation with them was wonderfully enlightening. Nobody could listen in a more friendly way to my account of what I was trying to do in the United States, but a few minutes were enough to show to me that it would be not only foolish but stupid to count on help from fellow-priests. Their attitude, their smiles, their good-natured shrugs, as well as all they said, recalled in a striking manner the talk of soldiers. Each man was too busy doing what you were doing yourself to do more than say "hello." To give assistance was impossible unless one were working in a team which we were not. All these men were active, and had been active for years, in collecting money. Good luck to me, but my chances were next to nil. The idea seemed more laughable than saddening. Each one of these men had been in a similar predicament many times, and their failures had not killed them. An entirely soldierlike view of the situation, and I understood it at once.

Meanwhile I was watching developments, for this was the most active dinner imaginable. There was music, the peculiar music preferred by captains of drives, and there were speeches. Every now and then a dapper little man, quite young, would rise from his seat at the high table and give the diners a piece of his mind. This drive had not been going as it should. Not by any means. Were we all asleep? Had we no real belief in the cause of the Church in France? Even the priests here assembled had been supine! It was unbelievable! Supine in their own cause! Catholic priests!

"Just listen to that little Methodist," one of the priests said, "he couldn't be half so outspoken if he were a Catholic; he makes me sick." But the others applauded and laughed good-humouredly at the Demosthenic Jack-in-the-box. A Drive-director could not talk differently; very like a preacher at the pastoral retreat, this one was.

Every now and then a local report would be read out loud, and the statistics I heard made me giddy. Burning zeal alone could account for such marvellous results. But how could my own diminutive cause manage to get wedged in between colossal efforts like these?

One of the reporters, a Catholic, had told me that the really influential speaker of the evening was Judge Dowling. If I could see him and get him to say a word for me at such a function as this, it would be a capital introduction to America. I took out my Foch autograph and read it over. There was a reference in it to the churches of France. No doubt Judge Dowling would think this letter a fine argument for his thesis and would turn full light upon it. My chance was here, within reach, a marvellous piece of luck. I said so briefly but forcibly on the back of a menu which one of the priests took at once to Judge Dowling along with the Foch letter. In a few minutes the Judge spoke, and the sound of his voice showed how delighted he was to be able to use Foch's letter. Visibly he had not counted on such a godsend. But his satisfaction blurred his memory—or, as I said rather harshly to him afterwards—his conscience. The Abbé to whom the letter was addressed was only vaguely alluded to and remained anonymous. My chance was lost. It was with some difficulty that I salvaged my precious letter which was being passed on from table to table.

Mrs. Gavin introduced me to Cardinal Hayes. She had told him that I had been the recipient of the letter just read with such solemnity and he had been impressed, but I could see in a moment that he had never heard of my repeated calls at his house and he had certainly never been told of my ill-fated circular. When I told him that there was a letter from Rome asking Cardinal Gibbons to suggest a collection, in all the dioceses, for Lille and Louvain, he raised his eyebrows. "I did not know that;" he said, "Cardinal Mercier will be here in a short time, I am afraid you will have to merge with Canon de Larsimont who is preparing things against his arrival. We shall see about the collection you speak of later. In the meantime, I must ask you to do nothing here in New York till this big Drive is over."

The request was too natural and too just. But where could I begin without encountering one of the multiform Drives? As for joining forces with the Louvain people I realized at once that it would be all too cuckoo-like. Their emissaries, dignified churchmen with the triple halo of Louvain behind them, had been working in the United States for more than a year and, Papal letter or no Papal letter, I could not decently take advantage of their efforts. I slept pretty poorly at the Holland House that night.

During the next few days while getting more information and more introductions I tried to raise a little money. This was not done in disregard of Cardinal Hayes' wishes, for—with two or three exceptions—men like Mr. Quin, the art-collector, or Mr. Burke Cochran—the people I then knew in New York were Protestants. Somehow these Protestants all seemed to know of my literary work and it made things infinitely easier than when I appeared as the mere mendicant. Most, or even all of these people, were Francophiles too, and I felt not only at my ease but happy with them.

Those of them who were purely literary—men like Mr. Burlingame and Mr. Brownell, of Scribner's, for instance—not only were helpful with encouragement and advice but they gave me money. It could not be much, but what they could give they gave. Not so, many others much richer than they were. I soon noticed in those a curious impossibility to give because they would rather not give anything at all than not give a sum that would look well on a list. Hinting that I kept no such list did not help. But I was given a lot of hospitality, even in the form of receptions, and I rather enjoyed at first being so lionized, for the cold French only lionize Anatole Frances, and I was not used to having any fuss made over me. But I soon discovered that what I thought was a form of sympathy was apt to be a form of vanity as well. Also a reception could be deftly transmuted into a literary gathering at which I was expected to say

"just a few words." Sometimes my hostess was interested in one
of the Drives and "would I not introduce a little appeal for it
with my praise of her activity?" I found myself, in that way,
giving a full-length lecture for some charity at the Colony Club,
and it took quite a little diplomacy to hint at my own work in
the course of the talk. John Finley's poem helped in such circumstances:

> Lille! 'Twas there
> They made for me a regal feast;
> But now we here who have the least
> Have more than they who had the most
> And played so gallantly the host;—
> And so, as my own prayer is said:
> "Give us this day our daily bread,"
> For those who hunger too, I pray
> In Lille and Laon and Saint Dié.

These verses invariably moved my audience. Three or four
times I was asked to speak for "struggling but very interesting
little French clubs," whose members surprised me by arriving
in fine cars and costly furs. I enjoyed hearing those women
telling me of their French experiences, but I soon learned to
interpret the enthusiastic phrase: "Oh, but we do love France,"
as covering the nuance: "Oh, but we do love ourselves in
France," so human and natural that I was ashamed to read any
real egotism into it. Sometimes too, finding myself passed on
to other rich people "who were sure to contribute" I felt bitter,
and my psychological acumen was coloured by the bitterness.
What I constantly understood was that the so-called charm of
my countrymen and especially women would not have been
half so appreciated if, being what they were, they had spoken
a different language. There is a magic in French words, in the
French inflections and in the cultivated French voice. I knew
it, of course, but the full revelation of its power came during
that summer in America.

My impression that, somehow, my literary connections would prove more practically useful than social influences, was fortified when I received invitations to attend the commencement ceremonies both at Yale and Harvard. As I had an official, though light, bond with Yale I was not very astonished to be invited there, but the Harvard courtesy was a pleasant surprise.

That year Harvard Commencement came first. The ceremonies, much more elaborate than anything similar in France, impressed me considerably. I stayed at the house of Bliss Perry who explained everything and everybody and, for the first time, I realized the place of Harvard in America. A forcible address by ex-President Eliot, young at eighty-five, opened up vast vistas, but there, as everywhere else, loomed the inevitable Drive. At the luncheon I met Mr. James Byrne who had just been made one of the Harvard overseers and I liked him at once. He told me he was a Catholic, and when I described to him the difficulties I now saw clearly in my path, he promised his concurrence in a tone which reassured me. The future showed that I was right in counting on one of the most intelligent and most truly Christian men I have met anywhere.

I also had a conversation with a tall portly gentleman who read from the platform a poem of his own, the Keatsian colour of which I liked. "I am a clergyman," he said to me, "when you are in New York my pulpit will be yours to ask my people whatever you may wish to ask them. My name is Grant, Percy Stickney Grant." He gave me his card. The next day was a Saturday and Bliss Perry took me to lunch at the famous Saturday Club. There were only seven or eight members at the luncheon. The presence among them of a son of Emerson and of a son of Oliver Wendell Holmes was one of those surprises which Boston holds in store and which make it so delightful. The same afternoon I was to meet Longfellow's daughter and a nephew of the poet who, with a carefully trimmed beard, was an absolute picture of his uncle. I sat next to President Lowell who, after some conversation and a few courteous questions, seemed to lapse into a brown study, sucking his cigar. Suddenly he asked me a question the unforeseen character of which still strikes me now after sixteen years. Would I give a course of Lowell lectures during the coming autumn? President Lowell had read *France Herself Again,* and he thought that I could easily bring the book up to date in six or eight lectures. Among the lecturers of the year were my scholarly countryman, M. Lévy-Bruhl, and Mr. Frederick Conybeare whose reputation I knew.

The proposal was flattering, but so unexpected that I asked for a few days' delay before accepting it. I wanted to be sure that I could do justice to such a course, and I had to cable Abbé Pautonnier in Paris, for this engagement would prevent me from resuming my college duties at the regular date. Very soon I saw the lineaments of eight lectures answering the question: Has France gained anything by the war? and I accepted. I did not suspect that what President Lowell was doing amounted to a complete transformation of my life. For the publicity freely given to Lowell courses is such that no sooner did my name appear on the list of lecturers than invitations poured from all parts of the country. Some of these invitations obviously would have to be postponed to another visit, and thus my habit of going to America every year was even then virtually established. Bliss Perry's kind face beamed as my conversation with Mr. Lowell was developing. I have never had a better friend anywhere than Bliss Perry, and I have long wanted to say so publicly.

The promises—richly fulfilled in time—of Mr. Byrne seemed to be the only practical result of my visit to Cambridge, but there was great encouragement coming from it. As I saw hundreds of thousands pouring into the Harvard Drive it occurred to me that if I could persuade the innumerable alumni who were contributing to give me fifty cents each it would mean the rehabilitation of one more dispensary in Lille. This vision, or this mirage, for it was one, kept me above discouragement many times and would have partly materialized had it not been for an absurd piece of ill-luck which I shall record later.

The Yale Commencement showed me how cordial even a big college could be. My usual correspondents on the Yale University Press, as well as Mr. Keogh, the librarian, whom I had kept posted in French literary developments for the past few years, were like old friends. I still recall the charming impression made on me by the Yale Press offices full of serious girls and of bright flowers. Mr. Keogh showed me the many rare books in his library. As we came away from the famous Elizabethan collection I noticed that his attention became concentrated on two feminine figures in black coming towards us. He soon left me, in considerable agitation, to welcome those ladies. They were two Frick ladies, world-famed Yale benefactresses. I watched the little interview, thinking of the possibilities which might also be latent in those women in deep mourning if only I knew them as Mr. Keogh did. "Foolish, foolish dream," as Thackeray says about that rich aunt he did not possess.

However, my friends the Parmly Days, introduced me to Mr. Brooks, president of the Telephone Company, and an important officer on the Yale Drive Committee. I told him of the aforesaid vision and, to my surprise, he not only promptly said that this was no foolish dream at all, but he volunteered to do all I might suggest. We soon entered upon a correspondence which became a powerful moral support.

I was also presented to Admiral Sims whose witty naturalness was irresistible, to one of the Wright brothers, a silent man with a fine domed head, and to ex-President Taft whose election I had seen, twelve years before, being nursed in Colonel Harvey's house. The contrast between Mr. Taft's bulk and his droll spontaneity made him both attractive and uncouth. He was astonishingly popular with the Yale alumni. But he was evidently a little puzzling to the many young American officers, Yale men in French uniforms, who were present. They had their ideas about hierarchical dignity.

I travelled back to New York with Mr. Taft and, during the two hours' trip, he let me talk to him about my mission with great patience and kindness. He seemed very much attached to

Cardinal Gibbons and insisted on then and there writing me a long introduction to him.

Somehow these few days in New England made a great difference in my outlook. I felt sure that the welcome given me in the two great Universities could be repeated elsewhere and, while feeling that it would be foolish to give up my chances on the Catholic side, I determined to visit as many colleges as possible, since Mr. Brooks might have his replica in a few of them.

Before leaving Boston I had called on Cardinal O'Connell. He gave me an appointment in a faraway church where he was giving confirmation to several hundred recent converts. I found him in the sacristy still wearing part of his episcopal vestments. After he heard me I saw a twinkle in his eye and he said: "I am glad that the French have discovered the value of money. They used to think any appreciation of it a low American characteristic, but I see they have changed their point of view."

"Your Eminence," I replied, "only fools can imagine money as unnecessary." I was not any too proud of the platitude of this retort, as I heard myself uttering it, but Cardinal O'Connell, who is evidently sportsmanlike, saw some fight in it. He laughed, and listened to me. He unhesitatingly promised to take up the collection, and his was, in fact, the first diocese in which it was actually taken up. A few weeks later he let me, with great kindness, address about a thousand Catholic women for whom he himself was speaking. I have not forgotten that occasion. The chairman of the assembly, a vivacious pretty woman, began her speech with the surprising statement: "You know—of course, you do know—that the Irish won this war." A New York singer had been engaged to brighten up the otherwise practical afternoon. When the singing began it turned out that the score was not in the tenor's voice and the accompanist declared himself unequal to making at sight the necessary changes in the key. All eyes were turned towards the Cardinal who, with a very good grace, went over to the piano and played the accompaniment as if he actually saw it printed on the page.

I called within a few weeks on all the Bishops in New England and on the Atlantic seaboard. They all were courteous, but most of them struck me dumb by the mere exposé of the financial burdens under which they groaned. On their desks I frequently noticed text-books of publicity the presence of which was eloquent. These bishops made me wish myself a rich and generous man instead of a quickly silenced mendicant.

With very few exceptions too the members of the hierarchy I then saw surprised me by their attitude towards France. It seemed dependent on a strictly Irish point of view, and this point of view had not been in the least modified by the European developments of the past twenty years. Readers of *My Old World* may remember that an ardent sympathy with Ireland was a tradition of my family and of the school in which I was educated. O'Connell was a hero of ours. His address to the men of Clare was frequently declaimed in the Elocution class. So I could not believe my own ears the first few times I heard the prelates I was visiting speak as if France were antagonistic to the Irish. And I was astounded when I found that the chief cause of this notion was the fact that, during the war, the French and the British had been in the same trenches. What the reasons for this alliance had been did not seem to be worth considering. There *had* been an alliance, and the French being, of course, pathetic and appealing during the war, had drawn sentimental America into the vortex. So it was that the British and Americans fought together a Germany against which the United States had no grievance whatever. The vital question of the freedom of the seas apparently did not exist. On the other hand, it seemed as if it were taken for granted that America was entirely Irish. The memories of my school-days made me feel in sympathy with that attachment to Ireland, but the lack of political perspective implied in all I heard rendered discussion impossible. I had to

content myself with the affirmation that not a single Frenchman
had ever heard the well-known dictum that England's extremity
is Ireland's opportunity. The French had welcomed Ireland's
independence, when it came, as they welcomed Britain's assistance, without historical reasoning.

There was another grievance against France: she was anti-
clerical in her government and the nation did not care. At all
events it did not show fight. The French had lost their faith. One
New England Bishop, now dead, told me that he would not send
any money to Lille University, but he would send some to
Louvain, and when he did so, he would be careful that this
contribution reached Cardinal Mercier from England. If it were
to cross France it might be confiscated by the French Government as monastic property had been seized in 1901.

I do not think much of a Scot's answer. But I found that a
few questions calmly asked worked better than argument. Had
my interlocutors never reflected that the history of the Church
in modern France is very different from that of the Church in
America? Here Catholics had been at first a tiny minority, and
their growth had not given alarm because the Irish were great
American patriots. In France, on the contrary, the Church had
long been exaggeratedly powerful and rich. Had she not possessed two-thirds of the land, the other third belonging to the
aristocracy? The fight against her had been largely political
and economic. The recent outbursts of anti-clericalism would
have been impossible if so many members of the French clergy
had not been hostile to that Republican form of government
which American priests were all taught to revere.

I invariably observed that the light thrown on the religious
politics of France by even this casual reference to history
worked in two ways: it was not pleasant to my interlocutor
that church dignitaries should be declared responsible for the
calamities which had fallen upon them, but there was comfort
in the reflection that, after all, they were not American but
arriéré European churchmen.

As for the discussion of French unbelief it was made easy by a mere glance at a book which was always within reach. It was enough to turn a few pages of the *Catholic Directory* to be satisfied that one good third of the religious orders of men existing in America, and more than half the orders of women were French. How could a godless country produce all those monks and nuns? Why was it that Rome canonized so many French Saints? Who were the so-called American martyrs? Seven Frenchmen! Somehow these questions, answered or not, generally closed the conversation pleasantly. With a great effort I would once more recommend the Lille collection to His Grace and sometimes a promise was the result.

Quite often I would visit a convent or two in the cathedral town where I happened to be. Nuns are charming. I never knew any who were not. The secret of their charm is their simplicity. Many of these American convents inevitably showed the American taste for luxury. I would be shown improvement after improvement and made to admire the new ball-room or the new swimming-pool. My guides' faces were radiant. Sometimes I pretended to be shocked. Too luxurious all this! Where was the vow of poverty? The sisters would laugh a little and blush a little. "Oh! Abbé! you are right. We will show you in the park the grave of our French foundress, and, close by, the log-house where she first lived. She was a Saint, Abbé. Our sisters in France still live on nothing. We shudder when we go over to the mother-house." This transparency of soul delighted me.

In time I saw Cardinal Gibbons. It was at Georgetown where he had ordained a few young Jesuits. An ordination is a long and fatiguing function and Cardinal Gibbons was eighty-five. I never saw the soul dominate the body as it did in that spare old man. In a moment he seemed to forget his weariness and, as we walked to his very light breakfast, he gave me the warmest welcome. He was full of intellectual vivacity accentuated by humour, but what struck me the most was the saint's simplicity. No notion of acting a part, no suspicion of being expected to act one had ever entered Cardinal Gibbons' mind. "Do you

know what we have been reading at my house lately?" he
asked. "Your book, *France Herself Again*! Fine book, but at
first we could not tell whether the author was Catholic or not.
It's only when those letters came from Rome that the Sulpitians
told me who you were." We both laughed at this double-barrelled encomium of my historical impartiality. I had a great
time with the Cardinal that morning. I went away with all the
encouragement I needed, and with the refreshment which the
vicinity of saintliness will always produce.

I saw Cardinal Gibbons again a few days later at the Baltimore and Ohio station in Baltimore. He had been travelling
alone and was looking for a taxi, wrapped in a coat in which
he seemed to be lost. "Oh!" he said, quite excitedly, "oh, Abbé
Dimnet! Why weren't you at the Pan-American dinner to-day?
I know you were invited, and I looked for you everywhere.
Wonderful gathering! Too bad. Too bad!"

Shortly after that Cardinal Mercier arrived from Belgium.
I had known all the time that Louvain was a name to conjure
with, that its destruction had been the whole world's sorrow,
and that the Louvain Commission which, for more than a year,
had been working with President Nicholas Murray Butler, must
have found things as smooth as I found them hard. But I
felt sure that the moment Cardinal Mercier himself appeared,
my slim chances would become even more uncertain. I had long
resolved to say so to the Cardinal himself if I had an opportunity for a real conversation with him. I was grateful when an
invitation came from Cardinal Gibbons to be his guest the whole
day Cardinal Mercier was to be with him.

I had not seen Mercier since 1893 when at an international
convention of Catholic philosophers he was chairman of a commission I attended. I had conceived immense respect for him
then. He was not forty, but he was already a master of mediæval
philosophy, and the thoughtfulness of his brow seemed to betray
as much resolve to understand other people's point of view as
to deepen his own. The beautiful eyes too were not merely the

eyes of a thinker: it was a rare experience to see a man of that type conducting an intellectual debate.

The Cardinal seemed to remember me when I was introduced to him before the high mass he was to sing in Baltimore cathedral. The war had made him even more emaciated and spiritual than I remembered him. A horrid thought came to me as I saw Cardinal Gibbons beside him: I had been wrong to regard the latter as a saint: he was only a fascinating gentleman. The saint was that other priest whose body seemed unnecessary to his soul.

That Baltimore day must have been hard for Cardinal Mercier. After high mass we were cinematographed for a long time; then the Cardinal received the press; after that he received Baltimore people. He spoke at lunch of course, then he received clergy. After that Cardinal Gibbons drove us out to his Petit Séminaire of which he was justly proud. There Cardinal Mercier spoke at least four times. He expressed himself in careful bookish English which, every now and then, might be a trifle uncertain but never caused anybody to smile. Cardinal Gibbons did not miss any of those addresses, but, in between them, he retired to lie down and in time reappeared, brisk and cheerful. He introduced one after the other all the teachers in the school, sturdy young priests marvellously excited over a football game going on outside and little inclined, it seemed to me, to hero-worship. Cardinal Mercier was, even when his energy began to wane, indefatigably kind to everybody.

As we drove back I spoke to him about my own work and frankly told him that I had never been so anxious to see again a man whose appearance I had also every reason to dread. During lunch Professor de Wulf, next to whom I sat, had with philosophical, or merely Flemish, frankness told me that the bracketing of Lille and Louvain in the Roman documents seemed to him a clever *coup*, but he was not quite sure of the authenticity of these papers. I made an extremely unphilo-

sophical reply, which I now regret, but in a day or two I
sent M. de Wulf the documents. Cardinal Mercier, of course,
did not show any such mistrust. His face became illuminated
with his heavenly smile as he said: "Do you know? we never
heard a word of this appeal from Rome until Cardinal Gibbons
told me about it." I had no difficulty in obtaining the Cardinal's
promise that he would not leave America till he had said in
public a word in favour of my University and the work I was
doing for it.

I spent the evening and the next morning with the Sulpitians
in the Seminary. Several of them were French but, according
to the tradition of their order, they had done all they could
trying to Americanize themselves. Their failure was touching.
It was easy to see that the students saw it too in that light:
they deeply respected their professors. I spent a delightful evening with those charming and holy men. Next morning one of
them, M. Bruneau, took me over the grounds. In the cool shadow
of the chapel-apse had been, or perhaps still was, the grave of
M. Nagot, a saintly ancestor of the present Sulpitians, whose
name I had heard many times pronounced with respect when I
was at Cambrai Seminary. In a quiet corner was a little graveyard where professors who had died in America were buried. It
was moving to see there, too, the grave of a woman, Henrietta
Blackstone. She was a coloured woman, a slave. M. Bruneau
spoke of her with reverence. Perhaps under that stone lay the
saint of America.

III

I had another whiff of French atmosphere when, a little later, I visited the two Canadian Archbishops. Montreal which is in reality a French city does not look it, not, at all events, like Quebec. I arrived there early one Sunday morning and went straight to the cathedral. Everybody in and around the station had spoken English to me but, walking into the cathedral, I heard, clear, sonorous and distinguished, the sounds of my native tongue. A bearded priest, M. Auclair, was in the pulpit. I listened to him as if I had never heard a French sermon before.

I soon found two former pupils of Lille University who had been there in my time. Nothing came of the help they promised me, but our reunion was pleasant. I also went to see the brother of a dear school-friend of mine who had been in Canada over thirty years. He was a gardener on a large scale. One of his daughters told me that he was not home, "he was in his field," and our biblical meeting took place in that broad open field. For some reason, perhaps simply because the words *"il est dans son champ,"* in the Canadian singsong woke up a chord in me, a thrill has remained attached to that interview.

I had a great time with the well-known editor, M. Bourassa. He had been against the entry of Canada into the war. For a whole hour he explained to me with extraordinary eloquence that Canada having been given up by France to the hated British in 1763, owed nothing whatever to the so-called parent nation. *Le Devoir*, his newspaper, would not help me from a pro-French, but merely from a humanitarian, angle. The French did not comprehend it, but Canadians had acquired a particularism, something like the Americanism of pre-revolutionary American plantations, even before the miserable treaty of 1763. He went on and on, and I listened to him with intense pleasure, for he is an admirable talker. Yet, suddenly, I could not help laughing outright. "You are the Frenchest Frenchman I have ever come across," I said to him, "all our qualities and all our faults intact! Don't be offended if I cannot help laughing,

227

hearing you explain so brilliantly that French you certainly are not."

I also saw the French Consul, M. Ponsot, who since made quite a career as Governor of Morocco and later as French Ambassador to Turkey. I might say that he summoned me. He had somehow persuaded himself that a lecture I was to give at the Public Library would be a denunciation of French anti-clericalism, and he wanted to protest. He was a strong, firm, almost stern man. You knew at once that he had principles, and that unlike many Frenchmen he would not be ashamed to express them. But there was also an obstinacy visible in this devoted servant of his country, and he was the kind whom you cannot interrupt, even if you feel you ought to do so. He orated a long time. When there was nothing more to say, and the Consul thought he had done all he could to awaken my torpid patriotism, I said to him: "Sir, you may not have heard an English proverb which says that a man must know his text before he preaches. You have been preaching without knowing your text. My lecture will be exactly the reverse of what you imagine it to be. Anti-clericalism is outmoded in our country, and you have been abroad too long."

Quebec looks and talks exactly like a French town. I loved it, and I loved its memories. There, as well as at Montreal, I was promptly taken prisoner by emissaries from the Archbishop and abducted to a cheerful room at the Palace. The atmosphere of that palace—where the Vicars-General and several canons lived in community—was delightful. The tone was given by one of the Vicars-General, Monseigneur Marois, an eighteenth-century pastel come to life. Nobody could be more exquisitely and traditionally French than he was. His vocabulary, quite naturally classical, was a joy. I made notes from it.

The Archbishop, Cardinal Bégin, was a tall, dignified man with an absolutely childlike nature which one could not help loving. He had evidently never acquired a sense of his own

importance as Canadian Primate, and showed charming instances of his simplicity. I saw him one morning knocking at
the door of the Diocesan Secretaries' office. One of the secretaries, a young priest, appeared, visibly flustered by his work
and exclaimed: "Oh, Your Eminence, we are atrociously busy
and . . ."—"Forgive me," the old Archbishop said, "I ask your
pardon a thousand times. I only wanted the time-table." His
politeness was not trying to give a well-deserved lesson: it was
pure Christian meekness.

A priest in the town, Abbé Nadeau, a graduate of Lille University, showed me extraordinary kindness. He hired a car and
drove me hundreds of miles through the Beauce district till
we found the auxiliary Archbishop, Monseigneur Gauthier. This
Beauce was a green desert with French villages here and there
and many isolated French-looking farms. It delighted me. At
intervals we crossed, on primitive bridges, a river the name of
which I liked to hear repeated, la Rivière Chaudière. All we saw
was romantic and fascinating. We stopped, to eat maple-sugar,
at two or three rectories, incredibly French. One of them belonged to the two priest-brothers of Sir Wilfrid Laurier, the
political orator: it seemed absurd that they should have a
brother who prefixed "Sir" to his name, and they were thousands of miles away from politics. M. Nadeau also asked two
priests who were studying English to come to me for a little
advice. It took a strong effort of imagination to comprehend
that those perfect Frenchmen were subjects of King George the
Fifth. They too, no doubt, had need of the same effort to really
believe it. M. Bourassa's voice was still in my ears: I thought
it sounded queer.

I finished my episcopal visitations in Chicago, where I was
welcomed by Father, now Monsignor, Thomas V. Shannon. He
is a man of extensive and varied erudition, he has a rich and
—probably—once violent soul which he has learned to curb,
and he has a rare capacity for friendship. I enjoyed my stay at
his rectory, and since then we have never lost a chance of meet-

ing. Mgr. Shannon introduced me to Cardinal Mundelein who
promised to take up the collection and did not forget. He also
took me to a convention of the National Welfare Council at
Notre-Dame University. I was much impressed by what I saw
at that convention. It gave me a high idea of the organization
and efficiency of the Council, and as soon as I returned to France
I described its composition and work in an article which *Le
Correspondant* published.

There were five or six Bishops present at that Convention. I
liked their informality: they wore their street clothes all the
time, they smoked incessantly, and when their tobacco began
to burn their tongues they would go to a fountain and quench
their thirst in that democratic manner. One of them, Bishop
Russell, of Charleston, was the image of an English squire. He
listened to the proceedings with an air of debating in himself
should he ride the white mare or the grey, but, when I thought
he seemed at his most aloof, he surprised me by a pertinent
remark expressed in a few terse words.

The two or three days I passed at Notre-Dame convinced me
once more that the Catholic clergy had too many troubles of
their own to be annoyed by other peoples'. One priest, a member of a religious order, thought it necessary to make that
plain in words which I should be sure to understand. Indeed,
he was shockingly boorish, whereupon I replied: "My dear Sir,
you have a French name, but you have not a French manner,
nor have you French manners." I found that this rather severe
punishment was given wider circulation than I thought, or
wished it would have, for that priest did excellent work in some
hospital in the Middle West.

The President of Notre-Dame, dressed exactly like a French
priest—for the college is another French foundation—gave me
excellent practical advice. So did the littérateur of the place,
Father Hudson, the editor of a religious magazine, a man of
refined culture. My conclusion was that my real chances were
not where I had imagined them to be, but with men in my own
line, writers or educators, whether Catholic or not.

The President of Chicago University, at the time, was Mr. Judson. We became acquainted through mutual friends. The Judsons, as long as they lived, showed me every kindness, both in Chicago and in Paris where they re-appeared every year. Mrs. Judson had a box at the opera and was constantly trying to give me good times to "make me forget that horrible job of money-collecting." She was the sunniest person.

I visited Cornell where I knew two or three professors. Mr. Orth who met me at the station one Sunday morning told me that, at that very moment, Dr. Henry van Dyke was preaching in the college chapel: would I like to hear him? I had never seen Henry van Dyke in his clerical capacity, and I had only heard him lecturing at the Sorbonne on literature. We went straight to the chapel where, in fact, Dr. van Dyke held the pulpit, but in his academic robes. He spoke warmly as usual. I had not listened to him two minutes before he alluded to the punishment of sin, adding in an emphatic way: "I *know* this punishment will *not* be eternal." The summer audience he was addressing consisted largely of schoolteachers, no doubt more conservative than undergraduates would have been, even sixteen years ago. At all events, a long ripple of surprise passed over the well-filled benches.

Dr. van Dyke seemed delighted when he found me in the vestry where Mr. Orth and I were waiting for him. He coloured deeply as he always did when he was pleased and, with his arm round my neck, introduced me to President Schurmann. He said all sorts of nice things which he capped with the joyous statement "and Abbé Dimnet has had a book on the *Index Expurgatorius!*" I said: "Yes, and I know of a certain sermon which, ten minutes ago, was put on the Index." President Schurmann seemed vastly amused. He had married off his daughter the day before and his house was strewn with rose-leaves, a custom I had not known before.

I gradually visited most of the colleges for men and women in the East, speaking at many of them. Penn offered me that honour and, two days later, Princeton followed. In Philadelphia

I was introduced to my audience by Miss Agnes Repplier who speaks as tersely as she writes, never condescending to use any rhetorical dodges. As she sat down she whispered to me: "I hope *you* can strike a spark out of them." I forget whether or not I did, but I remember going down from the platform to thank a young woman whose evident and vivacious comprehension had encouraged me through the lecture. A few weeks later this lady wrote to me. She was Katherine Brégy, the author of *The Poets' Chantry* and of many poems, as well as an excellent lecturer. Miss Repplier invited me to her house where I and Brigand, successor of her famous cat, hit it off beautifully, and I was treated to charming attentions punctuated with acidulated epigrams. For, Miss Agnes Repplier is one of the very few people who, writing or talking, seem to be themselves all the time.

Princeton was a great surprise: it is like an English duchess who somehow chooses to show you chiefly the eglantine charm of a country-girl. The aristocratic touch is given by the lyrical, but subtly lyrical, Cleveland Tower. That tower needs no bell.

President Hibben—like most of the Presidents, Provosts, Chancellors or Rectors I visited—had read *France Herself Again,* so that I required no introduction. He was a lovable person. When we became friends, and, after usually staying with Henry van Dyke at Avalon, or with his brother Paul at the Graduate School, I began to be a frequent guest at Prospect, I often heard his wife affectionately calling him a boy. In fact, under his Presbyterian sobriety was hidden all that is attractive in youth. His naturalness was taken for granted by all and unsuspected by himself.

Hibben had done a great deal for France which he loved without saying much. Yet, like most Americans of his day, he had been two years at German universities. He told me a story, the parallel of which I often heard without giving much attention to it, but to which he attached real importance. In the course of the year 1913 the German Ambassador in Washington, Count Bernstorff, called on him: he had approached other Amer-

ican alumni of German universities to ask them for a tribute
to their *Alma Mater* overseas, and he hoped President Hibben
would join them. Mr. Hibben was naturally willing, but he had
other things in hand at the time and begged for a little delay.
At Easter of 1914, meeting the Ambassador in Washington, he
told him that, having got rid of his other business, he was soon
going to send him the few pages he wanted. Bernstorff seemed to
reflect a moment, after which he said: "Oh! don't bother, it's
too late now." President Hibben had no doubt that Bernstorff
knew then that war was decided upon in Berlin. People who
believe that the Kaiser said as much to King Albert eight or
nine months before Easter of 1914 will think that Mr. Hibben
was right. Others will say that the Ambassador meant something entirely different. At all events, the story ought not to
perish.

President Hibben, while going about his study, asked me
questions relative to the North of France. He knew of the destruction of the Lille factories, and what I told him about the
sad plight of the University did not surprise him. He made
things easy for me by unexpectedly saying that American colleges ought to help. I told him about Mr. Brooks' and my plan
for asking the alumni of Harvard and Yale to contribute a trifle,
a dollar each at most. He immediately said that he himself
would send a similar appeal to Princetonians.

I spent some time in Providence which is a smaller Boston
with more primness in the appearance of its houses and people
than in reality. Culture smiles in Providence. I was the guest of
Bishop Perry. He took as much interest in my plans as I did
myself and, twice, invited to his house large companies to hear
me. He also introduced me to the President of Brown and to
many on the faculty. This was my first realization of how much
attractive scholarship can be waiting for discovery in the smaller
colleges of America. They recall the Sorbonne of my student
days which was only beginning to grow and had not forgotten
that, when it was at its most brilliant, it had a faculty of barely

twenty. Besides, Brown was all cordiality and its President,
Mr. Faunce, did all he could to encourage me.

This tour of the Colleges lasted five or six weeks and, although
no positive results came of it for some time, it taught me a
great deal. First of all, it made me familiar with American
psychology: I learned that you can be more simply human with
the people of the United States than with Europeans. It also
taught me the advantages of organization. All the wisdom of
America during those months protested against organization
which was declared to have become an end in itself. But to me
organization, in the point of perfection which I found it had
reached, was a complete novelty and a capital lesson. I could
not say enough about it in my letters to the Archbishop of Cambrai, to Monsignor Ceretti or to the Rector of Lille University.
Associated with it I could see all the time that devotion to ideas
which is often unrecognized in Americans but is one of their
most apparent characteristics all the same. Passion for action
is, on the contrary, constantly harped upon by foreign observers, but is accounted for by the youthfulness of the nation
or by a surplus of animal spirits. To me the sight of it was
positively a cure, for, during most of my life, I had neither seen
it in others nor wished for it in myself. No man who has had
the good fortune to soak in American life, instead of merely
writing down notes about it, will be the same person. He may
surprise, and will occasionally get abused for surprising, but he
will be the gainer, and even his critics will know it.

From the practical angle which was the one constantly forced
upon me this apparently desultory rambling from Bishop's
house to Administration Building was extremely useful, for it
gave publicity to my work. No money was produced, but many
towns came to know of a Frenchman who was as literary as other
Frenchmen, but was engaged in that same business of money-
collecting which in 1919 and 1920 seemed to be the American
vocation.

I was frequently interviewed and, when necessary, I learned

to go straight to newspaper offices and talk to the City Editor. My conversation with him never failed to appear in print the next morning. These interviews gave me chances which sometimes developed before I left the town, but they were often trying. I wanted help while the newspaper men wanted news. As my experience grew I learned strategy. I managed to steer the conversation so that it should converge towards something which was a more or less cleverly disguised appeal. I did not always succeed. Once, in Chicago, after several disappointments, I made up my mind not to be balked again. A reporter was to call on me very early in the morning at one of the more modest hotels in the Loop. I wrote a clear and, as I hoped, a rather interesting synopsis of what I wanted to say to my visitor. When he appeared I was writing letters—my eternal occupation—and I pretended to be too busy to stop. I handed the reporter what I had written and sat down again to my letters. In front of me was a looking-glass in which I could see the man as he read. He visibly liked the possibilities offered by that synopsis. When he got up to go I asked: "Will that do?"—"Yes, perfectly!"—"Well, then, please give a little space to those four lines I have marked in red pencil. It will be a kindness."—"Certainly."

Before the end of the day the interview appeared. It began: "No!" said the Abbé, a white-haired, bright-eyed Frenchman, excitedly pacing the room . . . ." Naturally the story did not contain the least reference to the unfortunate children of Lille.

During my stay in Providence, Bishop Perry took me one morning to the office of the *Journal*. He held the editor, Mr. Rathom, in great esteem, and I soon saw how right he was. Mr. Rathom, although a sick man, gave me an impression of strongly concentrated life and every word he said showed nobility of purpose. When the Bishop told him of my errand in America he bethought himself a moment and said that, as soon as some local drive was got rid of, he would make a public appeal for me in his newspaper. I had never dared to think of such a possibility before, but the natural way in which Mr. Rathom spoke

of it was a flash of light: I was partly a journalist myself, why
not count on other journalists, seeing that I noticed how vital
esprit de corps seemed to be in America? A few days later I
had no difficulty in obtaining a similar promise from my well-
tried friend, Ellery Sedgwick, editor of the *Atlantic Monthly*;
then from Mr. Williams, the editor of the *Transcript*; and—
once more through the kindness of Bishop Perry—from Mr.
Campbell, editor of the *Milwaukee Journal,* and from Mr. More-
house, editor of *The Living Church.* But my greatest piece of
luck came when, during a conversation with Father Wynne, the
well-known Jesuit, the latter said to me: "Catholics in New
York as elsewhere are crushed under the burden of their
churches and schools, but there is in this town one Catholic who
has never said "No" to anybody, and who will certainly help
you. I mean Mr. Robert Cuddihy. His *Literary Digest* has an
extraordinary influence in the United States."

I had seen *The Literary Digest* on many a table, but I had
never read it. I made a study of its formula and soon saw how
difficult it would be to wedge in an appeal in a review of that
kind. However, I wrote an appeal. When it was written I found
I could not sign it. Nor could I expect Mr. Cuddihy to endorse
it as it was. I then submitted it to three friends: Miss Repplier,
Mrs. Margaret Deland and Booth Tarkington who at once expressed their willingness to sign it.

As soon as I heard from them I went to the office of *The Digest*
and Mr. Cuddihy received me. I did not suspect that this publisher of a powerful weekly would be one of my dearest friends,
I mean the kind one has to write to frequently when one cannot
see him. He appeared, a spare man with a fine brow. He had
been working and I could see that his mind at first was not entirely on our conversation. When I told him of what I hoped he
would do, and prepared to show him my appeal, he said slowly:
"Probably you do not know that although I am a Catholic, *The
Literary Digest* is not, by any means, a Catholic periodical."
He went into a few details, all discouraging. "But," I said, "suppose this appeal was signed not by yourself or by me but by

three American writers two of whom are not Catholics, would it not make a difference?—"A tremendous difference, for it would almost be news!" Mr. Cuddihy said this with a joyful emphasis and a brightened face. He had dreaded to have to say "No" and here was a chance to say "Yes." In a few moments, as he went over the appeal and the letters from its three signatories, I saw that his soul was already in this new charitable venture. I have seldom experienced such a transition from anxiety to relief. I have also seldom seen such delight in being helpful.

Like the other publishers or editors who had promised me their help, Mr. Cuddihy needed six or seven weeks before he could print our appeal. All I did through the summer seemed to be, like that, at long range. Neither could I expect immediate response from an appeal which it occurred to me to send to the many American cities which bear French names, from Baton-Rouge, Louisiana, to Vincennes, Indiana. The same from another appeal to Catholic pastors which was rather in the nature of a lottery and might have raised eyebrows at the post-office. I possessed the original, in Cardinal Wiseman's own hand, of a letter which readers of *Fabiola* generally read on the first page of the French translation. How that rare autograph came into the possession of my uncle I do not know, but I found it, several years after his death, in his Bible, and, although only fourteen or fifteen at the time, I divined its value: I had brought it with me to America, thinking I might sell it to some well-wisher of Lille, but I thought a desire for its possession would inevitably inflame the imaginations of the Irish compatriots of Wiseman in America, and so promised it as a possible reward to contributors. It was not without a pang that I parted with that long-cherished letter.

As I spoke of my plan to various priests in New York and Washington, I was surprised to find that they had never thought of Wiseman as an Irishman. His name was too English. Was I

sure that the author of *Fabiola* was Irish? So, the first thing to
do was to write an article on Wiseman as an Irishman which
Mr. Michael Williams helped me to syndicate through the Catholic press. The week after, I wrote another article on the comparative scarcity of Wiseman autographs, as admitted by the
dealers. It was only after this preparation that the appeal to
Catholic pastors was sent all over the country. This appeal was
ultimately a great success, but not until several weeks had
passed and, in the meantime, my money was going fast. I was
so French in my aversion from borrowing that it is only as I
am writing this that I realize how uninformed I was in never
asking the Clews bank for a loan. The five thousand francs given
me by the Rector of Lille University had only produced about
six hundred dollars. I travelled constantly, and although I surprised porters by always refusing the Pullman where there was
a coach, my six hundred dollars soon melted away. Occasional
gifts like the two thousand five hundred francs given me by Mr.
Otto Kahn would keep me afloat a little while, but soon the wolf
reappeared at my door. My correspondence with the Rector of
Lille at the time was far from being sanguine.

I knew, of course, that the business of a mendicant was to
knock at rich people's doors, but how difficult it was! I have
seen people who did it gracefully and successfully, as a matter
of course. To me it was a torture. There was the difficulty, first
of all, to get round the fortifications with which rich people
naturally surround themselves. I soon learned that a coldly
polite letter from a secretary, accompanied by a cheque for
twenty dollars, was the most terrible of those defences because
it definitely closed the business of trying to arrange for a meeting. As I write I recall the names of famous American families:
they might have been in Kamschatka, so inaccessible they were.
Sometimes, on the contrary, I found myself unexpectedly face
to face with the magnates I was campaigning to get at. But this
invariably happened on the social plane. Partly because I may
not be sufficiently averse from it, and partly because my friends
insisted that a good deal of social life was necessary for the suc-

cess of my work, I appeared frequently at house-parties where my hostesses had invited the *Social Register*. Many of those hostesses were really interested and anxiously watched my conversation—a cozy little visit, they called it—with men or women who could have enabled me to go back to Paris, satisfied, the next day. But my interlocutors would invariably speak to me, in English, or especially in French, in the "tone of the world," and no north wind is as parching as that. I had a conscience, though, and I do not remember hesitating once about explaining the wretched business which had brought me to America, but I am also sure that not once could I find in myself the pluck for a definite request.

Exceptional kindness would occasionally help me. I was introduced, in Chicago, to Dr. Stone, of the Presbyterian church, who could, I was told, present me to the McCormick family. Dr. Stone asked me to kneel and pray with him, as, evidently, he did not think the undertaking any too easy. When we rose he said he would speak to Mrs. McCormick, which he did, and five hundred dollars were the result. I also met, through him, a charming Mrs. Stanley McCormick and Mr. Harold McCormick whom I also saw several times in the amusing drawing-room of Miss Kirkland (the "Madame X" of *The Chicago Tribune*). But of the last two I did not dare to ask any assistance.

In Chicago too I succeeded, after diverse outflanking manœuvres, in making the acquaintance of Mr. Martin Ryerson, the famous art-collector, a great Francophile. He showed me a dozen rare pictures by Lépicié, a French artist to-day in great demand but almost his discovery at the time. He saw I was keenly interested and showed me other pictures equally fascinating. In a few moments I felt that my interview with Mr. Ryerson was drifting away from its object, and a sort of panic made me articulate. "Do you know," I said, "that it took me many steps to make your acquaintance? I want assistance for a charity, and here I am, missing what I am sure is a wonderful chance because I *cannot* ask for money." Mr. Ryerson laughed and said he wanted to show me more pictures. We would talk "about less interesting topics afterwards." He gave me five hundred dollars, adding that he himself was collecting money, as well as works of art, all the time. "Everybody does it," he said.

This piece of luck happened when the first three or four summer months during which I did my preparatory work were over and moderate success was at last in sight. But during the early part of my visit hardly any money came. Meanwhile, more and more urgent letters from Lille were received. Finally the Rector wrote that the University Dispensaries were at the end of their resources and found themselves compelled to charge for medicine supplied to outside patients. This heart-rending piece of news completely upset me. I was in Buffalo. Walking down elegant Delaware Avenue, while ruminating how I could possibly send a little money over, it occurred to me that an exceptional effort should be made at once, no matter how painful it might be. Thee-thou-ing myself, as all the French do when they soliloquize, I said: "Just ring the bell of any of these rich mansions. Be something of a Franciscan at last! It is impossible that, if you persevere, help should not be given you." I rang a bell. A suspicious maid appeared on the other side of the screen. What did I want? No, you could not see Mrs. X like that. You should ask for an appointment. I went on to the next door, then to the next. The answer was always: ask for an appointment, or there's nobody in. The look was invariably one of mistrust. After seven or eight unsuccessful attempts I found a tall, thin, delicate gentleman pottering about by himself in the hall of his house. He led me in sorrowfully and I went straight to business. "Everybody comes here for charities," the gentleman moaned, "people think I am rich, but they don't realize that father has all the money and father has to spend a lot, and so there is after all very little money. No doubt people have told you about father." It was a bit pitiful, but it was above all funny, to hear this elderly man endlessly reverting to "father," for he told me much more and his progenitor could not be kept out of a single sissy sentence. No sooner was I out of the driveway than I

burst out laughing, and laughing made me feel the folly of
Franciscanism when one's face has nothing Franciscan about it
to work the least miracle with. I knew a French family in the
town. I went to them, and a glass or two of Beaujolais wine restored me to a sensible perspective and to equanimity.

In the evening I took the boat to Detroit where I arrived
before eight next morning. I went straight to an hotel, and by
nine o'clock I was in the office of *The News,* recently housed in
a magnificent building. I was extremely well received as if my
mortification of the day before had to find its compensation to-
day. I walked back briskly to the hotel and returned to my
room. I was amazed to find that my baggage had been taken
out and a woman had evidently taken possession, for there was
jewelry strewn on the chest of drawers. Not a thing of mine was
to be seen anywhere. I called the maid and complained. Where
had my bags been moved to? Who had given orders? The
woman was very much surprised. She had not heard of anybody being moved. The best was to see the room-clerk down-
stairs. "Number 618?" this self-possessed person said, "no,
nobody has been moved. Mrs. Jones has that room."—"Nonsense!" I said, "here's my key: 618! And I took the room less
than two hours ago."—"You registered, of course?"—"Why!
My name is the last but one on that page." But that name was
not my name; in fact, my name was not on any page. I kept
looking at my key which, of course, was the only proof of my
proprietorship, while the self-possessed clerk looked at me.
Presently he said: "I am sure I see what it is: you registered at
the hotel next door." I had, and the hotels were absolute twins,
but it is evident that if you ask in a certain tone for key 618 it
will be handed out to you and you can help yourself to Mrs.
Jones' jewelry.

A friend in New York had said to me early in August: "If I
were you I should get *them* in their hole. Go straight to Newport." Irreverent as it sounded, this piece of advice was evidently sensible and to Newport I went. A great deal is said about

Newport which leads one to form a completely wrong idea of
the place. I imagined it as a cross between Cannes—the exclusive Cannes of my youth—and gay Nice, with the loose appearance more in evidence than the exclusiveness. As soon as I
arrived I found how completely deluded I had been by inferences. There were no hotels, as hotels would have vulgarized
the town: I went to a small pension run by a Mrs. Walker, a
very good woman. The cottages stood coyly away from Bellevue Avenue or from the Cliff Walk, retiring, shady and as quiet
as English country-places where my lady never has to raise
her voice above a whisper in speaking to the servants. Leading
back to the centre of that dreamy city, Spring Street with its
eighteenth-century houses is all New England elegance and,
when the summer guests have left, actually returns to its original primness. In short, I was immediately conscious that the
first appearance of this capital of American luxury suggests
poetic meditation much more than agitation or intrigue.

How one could "get them" in the inaccessibility of this
silence would have passed my comprehension if I had not had
friends in the stronghold. I knew the dear old Misses Mason,
friends of Margaret Deland and ready any minute to walk back
into her books as into a magical mirror. I had also frequently
seen in Paris Mrs. David King who was a Catholic and at once
proved herself a friend. It was surprising that, no matter how
unlike flighty Newport these ladies were, they entertained a
great deal and their large houses were frequently too small.
Besides, on the more worldly side, I knew Mrs. Henry Clews,
Sr., who was acquainted with everybody as well as admired
by everybody. I also knew Admiral Sims and his wife, a sister
of Margaret Hitchcock's, a Paris friend of mine.

So, in Newport, even more than elsewhere, I had to live my
two lives, one serious, the other apparently frivolous. I gave a
few lectures. One, before the officers of the Naval College,
made me feel stage-fright for the only time in my life, and very
uselessly, for those "students"—as Admiral Sims called his
commodores and captains—were a perfect audience. All morn-

ing and late at night I would write letters to people whom I never could have tried to interest orally. The rest of the day I met ladies and gentlemen whose names the social halo had made so magnetic that they themselves did not seem magnetic at all. Mrs. Clews took me a few times to the "Beach"—the real one, separated from vulgar curiosity by impassable moral as well as physical hedges. It was easy in such a corral to meet three or four dozen magnates between eleven o'clock and luncheon. The ladies were still at that time so completely covered that they seemed dressed up and you caught yourself looking for their jewelry. Conversation went on, on the warm sand, as in a drawing-room. Nobody was very striking but everybody was natural, nice and welcoming. In the afternoon I would be whisked off to the horse-show to admire the performances of Miss Sears, and pretend not to hear the buzzing of conversation around me. For, contrary to the Beach, that horse-show was a veritable school for scandal. Once a lady said to me: "You know the Clews in Paris, I hear. Are they happy?" —"Very happy!"—"Well, now, how do *you* account for that? They are divorced."—"Yes," I said, "they wish they had never had to get divorces."—"*Tout ce que vous voudrez*," the lady insisted, "but they *are* happy."—"Oh," I said, "they have only been married four or five years."—"True," my interlocutor mused in evident relief.

Often before dinner I would walk the whole length of the Cliff Walk, getting my soul back into its proper mendicant condition. At that hour one hardly met anybody and solitude made one over. Once, turning a corner, I found myself face to face with a coloured clergyman, pretty poorly dressed and worried-looking. He looked up at me with an appealing expression as he seized my arm with one hand and my lapel with the other. "Oh! Sir," he said earnestly, "won't you contribute three dollars for the support of my orphans, poor little children who have neither mother nor father?"

"I'm afraid not," I said, "for if I did I would rob my own work which is none too successful either, and I am pretty poor just now."—"What is your work?" he inquired. I told him. "Oh! Sir!" the poor man exclaimed, "your chance is *so* much better than mine is."

The horse-show! The Beach! The talks in elegant drawing-rooms! Not much came from it all, but it was true: my chance was infinitely better than that of this poor Negro confrère. I gave him his three dollars from the fee paid to me by the Naval College—"for goods delivered" as the undiscriminating cheque said—and went on my way, thinking. Real Franciscans did not live Newport life, they carried neither sticks nor wallets, they stopped people in the street and, losing no time in vain parley, they told them what their soul was brimful of, and help came.

I found that somehow sensitive people read my soul pretty well, knowing that the horse-show only showed me tantalizing and unapproachable wealth. I sometimes felt conscious of sympathy which must have been born of commiseration. Money began to come. From Catholics first—the poor Irish servants of my friend, Miss Storer—and I remembered a saying of Mr. James Byrne, as we were discussing my chances: "The poor, of course," he had said, "give enormously." Later, from a Catholic audience for whom I spoke at that heavenly place, the Cenacle Convent. Finally, from many Protestant well-wishers.

The day before I left Newport, Mrs. Arthur Curtiss James, who had throughout been most kindly, gave a big reception for me. Almost four hundred people gathered in her fairy-like place, and it seemed to me as if, at last, I were touching my goal. Everybody was smiling and encouraging. People seemed to think that this last afternoon was going to be different from the others: it should be all kindness and charity. It was easy to address a gathering of people in that mood. I saw these friends deeply moved by the plight of a French town once so prosperous as poor Lille had been. If the ivory-box—a masterpiece of Chinese art—which Mrs. James kept near at hand, had been passed round at once I have no doubt that results would have exceeded expectations. But the collection was postponed till after refreshments were served, and champagne promptly re-

stored people to their usual horse-show state of mind. Not much
more than four hundred dollars were found in the ivory-box,
but Mrs. James rounded that sum in her own generous way.
Once more it was brought home to me that I ought not to count
much on gifts from individuals. The public appeals which I endeavoured to make urgent by innumerable letters were my real
chance.

My course of Lowell Lectures lasted from October 14th, 1919,
till November 7th. I arrived in Boston on October 12th and,
next morning, I moved on to Cambridge, where my friend Bliss
Perry was kindly offering me hospitality. By noon I was settled
in his house in Clement Circle.

The house was a scholar's home, tidy, orderly and infinitely
quiet. Perry was writing a book; his wife and his daughter
Margaret went about briskly but noiselessly, as professors'
women do.

Clement Circle is only a sort of driveway to the few houses
bordering it, not a real thoroughfare. So, hardly a sound came
from outside except the devotional angelus from St. Paul's
Catholic church in the next block. All round, as soon as you
crossed Huron Avenue, stretched in baffling similarity the shady
streets where only the squirrels never seem to lose their way.
Luckily one always manages to emerge on Brattle which, although quite a street, is as sleepy and poetic as the rest. Mere
Longfellow poetry, no doubt, the poetry of the copper beech,
of sere leaves and of white snow-balls, but poetry still alive,
alive and penetrating. Here and there the historic landmarks
of the place: Professor Royce's house, Professor James' house
(this is the person who, to us French people, will always be just
William James), Professor Santayana's house. Unitarian ladies
with pure blue eyes behind their spectacles show them to you
through the drawing-room window before pouring your tea for
you. Cambridge is a professors' community. I was invited two
or three times to undergraduates' clubs, but I used to marvel at

the scarcity of young men on the Yard, as tourists in Paris now marvel at the absence of *étudiants* from the Boulevard St. Michel.

Boston, to me, was mostly Beacon Hill. What is the fascination of that restricted, narrow chequered neighbourhood with its streets all akin and not a single spot which you can call particularly arresting? What makes plain Walnut and tiny Willow Street lovable? Bulfinch, who built the best houses, was a poet, certainly, but a poet like Emily Dickinson. He needs the collaboration of the visitor, and his façades require a setting. Elsewhere his austere grace would hardly strike a responsive chord. What we really feel here is what is felt in the Faubourg St. Germain in Paris, or in the Temple, in London, viz., the survival of a collective state of mind. America began here quite as much as it began in Philadelphia.

The Common, a step away, is too large for Beacon Street and, on sunny days, it is too park-like. Commonwealth Avenue, which pretends to be the daughter of Beacon Street, has much too grand a sweep for Charles or Brimmer Street. Urbanism has been at work there, not Unitarianism. As for the enormous modern Boston which beats around those few squares, and which real Boston only mentions with a smile, because it regards it as inexplicably foreign, it has always frightened rather than attracted me. There is a convincing look of being in earnest in the busy streets leading from the South Station to the Common, but how much they would lose if the Tavern Club and the *Transcript* office were not there, both of them full of subtle colour in drab surroundings! Boston harbour is too discouragingly vast not to be chilling, and the section in its vicinity is dourer than even the East India Docks quarter in London. Boston begins at the Charles River and ends where the hill expires near that perfection of a place of rest, the Granary graveyard.

I had good friends in Boston and I never understood what people meant by Boston coldness. Boston is admittedly self-sufficient (I once saw two Boston girls of nearly twenty arriving for the first time in New York and showing no sign of being flurried by the fact) but Boston is not cold. The Tavern Club is full of men who spread around them the atmosphere of 1820, but they are delightful men. Genial was the table of Mr. Rhodes, the historian, although I met there a Tory lady who seemed perfectly sincere in regretting the Revolution. Genial also was the home of Mr. Mark A. De Wolfe Howe. As for the exquisite little place in Willow Street where James Ernest King and his wife welcomed me so often it was warm enough to make me forget that I too had a home.

In Cambridge I met many interesting colleagues of Bliss Perry's, and two or three of the rare autochtonous families, but there was no time for social affairs. My Lille work went on as usual, with seldom less than thirty letters a day, all written in long hand, while my Lowell lectures were a heavy responsibility. I had full notes for those lectures entitled "Has France gained anything by the War?" but the skeletons from which I gave them were never ready till almost the time of delivery. I was compelled to concentrate and conserve more than I had ever done before. I seemed to be carrying the nucleus of each lecture as if it lay in delicate crystal and I was trying to save it from the shocks of over-work, worry or social agitation. I remember receiving as in a dream a lecture-agent who came proposing an attractive contract. I told him, in perfect honesty, that I was not a lecturer, at all events I was one only accidentally. I was collecting money for a charity. He stared at me in astonishment.

I had only been two days in Cambridge when I gave my first lecture in Boylston Hall. I was so full of my material that I hardly thought of the lecture itself. Through a lack of foresight, of which I have seldom been guilty since, I had not prepared my beginning, and thought I should just plunge *in medias res*. The secretary of the Lowell Institute was the late Professor Sedgwick who, as he should, thought the world of the Lowell foundation. He had been waiting for me in some agitation, and he proceeded to do all he could, in a gentle way, to agitate me too. The audience, he said, was larger, much larger than usual, because, as a rule, Lowell lectures were too technical to be popular. There were about six hundred people. Hard to please, they would be, those six hundred. Boston, you know. President Lowell was there too. In his box. He counted on an exceptionally good lecture. Unfortunately the hall was a very bad hall to speak in. After this preparation Professor Sedgwick suddenly changed his tone. He became reassuring, but much as mother reassures her little boy before the dentist's assistant opens the door. It would be all right, oh! it would be all right! The clock struck five and Professor Sedgwick pushed me through the dentist's door with the gentle force of the inevitable.

I was still without a beginning which could hardly have been born of my conversation with Mr. Sedgwick. As I walked from the door to the desk I suddenly remembered my schoolboy's vague hopes of seeing America, and the beginning I had been praying for appeared. "You remember," I said, "the two Venetian ambassadors who, after being shown through Versailles, were asked by Louis the Fourteenth what surprised them the most in the palace. 'To see ourselves in it,' one of them answered. Many years ago, in a cathedral-school in the North of France, a little boy would sometimes take advantage of a free hour to read Washington Irving's *The Sketch Book* which he loved; then he would open his atlas and, for a long time, he would pore over the map of the vast North American continent with its gigantic towns, its lakes and deserts, wondering: shall I ever see that faraway land? shall I ever really speak the language spoken there? The boy was doubtful, of course, but he had a faith in his future. Here he is, giving the Lowell lectures."

The eight lectures were a success. Not only my audience remained faithful to me to the end, but I could see that the thesis underlying the course seemed convincing to them: what France had gained by the war was less territory than the esteem of the world and the restoration of her own sense of dignity. What Sedan had lost her in 1870 Verdun had regained in 1916. Nobody would ever say now that a country rising in self-defence, as France had done, was a decadent country. All that France needed was a Constitution better suited to the national momentum produced by victory. Failing this the French would lapse from a sense of dignity to mere collective vanity and the pre-war opinion of the world concerning them would be revived.

Measuring the distance between what I hoped for in 1919 and what actually exists, I am sorry to say that the reform I was hoping for has not yet come. Partly on account of their lack of political initiative, partly because the world foolishly accused them of Imperialist ambitions braced by militarism, the French have left their irresponsible democracy where it was; their Republican constitution remains the work of Monarchists who did not believe in a Republic. The result has been what it is even in England where the democratic system is better rooted: a woeful lack of men, and wavering policies. France has not had the politics of her new strength, and the consequences of that deficiency in practical logic may be fatal to her. For, close by, are totalitarian states rapidly developing forces far superior to her own and growing every day more conscious of that superiority.

But in 1919 I was full of the hope that France would not shrink from her responsibilities and my audience shared the same hope. They showed it in a touching way at the end of my last lecture. I seldom experienced so much sympathy. Among the people who expressed it the most warmly was a woman who, constantly sitting in the same place, had gradually become a familiar figure to me. She had not been an encouraging listener. Bending slightly forward she would follow what I said with what seemed to me a decidedly hostile attention. For, when they are attentive men often scowl but women smile. The lady in question never smiled and I had finally suspected her of being either violently anti-French or narrowly conservative and trying to catch me in some unguarded assertion. I was completely mistaken: this lady had been friendly from the first, only her method of listening was not the usual one.

The lectures were reported for *The Transcript* by a young

journalist, the same James Ernest King of whom I spoke above. He was a little like Plato and I felt like saying, as Socrates did, "What beautiful things this young man imagines I am saying!" But nobody could read one's thoughts for oneself as accurately as Mr. King did mine, and I have always felt deeply grateful for his comprehension. Many of the invitations to lecture which followed my Lowell course came from readers of his articles.

IV

As I have said, my work for Lille was not interrupted by the lectures. My hearers knew of it. Most of those who flocked to the platform after my parting speech came with an envelope, large or small. But, even before that, the seeds I had many times been sowing in tears began to germinate. Mr. Edwin F. Greene of Chestnut Hill, whom I had approached like many other charitable Bostonians, asked me to lunch with half a dozen friends. They were businessmen who, after a few questions, told me that their little group was going to contribute a thousand dollars. Those men were quiet and undemonstrative. How grateful I was to them! Almost simultaneously the appeals published in *The Atlantic, The Transcript,* the *Providence Journal* and the *Harvard Alumni Bulletin* edited by Mr. M. A. De Wolfe Howe began to produce results. Money came in a steady flow, and Margaret Perry had to help me to read the letters accompanying it. I could not reply to every one. Yet, many were deeply touching. One, from a poor Irishwoman, a parishioner of the French Church in Isabella Street, in Boston, showed the heroism of charity. Many Harvard undergraduates also contributed and wrote to me. One of those young men joined to his own offering "five dollars from Mr. Poor who lives next door." Was it because of his name, or because of something quaint in the mention that he lived next door and yet was mistered by his neighbour, I was, and still am, particularly grateful to Mr. Poor. When I returned to Europe I sent several hundreds of those letters to Lille University, where they are kept, and all that a Catholic institution can do to show gratitude my Lille friends did. But it was inexpressibly painful to me not to be able to write to each one of my contributors individually. If any of them happen to read this book let them know that their charity not only moved me, but attached me forever to their country, the most humane country in the world. Since then I have had many opportunities to express this preference by word of mouth or in print. I might not have done so with the conviction I still feel had it not been

251

for their brotherliness. I might also not have repeated so indefatigably to friends far and near that no honest appeal should
ever be ignored, and that the poor songster in the Paris courtyards who humbly holds out his cap when he has finished his
ditty cannot be turned out bitter at heart, and that no matter
how little we give we should always give something. I know
that I was not so sure of all this before I applied in America for
assistance to the people of a town whose name was not known
to one giver in twenty.

In New York, where I returned after some lecturing in the
Middle West, I also found my affairs progressing satisfactorily.
There was a printers' strike at the *Literary Digest* office, but
Mr. Cuddihy faced it cheerfully as he does everything. He is a
man of incredibly resourceful imagination. If the *Digest* could
not be set up it should be typed and photographed and the result
would be the same. Soon the appeal signed by Booth Tarkington, Miss Repplier and Mrs. Deland appeared in one of those
photographed editions, and the response to it was immediate.
The first contribution came from Booth Tarkington himself who
"thought a man should answer his own appeal." Thousands of
small contributions came from people who were far from affluent, but big sums were not rare. A very generous Mr. R. L. Ireland, a citizen of Cleveland, sent a thousand dollars with the
sort of gruff letter which kind people, too constantly pestered
by mendicants, will occasionally write. Mr. Ireland said he was
under no illusions: most of the money he was sending would go
to office expenditure, perhaps to joy-rides, but it did not matter,
he was glad to do something for those poor Lille people. It was
a joy to be able to answer at once that every cent of that splendid
contribution would be on its way to Lille within a week. The
whole Lille Fund office was in my breast-pocket, and the only
secretaries I ever employed were lent me by friends for an hour
or two on exceptional occasions. I might have added details on
the extremely economical manner in which, between visits at
luxurious houses, I travelled and lived, for I played the game

honourably enough to make some of my friends quite impatient
at what they called my musty French notions.

The *Digest* appeal produced over ten thousand dollars. The
Wiseman letter collection came near to five thousand. So did
Mr. James Byrne's appeal to his Catholic friends, not including
two thousand five hundred dollars which came out, not of his
pocket, but of his bank, for he actually sold securities to give
me that royal contribution. It can be hideously true, but it can
also be deliciously true that nothing succeeds like success.
During November, 1919, some editors voluntarily republished
my appeal as they found it in other periodicals, and offers of
assistance were numerous. I was then the guest of friends for
whom I have so much affection that I shall not be able to express
it adequately. A Chicago friend of mine, Mrs. Bertha Holbrook
Clarke, had secured for me an engagement to speak at the
Isham House which was greatly useful to my work, for it was
the cause of my introduction to that queen of Chicago charities,
the late Mrs. Russell Tyson. As I was preparing to leave Isham
House, after my talk, I was confronted by a pretty but serious
face on which I read absolute sincerity. "When you are in New
York," the lady said, "please call on us, I want to do all I can."
She added Hotel Gotham to her card on which I read: "Mrs.
Charles Dyer Norton."

At the end of my first lecture in New York, Mrs. Norton was
once more waiting for me at the door. "My husband wants you
to stay with us at the Gotham, please say you will." In two or
three days I called. Mrs. Norton was out, but her husband was
at home. In fact, he was in bed, with a slight attack of the ear-
trouble which in a few years was to be fatal to him. I found such
a youthful-looking man that he was puzzling. He did not seem
to be thirty, with jet black hair and magnificent eyes. We talked,
for as long as he was not standing up he felt no pain. His disposition was as youthful as his looks. A lot that I said to him
seemed to amuse him vastly, sometimes because it sounded un-
practical, sometimes because it sounded quite shrewd and already American, and he thought I had no business to learn the

tricks so fast. The rapid working of his brain, the nimbleness of his wit, his directness, his boyish kindness, as well as a constantly perceptible background of culture, made him irresistible. A few allusions to friends whose names everybody knew, or to some of his interests—the city-planning of New York, the Metropolitan Museum, the American Academy in Rome—showed me at once that he was not merely the President of the First Security Company as I had been told he was. He said nothing of his political affiliations and it was only later that I heard he had been in the Taft administration. He spoke of his children: Garry was at Harvard, Lucia was at Smith where her mother had been, little Kim was still at Groton. I should like them all and they would like me, for I was going to move in at once. No delay was necessary: this hotel-apartment was big. I was puzzled by the name Garry. Well, it stood for Garrison: Mrs. Norton was a grand-daughter of the abolitionist. Kim was named after McKim the architect, an uncle. Lucia was named after herself, it was enough. I saw she was the apple of his eye.

In a day or two the Nortons' home was my home and it has remained my New York home ever since, although I also had many a happy visit with my Catholic friends, Mr. and Mrs. Cuddihy. Garry and Kim are men now, the kind of idealistic Americans who prefer their principles to their interest. They only read good books and can criticize even those. Lucia has become Mrs. Alan Valentine. She is an influential person, not merely because of her husband's position as one of the youngest college presidents in America, but because, as her father said, she is Lucia and has a gift. Their mother is a unique friend. She spends her life doing good in every direction, but she has a quick and sudden wit which never comes out of its scabbard unnecessarily or ineffectively.

Charles D. Norton knew everybody worth knowing in New York. He introduced me to many of his friends. I remember a luncheon at the Bankers' Club with three wheat magnates whose names are so well known that it is superfluous to mention them.

I was surprised by the unprofessional tone of the conversation. At the same time I could not help noticing that the characteristics which these gentlemen exhibited, one after the other, were absurdly similar to those I had observed many times in the businessmen of the Lille region. As they spoke I felt continually tempted to translate what they said into thee-thou French of the unpretentious millionaire variety.

Chesterton was then in New York, with his wife, on their first visit. Mr. Norton asked me to invite him to dinner at the India House. Chesterton was in a good vein and regaled us with many amusing verbal discoveries. He alluded to Charlotte Gilman Stetson Perkins but fumbled for her middle name and we had to help him. "She does puzzle one," he said, "with the names of those husbands she stratifies."

Two or three days later I took him and his wife down town. He had told me that Mrs. Chesterton did not like New York. She could not see what people found to admire there. This was long before the Empire State Building disarmed the criticisms of even the most antagonistic visitors. But the Woolworth Building was in its novelty and its florid decoration still seemed in good taste. I showed it to them and both saw its good points. Mrs. Chesterton wished to know the purpose of such a gigantic structure. I explained. I said that the top floors were used by Fordham University, and the very highest of all was the office of a Canadian Jesuit whom I had visited in his eyrie, Père Fortier. Chesterton's big body shook with laughter at the idea that a Jesuit was dominating the whole of New York. His wife did not join in the laughter. She was not to become a Catholic for many more years, but she did not approve of hilarity at the expense of anything religious.

Mrs. Chesterton went back to her hotel, and I then took her husband down to a barber shop in the basement. There was another phenomenon which kept Chesterton ravished and speechless. Stretched out full-length in the operating chair was the big body of, I imagined, some Hercules from a mining-camp in the West. The colossal frame was expensively clad in rich

English material; the strong legs were encased in dainty lavender socks. The shoe-shiner was lovingly at work on the shoes, a manicure was busy beautifying the formidable hands, while some mummifying process completely hid the face in a steaming napkin. "What on earth are they doing to him?" Chesterton asked. I knew about cuticle-lifting and could explain, but Chesterton would go on repeating: "Well! but why on earth . . . ?" I had to extemporize, in minute details, the giant's whole story and the life he must be leading at his camp. "What seems to you the last effort of effeminacy," I said, "is only one more effort of hard-earned money to get spent." As I spoke the bandage was removed and the face appeared, of an ashen colour which gradually heightened to purplish: it was a thoroughly good fellow's grinning face.

Every day I went over the long list of the many people I was to see in New York now that the Devastated Church Drive was over. In time I called on the poet-clergyman I had met at the Harvard Commencement, Dr. Grant. I found him in the parish-house of his church on Fifth Avenue and Eleventh Street. I had a most pleasant chat with him at the end of which he said: "My congregation is your audience, my pulpit is your platform; come the Sunday after next, say what you please and ask for what you will."

The codification of Canon Law had only been completed towards the end of the war, and I had no idea that the new canons forbade a Catholic clergyman to speak in a Protestant church, for, in many of our Alsatian villages, Catholics and non-Catholics use the same church as they might use the lounge of the same boat. But I had known all my life that no Catholic is allowed to take part in non-Catholic worship. Mr. Grant was aware of this too, and obviated the difficulty by saying that I could speak either before or after his service. The man made the same excellent impression upon me that I had received in Cambridge. I thanked him most heartily.

At night, C. D., as his friends called Charles D. Norton, asked me as usual how I had spent the day. I took out my note-book and went over the items. When it came to my interview with Dr. Grant C. D. put up his eyebrows and said: "Do I understand that you are going to speak in that church?"—"Yes, certainly, after the regular service." C. D. leant back in his chair, convulsed with laughter. "You've never heard of Percy Stickney Grant?" he finally asked.—"Just at Harvard, where he read a poem."—"Well, the long and the short of it is that you are trying to get rich people's money, and rich people hate Dr. Grant because he allows the wildest people, bolsheviks and such, to speak in his church. Your friend, Bishop Manning, dreads him like the plague. So do all sensible people, I think. You realize I am catching you on the brink of an abyss?"

The next day I returned to Eleventh Street. Dr. Grant was again in the parish-house. But I went through several rooms in it without finding him. After a time I gave it up and went to the Brevoort, my former hotel, where I wrote Dr. Grant a letter which I had to make sincere and plain, but not tactless enough to hurt a man who had shown me nothing but kindness. I said I had only known him as a poet; I had only heard the day before that he was an advanced thinker and, as I had been accused myself of being a Liberal, I was afraid the combination of our tendencies might be injurious to the cause of the poor people in whom he had seemed interested. So, I could only thank him for his suggestion which it would be wiser not to accept.

This note I posted in a mail-box just outside the Brevoort, one short New York block from Dr. Grant's rectory. I could have delivered it at his door myself, but he might have been back and I thought a written explanation would be better than difficult conversation. Well, that note never reached its destination. The day before the Sunday when Dr. Grant had said I could speak in his church, returning to the Gotham rather late for dinner, I found a special delivery message in which Dr. Grant said he would be pleased to send his car for me the next morning.

I must have turned pale with annoyance. I went to the telephone and explained. The person who took the message, a woman with a beautifully cultivated voice, said: "Oh, what a bitter disappointment!" I could have wished myself a hundred leagues away. I explained more and expressed my mortification, but the voice repeated: "Oh! but he will be sorry! What a disappointment!"

I re-wrote at once the letter which the post-office had so deplorably neglected and sent it by one of the pages. An answer came in a few days. I have kept it. It was most cheerful. It said, in part: "My liberalism is of such a meagre and ineffective sort that I am ashamed of it and of anybody who thinks you could be hurt in your appeal to Americans by any association with the Church of the Ascension. Your own Napoleon said he was surprised at the lack of inventiveness in politics. I am surprised at the lack of inventiveness in life, and especially in religion. We are a lot of 'copy-cats' as children call stupid imitators. Before I die I hope I shall deserve the name of 'an advanced thinker,' for at any rate I intend to qualify."

Shortly afterwards Dr. Grant sent me two volumes of his poems, many of which are extremely fine, with a classical ring to them. I was sorry when he died, and so were the Nortons though they never went to his church. C. D. often stopped at Grace Church on his way back from his office. He preferred his Anglicanism straight, and he was a constant reader of *The Imitation of Christ*.

To Mrs. Norton I owed the advice of a woman whose life was spent helping causes, as well as many introductions to people in her circle. One of these was Mrs. Dwight Morrow whose husband, also a frequent caller, had been at Amherst with C. D. The two men were great chums and I loved to see them together, but Mr. Morrow, a very shy man, could never be drawn out. Mrs. Norton also introduced me to a wonderfully kind, intelligent and efficient person, Mrs. Henry Loomis, sister of Dr. Stimson. I never knew anybody who could do good with such an unprofessional absence of effort and yet with such professional infallibility. She had the happiest nature and beamed her way through every difficulty. In a few weeks she began to drop hints about "some estate" she had heard of in Massachusetts and, to my boundless surprise and joy, she once came back from Boston with ten thousand dollars, from the same mysterious estate, which she handed to me. Mrs. Loomis was a frequent visitor to France. She had been thoroughly adopted by the French aristocracy. She, in her turn, appreciated what a nation owes to the preservation of individuals refined by century-old traditions, but her pleasure in their society never blinded her to the foibles of their class.

The last ten or twelve weeks of this, my first long visit, were divided between California and the East.

I started for Los Angeles from Chicago on December 28th, 1919. By that time I felt I began to know my various jobs as traveller, lecturer and money-collector, but, as professionalism crept into my life, it crowded out much of the zest I had found in trying to forget myself in the interest of my work, and fatigue came. I was especially tired of the endless letter-writing which kept me busy till late into almost every night. Add that I had had no vacation for fifteen months. When I settled for three days in the El Paso train I felt as if I did not want to do any more work and I began to think that, as some American friends of mine recommended, I would spend in bed my first week in Los Angeles.

To Europeans one of the greatest surprises in America is the slowness of most trains. Especially slow are the trains going to the west coast which still seem to remember the days when they were semi-experimental affairs crossing deserts on logs which did not dare to call themselves sleepers. But the very deliberation of those trains is restful, and the most strenuous Americans become lazy in them. In a few hours I admitted delightedly their somnolent influence.

But the trip west is also a wonderful experience. The vastness of America which would suffice to act on anybody's psychology is not monotonous like the immensity of Russia. There

is a thrill in passing from the soft hazy light of the East to the
sudden transparency of the atmosphere the moment you cross
the Missouri. Everything seems to become lighter and, as you
grow conscious of the phenomenon, you also know that your
cares, mental or moral, weigh less heavily on your soul. Our
ancient liturgies, like the Gospel of John—the Gospel of Greek
Ephesus,—are illuminated by the constant recurrence of the
talismanic word LUX, the Light. The Christian Greeks felt
what we all feel when the monotony of the western plains becomes transfigured by the brilliance of the western sky.

As you move west you also rise, and the higher you climb
the brighter burns your sun in the subtle atmosphere. Soon you
feel disoriented, far away, and the Spanish names of the places
you pass add to the sensation of remoteness. Bravo, Amarillo,
Santa Rosa are the names that belong there. They remind you
of the stony Castilian plateaus and introduce you quite naturally to what somehow you had never quite believed in, the
American desert. For many hours the desert is only sandy or
rocky emptiness and there is unspeakable sadness in the plain-
tive call of little vendors at the stations: "Desert holly! Desert
holly!" But the morning of the third day is unforgettable. What
good angel woke me up at early dawn to the scene which alone
would be worth the long trip? The noble hills peopled, but not
crowded, with those high-priests of the desert, the giant cacti.
The pagan sanctity of their assembly is enhanced by a sky the
celestial peach and orange of which no words can ever describe,
for it opens up a spiritual rather than a material world; it is
not a vision, it is a revelation. He who has had it will never be
the same man again.

El Paso, with its look of a frontier town, its soldiers, its long
files of mules, its airplanes patrolling the border; Yuma where
it never rains; Indio where the softness of California begins
cannot efface that morning impression. Yet, as your journey
draws to an end and the deep green orange-orchards between
the endless vineyards begin to appear, you become conscious of
what California has always given travellers, viz., the delicious

certainty that you are really arrived, a sensation I seldom had elsewhere.

It was six o'clock of December 31st when I landed at Los Angeles. The city was packed with people who felt rich, and it took me over two hours to find a bleak room at an hotel which visitors rightly seemed to avoid. At midnight I heard for the first time the chorus of factory sirens greeting the American New Year.

January first, 1920, at Los Angeles, was a day of Paradise and instead of staying in bed I was in the streets before eight o'clock. In less than a quarter of an hour I was on the old Plaza, Spanish and quaint. A Spanish wedding, all dark eyes and challenging smiles, filled the plain mission-church with such happy irreverence that it was not shocking. Outside, everything spoke of pleasure and wealth. I went from flowery hotel to flowery hotel; everywhere the same sign "No vacancies" warned me off. I finally made up my mind to take the one remaining room at the Baldy View Apartments, a simple place near the end of Grand Avenue. That room was close to my proprietors' private apartments, and I overheard every word they said. Separated from France by a continent and an ocean, the wife somehow was anti-French, the husband the contrary. He had been a Catholic once. He was a warm-hearted fellow with an innate gentlemanliness which even occasional "indulgence" did not destroy. Every time he got really bad he was very penitent and spoke eloquently of taking the pledge, but his wife was afraid he might pine away if he did and would not let him. During a few years I followed the history of that couple. George Moore had written it, word for word, twenty odd years earlier in *Esther Waters*: the man died and the wife had to go into domestic service.

Los Angeles, in 1920, was immense though unfinished. Where the Italian whiteness of its suburbs now gives an inhabited look to its happy hills, were ugly oil-fields or palm-tree avenues awaiting builders. The plans for the city were evidently gigantic

but perhaps they would remain mere dreams. I had a luncheon
engagement that first day with a dear old friend wintering at
Pasadena. I was told that the West Pasadena trolley would set
me down in sight of the hotel. It did. Two people assured me
that I would see the hotel on the hill as soon as I turned the
corner. There, in fact, stood the hotel. I was a little late and
hurried up. A page took my card and disappeared with it. He
never returned till a quarter past one when he gave me back my
card with the announcement that there was no such person as
Mrs. Joline at the hotel. I ran back to the street where a providential Japanese gave me a lift in his jitney down to a cross-
roads full of tramcars going in every direction. Nobody could
tell me where the hotel was, or what car I should take. I was
getting fretful when a tall elderly man with long white locks
came up to me with a smile and, to my astonishment, spoke a
Latin sentence:

"*Omnes isti sunt viarum ignorantes et non pauci stupidi.*
(These people never know the way to anywhere and many are
fools.)"

"*Patienti dicis!* (I know it and suffer from it.) *Hispanus es?*
(You are Spanish?)"

"*Nequaquam! hibernus sum.* (No indeed. I am Irish.)"

"*Qui fit ut sermo tuus auribus meis gallicis sonat familiaris?*
(How is it that your Latin sounds familiar to my French ears?)"

"*Et ego in ludo Gallorum studui.* (I was at school in France.)"

"*In quibus Galliae partibus?* (In what part of France?)"

"*Cameraci.* (At Cambrai.)"

So this man had been educated in my own school, had been
there ten or twelve years before I entered and knew all my
teachers! His name was Dayton. As he said so to me my trolley-
car came up and I hastened to where a very hungry and cross
old lady would be sure to scold me for being late.

I very nearly missed another appointment at an elegant school
the same afternoon. Even in 1920, nobody walked, because
everybody drove, in Los Angeles. As usual the roads were
scantily marked and the house-numbers played their game of

hide-and-seek away from the street-entrance to put off enquiries. Moreover there was nobody to enquire of in those immense avenues. Unfamiliar stars were beginning to wink mockingly at me over the sierra when another Japanese, a little gardener, left his hose to direct me in recently-acquired English. The school was the last house in that part of the world. Just beyond it began the geometry of an oil-field with the tock-tock of its automatic wells.

My work was not difficult in Los Angeles. Bishop Cantwell promised me without the least demur to take up the collection; a Frenchman, M. Brunswig, introduced me to his many friends, and a fortunate circumstance put me in touch, almost from the first, with a group of people who took as much interest in my work as they did in their own. I had met in Boston two charming Misses Metcalfe who lived in Los Angeles and gave me a card to one of their friends there. This lady, Miss Katharine Douglas, was a young woman of such ability that you felt as if the magnetism which she also possessed were superfluous to ensure her success. She was engaged in relief work for the Near East and everybody recognized and admired her capacity. Almost without knowing how I found myself one of the extremely congenial group who were associated in her work. The leader was a man of remarkable driving power, Judge H. N. Wells. I shall always be grateful to Judge Wells for the generosity with which he not only advised me in every way, but prevailed upon another gentleman on the bench, Judge Craig, to make a public appeal for Lille University. As usual I got interviewed by reporters, I wrote articles in the local newspapers, I called on scores of people and wrote to hundreds, but I found everything infinitely smoother in the gay atmosphere of Los Angeles than I had anywhere else. Pretty soon I experienced a queer feeling: the drudgery of money-collecting which had been a trial was quickly turning into a routine. The small amount of psychology or diplomacy necessary to open the hearts and purses of people became alarmingly natural. For diplomacy is not Christian, it belongs to serpents rather than to doves, and psychology procures such an easy acquisition of power that one has no cause to be proud of it. I almost regretted the days when I had to toil a great deal for very small results. The whole band of us mendicants frequently lunched together at The Roma or The Angelus, and those parties were so light-hearted that they put me in mind of the *Jolly Beggars*. I hated the unkind thought when at two o'clock sharp I saw everybody bravely going back to their offices, but it would pursue me, and I remember thinking a little uneasily of Cardinal Mercier who was touring the country on exactly the same errand as mine and was being fêted everywhere.

In sixteen or seventeen days Judge Wells' and Judge Craig's assistance added six thousand dollars to the sixty-eight thousand I had already sent over. Just then a cable from the Rector of Lille University informed me that our Archbishop, in consideration of my literary work in the past and of my present charitable efforts, had made me a Canon of Cambrai Cathedral. I remembered the hoary gentlemen whom in my school-days I saw slowly moving in ermine and scarlet about the cathedral, and a vivid sense of the brevity of life came over me. *Et ego.* . . . Then I could not help smiling. Most canons I had met did not know exactly what they had been canonized for; I not only knew what for, I knew for how much.

San Francisco was a delightful experience. It is one of the few American cities where one actually feels inclined to dream, listening to the musical purring of the wire cables endlessly rolling under the tracks on the steep avenues. There are flowers everywhere and the people are courteous and smiling. No city can show pleasanter society. Nowhere have I met with so many people who knew the niceties of the French as well as those of the English language, and regarded Paris as their own city.

I went to the Rectory of the French Church. An old man of the name of Gobeaux, half sacristan, half doorman, opened the door for me. He had not uttered twenty words before I told him that most undoubtedly, he came from some place less than ten kilometers away from my native Trélon. "Yes," he said, without showing the least interest in my divining powers, "Yes, I left Baives in 1892 and since then. . . ." A long tale of woes in the wake of an unlucky French count followed.

I made the acquaintance of a delightful French family, the de Latours, and through them of many people whom I shall always remember with pleasure: the de Guignés, the Parrotts, Mr. Richard Tobin, Mrs. Lord, the McEnernys, Mrs. Hill and many others. I lectured in nine or ten places including Berkeley and Stanford. Stanford, with its innumerable arches and palm-planted quadrangles, seen for the first time by moonlight, was a magical vision. My friends, the Guérards, were not there as yet, but the President gave me a delightful welcome. So did the charming Barrows at Berkeley. Twice I met my dear New York Cuddihys, by mere chance, as if Providence wanted to make it clear to me that here were real friends, the kind it would be un-forgivable to waste. I had had a little private controversy with Mademoiselle Rebecca Godchaux, a woman of great culture. I went to see her to make up matters and found a Jewish family who, though born in America, were as Parisian as if they had never left France. Mlle. Godchaux' brother introduced me to Mayor Rolph who insisted on my being present, seated at his right, at one of the meetings of the supervisors, and finally in-vited me to address that rather intimidating body. The mayor reassured me by whispering about two or three of them, the most eloquent ones, that they were mere politicians and even shady characters. In the course of that meeting a wire was handed to the mayor. He rose, bent forward and, in a whisper more elo-quent than a long speech, broke the deplorable news to the as-sembly; the results of the census were now known, and Los Ange-les beat San Francisco by 5,600!

I went back to Washington and New York via New Orleans which I still found so French that I have never become ac-customed to the English translation of its name. A couple, quar-relling over a car, were the first people I heard speaking in

French. After passing them I retraced my steps and said to them:
"If you knew the harmony which your French is to my ears you
would not use it to fight." They laughed.

In Washington I met, at the house of Mr. David Jayne Hill,
Blasco Ibañez who was just finishing a long tour of the United
States. He was tired and half sick and, like M. Duhamel, found
fault with everything. Sensitive to a degree, he had been overwhelmed by the immensity of America and retained a frightened
look. He showed touching sympathy with American husbands.
"Oh! les pauvres! les pauvres!" he repeated.

Senator Lodge invited me to lunch at the Capitol House and
to dinner at his own house. This irreconcilable enemy of President Wilson was gentle and soft-spoken. He showed us a letter
written to him forty years before by the former President, sub-
mitting an article for a review which Mr. Lodge edited, and still
signing himself Thomas Woodrow Wilson. Both the style and the
penmanship of this letter were admirable and to my surprise,
Mr. Lodge handled it almost tenderly. He asked me pertinent
questions about French politics. "The Versailles Treaty is a
misfit," he said, "absurdly complicated by the influence of Mr.
Wilson. France was duly informed that we could not ratify;
she should have simply annexed the Left Bank of the Rhine." I
was surprised. Senator Medill McCormick, who was also present
and had so far acted like a very submissive disciple, said: "What!
create another Alsace-Lorraine!" Senator Lodge looked at him
with a distinct expression of superiority, and said: "Annexation
of the Left Bank would have given France and Europe sixty
years' peace. You may live long enough to see that the present
peace will not last thirty years."

President Wilson was already a very sick man. I believe it was
during the same week that I saw him from the windows of his
neighbour, Mrs. Adolph Miller, who had invited Mrs. Houston,
Mrs. Frank West and myself to see the ex-President serenaded by
colourful Shriners. Mr. Wilson stood at the window, leaning on
his wife's arm and heavily weighing on a cane. Just as I felt inclined to label him as completely broken down he sent over the

crowd an eagle's glance which revealed what the man must once have been and made me feel deep sympathy for him.

My last four weeks were spent at the Gotham in New York, in the delightful company of Mr. and Mrs. Norton, but I gave more than twenty lectures during that time in various cities in the East as well as in New York. After a lecture at the Town Hall Mr. Ely invited me to a luncheon he was giving in honour of Lord Dunsany for whose consummate art I have great admiration. Lord Dunsany, like myself, was a frequent contributor to the *Saturday Review*. I sat next to a lady whose mental activity under a quiet demeanour delighted me. She was a poet and took particular interest in French poets. I mentioned Angellier and she said she knew him; she had met him in Florence. "Yes," I said, "you met him at the Uffizi, standing on a scaffold and taking minute measurements of some antique, but you also sat next to him at the pension where you both stayed. I do not know your name, but you are Theodore Roosevelt's sister." All these details had remained in my memory from a narrative of the same incident given me by Angellier seven or eight years before. Mrs. Douglas Robinson was considerably surprised. I liked her and this chance meeting began a friendship which lasted as long as her life. Nobody was truer to her friends. People imagined that her loyalty was entirely spent on her famous brother, but in reality she had lots to spare. She was extremely natural and, like most poets, she was childlike. Her political antagonisms only seemed violent or cruel because she expressed them without any diplomatic reticence.

A year or two after we became acquainted she said to me: "You probably don't know what Wilson and Harding talked about in the car which took both to the Capitol on the latter's inauguration. I asked Mr. Harding and he told me. He told me he had not expected to find Wilson physically so disabled, with his valet almost lifting him into the car and placing his weak hand for him inside his waistcoat. There was no conversation, and Harding not knowing what to say told his predecessor that, the

day before, he had received a letter from his sister—a missionary's wife in Burmah—and the letter gave touching details about
the death of a pet calf-elephant who positively said good-bye to
the whole household before he expired on the lawn. Suddenly
Harding noticed that Wilson was much affected by the story, with
tears rolling down his cheeks, and hesitated as to whether he
should take his companion's handkerchief out of his pocket to
help him, or should he pretend to look away and say no more.
He thought it wiser to look away." This story which to me seemed
pathetic, because of my compassion for a stricken man, as well
as of my love for animals, only affected Mrs. Robinson as being
minor history. To her Wilson could only be the man who twice
beat the political party she naturally favoured. But in everyday
life she was kindness itself, and I never knew anybody so truly
beloved by her servants.

My last fortnight in New York seemed incredibly short with
lecturing, letter-writing and constant conferences with Mr. Byrne,
Miss Marbury, Mr. Cuddihy, Mrs. Cecil Barrett and especially
Mr. Brooks who was giving the finishing touches to our appeal
to the Harvard, Yale and Princeton alumni.

One morning I called, at One Madison Avenue, on the director
of an office which I had been told was a sort of liaison between
the Government and private charities. I have forgotten the name
of that bureau. I explained what I had been doing in America.
The director showed some mild professional interest and asked
to see "the account-books of my organization." I produced the
note-book out of my breast-pocket and showed to the gentleman
the pages devoted to Credit as well as my list of reluctant ex-
penses. The director scrutinized me for a minute or two with a
puzzled expression, then burst out laughing. "How much have
you taken in?" he asked.—"Nearly a hundred thousand dollars."
—"Well, everything can happen," the hard-boiled specialist concluded. It was only the next day that it suddenly occurred to me
that I might have been for months on the narrow edge of legality,
and wrote to the director that every penny which had come to me

had been at once deposited with the Clews Bank and sent over to Lille by that bank. I supposed my accounts could be audited there. I then understood why Mr. Byrne and Mr. Brooks never signed anything I wrote without weighing each sentence as if their lives depended on its unimpeachableness.

A day or two before I sailed C. D. Norton winked me to his room and gave me a cheque for five hundred dollars. Instead of thanking him I asked, in my surprise, how much he had been giving away in the past twelve months. C. D. reddened and stammered a little, but I extracted from his modesty that his contributions to the innumerable appeals then circulated had exceeded fifty thousand dollars. Whereupon he said: "No more of that, I want you to criticize these few pages I dictated this afternoon on behalf of our Academy in Rome." It was a perfect specimen of classical English, relieved here and there by happy original expressions which came naturally to my friend. I touched these with my pencil and said: "Do not believe the gentlemen down town who will advise you to change these phrases."

The same evening I was dining at Mrs. Cuddihy's at 270 Park Avenue. Her five married children and the two then unmarried daughters were there. Also a few friends. That was my first experience of the Cuddihy tribe with their naturalness, their kindness, their humour and a general irrepressibility which can never even remotely suggest bad taste. There are no Christmas dinners like those of that family. After dinner I noticed a little manœuvring to back me into the curve of the piano. Elsewhere this would have been followed by a little request "to say just a few words." Instead of that, one lady after the other filed past me with a curtsey and a smile while some small article under which money could be concealed was placed on the piano beside me. Little Emma, the youngest of all, came last with her archest smile and two thousand francs. Like Booth Tarkington, Mr. Cuddihy had thought a man ought to respond to his own appeal. I have found it hard to wait sixteen years to narrate that charming scene, adding that many more little episodes would be worth narrating of the Cuddihy family.

My last evening was occupied by a lecture at Columbia. I returned to the Gotham, packed up, and when that was done I wrote three different articles destined to inform the readers of the Harvard, Yale and Princeton weeklies that our (Mr. Brooks' and my) appeal for Lille would be mailed to them within a week. At four a.m. I tumbled exhausted intò bed. At ten I was on the S.S. *Rochambeau* and my longest experience of America was at an end.

I never cross the ocean after a strenuous eight or ten weeks in the United States without awaiting the moment—five or six hours after shoving off from the dock—when the rushing, the knocking, dragging and shouting coincident with departure subside and deep silence, relieved by the breathing of the boat, sets in. It is a great time for also establishing silence in one's own soul. I remember how I welcomed that great beginning of rest, and how sorry I was that one of the passengers was an old American who, bitter and ulcerated, was leaving his country because he could not bear the infringement on his freedom which he regarded Prohibition to be. I wanted everybody around me to be peaceful and happy.

The second day out I was jarred by a radio from Mr. Brooks saying that a group of Yale architects wanted to adopt Lille and had asked him to stop our own campaign as their plans were on a scale which did not admit of weak collaboration. The French architect Gréber would give me all necessary information in Paris. I had misgivings which further developments or rather the complete absence of any developments were to verify. M. Gréber was vague and even evasive. It was not till a year later that I could trace the originator of that so-called Yale plan. He was so nice that I still dislike remembering how unpleasant his confession was to him. The whole thing boiled down to an after-dinner conversation of four architects, Yale men, who thought it would be a fine thing to "do something for a French university" and told Gréber, who mentioned Lille. The amorphous thing would have been still-born if an officious woman had not placed it under the microscope of a strong imagination. The contrast between our long effort and this hot air would have poisoned my voyage if I had known the full particulars of the affair, but I only had presentiments and they were not enough to upset the state of mind which the repose of the boat was not long in creating.

Here then I was. Ten months before I had been on another ship planning, hoping and wondering instead of taking stock as I now did. I was full of illusions then, counting on things which turned out to be impossible and not anticipating many developments which actually took place. If I had been told that, by the time I sailed again, a hundred and three thousand dollars would have been sent over and Lille University lifted out of the morass, I could scarcely have believed it. People who did not know me, or who only knew me through print, had done it. They had been touched by what I had told them about a city the name of which was so unfamiliar that they did not recognize it when they mentioned Lisle goods. How could I not be grateful? How could I escape the conclusion, since then so often forced upon me, that in no country has an idea, helped by an image and, if possible, by an emotion the chance it has in America?

Unforgettable little touches in thousands of letters I had received would re-live in my memory. It is true that I could not escape the wretched law of human nature which causes us to forget ten kind turns when one unpleasantness happens to mar the picture. I could not help remembering my first four months and the valley of despair they had often threatened to be. I still had in my ears the verdict of a woman-friend: "Do not expect many people to help you; many spend to the limit,

up to the last dollar; no! they won't be able to give you a
dollar." How often this had been true! But, contrary to what
my friend imagined, it had been true of people whom I saw
jauntily giving two-dollar tips to waiters, or treating themselves
to expensive cigars. These people, from vanity or from intricate
psychological motives which I now know well would not give
a dollar. They would give gregariously, or whiskily, or to girls,
but they had to be moved powerfully, and often they must have
gone through a course in giving. I had been infinitely grateful
to readers of my appeals in the press till an experienced editor
damped my feelings by pointing out that only two in a hundred
such readers actually gave. A college-president also showed me
a newspaper clipping stating in a matter-of-fact tone that out of
the twenty thousand Harvard alumni in New York, only four
thousand had contributed to the Fund destined to raise the salaries of their former professors. An army of sixteen thousand had
coldly stood aloof. It was only by degrees that it dawned upon
me that it was unfair to imply that *all* the readers of a newspaper
or review discovered a three-hundred-word appeal, or had not
had their attention diverted from it, or had not forgotten it, or
had not been irritated by it because the limit of their capacity
for coöperation had long been reached. An intelligent French
nun in New England had once told me that "more French gave to
charities if Americans gave more." The epigram stayed in my
memory, as epigrams will, but I was not sure it was more than
a jingle of words. I knew my compatriots and they might have
a score of excuses for their individualism, but it was useless to
pretend that they were not shy of coöperation. Useless also to
deny that ideas were their playthings infinitely oftener than
their poles of attraction. This accounted for the undeniable fact
that the poor French gave more readily and more generously
than the imaginative and talkative rich.

Altogether I could not but admit that America had treated
me with extraordinary kindness. During a period when I might
easily have felt like an interloper I had not even felt like an
alien. My belief in the welcoming disposition of the New

World, exaggerated as it must have been, had never been shaken by any real disappointment. I had mostly met equals, gentlemen, often brothers in occupation or tastes. When I had associated with other classes I had been struck by their kindliness, and in the case of poor Catholics, by their saintliness. Mr. Santayana was right: the average American was a thoroughly good fellow.

Not once had I been confronted with religious antagonism. Perhaps it was because I did not believe in it and it did not dare to show itself. But I have still to encounter it, though I am often conscious of astounding ignorance, and that makes it difficult for me to follow my friend André Siegfried in his explanation of America by Protestantism.

I had not been in the melting-pot, but I had been in a vitalizing atmosphere. Tired though I was physically I felt more energy than I had brought over ten months before. I had learned to regard coöperation less as a virtuous effort than as a natural duty. America, noticing this attitude, had adopted me and taught me methods which only cynics can deride. A completely different future from that which I had cherished had been offered me and accepted. My very literary ideas were being modified. I have not the least doubt that, had it not been for my American baptism of 1919–1920, I should never have felt like writing books for others. I should have gone on writing them for myself, and the just penalty would have been dealt to me.

Such were my thoughts as the *Rochambeau,* pushed along by a friendly gale which never for an hour diverted her from her course, was swiftly carrying me home. One afternoon, a Sunday afternoon, we saw the bright green coast of Cotentin. Shortly after, I was surprised to hear my own language spoken by stevedores and little children on the quays of Hâvre. In a few more hours I found the huge key of my rooms lying on the window-sill where I had left it the year before and, although everything was the same, everything was different. I remem-

bered a sort of revelation that it would be so which I had had
one bright morning in Los Angeles as I went up steep Grand
Avenue from Sixth Street.

I had returned to Paris with a list of thirty-nine lectures
promised to a variety of organizations in America. So, before the
end of 1920, I re-crossed the ocean to meet those obligations.
My boat was the old *Savoie,* quite gorgeous for the period,
and showing no sign of age although she was to be scrapped
on her return to Hâvre. She was packed and I had to chum
with a passenger of Swedish origin whose company was far
more enjoyable than my dislike of any such arrangement had
led me to suppose. This companion of mine knew interesting
people in Paris and had been the guest of Madame Laborie,
the widow of Captain Dreyfus' famous counsel. It was still bad
form in 1920 to draw people out concerning the notorious
Affair, and consequently I refrained from asking questions.
However, my room-mate once reverting to his conversations
with Madame Laborie I merely asked him whether or not he
had been able to infer the lady's own opinion of Dreyfus. The
answer seemed interesting enough to be noted at once. Here
it is: "Oh! Madame Laborie told me that her husband always
believed that Dreyfus was innocent of what he was accused of,
but constantly dreaded that he might unexpectedly own up to
something worse." Let it be recalled in qualification of this
statement that Laborie had had difficulties with his client about
the honorarium he charged.

I had an invitation from a friend, interested in gold and silver
mines in Mexico, to visit his camp in Sonora. I was glad to
accept. On my way from Los Angeles to New Orleans, the winter
before, I had broken my trip at El Paso in order not to leave
the borderland without getting a glimpse of Mexico. I had
crossed the Rio Colorado on an endless bridge and I had spent
two or three hours in Piedras Negras. People did not go there,

as they constantly went to Tia Juana, to escape from prohibition, and the little place was surprisingly native. Women in mantillas were cooking greasy things on *braseros* smouldering under the trees of the public square. Unmilitary soldiers in immense hats and espadrilles watched them as if they were doing something unheard of. Mules also looked on.

I went into the church. I might have been in Andalusia. The same golds, the same reds. The same effort to produce a violent impression. Before the long-haired, beskirted Christ a kneeling woman was adjuring, even more than praying, while fanning herself all the time. Where were the Americans I had been accustomed to, so afraid of not looking like everybody else, so liberal in giving of the superficial in their souls, so disinclined to let you into their really intimate? Just on the other side of that dreary bridge. I retraced my steps accompanied by saucy urchins sucking bits of sugar-cane and declaring everything *bonito*. All that is Spanish has an extraordinary hold upon me. I wanted to see more of this wild Mexico and my friend's invitation was welcome.

I arrived at Tucson at four o'clock of Christmas night, a soft velvety night. By five I was in the cathedral, founded by a French bishop and still served by bearded French priests walking, as French priests do, up and down the aisles as they said their breviary. My friend was not at the hotel where we had agreed to meet. The hotel-manager felt sure he must be at Nogales where, in fact, I knew he frequently stayed. So to Nogales I went by stage, arriving there in time to see an extraordinary sunset the glow of which encircled not the west alone but the whole flaming horizon. My friend was not there. I went to an hotel and waited patiently, visited every now and then by a little mouse which a cracker or two made quite tame. The hotel was a very simple wooden structure. I took my meals in a restaurant near-by which had been a haunt of rough frontiersmen and still showed the traces of their revolver shots in its ceiling. It was now deserted and painfully quiet. So was Nogales itself, where an elderly

English couple and myself seemed to be the only strangers. We ran into one another at intervals by the wire-fence dividing Mexican from American Nogales. Negro soldiers were frequent there too, looking at nothing through the chicken-wire.

Finally my mining engineer turned up. He had been frantically looking for me, and had telephoned my hotel several times. The last time the manager had answered: "No, Abbé Dimnet is not here, but Abe Dimnet is, writing all the time." This was not the only time I have been rechristened Abe; in spite of Lincoln, it is not an exciting experience.

We left early in a specially constructed Ford which thought nothing of shunting into the torrent-bed when the trail became uncertain. Few days stand so vividly in my memory as that day still does. I knew that Northern Sonora was largely a desert but the word desert connoted rockiness and sandiness; so, what I was introduced to, almost on leaving Nogales, was a captivating surprise. The Sonora desert is not a desert at all, it is a glorious solitude, green and rich, where nature has played at appearing civilized as English landscapists play at making their parks wilder than they would naturally be. For the cotton-trees, tall and graceful, amuse themselves by falling in rows, and, dozens of times, I was fooled by clumps of mesquites looking so like apple-orchards that the absence of a farm suddenly transformed their happy familiarity into the melancholy of a French battle-field. It took me an hour or two to realize that all this wealth of greenness was not for man, but for coyotes or jack-rabbits, for red-necked vultures greedily watching us from dead trees, or for a bird whose long and deep whistle searched one's very soul.

A few human habitations made the solitude even more solitary. I remember a comfortable bungalow separated from a brilliant creek by a tall bamboo-hedge. Two women stood near the gate, one in a leather coat and bright red skirt carried a basket on her head, the other, perhaps her daughter, all in red, was combing her dark hair which fell well below her waist. I wished for

an Etruscan vase-painter even more than for a Gauguin. Towards
evening we passed a smaller cottage at the foot of a hill of giant
cacti. The woman was preparing to close her shutters. My friend
slowed up and asked in Spanish if she had any eggs to sell. Without turning her head the woman answered: *"No, señor, no hay!
Nada."* Her voice was as clear as silver and seemed to ring
through the solemn landscape. Another thrill was the sudden
appearance of an all but intact Spanish church standing by itself
in a wood, at present more than thirty miles away from any community. Only trees were now the parish, with a few brick-tombs
to recall that long-extinct life had once been active in that place.
It was night when we reached the camp which consisted of two
bungalows separated by a few hundred yards and of the rudi-
mentary mining plant itself. No sooner had the night really
closed in than a coldness of a kind I had never experienced
gripped the air as the stars shone with increasing brilliance. I
slept under nine blankets which were very necessary, yet you
could stay outdoors many minutes before feeling that it was
unwise to do so, and the Mexican chauffeur who had driven us
slept in the cart outside. A similar phenomenon surprised me
during the daytime: the December sun was scorching and the
earth exhaled such heat that, several times, I actually looked
round for embers, yet all the time the pure subtle air was cold.

I stayed four or five days at the camp. I saw the end of the
Christmas or Noche Buena festivities. They began in a touching
extemporized chapel made of cactus branches hung with sheets
and decorated not only with holy pictures but with family photographs. They ended in outdoor dances stimulated by dangerous
cactus brandy. After two or three days these subsided, and the
natives went back to their favourite occupation of warming themselves at little stoves—made of a can in which a few sticks mirac-
ulously burn—and looking vacantly at things over the blanket
they hold up to their face. The most active person in the camp
was a little fellow of barely five who appeared two or three
times a day, carrying a can of milk or a basket in one hand

and clinging with the other to the mane of the tall horse on whose
neck he rode. A Chinaman cooked for us. No one ever concealed
so well the mystery of his race under the empty universality of
his name, Charlie. One night we dined at the other bungalow
belonging to the foreman. He lived there with a young wife and
a youngish divorced mother, a doctor by profession. That evening the ex-husband, himself a physician, appeared just as dinner was announced. He seemed on the best of terms with his
former consort and it was lucky, for the exiguity of accommoda-
tion in the bungalow raised difficult problems. I had been a
great reader and a great admirer of Bret Harte. The conversation
of this physician solely and passionately interested in mining,
that is to say, in gambling on mines, fascinated me. I had not
expected that such a western type could still be possible. All
those people were kind.

My friend did all he could to give me a good time and drove
me all over the country, rich in Spanish dumps full of this or
that ore, dumps of hopes they rather seemed to me. Those aged
hillocks were overrun by *choyas*, a vicious kind of cactus which
actually stretches out its prickly branches when it sees you planning to go and keeps you where you are with the pertinacity of
the mining passion. Once or twice we met an old Englishman,
thin and drawn and apparently exhausted by years of patient
expectation. He roved about those dumps with a hungry unsatisfied look in his eyes.

We did some sight-seeing. My friend showed me a conclave of
boulders on which were what he felt sure must be hieroglyphs,
but which I thought were only mineral deposits of fanciful shape.
I was much more impressed, and of course convinced, by the
enormous tiers of a gigantic theatre cut into the side of a mountain. The feeling that this theatre was in absolute solitude, and
had for several hundred years been awaiting spectators who
would never come was overpowering. A short distance away from
this grand scene my friend who, unfortunately, was an excellent
marksman, killed a coyote far beyond what I had imagined would

be the range of an ordinary rifle. The poor animal had just been drinking out of the brook and was giving a cheerful bark in evident enjoyment of the perfect morning when he was hit. To see his happiness collapsing into death darkened the whole day for me.

On our way back to Nogales we stopped at the little town of Magdalena. I remember its sidewalks, almost three feet higher than the causeway, its streets bordered with oleanders and dark orange-trees, its cool houses, wide open to the sun, all showing a crib on a small altar with two candles on either side of the Holy Child, a primitive bed on trestles and the inevitable Singer sewing-machine. I remember the priest, in cassock and biretta, thrusting a shovel into a heap of mortar to try its consistency and be sure it would be worthy of the addition he was making to his church. Also a striking parade of horsemen in vast sombreros preparing for the horse-race. I have not forgotten either the Lille-born doctor who turned up at the Chinese inn and easily detected my nationality in my pronunciation of Spanish while I could scarcely believe it possible that the mere use of the Spanish language should have given *him* his Marseilles accent and his gesticulation. But what I can remember better than all the rest, and yet feel utterly at a loss to explain, is the strange certitude which took hold of me that this little town knew the secret of happiness and that the warmth of its sun and the coolness of its air were both trying to whisper that magical spell in my ear. Few places have seemed so eloquently confidential to me.

As we drew near the American border we were stopped by a polite gesture from two Mexican customs officers in immense hats and carrying funnel-mouthed blunderbusses. They were courtesy itself and were a strong contrast to the neutral and mechanical person who searched our luggage as soon as we were on the civilized side of the chicken-wire again.

My train was a few steps away and, in twenty-four hours, I was giving my first lecture in Los Angeles.

V

As I said above, I gave thirty-nine lectures in less than eighty days during the early months of 1920. I had arranged my own tour and, of course, I had been more mindful of distances and night-travel than the usual agent would have been. Moreover, the winter was exceptionally mild. Also, I seem to have been sixteen years younger than I am now, and that counted for more than I am inclined to imagine at present. I never felt tired and rather enjoyed the endless travel, engaging unknown people in conversation with truly American simplicity and meeting several interesting men and women. I had lunch in the dining-car once with a young Mexican seminarian whose spirituality permeated even a distinctly man of the world's manner. He recalled forcibly to me the saintly Archbishop Ruiz y Flores—met the year before in the house of Monsignor Shannon—and he never suspected that he preached a sermon without words for me. Another interesting cleric was a young Russian priest whose delight in theological subtleties and inclination towards theological irritability, *odium theologicum*, were a study. I felt as if I were listening to one of those Greek hair-splitters who have made the accounts of the great councils such a complication. He was a lover of liturgical niceties too and spoke with crushing contempt of a ritual practise *qui remonte à peine au septième siécle* (practically unknown before the seventh century). Around us lived millions of Americans who never took any interest in the past, and to whom the seventh century was as nebulously indifferent as the reign of Rameses. I could not help laughing.

I was also amused on another occasion when I overheard a college boy trying to quote to an older man, uncle or grandfather, a passage actually remembered from an article I had recently contributed to *Harper's Magazine*. That student could only recollect the general tenor of the passage and ineffectually stumbled on the wording of it till I could not bear it any longer and said that I too had read that article and could reproduce the passage in question word for word. Whereupon the young man borrowed the head-waiter's pencil and wrote down, from my dictation, on the back of a menu: "American women expect, very rightly too, from their husbands the attentions which most Frenchmen receive from their wives. The American husband expects nothing, and for what he receives the Lord makes him truly thankful."—"That's me," the elderly gentleman said good-humouredly.

It was delicious to be in America again, travelling and lecturing as during the year before, but doing it with no responsibility except to myself. Yet, at first, I felt a little like the Prisoner of Chillon so unused to freedom that he was afraid of it, and I missed the bracing consciousness I used to have of working for others. However, I got over that as I noticed that many of the people for whom I lectured asked a little anxiously whether I was still collecting money for that stricken French town.

My lectures themselves were no trouble. I was treading familiar ground and I was free from the anxiety I had at first lest interest in the reactions of my audiences should make me lose the thread of my argument. One evening, lecturing at Berkeley for the University of California, I left my glasses on the boat which took me across the bay but only missed them a few minutes before beginning to speak. I was much annoyed and, during the whole lecture, I was teased by the thought of those glasses, fondly wondering where they might be, and seeing myself writing a longish letter about them. There is no doubt that a considerable portion of my consciousness was concentrated on those unfortunate glasses and not on what seemed to be the important issue between my audience and myself. Yet, the lecture was an unmistakable success, the President of the University then and there inviting me to give a whole course next time I was in America. I quoted this instance several times when lecturing on thinking to show that our real thought lies much deeper than the stratum we express in speaking, and that what we call our distractions are, after all, our real interest.

I lectured, during that winter, in all the principal American colleges of both men and women, but it was a charming experience to discover the smaller colleges: Mills and Pomona in the West, Wells near its beautiful lake, and, after a few interesting contacts with Pennsylvania Dutch communities, especially Bryn Mawr which of course is small only in size.

I had two friends in Bryn Mawr: Miss Eunice Schenck, now Dean, and a brilliant student, Miss Clorinda Garrison, niece of my friend Mrs. Norton, so I saw a great deal of both the faculty and the undergraduates. I was keenly interested in the quakerism of Bryn Mawr and was preparing to gather a sheaf of notes about it. But I never discovered the least quakerism, except political idealism, in the place. The girls who were supposed to be weaned from music, sang admirably during meals. There were no quiet times—although the College was entirely free from the excitement I have sometimes detected elsewhere—and there was no thee-thouing. Miss Thomas, who was then President, was the most hospitable person, and full of geniality and humour. I was invited to stay over Sunday and the Sunday dinner was quite a function. I admired the very pretty dinner-card in front of me. Miss Thomas said: "I had a much prettier one for you, bought in your own Paris. But my secretary said: 'Oh! Miss Thomas, you can't use this card for Abbé Dimnet!' so I had to refrain, and now I regret that I did."—"Please let us get the card," I said. The card came—I still have it—and it was a distinctly Frenchy, Montmartre card, done by an excellent artist, but certainly in no Quaker spirit.

Miss Thomas also said: "Abbé Dimnet, I've read your article in *Harper's Magazine*. You said that we *all* believe in Purgatory: I don't."—"Yes, I am sorry, Miss Thomas, but you do."—"I certainly do not."—"Why! Miss Thomas, I am almost sure you don't believe in Hell."—"No, of course, I don't believe in Hell." —"Well, I can scarcely imagine you sure that you will go straight to Heaven."—"Nor can I."—"Well, then, you believe in Purgatory, which is a beautiful doctrine, only you don't like to call it Purgatory, any more than Mrs. Besant did."

The conversation turned to politics. Miss Thomas was a great traveller, and few people could travel as intelligently as she did. She had just finished a tour of the French colonies and had carried home the admiration for Morocco which all visitors conceive. She could not say enough in praise of Lyautey, and finally she said to me: "You will not realize the full meaning of being a Frenchman till you see what that man has accomplished in a few years."

Miss Thomas was the only great Francophile at that dinner. I heard the criticisms of France habitual in 1920. France was militaristic as she had always been: why didn't she demobilize her now unnecessary army? The spirit of hegemony was still alive in her: visibly she was striving to make a solid block of Central Europe and dominate it. One professor, of Swiss origin, who evidently was a pioneer in admiration of the Soviets, resented French support of Poland as a covert antagonism to Russia. At the same time he was eloquent in advocacy of what he called a Christian spirit in politics. All those criticisms, after sixteen years and in view of the situation of France at this writing, sound ludicrous enough. France, the ally of the Soviets, is now blamed for her pacifism and for her antipathy for hegemony the new name of which is political responsibility. I remember prophesying to the ten or twelve at that dinner that it would be so, but it is the fate of political predictions that they are forgotten by the time they are verified, or the people to whom they were made are either dead or, which is worse, have persuaded themselves that *they* were the prophets. Philosophy is better than second sight, after all.

In Washington, where I spent the last ten or twelve days of March, I also heard European politics frequently discussed. Secretary Lansing's book had just been published and was seen on every table beside the first bouquets of early lilacs. It provided the subject of innumerable conversations in the drawing-rooms of Senator Lodge, or of Mrs. Houston, of Mrs. Adolph Miller and Mrs. David Jayne Hill where interest in politics was dominant. Colonel House valiantly defended Clemenceau whom he

seemed to regard as the great man of the war. Frank Simonds
did not concur. I liked Simonds very much. His library was a
statesman's, not a journalist's, library. His very American point
of view had not acquired as yet the exclusiveness it was gradually
to display, but it was felt under the smouldering passion which
Simonds' wit and smile vainly tried to conceal. Simonds' information on the internal politics of most European states gave
one a delightful sensation that, whatever one might say, not a
single nuance would have to be explained.

André Tardieu was frequently mentioned: the man could not
pass unnoticed anywhere, and his New York office had counted
for more, during several months, than the Embassy itself did.
In America as in France Tardieu seemed to be an object of
animadversion when he was not an idol. A good judge of men
told me that "he had never met anybody with such marvellously
equipped intellectual machinery." A former member of the
Cabinet, on the contrary, regarded him as what common parlance
calls a go-getter and said as much with evident resentment.

While I was in Washington Viviani arrived on an important
mission and was at once the cynosure of attention. The man was
so eloquent that many people who knew no French eagerly tried
to hear him speak. On the other hand, he was reported to be an
avowed atheist and this reputation considerably hindered his
action. It also gave the unthinking a totally wrong idea of the
French. There being a large amount of legend in the atheistic
reputation of this ex-Prime Minister, I thought it only fair to
attempt a portrait of Viviani and did so in a lecture which I
gave in Mrs. Adolph Miller's drawing-room. Viviani was famous
as the man who had bragged about "extinguishing the stars in
Heaven." His atheistic reputation was largely built on that metaphor. As a matter of fact, eloquence and fine phrases being the
curse of French political life, Viviani as a young deputy had
been much struck by Jaurès' first Socialist address in which this
famous orator reproached the Liberals for "silencing the old
song which had been lulling human woes." His allusion to the
extinction of the stars of belief belonged to the same beautiful

rhetoric as Jaurès' *vieille chanson*, and, like it, was more a denunciation than a proclamation. I said so to my audience and
the simple explanation was taken up by the press to Viviani's
great relief, for, totally indifferent to Theism or Atheism as he
really was, he had been in America long enough to have heard
that Mr. Taft's theology had not been a help to his political ambitions.

Madame Jusserand was in my audience. Cardinal Gibbons
had just died and I asked her if she was going to the funeral.
She answered in a typically French sentence: "We have received
no instructions."—"Why!" I said, this is going to be the funeral
of a great American even more than that of a great churchman."
In fact, the silence of the French cable about what the Ambassador should do was as unfortunate as the extinguishing of the
stars. Madame Jusserand was a delightful hostess, a perfect
blend of American and French gifts. Her husband was, and remains after more than a decade—a long, long time in Washington—the incarnation of superiority veiling itself under charm.
But he had entered that phase of life during which men call
wisdom the indifference born of fatigue. What struck one in what
his shrewd psychology endlessly extracted from the American
scene was his conviction that Time was a much greater diplomatist than ambassadors. When things seemed to be favourable
expect them soon to appear adverse. When the reverse, be of
good cheer, for America is mercurial and wisdom can afford to
give levity a little leeway. Probably the constant changes of
Foreign Ministers in Paris had given him a similar lesson and
he had gradually come to a wait-and-see philosophy which was
well exemplified in Madame Jusserand's answer.

I was distressed, for I saw clearly that the Ambassador's non-
appearance at a national funeral would be fatal to his reputation. I wrote to M. Viviani urging him to be present at the ceremony. The answer came promptly: the French statesman would
attend the funeral. This was sure to be a great encouragement
to M. Jusserand. I kept constantly in touch with my friend,
Professor Chinard, of Johns Hopkins. In a telephone conversa-

tion we were having M. Chinard bethought himself that Cardinal
Gibbons had been given a high grade in the Legion of Honour,
and that this particular alone made the presence of M. Jusserand
at the funeral a necessity. In fact, this consideration brought the
Ambassador at once to a decision. As for Viviani, he not only
assisted at the funeral but he asked the Sulpitians to take him
to the Seminary, and after going over the Seminary with them
he asked two on the staff to show him the sights of Baltimore,
and altogether, treated himself to a debauch of clericalism the
whole day.

A Brooklyn newspaper was shocked at this display of liberalism and angrily insisted that a man who extinguished the stars
should not show his face at a Cardinal's funeral. I replied, in the
New York *Times,* less than two hours before sailing on the
Lorraine. I counted that during my three months' visit I had had
to write more than twenty such letters in defence of France.

During the voyage it occurred to me that, although many
American friends of France did not hesitate to do voluntarily
what I felt it my duty to do whenever my country was unjustly
attacked, it would be infinitely better if that defence were entrusted to a specialized organization. I gave the idea a good
deal of thought, and gradually the lineaments of that organization became clear in my mind. I saw it primarily as a purely
American affair. It would not be difficult to keep it free from any
French pecuniary assistance but no French influences should be
admitted into it. The name of the organization, as I conceived
it, should be: an American Association in defence of Truth and
France. Truth first and foremost: the inevitable shortcomings
of French politics were not to be palliated. Practically I visu-
alized correspondents in the chief American cities who would
watch the local press and redress it on occasions. Whenever they
happened to lack information they would communicate with an
office in New York which I hoped either my friend, Nicholas
Roosevelt, of *The New York Times,* or my other friend, James
Ernest King, of *The Boston Transcript,* would be willing to run.
This office would, when necessary, ask information of a Paris

bureau, the counterpart in my mind of what M. de Chambrun's French Information Bureau became in 1935 in New York. The only French collaboration would be at the Paris end. There would be and should be no suspicion of propaganda anywhere. The sole object of the organization would be information and the redressing of injustice which must appeal to American fairness.

Shortly after my return to Paris I went to the Ministry of Foreign Affairs and spoke of these plans to my friend M. Dejean, Director of American Affairs. He put me in touch with M. Jean Giraudoux who, although busy writing a play, showed interest in the idea and spoke of it to M. Paul Morand. The latter may have given it whatever time the writing of a novel left him, but I found later that the files of the Department were not in perfect order. It soon became clear to me that while I expected some collaboration, my interlocutors were in the habit of giving none. I also discovered that M. Poincaré who, at the time, was running the Quai d'Orsay, had been approached by rival planners and my chances were slender. I spent considerable money printing preparatory literature, after which the Quai d'Orsay opened an Information Bureau in New York very much on the English plan and endowed it with twelve million francs. When the twelve million francs were spent the Bureau shut down, and the incumbent was promoted to a diplomatic post.

In the Spring of 1923 I was asked by President Garfield, of Williams College, to act as French spokesman at the Williamstown Institute of Politics. I was very much flattered by this invitation, for the Institute, in those early days, was not only an extraordinary success but a model of what political symposiums should be.

I arrived in America early in May and fulfilled lecture engagements, until mid-June of an extremely hot summer frightened people away from lecture-halls. I had not been in America the year before, and I gladly took advantage of extensive travel,

during those few weeks, to feel the pulse of American opinion
before meeting that opinion, crystallized and systematized, in
my Williamstown audiences. Imponderabilia count for very
much in that kind of investigation. At a big banquet given in
Chicago to Overseas Girls—the hundreds of brave American
women who enlisted with their men—I was struck by a peculiarity which apparently was passed unnoticed by everybody
else. The words "in France" constantly recurred in speeches as
well as in songs. To the boys and girls who cheerfully sang them
as they danced between courses they evidently had no reference
whatever to the country of my birth. They merely meant the
spiritual location where those young people had displayed the
unconscious heroism belonging to their age. They simply were
synonymous with the other happy syllables which I could hear
floating about on gay notes: "over there, over there." General
Dawes sat next me, much to my joy, and I pointed out the nuance
to him. He had not been aware of it, but he saw at once what I
meant. "I suppose," he remarked, "that your boys say: 'in Morocco' in much the same spirit." The similarity was obvious and
I felt in full the cruelty or, at all events, the cruel indifference
of it, for in 1923 the soreness of the war was as painful as ever.

Another remark of a less subtle character made such an impression upon me that I can always inwardly hear it when the
least occasion recalls it. Dining at Sir Robert Falconer's, in
Toronto, I had an interesting conversation with the Canadian
Representative at the League of Nations. This gentleman soon
felt sure that I was not the kind of Frenchman who cannot take
the least criticism from a foreign observer. He looked at me
with a shrewd smile as he asked: "But why do you always send
orators to Geneva?" The question called for a repudiation of
much that is specifically French. I could only answer it in the
words written by Julius Caesar about my presumed ancestors
twenty centuries ago: "*Rem militarem et argute loqui*—the
French are good soldiers and they are fine talkers." Unfortunately what our bravery does is but too often undone by our
oratory.

About June 20th I settled in a quiet country-house in Maryland, belonging to my friends, the Alvords, and started on the immediate preparation of my lectures. Maryland, with its isolated farms on a tree-grown hillock, its neglected but poetic country-houses behind an unkempt coppice, its Negro hamlets at a turn of the road and its handsome horses freely roving about the cornfields, is a strong contrast to the woodsy Indian solitudes of New England, with their broad shady streams, their dykes and their family graveyards hidden under brambles and nettles. I used to go bicycling along unfrequented lanes, to the wonder of the hillbillies who never saw a gentleman riding a bike. "Who may you be?" they asked sometimes. I loved their curiosity and their tolerant interest in my strangeness and foreignness. Sometimes my friends drove me farther afield into the redness of Virginia, or along the Frederick road, as genuinely ancient as the so-called Old Post Road running north of New York is artificially so.

The days were hot on the parched land with quails endlessly repeating their Latin plaint: *sustuli, sustuli,* and the redbird whistling his human note. The nights were full of fireflies, unexpectedly turning off their little lights, while dry-bodied breakable insects banged like missiles against the window-screens. I felt far away from home, from my cool Trélon forest, but the sensation was pleasant.

Every other day I drove into Washington and spent five or six hours in the Peace Library, close by the White House. The staff were particularly interested in Williamstown and gave me an assistance which the Paris libraries forcibly recall by never offering it. Washington proverbially terrifies people in summer, but I liked it because its disappointing passivity during the rest of the year is less noticeable when the heat puts everything to sleep. Moreover Rock Creek Park, the romantic Oak Hill Cemetery, as well as some old streets in Georgetown are delightful oases which one can have almost entirely to oneself.

Ambassador Jusserand was in town, faithfully doing the mys-

terious things which Ambassadors are supposed to do year in
year out. I went to see him and asked for his opinion of Williamstown and what line of argument he thought I ought to take there.
He did not hesitate one moment. He regarded the Institute of
Politics as little better than an academic circus. The questions
treated there had much better be let alone. Time would provide
the only possible solutions. Hundreds of people were flocking to
the pretty little town to see a Frenchman and a German fighting
in a cockpit. The newspapers were already full of the prospect.
Undignified, all this, undignified and useless. We went in to
lunch, a charming luncheon with prohibited red wine glittering
in the decanters and not enough guests to encourage the usual
hubbub of conversation. The ambassador liked his audience. He
opened up the stores of his marvellous knowledge of American
history and kept us interested till late in the afternoon. That
man knew his eighteenth century as Lenôtre knew the French
Revolution, almost hour by hour.

Two days later I went up to New York to pay an official visit
to Mr. Bernard Baruch, the angel of the Williamstown Institute.
I found him in the kind of office usually preferred by modern
magnates of business, viz., a vast empty room only illuminated
by a few museum pictures and, seated at a historic Louis-Seize
table, virgin of anything except a telephone, the magnate himself.
I liked Mr. Baruch. I thought his ideas were in remarkably neat
order and he expressed them both tersely and warmly. He was
entirely clear about the object of the Institute of Politics: it
was a place where the truth should be told about politics and
economics. The whole truth, facts and figures. Mere display of
culture or erudition was out of place there. Mr. Baruch looked
at me with a curious expression. "I hope," he said guardedly,
"you're not going to talk about the eighteenth century. European
lecturers know altogether too much about the eighteenth century." I laughed, and I was glad that the entrance of a tall impressive daughter left Mr. Baruch no time to ask me why I
laughed. I returned to Washington the same day and resumed
my work at the Library.

I had been conscious, almost on landing several weeks before, that American sentiment had been somehow turned against France. The stories about trenches or water which had to be bought by poor American doughboys had begun the transformation. I found the change even more marked in the newspapers or reviews, the files of which I patiently went through.

The chief grievance was obviously the occupation or—as many journalists malignantly put it—the invasion of the Ruhr. Intelligent people like President Hibben or the men I met at Mrs. Douglas Robinson's had no doubts about the real character of this move: it was a manœuvre to expedite payment of Reparations and nothing else. Mrs. Robinson repeatedly said: "We, in America, were beginning to tire of France's ineffective protests at international conferences. Now she has taken her affairs in her own hands, and it is as it should be." But to people not so well informed about European affairs it seemed to be an act of war accomplished when all the world was craving peace, a wanton display of force at the expense of the underdog, or the wreaking of revenge in cold blood.

The presence of black troops in the Ruhr seemed to add insult to injury. Americans resented it with all the force of prejudice, and British interpretation of the presence of those troops was anything but benevolent. People constantly alluded to this point in their conversations with me. I would reply that, judging by the lynchings, the American Negro was undoubtedly inferior to ours, yet there were American coloured regiments at Nogales, Arizona, and I had myself seen one quartered in that Frenchest of French towns, Blois, six or seven months after the Armistice. Where was the difference? Who had ever said that the Germans were more sensitive than the French? Answers to these questions showed embarrassment, of course.

Many times my interlocutors evaded a direct answer by saying that, black troops or white troops, the Reparations were unjust or impossible. They did not read, as I did, the impassioned though technical books of Mr. J. M. Keynes. But they heard the virulent denunciations of Signor Nitti—the Italian ex-Premier—

who made as much noise at the time as he has been quiet since. And Americans love the repetition of strong expression. Most people did not realize that the bill for Reparations was inflated by Mr. Lloyd George's famous contention that "lives had as much right to indemnities as chimneys." They did not know that it was Lord Cunliffe who insisted that Germany could pay three hundred billion francs. And they had forgotten, if they had ever heard it, that the German negotiator at Versailles, Count von Brockdorff-Ranzau, had admitted—wrongly it now appears—that his country could pay a hundred billion. Most people repeated the well-known argument that the transfer of wealth from one country to another raises impossible problems. When I asked them whether or not this theory applied to the payment of Europe's debts to America, they laughed good-humouredly as Americans do, and remarked that I knew "how to make a point." This was praise I was to hear often at Williamstown but, as a rule, it meant a refusal to think logically and therefore could not be said to be either extremely flattering or wisely critical. Sometimes they counter-attacked by asking me if it was true that French people paid no taxes. I knew that this extraordinary notion—which I found lurking even in apparently good minds —arose from two causes: in the first place, the Income Tax compared with other French taxes was a negligible affair whereas it is the whole thing in America; in the second place, the French farmer—who was from beginning to end in the trenches while the American farmer was selling his wheat at a miraculous price —was lightly taxed as a reward for his war-record and also to help him to produce his flour more cheaply. But the absurdity of the charge invariably made me feel ironical and I would admit with great seriousness that the French paid no taxes because they knew the secret of gold-making which enabled them to keep up formidable armies as well as to lend money to everybody in Central Europe. Americans love a joke, but they resent irony. Once an indignant Bostonian young matron told me that I was "an unserious unmoral man."

But the chief grievance against France had been caused by
the Washington Naval Conference in 1922. Allusions to it teemed
in all I read or heard. At first I could not understand it, for
France had been treated worse than shabbily by her former
Allies at that conference. Before the war the French navy was
second only to that of Great Britain. But during the war the
French Naval Arsenals stopped making the steel-plates with
which warships are built and produced nothing but shells. Hence,
by the end of 1918, an extraordinary decrease in the French
naval force. Yet it was by that ghost of a navy that the French
requirements were measured at the Washington Conference. The
result is well-known. France in the final decision was bracketed
with Italy, the Italy of 1922, who had no vast Colonial Empire
to defend. Japan was allowed a navy a hundred per cent larger.
Britain and America gave themselves the lion's share, each with
a navy larger than those of France, Japan and Italy combined.
This agreement had seemed bitter and bitterly puzzling to French
opinion. Yet, what I constantly read or heard in America was
the reproach that at Washington "France had been rocking the
boat." She had appeared as a nervous woman, even as a spoilt
little girl, whom her seniors had only made to behave with great
patience and considerable difficulty. I gradually found that this
"naughty if charming little girl" idea was at the back of many
American heads. Two of my best friends, great and influential
Francophiles, entertained it. The fact is that there had been
a little too much sentiment in the coöperation of America with
France. Barely one American in twenty realized that President
Wilson had declared war not primarily to save France but to
defend the freedom of American trade. This mistake was com-
prehensible when I remembered a conversation I had with an
English M. P. in 1914. This honourable gentleman did not realize
either that his country was defending itself and nobody else in
Belgium. He complacently read pure idealism in the British
intervention. Both in England and in the United States there had
been so much sympathy with Belgium and France that gradually the original cause of intervention was forgotten, and now the

"bleeding martyr" of the adjective-loving French orator—
copied by a thousand newspaper men—had become the "naughty
little girl." France was a minor, and all she was expected to do
was not to rock the boat in which benevolent sages were trying
to row her to safety by reducing her navy. There was no idea
of French history, no conception of the enormous political capacities of the actual French Empire, no realization of what Frenchmen under the guidance of such a giant as Lyautey, for instance,
can accomplish. The gulf between that reality and the "little
girl" delusion was so obviously impassable that it almost dis-
couraged effort.

What had happened in Washington the year before was that,
once more through the fault of politicians, France had not been
properly represented. As usual an orator had been sent. It was
in vain that this orator was Briand, the prince of eloquence, the
most illustrious European idealist, and the Frenchman whom
Americans seemed to prefer to all other civilians. M. Briand
spoke no English and his oratory was wasted. Moreover, he
had sailed with the absurd notion—summed up in one sentence
at the end of an extremely misleading series of articles by M.
Stéphane Lauzanne—that "in Washington France would sit in
a comfortable chair while Britain sat on the hard stool." This
idea of a serious naval antagonism between the United States
and Great Britain was laughable, but Briand had taken it for
granted. He imagined that the question of the freedom of the seas
would raise an impassable barrier between the two great English-speaking nations. No sooner was the conference opened than
he found himself confronted by that epitome of English qualities, the suave and debonair but unshakable Lord Balfour, and
the reality appeared.

Americans do not, as a rule, love English people: they think
them patronizing and always know they are regarded by them as
colonials, or as democrats in a sense quite remote from the comfortable connotations attached to the word Whig. Marie-Antoinette saw Benjamin Franklin in exactly the light in which

modern conservatives see M. Litvinoff, and probably most English people took the same view. Something of that unfavourable opinion subsists in spite of the slow changes worked in its appearance by the chemistry of time.

But without loving them in general, Americans *like* the British and often are fascinated by them. Any Englishman with decent manners and a decent way of expressing himself, is an aristocrat in the eyes of the average American. The language largely does this. Americans who cannot mock enough one of their own countrymen returning from England with what they call an Oxford accent delight in the sound of English English. Moreover the aloofness of the Englishman makes his first smile or his first joke a joy to the cordial and welcoming American. He feels as if the Revolution were forgotten, and blood was thicker than water, and bygones were bygones at last. This accounts for the fact that while a Frenchman naturalized American always looks and acts like a converted Jew, an Englishman in the same position is absolutely at ease because he feels welcome and really coming into his own. The obverse is hardly ever true: even a Henry James never quite becomes English, no matter if he is legally naturalized and votes Conservative: he knows it and, in a perfectly polite manner, he is made to feel it to the end.

Balfour towered above everybody else at the Washington Conference. He knew what he wanted as nobody else did. And people around him realized it and were grateful to him for the grace with which he dominated everybody without in the least appearing domineering. He liquidated the Japanese alliance with the lightest touch and got all he wanted without demanding anything. Never was the superiority of a perfect specimen of an ancient race acknowledged as it was there. A year later I found the impression of it enduring even in that America where a year is an age. A few individuals here and there resented and resisted it, but almost invariably they had to appear somewhat loud and uncivilized while doing so and this was another triumph for Lord Balfour then happily reading philosophy in his Whittinghame house.

So, what with this success and the Ruhr and the blacks and foolish returning hints that Paris was more immoral than Berlin, or that French families were shamefully restricted in comparison with the prolific American families (of 1840), what I found as I read and talked in Washington was that the British were at the zenith while the French seemed to be regarded as mere Latins.

Yet, it was not difficult to find that this was more an appearance than a reality. Like M. Jusserand I have now had enough experience of Americans to see them get in and out of love with France several times. I know that when they criticize French Cabinets, or French hotel-keepers, or French telephones, it is with the understanding that these criticisms do not touch the French nation itself. Americans retain a historic sympathy with the French. Poor Lafayette has suffered the fate of all symbols that have been in use too long. Not so Rochambeau or De Grasse who are obscurely known to have been more important than their popular compeer. The upper strata in American culture or art, as well as in society, are invariably Francophile. Americans of Huguenot descent rank with the Dutch aristocracy of New York. This is felt by the rest of the nation who have not the same knowledge of the reasons underlying this sympathy. When criticism of France is in fashion, people indulge freely in it. Discuss it with them, showing where it is groundless or exaggerated, they laugh like school-boys caught in an ignorant statement, or they plead their everlasting youthfulness. During the years 1930–1935 the most Francophile Paris correspondents could not send a letter to their New York newspapers without some carping remarks at the expense of France. When I would point out that these remarks were visibly out of tune with the articles themselves, the writers invariably admitted that editors expected such criticisms, but they had no importance in comparison with the gist of the statements surrounding them. Teasing of this kind at the expense of the British would never be encouraged, because editors know that it would not be forgiven. In the case of France it is only regarded as harmless foil-play,

as the give-and-take of a little satire permissible between people
who, in spite of different languages, are temperamentally alike
in many ways.

Of all this I was conscious as the time drew near when the
1923 session of the Institute of Politics would be opened.

The 1923 session of the Institute of Politics was opened on
July 27th. I arrived at Williamstown the day before and settled
at the Greylock Hotel which I preferred to a villa graciously
offered me by the administrators of the Institute. My first impression of Williams College, infinitely peaceful on its lawns, is
still fresh. Somehow I was fascinated by little flights of happy
finches frisking about President Garfield's house and coquet-
tishly displaying their semi-circle of white feathers. All round,
the horizon was shut in by the graceful hills which give the place
its secluded appearance but make it tropically hot as soon as
the sun has risen above them. Yet, everything had to be made
so comfortable for the eight or nine hundred people attending
the session that every morning there were big fires in all the
public rooms at the Greylock.

I soon saw the characteristics of the Williamstown crowd. They
were mostly elegant New Yorkers or Washingtonians summering
at places like Lenox but anxious to give some seriousness to their
vacation. That Williamstown was in fashion required no demonstration. I even discovered before long the usual sprinkling
of *jeunes filles à marier*. Yet the general tone was Genevan, subdued and collected. Two or three ladies whom their beauty or
elegance rendered a little conspicuous were tacitly made to feel
that they were not playing the game. Picnicking by the cool
creek was authorized, but bridge-playing had to be kept a bit
furtive. On the whole, the atmosphere at Williamstown was that
of a Wisdom School where it was nice to be and where it would
even be nicer to have been. I knew many of the visitors. They
were admirably discreet, content to recognize one with a nod

and a smile, and at first I imagined that I was going to have all my time for my work.

I was soon disillusionized. There was a strong body of pressmen superintended by my friend, James Ernest King. Several of them called every day as soon as they had read the morning papers. They were a fine class of reporters—Mr. Stanley High was one—and I enjoyed my talks with them, but commenting on the news for them would have been a joy in itself. Needless to say that the telephone buzzed incessantly.

This was not all. Most of the work of the Institute was done at Round Tables conducted by men like my friends Boris Bakmeteff or C. Dewitt Poole, or by experts like ex-ambassador Morgenthau or Mr. Philip Kerr, or by technicians like General Bliss, Mr. Culbertson, Mr. Blakeslee, M. de Sanchez, Mr. Hornbeck and several others. I, like the other lecturers, was expected to appear at those Round Tables, sometimes to conduct them, and this could not be done without serious preparation. Finally, there was a semi-official representation from Washington, consisting of Admirals or Generals who invited us to luncheon parties very like symposiums. As my six lectures had to be got ready in spite of it all, I had to live all the time with my thoughts and, much to my regret, I neglected, or apparently neglected friends some of whom were grieved by my effort to retire. They did not realize how difficult it was, under such circumstances, to give six lectures in seventeen days.

My fellow-lecturers were Sir Edward Grigg, M. P. and former secretary of Mr. Lloyd George; Señor Zeballos, Minister of Foreign Affairs in Argentine, and Count Harry Kessler, lately Ambassador to Warsaw and a semi-official representative of Germany at the League of Nations.

Sir Edward Grigg was accompanied by a nymph-like young wife whose beauty and independent manner attracted a good deal of attention. He was a typical British Liberal, which his recent connection with Lloyd George emphasized, but he was as interested in Imperial problems as any Conservative might

be and, soon after his American trip, he became governor of
Kenya. His course was largely devoted to the relations of Britain
with her Dominions. I remember his concluding his first lecture
with the statement that Britain had hitched her chariot to three
stars: justice, freedom and peace. As we walked out of the hall
a lady, related I believe to the Garfields, said to me: "That celestial chariot sounds well, but I have just returned from Egypt."
Few people were sceptical like this lady. Slightly old-fashioned,
Sir Edward was convincing by that something superior which
Voltaire says belongs to the unruffled reasoning of the English.

Sir Edward Grigg was practically understudied by Mr. Philip
Kerr—now Lord Lothian—who had been a speaker at Williamstown before, and had also been attached to Mr. Lloyd George's
cabinet. He was a youthful, amusing person, full of naturalness
and spontaneity. Once he accosted me with the declaration: "I
don't like your politics, but I love your lectures: you know the
lecture-business inside out." I am afraid that he too meant that
"I knew how to make a point," for his apparent facility in con-
ceding what you pleased was accompanied by a strong capacity
not to be influenced by the concessions. Moreover, although he
had already had considerable political experience, he was only
well-informed on problems immediately connected with British
interests or with Germany, and he treated the rest cavalierly. A
few years later I met him as he was leaving the home of M. Léon
Blum with whom he had had a long conversation: he had never
known or suspected that M. Blum was a Socialist. The refined
tastes and ways of the Socialist leader had only suggested a
Liberal politician, but I was astonished that Lord Lothian had
interviewed M. Blum without inquiring who he was. Much as I
too dislike the marquess' politics, I like the man and it is always
a pleasure to run up against him. He was constantly in the breach
at Williamstown and showed a good-humoured bravery which
people admired without being always conquered by it.

Señor Zeballos was undoubtedly the most interesting figure
at Williamstown, for he possessed immense legal and political
knowledge, he was an international personage, and he discussed

the Monroe Doctrine in his course with such thoroughness that
it did not occur to one to call it fearlessness. Those lectures were
admirable pieces of robust work. Unfortunately this vigorous
thinker was an old and tired man whose voice did not carry in
the hall beyond the first three or four rows, and whose English
sounded so foreign that it could not be understood even by those
who heard it. It was agony to sit there watching him waste his
wealth of intelligent knowledge. He felt out of it in Williamstown
and in the United States as well. He was going to Europe immediately after the end of the session and it was evident that
he would be infinitely more at home in Paris than where he was.
Once I met him at the door of a Williamstown druggist looking
doubtfully at a little box of medicine. It was plain bi-carbonate
of soda, but he hinted that he would be glad when he could buy
the stuff at a European pharmacy. All that was American was
alien to him. His melancholy appearance only foreboded a
catastrophe: he fell dead as he landed in Liverpool. His death
grieved me, for I respected the man deeply. It also lost me an
invitation to lecture in Buenos Aires which I had gladly accepted.

Count Kessler was a refined thoughtful gentleman whose pensiveness was apt to be pathetic. I have never known whether or
not he was exceptionally religious, but he often appeared to me
as a monk who had gone back to evening clothes. He had an
Irish mother and a French brother-in-law and the Keltic had
largely eliminated the German ingredients in him. He could be
full of animation as he recounted amusing experiences in three
or four languages which he spoke like a native. Yet this inter-
nationalist was at heart an uncompromising German and his lectures showed it, even when he tried to make them appealing. His
antipathy to Poland and his capacity for propagandizing against
France—which he liked—revealed the nature of his patriotism.
I noted in my Diary: "It is frightening to reflect that Count
Kessler is a real German Liberal; of course, there will be another
war." We were soon in the cockpit which M. Jusserand had so
ruefully anticipated. Neither of us was perfectly dignified. But
no Frenchman could have left unchallenged the statement that

France was as responsible for the war as Germany. France doubt-less appeared militaristic under Francis the First, Louis the Fourteenth and the two Napoleons. But it was only an appear-ance, for history leaves no doubt that not one of those monarchs was really loved, whereas the Germany of 1914, long before the Germany of Hitler, was well represented by a popular Kronprinz who could hail war as *frisch und lustig*—fresh and cheerful— when frightfulness was at its most sanguinary. I had seen it with my own eyes, and my memory was still full of the images of murder and destruction.

Count Kessler also relied on the remoteness of Americans from European history when he devoted a whole lecture to the long struggle between France and "Germany." Not one in ten in his audience could have a clear notion that the Germany against which the French *ancien régime* fought so long, had little in common with the inflated Prussia which now goes by that name, and was really Austria. My own lecture the next day was entitled "Reconciliation" and had long been planned to explain that capital difference between the "German Empire" (merely dating from 1871) and the historic "Empire of Germany," or Holy Em-pire, which Prussia detested. Many people stared as they heard me allude to a war of Prussia against Bavaria in 1864, to another war, in 1866, against Austria, or to racial differences between the Prussians and the Germans. As a shrewd Bostonian said to me after the lecture, people could save a lot of foolish emotion if they would learn history. But what I read on many faces was merely the typical American feeling that "Europe never can be understood; it would take a lifetime to understand Europe." Yet they realized that, this time without any polemical intention, I was giving an historical lecture every paragraph of which hap-pened to be a refutation of what had been said, the day before, from the same platform. The effect was considerable as the press of next day showed. Count Kessler himself good-humouredly ad-mitted it at a tea which I gave for my fellow-lecturers. I felt that afternoon how much more European than the British Germans are. (Intelligent Jews in America also invariably strike me as

more European than the most travelled New Englanders.) A
literary man like myself, Count Kessler seemed only separated
from me by infinitesimal differences, yet dining, the same day, at
the house of Sir Edward Grigg, I felt more *en rapport* with him
and his wife and even with the avowedly pro-German Philip Kerr.
The reason is no doubt that the French have never yet had with
the Germans the kind of conversation which leaves no dark suspicious spot untouched, whereas they have had it, on several mo-
mentous occasions, with the British. I had been able, only a week
before, to devote a lecture to a denunciation of Mr. Lloyd George
—the greatest liar in history, as Mr. J. M. Keynes said. Yet Lloyd
George's two former secretaries did not bear malice, and they
laughed when I told them that Mr. Baruch had forewarned me
against lecturing on the eighteenth century. They also admitted
that I knew how to make a point when they blamed France for
nervously insisting on security, instead of trusting to the future,
and I answered with a frank argument *ad hominem*. I pointed out
that France has several hundred kilometers of a difficult frontier
to defend against a Germany which has invaded her territory
three times in a hundred years. On the other hand, Britain refuses
to share with France, a former ally, a frontier of barely twenty
feet—the Channel tunnel—which two Eton school boys with machine guns could defend against a whole French army if they
did not prefer blowing up the whole frontier and flooding the
tunnel at one blast. Yet this frontier was refused by Britain,
entirely for military reasons. D.O.R.A. seemed to show more
nervousness than France but, being British, she had no idea
that she did so and, no doubt, plumed herself on taking no
chances. For years there was a curious contrast between the re-
spective attitudes of France and Britain. France prayed that
Britain might increase her military forces. Britain, on the contrary, showed evident relief when the efforts of French Liberals
reduced the military service from three years to eleven months.
Her satisfaction only lasted till Germany unexpectedly reappeared with a brand-new army of extremely doubtful cousins.

The subject of my lectures was, as I said above, France and her problems of the moment viewed largely in connection with her former Allies' policies. I strove to make French political conditions clearer and, without holding a brief for the League of Nations, the World Court or anything definitely involving America in the entanglements of the rest of the planet, I endeavoured to give my audience a consciousness of the role which willy-nilly their country could not but play in international affairs.

A considerable number of the Americans attending the session were Francophiles. Yet I found in them, as in their less travelled countrymen, a puzzling uncertainty about that France of 1923. They were inclined to think of her at the same time as Militarist or Imperialist, and yet as specifically Latin, with incomprehensible impulses resulting in constant changes of government giving her a weak and almost Caribbean appearance. Conciliation of exaggerated ambitions with vacillating politics seemed difficult to my audiences.

The answer to this note of interrogation was however easy. A French government had little in common with the government of the United States. The American Constitution had been the outcome of a revolutionary crisis which made a strong Executive a necessity: it was not surprising that the first American President should have been a General. The Constitution of the French Republic, on the contrary, was the result of a purely political compromise. Indeed it had been the work of a Royalist, decidedly anti-Republican, assembly which had only framed it as a temporary makeshift, because the three Monarchist factions composing it could not choose from among three Pretenders: a Bourbon, an Orléans and a Bonaparte. This accounted for the fact that a French President had no power, that the real ruler of France was the Chamber, and that, when this ruler changes Prime Ministers, the change has no more significance than when the President of the United States changes his secretaries: invisible bureaucrats carry on.

The oft-repeated accusation of Militarism and Imperialism was more difficult to refute, for the French had retained, in 1923, the largest part of their army of 1919, this army was in the Ruhr and the effort of French diplomacy to strengthen Poland and give more cohesion to the Little Entente was denounced as "colonization." The superficial conceit which has been a French fault ever since there has been a French nation was not likely to modify the impression produced by the presence of French troops in Germany or of French generals in Poland. Useless to add that adverse propaganda was making the most of even the slightest appearances against France. I did my best to place the situation in its true light. The explanation of the occupation of the Ruhr was, of course, the desire of France to obtain Reparations. In fact, as soon as the Dawes Plan became a possibility the Ruhr was evacuated. As for the action of French diplomacy in Central Europe, it found its natural explanation in the craving for security. Only people who know what invasions mean can realize the dread of being invaded. I constantly heard even intelligent people asking me the naïve question: why can't you live with Germany as we live with Canada? The answer, of course, was that France lives with Belgium as the United States lives with Canada—the frontier is undefended. But I could not help pointing out that the Mexican frontier is closely guarded by American troops and yet Mexico is a delightful neighbour compared to the Germany of 1815, 1870 or 1914. Unfortunately such arguments strike people as mere dialectics. They silence more than they convince.

Americans are so fundamentally honest that they believed me, more than my logic, when I told them that whatever may be the actions of its rulers, or however evident its military qualities, the French nation is at heart pacifist. The tendency of the electorate to return Liberal majorities to the Chambers was proof enough of this. The astonishing ascendancy of M. Briand—who during ten years directed the foreign politics of France—was another proof. But the notion of a militaristic France was so deeply rooted that between 1924 and 1934 the ship's reporters never once met me at the dock without asking me if France was not going to declare a preventive war against Germany.

To-day nobody in the world would dream of repeating that France—although she is feverishly re-arming—ought to be called militarist. The real situation is so clear that even a child must see it. On one hand there are two Empires—the British and the French—which have lost the Imperial spirit. On the other there are two nations—Germany and Italy—which possess that Imperial spirit but have no Empires. Signor Mussolini has many times drawn the conclusion. *Experientia magistra stultorum.* It is unfortunately true that Italy is more admired for acquiring strength and ambition than France is for having listened to international pacifist preachers. The lesson of history that advisers do not pay the pipers is always learned too late. I am tempted to forgive my French countrymen when I remember that the whole world indefatigably repeated to them: Be of good cheer, get over that nervousness, everybody wants peace. But the world has now changed its mind.

Nine in ten at Williamstown were for the entry of the United States into the League of Nations. They had been Wilsonians, they were proud of the American origin of the League, and they did not want the moral benefit of American intervention in the war to be wasted. Their culture put them above the platitudes which were already beginning to fill the press, viz., "America was cleverly drawn into a war which was not her war; she was taken in by wily statesmen infinitely more clever than her own; all European nations were ungrateful; the more remote they were the better." Yet they could not be entirely free from the basic American ideas concerning Europe. Used as they were to speak of America as a continent occupied by one nation, it was almost impossible for them to form a clear conception of the jigsaw-puzzle division of Europe with its racial, linguistic or religious differences. I heard even intelligent people wondering: why don't you have the United States of Europe? Europe, endlessly intriguing or fighting or whining, seemed stupid and her stupidity was irritating. How could she be so antagonistic to the notion of unity, even if unity had to be built on compromise? Could she not see how much happier God's country was? The intellectual conclusion to which this psychology could not but lead was: we want to enter the League of Nations because it is natural for us to feel brotherly, but we do not want to get entangled in purely European affairs. Gradually the correction was made: we can be brotherly without the League of Nations—which is sure to entangle us—therefore let us keep clear of the League.

Many Europeans are annoyed by the endless repetition of the statement: "We do not want to be selfish but we do not want to be entangled." For the repetition is endless, and even political writers of the first order cannot avoid it. It is not rare to hear Europeans, tired of the formula, attaching to it the label of hypocrisy. Yet the American is no hypocrite: he honestly wants to help, but he cannot forget that the Pilgrim Fathers, who still somehow fashion his soul, turned their backs on Europe without any idea of returning there. What there is of kindly feeling in the phrase "the Old Country" was attached to it by later emigrants. Interest in European nations belongs to culture or to families caring for an ancestry.

I do not think it possible for a country like the United States to persevere indefinitely in an attitude which might seem logical when it took a month or six weeks to cross the Atlantic Ocean, but which must appear less and less so as the increase of speed will reduce the dimensions of the Earth. Contingencies will do what no amount of preaching has so far succeeded in doing. But in 1923 nobody would even see the germs of those contingencies. A surprised smile or a sceptical shake of the head would meet my allusions to the fact that the role once assigned in the world to Great Britain must now belong to the United States as well. My audience were so grateful to be a happy country that they did not wish to be anything else. Only once, in New York, did I meet a lady who said definitely: "The big wheel of the world is now here," and I felt sure that even she did not contemplate any responsibility.

Yet, my last lecture in which I insisted that the reconstruction of Europe could not be effected without American concurrence was the most successful. I had had no experience of an American ovation, and while its extraordinary warmth moved me deeply, I felt as if I had no right to so much enthusiasm, and I was out of the hall, blaming myself for churlishness, long before the applause subsided. On several occasions since, the American public has tried to make me feel that I was somehow adopted. As I write this, I cannot refrain from saying how deeply, every day of my life, I appreciate the distinction—it has transformed my existence—but the revelation that henceforth I was to be something more than a sympathetic foreign observer came to me on that seventeenth of August, 1923. I have long wished for an advance of our still narrowly nationalistic civilizations that would enable a man to be a citizen of two countries at the same time.

I touched lightly on the debt question during my Williamstown course. My feeling was at the time what it has remained since: I did not think that America could count on payment for the munitions she sent to the Allies after she declared war. For, during many months, those munitions were used by Allied soldiers who lost their lives while using them and so saved American lives. But I also thought that every penny loaned to Europe after the Armistice ought to be paid back.

A few months after my Williamstown experience, Colonel Harvey, in Washington, arranged for me to have an audience with President Coolidge. I was surprised to find the so-called taciturn President much more talkative than he was supposed to be. He actually made conversation and I was astounded to hear him remark—as I told him that I had known Colonel Harvey over twenty years—that "in that case I ought to know all his prejudices about things and about people." But when a turn of the interview gave me a chance to tell the President of the line of argument I had followed at Williamstown concerning the debt, he rose precipitately and said that he saw the next man coming.

I had a few days in New York, after the Williamstown session, before sailing. Mrs. Loomis invited me to a dinner, in Tuxedo Park, which she was giving to General Gouraud. The dinner was excellent, but owing to the complete absence of wine—our hostess was a law-abiding Presbyterian—there was about it the something melancholy which belongs to things unfinished. Gouraud felt it and tried to express the nuance with soldierly frankness. Looking fixedly at Mrs. Loomis he said: "Madame, your dinner is very good. Very good indeed is your dinner. In France we always eat too much because everything is too good." Mrs. Loomis knew French very well and registered the double-barrelled compliment with the admirable ease she possessed.

A few days later we were on that perfection of a French boat, the S.S. *France.* The Friday luncheon was a culinary triumph and everybody had been over-eating when crêpes Suzette made their blazing appearance. I saw Gouraud who sat opposite me at the Captain's table fumbling at his belt with his only hand before he started on those crêpes. "Oh! General," I said, "don't you think that in France we always eat too much because everything is too good?" The General looked at me with a queer composite smile, trying to remember something.

Gouraud's presence on the boat nearly caused a catastrophe. A poor French ex-soldier, who wrongly imagined that he had not quite done his duty during the war, could not bear the sight of the mutilated and extremely impressive General. He jumped overboard, and during half an hour we circled around trying to rescue him. The Captain said to me: "Don't be shocked. When the boat is close by him, he'll sink. They always do." But this man did not. He was hauled up unconscious but still alive. With great kindness Gouraud visited him every day.

We had many interesting conversations which M. Bédier, the great scholar, often shared. Gouraud has a first-rate and remarkably equipped intellect. I noted down a number of his judgments.

What could not be recorded was the poetry of his descriptions of Africa. I have no patience with Radicals whose pacifism causes them to speak patronizingly of even great soldiers. Men of action can only be appreciated by their peers and should never be depreciated by critics whose capacity to struggle with the world has never been put to the test. Bédier showed touching deference to one of his country's foremost defenders.

Shortly after landing I made up my mind to move away from College Stanislas. The resolve cost me a great wrench, for I loved the College, and the rooms where I wrote *From a Paris Balcony* had become part of my consciousness. But I could not, year after year, keep asking for leave of absence to go to America. Once in a while I still conduct examinations at the College and I never find myself in the rue Notre-Dame-des-Champs without almost unconsciously swerving into the familiar park. But the apartment in the rue Chanoinesse where I have lived since 1923 has gradually become equally dear. It is only a stone's throw from Notre-Dame whose clock regulates my work. In fact, it is within the precincts of the Cathedral Cloister, and the stones of long-departed canons pave the courts. My little street is full of associations: Héloïse lived in the even narrower rue des Chantres, close by. All that was most mediæval in the Middle Ages once crystallized here: indeed, my rue Chanoinesse has an air of running away from banality and modernity. I should find it hard to live elsewhere.

This nook has also for me more recent associations. During nine years my friend, Henri Bremond, himself a priest, and an illustrious writer, lived in the next apartment. I could hear his voice from the desk on which I am now writing. His presence and the consciousness of his indefatigably active thinking added to the studious atmosphere of the place. Every day, either of us would visit the other, but anxious, as we both were, to save every minute for our work, we abode by an unwritten rule never to sit down in each other's study. Bremond's death has left a wistfulness over our house, although his apartment was at first taken

over by my old friend Hilaire Belloc, and is now occupied by
a writer for whose concentrated work I have the most sincere
respect, M. Charles Du Bos.

VI

Ever since 1923 I have never missed a single year revisiting America. In May or June, when the Spring is here and Paris is at her best, and I ought to be content with the lazy pleasures which the warm weather provides, I begin to experience a craving for the faraway shores left a few months before. It is a strange thing that I should thus periodically want to be in a country where I have at no time dreamed of settling permanently. I have never been able to analyze that longing in a satisfactory way. It is true that my easiest work is done in America, that my chief success has been and still is there, that I feel nearer to an American audience than to even a French one, that I see my books more frequently on American counters than elsewhere, above all, that I have in America friends whom I wish I could see all the time. But those obvious causes are probably not at the bottom of the attraction I feel. All told, I want to be in America because I am happy there, not because it is God's country, or the land of the free, or the land of opportunity, or anything that fills the tomes of political students or the biographies of adopted Americans like myself. The joy I experienced, almost thirty years ago, in repeating to myself at Deal Beach, in the garden of the Harveys: "This is America, I am actually in America," is what I want to revive. And I want to revive it probably because of the wish I had in boyhood to see my boat sailing into the broad mouth of the Hudson River, entirely imagined from the map. My soul is cold and indifferent when I go up the rue de la Paix, it is alive when I am in Madison Avenue. I keep secret foolish note-books in which sections of New York, Chicago, San Francisco or San Antonio are described in minute detail, a well-known symptom of love. And when I meet French or English friends who express their sympathy with America, I feel like the legendary Englishman who helped himself to the whole dishful of radishes because nobody liked them as much as he did. Yet, as I write all this, I know that it will give pleasure, not only to dear friends, but to hundreds of Americans whose welcome was partly meant to

311

attach me to their country, and I rejoice at being able to write it sincerely.

Summer is also the time when I begin to think of the subjects I shall have to treat in America and, as I visualize my customary audiences, the sensation of America becomes intensified. The choice of lecture-subjects is all-important. Some which at first seem attractive and rich in possibilities are only pretty nobodies which, after deceiving me, also deceive my American correspondents. It requires diplomacy to convince them that I made a mistake. Sometimes, too, Madam Program Chairman not knowing which of two subjects she prefers wants me to fuse them both into one lecture, a fatal mistake which neither of us must be guilty of. Other subjects turn out to be taboo. During two or three seasons one of the lectures I offered was "Anatole France and the New Literary Generation," a study in the inevitable eclipse of a great name. Only once—at the charming little college at Northfield, Minnesota—did I succeed in persuading my audience that I did not rejoice in a literary injustice. Finally I had to give up that subject, but people perversely go on asking me to choose it that they may misunderstand my treatment of it.

September I always spend at Trélon, my home-town in the forests. When the swallows begin to assemble on the telegraph wires I go back to Paris and, shortly after, I am on the liner, mostly a French liner, which provides a dreamy transition between my old world and my new world. One night I am awakened by the vibration of the ship in reverse motion. An hour or so later she comes to a standstill and, looking out into the cold gray morn, I see suspended and aërial, as it were, on its sloping lawn, a white timber-house which has been my landmark for many a year. When the ship moves on again the jagged line of the New York Towers soon appears. It gives me a thrill which no repetition can diminish. Yet, no sooner am I off the dock than everything seems familiar: the taxi, the driver, the Highway, the red teeth of the cross-streets, the passers-by, very English-looking as long as they do not speak, the gloved workmen, and even the new buildings announced far and wide by the sound of the drill. Finally East Seventieth—always misunderstood by the driver who would like me to call it East Sevenny—and the usual welcome on the ninth floor, and my room, with already a pile of letters and a few memoranda waiting for me. Five minutes later I take up the receiver which gives me the recognition of a friendly little spark, the telephone girl says "good morning," a courtesy unheard of in Europe, and lo! I am talking with exclamatory friends. When I return to my desk I become suddenly aware of the cypress terraces of a tall house on Seventy-first Street, and I look out of the window. Here are the green copper-roofs of Mr. Frick's house; there's the Park with its sheeny black roads and the motor-cars apparently glued upon them; far away, towards the Bronx, I recognize those cubistic buildings which were there last year. I know I am back in New York.

I shall never know America as well as a native does, because an American—though knowing about his country infinitely less than he imagines—has accumulated more subconscious information about it than I can ever hope to gather. But I am more interested in America than Americans are. Probably this superiority would be forfeited if I actually lived in the United States. The French New Yorkers of my acquaintance wilt the moment they cannot go home every year, whereas I land, autumn after autumn, full of refreshed curiosity. It is still an adventure for me to take the Twentieth Century to Chicago, familiar as that city is. The Pullman may be capriciously heated and poorly ventilated, and I may resent the lack of semi-privacy which the traveller enjoys, with a little luck, in the compartments of a European train, but I am never bored when I travel in America. I spend hours studying the landscape which I am the only one to look at. During my early trips I was a victim, like everybody else, of the fallacy that you can see America from the carriage-window. I used to deplore that the country was over-populated, that it lacked forests, above all, that it only showed you incipient suburbs instead of what we call a village. Now that I have driven, bicycled or tramped many times away from the deceptive thread

which is all one can see from the train, I know how to interpret
the lay of the land and the horizon-line. Behind those garden-less
farms or wall-less gardens which still offend my European eyes,
I imagine secluded homesteads under spruces which I like to
hear being called cedars. The certainty that unbroken stretches
of the great American solitude subsist a few miles away from
the banality born of railways is enough to transform what I
actually see.

I also study my fellow-passengers as soon as I am rid of the
annoyance of being studied by them. This is done by the magical
trick of substituting a black tie for my Roman collar. In a twinkle
I cease to be a public character or public property. I am also
protected against tiresome confidences. For I have often found,
in Europe as well as in America, that a Roman collar exerts an
incomprehensible attraction over people who, "having been indulging," are dying to tell you what good boys they are. Not
that my fellow-passengers are really deceived about my ecclesi-
asticism. A score of signs, besides my general blackness, leave
them no doubt about this, especially if they happen to be Irish,
which they frequently are, but they realize that the disappearance
of my collar means that I have retreated into myself and they
are just ten minutes too late. Moreover, the porter soon brings
me the little table on which I have done so much comfortable
work in the past, and as soon as they see it strewn with notes for
my lectures, people cease to wonder why I seemed at first not
to be playing the game. I can work in peace.

My lectures, when I leave Paris, seem to be quite ready. They
repose, neat and alphabetical, in a special valise. In each dossier
lie two separate envelopes. One contains the notes which I made
in my first contact with the idea without which there would be
no lecture: they are of all shapes and sizes, rough-looking, inky
and incorrect. The other envelope protects three or four largish
sheets covered with obviously synoptical indications, here and
there underlined in red pencil. These sheets are the outline of

the lecture, as, sitting in my peaceful flat in the rue Chanoinesse, I saw it logically developing. The completion of this outline invariably leaves me under the delusion that my work is done and I need not worry about it.

But I no sooner look at one of these skeletons, after landing in America, than I feel how truly it deserves its macabre name, for its logic is as cold as death. A few newspapers read, a few conversations overheard, a few faces scrutinized leave me under no doubt that a lecture prepared in Paris refuses to be delivered in America: it has to be rebuilt, life has to be infused into it. I have rebuilt some lectures more than twenty times, because I have never been able to give twice over the same lecture from the same skeleton. I do not give myself the trouble of courting a subject afresh from conscientiousness, or because I am afraid that somebody may have heard the lecture in another town, or from any such unselfish motive. I rebuild my lectures because I possess the unfortunate gift of hearing myself delivering them, and the one of my two selves who speaks knows that the other self who listens cannot bear to be bored. That is why I must have been seen, on innumerable occasions, rebuilding lectures in the train.

I cannot be happy on the lecture-platform unless I am sure of two things: in the first place, I must be certain that although I have no memory I shall not be teased by anxiety concerning the sequence of what I have to say; in the second place, I must be able so to forget that I am giving what is called a lecture that I shall be like one of the audience, discussing some interesting points with them. In my own vocabulary I call the first requirement "a thread," an Ariadne's thread, while I call the second "contact." There can be no contact unless I am sure of my thread.

I pity lecturers who have to read from a manuscript, for pitiful it is to waste the reserves of human sympathy latent in an audience. But sometimes I envy the many lecturers who can memorize what they have to say and fear neither the treachery of memory nor emotion, nor any foolish incident like the sudden entry of a camera-man indulgently telling you to go on with your talk. In order to enable myself to speak for an hour or more I have to store up an enormous amount of material, for I invariably forget many things in which I have taken real interest. A twist of a sentence, the unexpected change of a simile, a few words in answer to a smile or a questioning expression on a face, and a whole train of thought gets displaced and vanishes. I never give an hour's lecture without material enough for a two-hours' talk.

The thread which helps a man destitute of memory to wend his way through this labyrinth of data is merely the simple and natural unfolding of an absolutely simple and natural idea. At school in Cambrai I read Maury's celebrated *Treatise on Eloquence,* and I noticed with astonishment that this writer, famous in a sophisticated epoch like the eighteenth century, insisted on a discourse being based on such an obvious statement as can be grasped by a peasant or a child. This is the kind of advice which does not appeal to an ambitious schoolboy. Many times I found myself seduced by a brilliant formula, sometimes a mere witticism, on which I imagined that an essay could be built. On each occasion I discovered that the brilliance is exhausted as soon as a few lines have been written and barrenness is the punishment for vanity. So experience taught me that the real method for doing without memory consists in treating a subject in such an uncomplicated way that it will not require any memory. Surely no memorizing is necessary to give a lecture on "Feasts of the Mind," for instance, beginning with an analysis of the most elementary of those pleasant mental conditions, reverie, going on through a natural gradation to the concatenation of causes and effects in an historic development, and finally dwelling on the enjoyment one can find in philosophical abstractions. One needs only to think, not remember, such a sequence.

This method offers another advantage: it leads the people who are listening to you on from one idea to another, and there is nothing for which a man is so grateful as to be given the impression that, during an hour, he is made to use his brain without any interruption, without being conscious of a gap or annoyed by a snag. A lecture should be like an hour on a placid stream down which we float without even being reminded that life is but a dream. Nobody should invite people in to make them work.

With a large provision of ideas and an absolutely clear distribution of them, contact with the audience becomes possible and even inevitable, because no phantasm creates the anxiety imprisoning the worried lecturer within himself. He forgets he is bothering with the thing technically called a lecture, he is only conscious of an idea and of fellowmen interested in that idea. He is going through a completely human act and feels vitalized by it. Hence a sense of freedom, nay, a sense of adventure, for the interest felt by the audience reacts on the lecturer's curiosity and trebles his mental energy. I have been conscious of that delightful excitement too many times ever to run the risk of forfeiting it: my lecture is as full of unsuspected possibilities for me as it is for the most receptive among my audience. Instances are not easy to recount. I may say that once, lecturing for a club on Long Island, I hit upon a definition of culture as "the subordination of emotions to ideas," which may illustrate what I am saying. I shall have an occasion later on to say that my book on *The Art of Thinking* passed from the stage of mere notes to that of as vital an exposé as I am able to produce through the process of lecturing. But the unkempt memoranda I described as being the first outcome of loving interest in a fecund idea must never be lost sight of. There, without any effort at organization, lie the apparently inert things which are no sooner brought into contact than sparks begin to flash out of them. The words underlined in red in my skeletons refer to those simple but pregnant ideas. I have seen inquisitive newspaper men, who insisted on looking at them, puzzled by their apparent lack of meaning. In fact they are more like Chinese ideograms than like ordinary

English or French words, for I often do not know in which language my outlines have been written.

By dint of looking out at the landscape, or of looking within myself at ideas which contemplation gradually makes phosphorescent, I finally arrive at my destination. Lecturers are full of funny stories about their experiences, and I myself could tell a number. But I have no doubt that my readers have been treated to such narratives often enough not to crave any more. Suffice it to say that it is so pleasant to be met that it becomes unpleasant not to be, but, on the other hand, being met is something of an anxiety, for the contrast between the self-collectedness which you try to preserve and the frequent excitement of the people who meet you is disquieting. Once I was met up the line, at six o'clock in the morning, by an extremely kind woman-friend who got me tumbling, unwashed and unshaven, out of my upper berth with an imperative *"Levez-vous!"* There lives no kinder person, but one's first experience of a levee is intimidating. I always know by the look of the people who meet me whether I am going to be protected against reporters or delivered up to them, taken to a quiet room or led to a house full of electrified guests. I always know, too, the worried expression of the bookseller who wonders whether I will not go at once to his shop "already full of people wanting autographed copies of my books." People ought to be told that the little flame which has to blaze up during a lecture is as vacillating as that of the clay-lamp of the Catacombs, or to change the simile boldly, that your lion will not roar if he has been over-lionized. Americans, I shall never tire of repeating, are the most cordial people on earth, but their cordiality makes them excitable and talkative, and it is a mistake to talk to death a man who, in five minutes, will be expected to do such an ambitious thing as talking an audience to life.

In most cases your audience is only too full of life, or of what it calls life, already. You know this as you go up the aisle or peep through the hole in the curtain. You realize that it will take

quite five minutes to let agitation subside. The best is to step up
to the desk and fuss over the light, or the glass of water, or your
own glasses as long as possible to let people forget the last excitement, or the sentence, pleasant or irritating, still buzzing in
their ears. Meanwhile they can make up their minds whether
you are "the aged philosopher" or "the white-haired but youthful Frenchman" the newspapers have described. The important
thing is to bring them to a state of mind in which you need no
longer fear that, in case anybody comes in late, the whole audience will concentrate upon *them* as if they had been long and
eagerly expected. In time you feel that they begin to read your
thoughts. They see clearly now why you have been trying to slow
down matters. They smile recognition of your psychology. You
smile too, and your contact is made. If you then begin in any
arresting way, with a question, for instance, or a reference to
the morning paper, you may in a few moments capture as much
of your audience's attention as a lecturer can ever hope to annex
or an audience is capable of giving. If the hall is neither Gothic,
nor long and low; if your voice fills it in such a way that no
attendant will have to walk up stealthily to your desk with an
amplifier sure to rob you of half your personality; if the lights
above you are not so glaring that you will be dazzled by them,
or the lights above the audience so dimmed that you will not
be able to follow the effect you produce on any physiognomy,
you will be able to retain the contact to the end. I remember exquisite minutes when, with a tension of all my faculties, I have
pursued an elusive nuance while the audience visibly collaborated in my search. There is no greater pleasure than the perception of a mental communion like this.

A Forum frequently follows the lecture. A certain amount of
danger to the lecturer results from it, but it makes that little
ordeal infinitely more exciting than the put-up job audaciously
calling itself a debate. The real annoyance is not heckling, which
can always be punished in a moment by a few retaliatory questions or by merely calling it heckling. I have done this many

a time to the evident satisfaction of the audience and sometimes even of the heckler himself, ready to regret a little horseplay and laughing at himself with good-humoured embarrassment. What is annoying is irrelevance, which is often the result of honest curiosity but which makes everybody uncomfortable. A great deal of tact is necessary to answer an irrelevant question.

Characteristically American is the ceremony inevitably following a lecture. Scores of people file past the lecturer to shake hands and say a few words. An English audience is too shy or too respectful of your privacy to do it. I addressed over two thousand people once at the City Temple, in London, and the audience seemed as enthusiastic as any in America. Yet, when I found myself in the stream of my listeners going down Holborn, nobody thought of stopping me to ask a question, nobody even nodded recognition. The crowd did not wish to trespass on my recovered anonymity, or seeing me carefully wrapped up against the evening coolness they thought it would be unkind to delay me and politely pretended to look away.

I appreciated this discretion, but I should not like to see it copied in America, where it would be instantaneously transmuted into a pose. Americans must be warm. European lecturers often speak with cruel incomprehension of what they remember being said to them by people filing thus past them. It is true that there is a good deal of apparent artificiality in what many of them say: you get nervous at the prospect of one more mentioning your "message." But the cliché is only trying to convey appreciation. You must also expect plenty of egotism. ("Daughter is in your own country. She knows French very well and she's seen all those châteaux!") But here again you can detect an effort to express sympathy with your country and your language, or admiration for those châteaux about which you said not a word, and how can the poor old lady do it without mentioning Daughter instead of concentrating on your sacred Self?

Every now and then you may encounter frankness: "You said this or that. I don't believe it."

"Well, all the Washington papers say so."

"Do they? I don't believe them."

Eavesdropping lady: "May I ask who you are?"

"Yes, I am Mrs. Tremont. I hate the French."

"Where are you staying?"

"With my daughter, Mrs. Foley. She hates the French too."
The dear old lady is deaf and funny. There is not an ounce of
hatred in her hate. Why should you mind?

Moreover there will always be two or three people who, shyly
and briefly, will say something summing up months of reflection
so touchingly that you feel ashamed of having elicited such
confidence by a mere lecture, or by a passage in one of your
books far superior to your normal attitude towards life. Those
are the people whose presence delights but also intimidates
a lecturer.

American writers, even the most sensitive to criticism from
outside, are hard on American Women's Clubs. Their attitude
is in fashion, and fashion is thoughtless. Why should a writer
express himself as if there were more foolish people in a club
than elsewhere? Or why does he imply that no foolish people
ought to be members of a club? As a matter of fact, the proportion of silly individuals is probably less in a club than in the
community at large. And why should silly people be debarred
from a chance to grow less silly? One great fact strikes the observer in America, viz., that mental progress in the United States
is largely produced by life, by activity, by campaigns in pursuit
of simple practical ideals. Collective thinking is more visible
there than in Europe less gifted for coöperation. A tremendous
amount of kindness transmuted into thought is alive in the wom-
en's clubs of America. A tremendous amount of energy is skil-
fully harnessed by their officers.

I admit that these officers cannot manage a luncheon: they
seldom give you enough to eat and they never give you anything
to drink. But they manage their serious affairs in a remarkable

way. I have been invited a few times to witness their interior proceedings before my lecture. The amount of sense, of courteous individuality, or of graceful unpretentious eloquence I have seen displayed during such sessions was apt to be intimidating and I prefer to avoid it. America can produce a more impressive list of distinguished women than any other country, and those women have all been trained in clubs or in Leagues. It is useless to add that a sure instinct has taught them to save their womanly attractiveness while acquiring the qualities supposed to be the apanage of men. They all know that a quick-moving argument supported by accurate data and expressed in terse language is in some danger of sounding positive, and they take their precautions in consequence. Nobody accuses them of being man-haters.

In the wake of the lecturer invariably appear the reporters. It is impossible to know them as I do without feeling profound sympathy with them, with their hard work, their constantly taxed industry, their suppressed personality and, above all, the patience with which they sometimes endure indignity at the hands of their employers. But it is also impossible to know American reporters as I do without being very much on one's guard against them.

During many years I used to meet the old-fashioned ignorant reporter who only knew one question: "What do you think of America?"—and did not at first suspect you were laughing at him if you began "America extends from the Atlantic to the Pacific Ocean. Its population is computed at, etc."

There are still left extremely simple-minded ones. I remember a nice honest-looking fellow in a western city asking me: "Those Brontë sisters that you spoke about at the University, what religious order are they?" I laughed, and the reporter said rather pathetically: "Did I say something awful? Don't mind me. I am the lowbrow at the office, but our Mr. Grimes will call on you this afternoon, and you will have a fine time with him."

There are also the angelic-looking girls who produce their pad and pencil and, noticing that you are unwilling to do all their work for them, promptly admit that they never heard about you and have not the faintest idea why they were sent to you. Say anything, they will write it down without a thought. You forgive them much more readily than the equally pretty husseys who break into your hotel-room, pry into everything as they ask you mechanical questions, and finally pounce on the MS. on your table with a "What is this?" which you are vainly hoping not to answer. South-western lady-reporters, these. The same are entirely indifferent to your personality, but will keenly record such trivialities about your appearance as the way you part your hair.

However, it cannot be gainsaid that there has been a vast improvement in reporters during the past ten or twelve years. Sometimes you actually find yourself interviewed by a University professor whom you would love to interview yourself. The best newspapers also employ real psychologists who talk with you three-quarters of an hour without jotting down a single note and manage, the next day, to reproduce the movement and colour of your conversation while giving more than a sketch of your characteristics. Philosophically-inclined reporters appear also, once in a long while. I remember a Hindoo gentleman in San Francisco who never asked me a personal question and did most of the talking, yet turned what little I told him to remarkable account. One is deeply grateful for such treats.

They can only be exceptional. Yet I feel inclined to say that out of ten reporters six nowadays are college graduates and gentlemen. They know the significance of the words you use, and aim at giving a certain unity to your interview which implies a literary preoccupation. But in spite of their culture they are handicapped by the legacy they have received from inferior interviewers, their seniors, or by strict injunctions given them at the office. Professionalism soon becomes visible in their general deportment and changes even their voice in a bizarre unnatural way about which I am never mistaken. They also seem uniformly trained to look for something sensational in what you say to them. I have never known one who, either from a desire to make you administer his own criticisms to America, or in order to enliven his story, did not try to make you say unkind things about the United States, especially about the American women. You see them smiling with delight as you seem to get perilously near the pitfall, or crestfallen as you extricate yourself. Needless to say they would love to entice you into a discussion of American politics or judgments on American politicians. Once, on the boat, surrounded by six or seven sea-front reporters whom I had diplomatically brought to a natural conversation in their natural voices, I heard universal laughter at some statement made by one of them. I asked what the joke might be and, being told that Mr. So-and-So had just said that "only Jimmy Walker could get America out of the depression," I laughed feebly for company. Although I had never said a word about the ex-mayor of New York, whom I only met much later, in Holland, the remark concerning him was coolly saddled on me the next day, in one of the most important newspapers in the city. When I complained I was told that it is a rule of the game that "what you do not contradict can be reported as being your own opinion."

Such things teach you wisdom. Pure mistrust would not be wisdom for it would be resented. It is much better to learn the aforesaid rules of the game. They are not mysterious. If you resolutely and openly taboo certain subjects, with just a smile, you will be understood and you can talk freely and sincerely about all other topics. But caution will still be necessary and, for a time, you will have to be what Paul Valéry says that Mallarmé used to be, viz., "an extraordinary man! he was actually seen to be thinking before he spoke." I owe reporters that unique experience, entirely different from the mental preparation of a public speech. It gives a man a high idea of what human expression could be if, like reading, it had not been made fatally easy and practically mechanical.

I have never known a reporter to escape the influence of that

effort to give him of one's best. Not infrequently the conversation
ends confidentially, on the spiritual plane. When it is not so,
the reporter easily regards his interlocutor as his game, that is
to say, his enemy, and sometimes suddenly hardens at the moment of departing. Then woe to the person interviewed, for the
reporter's story will deserve its unfortunate name. The rules of
the *genre* have nothing in common with the rules of the game.

A reporter's story is as interpretative as an impressionist's
picture. Only, in spite of numberless experiences and of innumerable declarations, the public does not know this, or, while
knowing it, does not believe it. The waywardness of most stories
is an immoral thing against which it is surprising that American
opinion does not rebel. On four different occasions before 1937
I have been interviewed about successive works of Mr. Sinclair
Lewis. I am not sure that I have much personal sympathy with
this novelist, and his books show flaws which my literary conscience compels me to point out. Above all, I am often irritated
by his satire of America, because I am sure to find in Europe
prejudiced readers who will not fail to tell me with a certain
smile: "Here, at all events, is an American who tells the truth
about your America." Such readers naturally fail to notice that
Mr. Sinclair Lewis is the kind of modern artist who is more
inspired by ugliness than by beauty. All this I have said, on all
four occasions, to my reporters, and it has been reported, more
or less faithfully, in that fist-on-the-table tone habitual in stories
from which nuances are carefully banished. But, on all four occasions, I also pointed out that, in spite of his shortcomings—
which are those of a former newspaper man—Mr. Lewis is a
powerful writer who deserved the Nobel Prize given him in 1933
better than any other American writer. Now, this all-important
statement has *never* appeared in any one of the interviews I am
speaking of. Such "economy" of what a man declares to be the
truth is certainly not to the credit of the press.

It is true that nobody, except the reporter, knows what becomes
of the latter's prose "at the office." Several reporters have told

me that they type every day some three thousand words, two-thirds of which get expunged by the city editor. This mysterious person's influence can be detected, by internal analysis even of the most cursory description, in the clumsy stories he publishes. But once I actually saw him in action. While we talked he worked, and I saw with amazement what his absent-minded pencil could do, how it zig-zagged, and deleted, and inverted whole blocks of composition, and ruined the story without showing it the mercy of completely destroying it.

I have never been clear about the duties of the gentleman called the re-write man. All I know is that his name is terrifying and would suffice to paralyze any reporter. But I have no doubts about the baneful influence of the other formidable person who writes the headlines at the office. It is obvious that he makes it a point, or is strictly enjoined, *not* to read the stories submitted to him, for he continually contradicts their contents. He probably runs his eye rapidly along the copy till he finds a word which can be so magnified as to produce a sensation, and he promptly magnifies it. Once, in Los Angeles, eating breakfast in that sanctuary of peace, the University Club, I was startled to read in large alarming letters: "War-god on March; Europe Seething with Strife." These headlines merely referred to the difficulty between Poland and Lithuania, so old and stale that only specialists, in Europe, still go on watching it. The Vilna correspondent had tried to enliven his story by risking the affirmation that Central Europe was seething with *interest*, and it was on that innocuous phrase that the headlines man had built his blood-curdling title.

Another time, in Boston, I was interviewed by a scholarly, gentlemanly Irishman. The reporter was leaving when he bethought himself: "Oh! but," he said, "we have not said a word about Prohibition. Do you consider it a noble experiment?" This question, about 1930, was still ticklish, and I preferred dictating the following answer: "Prohibition may have begun as a noble experiment, but as I see it practised in America, it is not a noble experiment any more." The next morning this sentence was printed, word for word, but the headlines man had retranslated it as: "Abbé Dimnet says Prohibition Ignoble Experiment." I found, that same day, several elderly Boston friends of mine grieving over the injustice of my statement, and we had to toss off stiffish cocktails to make them forget the indiscretion.

Every now and then the inaccuracy of the headlines man becomes actual falsification at the hands of some superior officer. In December, 1935, a Washington, D.C., newspaper man asked me if I did not think there was real dictatorship in the United States. I disagreed with all possible emphasis, but the interview appeared all the same under the title: "Abbé Dimnet says peak of Dictature in America." Needless to say that an indignant letter I sent to the editor never was published, but the reporter let me know that he was in no wise responsible for that little piece of infamy.

The conclusion I cannot help drawing is that Americans ought to be constantly on their guard against press reports. This is a sweeping statement and it ought to be qualified. It does not apply to the weekly or monthly reviews (as distinguished from magazines), and I have said many times that the average American reader would be a gainer, both in information and in political formation, if he would resolutely make up his mind to be satisfied with two or three weeklies of conflicting tendencies, or with the Sunday supplements of the best metropolitan or provincial dailies. However, this again ought to be qualified for it applies more to the news than to its interpretation. It would be sheer injustice to deny that a fair picture of world politics can be obtained from the editorials in most of the daily journals of America. They show as much political sense as those of Great Britain and less bias. I have been surprised many times to find that they are nearer the important realities in even French politics than those of famous French dailies, seldom free from a curious fringe of abstraction.

But the news, as given in nine out of ten American dailies, is not entirely reliable. It shows a longing for sensation which vitiates it. An American correspondent who is an honest pacifist will often give the impression that his professional desire for excitement would welcome a European war. His unsuspecting reader in the United States is never low enough to reflect that his business might profit by such a war, but he is influenced by the rhythm of what he reads and gradually counts on war which is one of the ways of bringing about wars. Or he shrugs his shoulders at the incorrigibility of the abstraction he calls Europe, for numberless American readers speak as if they were unequal to the extremely easy task of distinguishing which nations in Europe are for war and which are for peace. Even American statesmen occasionally show the same incapacity in a surprising degree.

Sensational also is the transformation of a little agitation in the streets of Paris into a riot which terrifies the New York relatives of students spending a year at the Sorbonne. Speak to a correspondent of the event which, only a week or ten days before, he has described as a catastrophe, he will look at you blankly and uncomprehendingly: last week's news only interests the monthlies; you do not know the rules of the game. Apart from their virtues as news the correspondent is indifferent to the events he relates, often in the tone of his colleague on the sports page, and this indifference is contagious and affects his readers.

On the other hand, there are times when the atmosphere of America is subtly felt by pressmen to be antagonistic to the publication of certain news. Then the news is withheld. During the years following the occupation of the Ruhr, there was in the United States a distinct pro-German tendency which could be accounted for by various causes. But it is astonishing that this tendency should have resulted in the deliberate suppression of a historic document of such importance as the machiavellian letter of Stresemann to the German Crown Prince after his Swiss negotiations with Briand. This letter was indeed published by *one* great New York newspaper, but I never succeeded in having it appear in any other. I remember the surprise of a Harvard professor's intelligent wife when I showed her the text of that famous letter and her exclamation: "Can't we hear the news, even garbled?"

This is a frank criticism of the American press, but it is meant as constructive criticism and not as mere carping, of which I am incapable. The newspapers of America not only have always been uncommonly kind to me, but they are so admirable, in many respects, that I can hardly do without them and they are sent to me in Paris by a thoughtful Boston friend, Mrs. Locke. Their shortcomings can be charged partly to the inevitable commercialism behind newspapers, partly, as usual, to American youthfulness. Complex as it is, the press of the United States is chiefly, at bottom, one of the national sporting grounds, and it seems to be enough if one plays there briskly, ably, happily, even at times a little roughly. There is nothing vicious in the sport, and I have no doubt that whenever the immorality of "the sensation at all costs" is realized it will disappear more quickly than it came. The press can never be a public service in the totalitarian sense, for it lives on the free expression of opinion. But it is evident that at least the same qualifications ought to be expected and demanded of a newspaper man who teaches fifty thousand as of a college professor who only teaches fifty or a hundred. As soon as the public really sees this, there will be courses in press ethics as there are courses in medical morals, and the blemishes of the press which everybody deplores will belong to a past only saved from being called disingenuous because it did not know it was disingenuous.

A lecturer does not derive his impressions of American culture solely from the clubs he visits: he is frequently invited by Universities, or by organizations connected with Universities, and occasionally by schools.

Though my first American visit in 1908 was, as I have related, more of a psychological experience than an investigation, I could not help bringing over with me my professional interests, and I

endeavoured to obtain some information concerning education in
the United States. I visited Columbia, Harvard and the Catholic
University in Washington. I also devoted an afternoon, in some
library, to the catalogues of the chief Universities.

These catalogues appeared enormous to a Frenchman. Everything seemed to be taught, including ancient Irish, and the number of specialists necessarily corresponding to the number of
specialties, there must be in America an army of professors
worthy of teaching in Universities. Yet I was struck by the fact
that few names seemed to be universally known in comparison
with those familiar to me in the great centres of knowledge in
France, England, Germany or Italy. Another peculiarity was
even more disconcerting: the teaching of French was obviously
divided between German professors who taught little else than
mediæval literature approached from a purely philological
angle, or by French instructors who, judging by the humility of
their degrees, would only have been allowed to teach little boys
in the secondary schools of their own country. Did the Presidents
of American Universities know nothing about our *agrégation*?
And how could one explain the unexpected proportion of foreign
names in all the catalogues? Colonel Harvey did not seem willing or qualified to answer my questions. Mr. Miller, the editor
of *The New York Times,* merely said that higher education was
a problem in America. He shocked me by speaking quite naturally of Princeton as Princeton College, not University. I carried away the impression that the hundreds of American Universities mentioned in the directories I consulted must be different
from ours. Only one definite picture remained in my memory:
the grounds of Columbia were alive with young men and women
attending the Summer Schools—I was surprised and delighted
to see many nuns among them—and they all looked happy. But
the books I saw in their hands were mostly elementary textbooks.

My information concerning American education became considerably enlarged during the years 1919 and 1920. I spoke in
at least twenty-five colleges. The splendour of their buildings,

the wealth of their libraries and laboratories, the vastness of their enrolment, their apparently inexhaustible resources acted powerfully on my imagination. I was so situated at the time that I could not help being particularly impressed by the devotion of their alumni. How different it was from the cold esteem which we Frenchmen retained for our Universities. It is true we did not live in them, indeed we hardly knew anybody in them by name. As usual, we insisted on remaining on the purely intellectual plane, whereas Americans were tenderly attached to the colleges, famous or obscure, in which they had passed from adolescence to manhood.

I was also struck by the fact that so many Americans I met had had a University education before entering on their professional training. It was not so in France where only future teachers gave themselves the literary culture—wonderful indeed —provided in our Universities. Whereas French students, intended for the law or medicine or a scientific career, passed at once from the *lycées* to the Schools dealing in their own specialty, graduates abounded in the United States. I would frequently catch myself imagining what Fourmies—a town of some twenty thousand inhabitants, five miles away from my native Trélon— would look like if it had grown up in America. There would be a small college, a big high school, a good library, two or three fine bookshops, two prosperous Clubs, and a newspaper which would put the present dowdy Fourmies Weekly to shame. Statistics telling us that out of every hundred and twenty Americans one is attending college, there could not be less than a hundred and eighty undergraduates in the town, and the number of Fourmies people who had passed through a University would not be inferior to four or five hundred. This élite would buy more books, subscribe to more reviews, and get up more concerts or lectures in a month than the actual Fourmies does in two years. My note-books of that time show that another feature was a constant matter for astonishment to me, viz., the abundance of verse printed by local periodicals which might have been supposed to be indifferent to poetry.

Over against this optimistic estimate was an ignorance of the general canons of literature which I frequently noticed and which I could not reconcile with graduation from a University. I noticed this at first when friends invited me to the theatre: the play was judged according to the amusement it gave, never by its approximation to a masterpiece. The personality of actors was discussed, but not their interpretation of character. The excitement of a Paris house over a new Phèdre or a new Alceste was unheard-of. Gradually I found that books also fell into only two categories—good book, dull book—merely indicative of the amusement they afforded. The same with pictures: a landscape or a portrait was judged entirely apart from its artistic treatment, while painted anecdotes were a joy. Clearly, the reasoned appreciation of works of art, the natural result of education, was exceptional. Once, at the Chicago Opera, a friend of Mrs. Judson's, my hostess, created a scandal, while he delighted me, by saying aloud as we left the box after a performance of *Madame Butterfly*, "Good opera, as much as you like, but a vulgar play!" Such independence evidently shocked people; if so, what was the good of multitudinous graduation?

Another observation gave me food for thought: all the institutions of higher learning which I visited were invariably dissatisfied with themselves. My guides through the magnificence I admired on every campus surprised me by cynical remarks on the system, on the trustees, on coeducation, on vain disputes concerning methods, above all on the indifference of undergraduates to their work and preference for what was called the college-life. In fact, I was never interviewed by the reporter from the college Weekly about studies in French Universities: the interest centred elsewhere. The young man was astounded to hear that French undergraduates hardly knew one another, had no notion of dormitories—the *Cité Universitaire* was not even planned at the time—played no games, organized no balls and did not even suspect that there was such a thing as intercollegiate activities. I gathered that an American University was not specifically different from any other American community: the routine of daily life was the real interest. A French University meant preëminently the Faculty; an American University meant the student-body. By slow degrees it was borne in on me that a curious relation, a reciprocal and rather affectionate contempt, prevailed between American professors and their undergraduates. No racial difference could be as marked as that one.

More surprises were in store for me. The first came in October, 1919, when I found myself in a small group of college girls seated in a little railway-station outside their campus, and intermingling a giggling conversation with a little school-work. I could hardly believe my own eyes when I saw that the book in their hands was a text-book of German meant for very young beginners. Elementary teaching went on, then, in the parklike campus I could see on the other side of the railway. This accounted for the fact—which I soon discovered—that many University professors taught as much as nine or ten hours a week (vs. sixty hours *a year* in French Universities). Such a heavy schedule evidently stood in the way of scholarly research and would have been impossible if a portion of the time had not been consumed in recitations or other elementary school-work. What I was compelled to infer was that young men and women must carry away from their four years at college the notion of a prolongation of school but no idea of a University. The older professors submitted to this state of affairs, sometimes passively, sometimes cynically. But here and there I found younger men with alert analytical faculties, undisguised radical tendencies, and a sort of general Frenchness about them, who showed their contempt for the system unequivocally. These young professors, in spite of their intellectuality, were popular with their students who seemed to be lifted up by them from boyhood to a promise of maturity and were grateful for it.

But my greatest surprise was the number of degrees conferred every year on indifferent seniors (49 doctorates in 1933 at one of the larger Universities!). Graduation seemed to be a matter of course. At the other end, admission to the University appeared to be ruinously easy. Entrance examinations have benefited by the reforms effected in the chief Universities during the last ten years, but in 1919 the students whom I would cross-examine on this all-important point were surprisingly vague. Often mere graduation from high school, or a principal's certificate, appeared to have been sufficient for admission.

Columbia, in spite of my friendly relations with President Butler, was always too big an affair to invite investigation. Harvard, Yale, Princeton, Chicago and the University of California commanded respect by a spirit which, even when it found obstacles, was evidently scientific and has ultimately triumphed. But for a long time I thought that the smaller men's colleges, and especially the women's, were nearer than any other to the higher learning. I conceived great respect for Amherst, from what C. D. Norton told me about it. In the women's colleges I thought I invariably found more appreciation of literary or artistic beauty, as well as a superiority over sports which were considered as recreation, not an occupation. Finally, I was conscious there of a collectedness which I found sadly lacking in coeducational colleges especially. But this impression was not sufficient to remove the conviction which I gradually formed that there was more school than university in the establishments of Higher Education in the United States, and that the word "college"—inevitably associated in a French mind with secondary education—was decidedly appropriate.

The concatenation of causes and effects in this state of affairs would have appeared to me clearly if I had had more knowledge of secondary education in America. But I only knew half a dozen excellent girls' schools of the Rosemary type and three boys' schools—Saint Mark's, Groton and Saint Paul's—which may, and do, criticize themselves with the sincerity made easy by approaching perfection, but are really the perfection of American schools, and would seem near perfection anywhere. For the ancient ideal embodied in *mens sana in corpore sano* is realized in those schools. A wonderful admixture of freedom and discipline creates a habit of unobtrusive candour in the boys brought up there, and they are prepared for their social role without a trace of the snobbishness unjustly ascribed to them by class jealousy. Indeed I have never heard social differences as much as alluded to by the headmasters, and the faults inherited with wealth are combated without the least reference to wealth.

There, as in the colleges, I find the younger masters nearer to the European type, more interested in pure literature and more anxious to rival Mr. Thornton Wilder than their seniors, too interested in the school-life to think of writing books. Literature may not be taught critically; Latin or French texts are not dissected as they would be in a Paris *lycée*. But creative literature is not merely encouraged, it is expected with that certitude which inevitably produces it. Poetry, fiction, essays of all kinds, including the humourous, are the results. To my regret, philosophy is not part of the curriculum, and boys who will not take it at college may always be posed by nuances of language or references to doctrines in what they will read. Yet, moral or political issues are kept in the foreground and frequently discussed. On the whole, my impression in 1919 was that the ideal of Universities—culture—was much more in evidence in these schools than in the colleges I constantly visited, and as I mentally classified them as high schools I was inclined to think highly of American secondary education.

This impression was fortified by the fact that while, as I said above, American Universities are articulate in self-criticism, American high schools are loud in self-praise. President Coolidge, during the audience to which I referred, more than gave me to understand that I should be amazed at their superiority; and the parents I heard were equally satisfied with them. A book

edited, in 1933, by Mr. Charles A. Beard also regards them as
the peak of excellence.

Gradually I came in contact with a few families whose children were educated in the public high schools. I met the teachers
and two or three principals, and my professional interest in
text-books and in pupils' copy-books soon showed me the methods. It is difficult to speak harshly of American teachers, mostly
charming and charmingly sincere women, not exactly devoted
to intellectual apostleship, but devoted to their pupils, and personally deserving of all respect. Yet truth compels me to say
that when I found that these ladies, many of them young and
planning to marry away from their job, were doing exactly the
same work that my brother *agrégés* were doing in the *lycées*,
surprise made me dumb. For one Lizette Reese France has many
hundreds of gifted literary men—not women—teaching her boys.
Let me repeat what has been said so often, viz., that the com-
petitive system and a truly literary or scientific spirit have raised
French secondary education to such a level that if all the professors in the French Universities were swept away by some
catastrophe in one day, their chairs could be filled, the next
day, by professors from the *lycées*. A similar substitution of high
school teachers for University professors in the colleges of
America is unthinkable.

But while French teachers only take a remote, an almost
theoretical interest in the happiness of their charges, the idea of
the child's happiness is paramount in the minds of American
teachers as it is in the minds of American parents. This is especially noticeable when one meets French women transplanted to
the high schools of America and converted to the worship of
happiness at all costs prevalent there. They, like all converts,
are more vocal than their native colleagues and they show you
that, beyond the possibility of doubt, the object of American
secondary education is not, even remotely, preparation for the
Universities. No idea of intellectual differences between students
is ever given in the high schools because it might cause discouragement; the top boy of the English schools is replaced by

a top girl admired for the qualities which make a girl "popular" in America. The models of literature are often chosen from current fiction, less intimidating that the English classics; Latin and even French are toyed with so as not to produce an idea that even those who teach these languages have only a smattering of them, for that too would be discouraging as well as scandalous; ninety-fives are showered on home-work which ought to be severely reprimanded; graduation is a matter of course: a young friend of mine in a supposedly distinguished high school was graduated with no less than three hundred and forty others in a class of three hundred and sixty. I saw the endless list, and when I asked why another battalion, of over three hundred, were graduating with honours I could not obtain a satisfactory explanation of what those honours were. Yet, the marvellous capacity of America for healthy and simple emotions lends such a glamour to graduation, with white dresses, flowers and choking parents, that I do not dare give it the name it undoubtedly deserves. The notion that it opens the door of most State colleges is painful to anybody truly interested in the intellectual future of America. I once crossed the ocean with the principal of a big high school in Philadelphia. He knew the truth and spoke it fearlessly, but when I asked him why he did not print it, he replied that it was for Harrisburg and Washington to do that, and principals did not print anything.

Since then, two things have taken place which must inevitably raise the standard of the high schools considerably. In the first place, Mr. Abraham Flexner has shown that, as long as the inadequacy of secondary teaching compels the Universities to include a college, that is to say, devote two years to mere high school studies, real University work must be postponed till after graduation, a contradiction in terms. In the second place, the ruthless reforms accomplished not only in the chief Universities but even in a few modest colleges must have a beneficent consequence: requirements for admission to college becoming stricter, the level of high school education will have to meet those requirements. Already Saint Louis, Louisville and, I believe, Philadelphia have substituted men's teaching for women's in the high schools, and insist on real qualifications. The next step must be sincerity in graduation which will mean sincerity in the grading of school-marks as well. The notion of failure will have to be introduced into the high schools as it exists in schools preparatory to West Point or Annapolis. Will this mean the end of the Era of Happiness in schools? It would be a pity. But the Era of Happiness may soon appear to have been merely the Era of Facility, a poor time. There are Americans still living who knew other methods in the not faraway days before a formidable influx of aliens fatally evolved the so-called easier methods. Men of my own age in America have been like myself taught their philosophy in Latin and thought the method perfectly natural. The authors of the excellent articles which the American monthlies printed fifty years ago had been taught in schools which were not afraid of grading talent in industry, and produced an aristocracy of minds. Happiness by levelling was unknown then. Yet those men never said that they were unhappy schoolboys. Memoirs abound to prove it.

One Sunday in 1920 a friend of mine in Washington, Mr. Frank Bright, took me to see his father, a man of about eighty. I found the old gentleman reading in a large black book and, it being Sunday, I imagined that book to be a volume of Sermons. When I came near, the reader looked up and said: "Ah! you catch me reading a frivolous book on the Sabbath!" The book was Plutarch's *Lives*, and it is true that Plutarch is the Maurois of antiquity, but the present generation has forgotten it and will have to become used again to that notion before American colleges can really be called Universities. I cannot think it will take long, and I feel inclined to hope that the conjunction of American creativeness with a more severe mental discipline will soon bring about the Golden Age of literature in the United States. What is already noticeable is the excellence of the scholarly output of University professors. Once my friend Shorey, of the University of Chicago, said to me, with well-founded pride, that no student need seek in Europe scholarship which he could find "right there, on the campus." This statement would be true now of at least seven or eight Universities. The only thing that is still needed is a preparation, as well as a craving, for the culture now offered in plenty.

VII

I have been on nineteen lecture-tours in America; I have been in every State except four; I have scrutinized thousands of American faces and shamelessly listened to thousands of American conversations; I have acquired the memorandum habit, and so, many things I have heard survive more or less in my diaries or dossiers; I can say I know thirty or forty American men and women intimately; I am no longer surprised at any of their reactions or at their silences: I can predict them; I can imagine those friends in hypothetical situations and, being a pretty good mimic, I can impersonate the attitude they will adopt; there are still a few Americans who will shout at me because, not being a "citizen" I am not supposed to understand English. The same are apt to explain to me that the essence of America is a passionate love of freedom. But of these there are very few: most people in the United States say, on the contrary, "How well you know us!" or "When are you going to write about us, at last?"

All this is true and encouraging. And it is also true and encouraging that I, like everybody else, at first brought over to America my European superiorities and prejudices. It took me several years to shake off those prejudices, and to see America as it is instead of seeing it through the prism of deforming words or tyrannical formulas. I have gradually come to like America with a mental approbation instead of merely loving it from a sentimental inclination; a sort of subtle naturalization, far more real than mere "papers," has by degrees tied me to it: the first time I saw the new Union Station at Cleveland and felt I was finding deep pleasure in a typically American achievement I checked myself inwardly with a "Cautious, there! Don't be quite so American." Often, now, when I hear the United States misrepresented in Europe, instead of flaring up in irritated defence, I content myself with the more effectual device of shaking my head, as a polite American would do. I do the same thing as I read book after book about the United States.

Yet, I have not been eager to "write about America, at last," and the longer I have waited the more difficult the task has become. For, new books of American impressions or American systematization are published every month, and there is not much that is new in any of them. Everything has been said. I never look into the earliest systematizer, Tocqueville, without concluding that he saw clearly all that was worth scanning, and glimpsed all the rest. As Montaigne said, all we do is to *entregloser* one another, comment upon the other fellow's commentary. What is the good at this time of day to enlarge on what is English in America, and what is so un-English that it invariably irritates the British? I used to imagine there was a certain novelty in what I noted concerning the influence of the English language on the physiognomy, the gestures and, ultimately, the psychology of even a recent American. But I found that that, too, had been said more than once and was only new to me.

I used to hold up to contempt the rashness of casual foreign observers who, like M. Duhamel, see the United States through an angry certainty that all that is damnable in modern trends comes from America, because it began there—a palpable fallacy —or who, like Count Keyserling, sprinkle a book of impressions with not very deep philosophy. I have changed my mind. The mere impressions of Count Keyserling are Count Keyserling's all the same, and Duhamel's tantrums, no matter how unjust they may be, are never far from literature. On the other hand, it is noticeable that natives who know the imponderabilia in their own atmosphere inevitably escaping the foreign observer, never feel inclined to describe their national characteristics: they content themselves with satirizing them. The more like a native an adopted American becomes the more he feels inclined to limit himself to pointing out what he would like to see corrected in the United States. But to write for America is very different from writing about America.

Then, everybody travelling in a foreign country has been conscious of the melancholy fact that he is more impressed by what goes against his own particular grain than by what he approves of. Many of the notes I have accumulated in the past twenty-eight years may have been supplemented or corrected when I sorted them, but they were originally adverse. The reason, apart from the picturesqueness or literary appeal of satire, is that although I never make a carping remark about my friends—because I discover extenuating circumstances for what displeases me in what they say or do—I can make such remarks about unknown people whom the mean human nature in me dislikes for the mere reason that I do not know them. *Peregrini!* Yet, the impression I finally retain of even common or aggressively nationalist Americans—generally of the second generation—is favourable, because I have inferred from innumerable street-scenes the certainty that their qualities outweigh their faults. Moreover, I have often found in them a sensitiveness—born of a complex—which makes them pathetic, or a humble submission to criticism which disarms criticism. Add that I have contracted in Europe the habit of appearing as an apologist of America and this habit has created a bias against which I ought now to be on my guard. I do not care much if American critics—who at heart may be narrow nationalists—accuse me of "soft-soaping" their countrymen, but I am as afraid of being unduly indulgent as of being unduly severe. The entity which we call America—the annoying America endlessly preaching at Europe—may make me unjust to the abstraction called "the American" and ultimately to the Americans in flesh and blood whom I know. I feel I am between Charybdis and Scylla, and am the more afraid of these generalizations which, however, I am bound to make.

For I must admit to myself that I have evolved my own idea of America and the Americans, and it does not matter if that idea is more negative than positive, since what I feel sure Americans will *not* do corresponds to what I feel inclined to predict they will do. So, in spite of the difficulties stated above, and in spite of the laziness or passivity left by many useless debates on the subject of the United States, I will not shirk the task of giving the reader at least an impression of my own impressions. This can best be done by culling notes from my diaries and transcribing them as they stand, for most of them were written in English. I see no other way for me to keep in contact with a fast-receding past, or for the reader to keep in contact with me.

VIII

New York, May, 1919. **

There is a certain Englishness in all I see. I am conscious of it
even down town, in spite of the skyscrapers. The language, of
course, adds to the impression. But the sensation of restfulness
produced by London is replaced here by exhilaration. I look in
vain for the typically Saxon type abounding in the London shops
—solid stolid strength which, centuries ago, was probably accompanied by the same happy confidence I notice here, but the
confidence has gradually been toned down to the modern Englishman's imperturbable sense of security.

Here, young strength is so optimistic, so buoyant, so convinced
that everything will be all right, that the impression at first produced by strength makes room for another: strength does abound
in the United States, but, after all, it is not necessary, because
everything is all right, everything will be all right. A few scowl-
ing faces showing an excess of will power and a number of
surprisingly clerical faces do not detract from the general effect.
These people are happy: their elastic gait declares it, their
cocked cigars proclaim it; and they seem never to have been in
the school of sorrow. Hardly any faces show sensitiveness. The
only exception I have seen to-day was a slender old Negro with a
finely chiselled face and long un-African white locks hanging
over his shoulders. He was walking slowly up East Thirty-ninth
Street and stopped for a long time in front of a house which interested him particularly for some reason.

Even women offer the same characteristic. Many of them
move lightly on small agile feet, looking straight before them.
If their glance encounters a man's, contrary to European tradi-

** NOTE:—The reader will no doubt observe that the following entries
from my diaries are not chronological. There is, it is true, a certain logical
sequence in them, but it need hardly be pointed out. If it were it would
provide the elements of a didactic exposé of what I feel about America,
only didacticism is precisely what I want to avoid. My impressions of
America, most of them more than favourable, must remain only loosely
connected, as they came.

tion they look him down. No immodesty in that, no modesty either. A few girls smile at me, "speak to me," my companion says in a curious idiom. Catholic girls, no doubt. Some elderly ladies do more than look me down: their auger eyes search my very soul for horrid things like sloth or drunkenness, which they are sure must be lurking there. When my bad conscience is betrayed by my annoyance at being scrutinized they search harder and deeper. I have seen thin weary faces like these in England, in the North Country, but they were pathetic, not reproachful. When I make up my mind that these auger-eyed American old prophetesses must have been difficult to live with, one of them smiles at me for picking up her umbrella, and lo! the smile is full of sad gentleness. It is an extremely touching smile. At all events these poor old souls have suffered, I see it now. If their eyes have grown sharper, it must have been in expectation of worse to come. They are like palsied people who always look hostile, poor dears, because they are always frightened. They don't think I am a hypocritical Papist or a salary-drinking rascal.

In front of the Library, where the crowd is at its densest, the stream of passers-by becomes slower, astonishingly slow in fact, but nobody seems to mind. I have noticed the same indifference when the Madison Avenue trolley-car has taken seventeen minutes to creep up four blocks. English people would sniff and shrug and plan letters to *The Times*. These, their active descendants, out-British them in passivity.

Passing Central Park I notice that five or six little boys, the oldest not above ten years of age, have made a huge, a frightening bonfire. Nobody seems to care, and the urchins look around for approval. Already in 1908 I had been struck by the pleasure which railroad-men found in raising big pyres of sleepers lying by the tracks. A probable survival of pioneer days when timber had no value. In France all that wood would be carried or wheeled home. Only last month in Meudon Forest, within sight of the Paris steeples, I saw mediæval-looking old women dragging along big faggots and infinitely more mindful of their luck than of their exertion.

New York, February, 1920.

An American is a man who wants something. He wants it, wants to get it, does not wish to want it, wants it. He knows that everybody in America is like him. I was surprised the first time I heard an American woman calmly asking: "What's in it for me?" But, since then, I have heard it at least half a dozen times. The question is entirely natural. It seems to be a sort of idiom, an implicit quotation which does not shock anybody. I have used it myself—with the apologetic commentary of a smile— once or twice during my Californian campaign, and nobody showed any suspicion that I might be joking. The reaction of the person who hears "What's in it for me?" is expressed in an immediate "Why! of course . . ."

The French have dreams, wishes, hopes but their object is not quite their own, it is imposed upon them from outside, hardly ever chosen by themselves. Antiquated society. No chances. No room for initiative. Hence the resignation to one's circumstances, and, as men must have an escape, the endless dreaming about possibilities. The conversation at Henri Lorin's was full of ifs, and, in spite of its seriousness, it was desultory. I hardly ever knew it to revert to the same subject two Sundays in succession. Talking about reforms was an object in itself. Under it all lay the certainty—probably bequeathed by the French Revolution—that an idea, if cherished long enough, must inevitably materialize and can be left to itself.

The one thing which French soldiers, who can be prevailed upon to speak of their war experiences, seem to have enjoyed in that dull and long-protracted misery is that trench-life gave a chance to their long pent-up resourcefulness as well as to their capacity for self-sacrifice. You would surprise them by saying that it gave them a chance to feel as people do in America. Yet, that is the truth.

Williamstown, August, 1923.

I am here in a perfect *vivier* (fish-pond) of intelligent Americans. Yet I am more struck by the intensity of their political aspirations than by their intelligence, by what they want more than by what they think. How do I grade the strength of personality in a Latin? By the impression made by his intellect and mental equipment. What is called his character is secondary in my appreciation. His power will, of course, when I come to know him better, be increased by my realisation of his integrity, but he will chiefly dominate me by his influence over my mind, by his ideas more than by his ideals. I feel this every time I talk with Señor Zeballos, or with that Parisian-looking young Minister of Colombia, so full of nuances. I feel it also with Count Kessler who is not a Latin but might be one and acts like one the moment he can draw aside the veil of melancholy left on him by the disaster of his country. Probably it is a European characteristic. The sense of personality in a European is produced less by his consciousness of the mental power he happens to possess than by other people's consciousness of it.

Not so in the Americans I meet here. They are interested in ideas, keenly so, but you see them at once transforming your ideas into their ideal and ready to champion them, to devote their energies to them as soon as they cease to be purely intellectual. In a minute your thoughts become part of the American's personality and add to the tenseness of his will. You were a mirror, he is a force.

New York, October, 1924.

Americans working on behalf of some idea soon become so devoted to that idea that they do not mind disappearing behind it. Those splendid missionaries are invariably modest. Yet the average American is not modest. He is self-assertive and uninterruptedly conscious of his ego, of being Peter or James rather than Tom. I used to notice the same thing in obscure British officers during the war. All those so-called nobodies, who would never rise above the rank of captain, thought themselves somebody and impressed one in consequence. I do not like being slighted or even unrecognized, but to be made a great deal of makes me feel uncomfortable. Not so those Anglo-Saxons who have such a belief in the human equality of dunce and genius that it gives them a strange superiority. Ego, ego describes and explains them. To be sure, it produces the splendid quality which we French people hardly ever pray for, viz., the capacity for taking on responsibilities. It is also true that, in the case of many Americans, this can coëxist with lovable modesty, as in C. D. Norton who watches his own development and, curiously, says even now that "he will arrive late." However, it is frequently associated with egotism in the full sense of the word. Faults are not easily acknowledged by Americans. Catholics who are accustomed to confession and are encouraged to practise humility are better than the others in this respect, but even they show that national characteristic.

The only fault that Americans gladly admit is hastiness, but hastiness is not regarded as a fault. "I got mad," sounds nice. A fool never says: "I was such a fool that . . ." He says: "With my usual impulsiveness I . . ." You are not blamed either in America for admitting: "I am as proud as Lucifer." What surprises me the most is that this attitude of self-defence at all costs, based on self-appreciation, is so rapidly taught to immigrants that it seems entirely natural to them in the second generation.

I always feel inclined to think that there is something biological in that assertiveness. Good food, good air, and not too much study make strong American boys: why should the consciousness of their personality be exiled to their brain instead of tingling in their whole body? I am frequently surprised by references to bodily violence which are tabooed in Europe. Even gentle refined women over here smile approvingly when the narrator comes to "Well, I took off my coat . . ." There is a philosophy behind this attitude.

New York, November, 1919.

It is good form in America to exhibit moral and religious
principles. I constantly hear men expressing them articulately.
The strange shame which we call *respect humain* does not exist here. One is led by the extreme seriousness of many American faces to expect a certain amount of puritanism in the moral
attitude, but the frequently recurrent expression of principles
echoing the pulpit always surprises me. I am inclined to account for this explicitness by a desire to buttress the speaker's
personality, to help it in its effort to secure an object. The man
reassures himself and fortifies his action by connecting it with
universally admitted truths. I know it works for I am always
impressed by these little lay sermons, by the earnestness they
reveal, and I wish the French were not so far away from the
same habit. But far away they are. Our national dread of in-
fringing on the other fellow's freedom lest it might give him
a chance to infringe on ours, is probably at the root of this
aversion. Perhaps also my countrymen are afraid that a declaration of principles may be interpreted as a moral creed by which
they will be bound, in sexual matters, for instance. We can
speak with great vehemence in defence of a position which we
regard as true, we like to convince and we love to confute, but
we seldom say anything likely to influence another man's conduct. Even patriotism, which is the religion of many Frenchmen,
is not missionary. We can print appeals founded on principles,
but we hardly ever speak them. Americans do so all the time
with the naturalness of spontaneity. What they refrain from is
the expression of emotions which, on the contrary, is habitual
to us. Yet Americans are emotional. What restrains them is the
language they brought with them from England.

Chicago, October, 1927.

Rich American bankers or industrialists will harp on the use-
lessness of wealth. They are evidently sincere. Yet, they are philanthropists which is as much of a luxury as being a patron of
the arts. They often show simplicity in their way of living and

prefer it. Mrs. G. finds real pleasure in the tiny garden she cul-
tivates on the roof of her ballroom. A French railway-crossing
guard would turn up his nose at it, but she shows it to her
friends with great pride. Marie-Antoinette at her hamlet, of
course. Or well-off Tolstoy in a moujik's smock. Your millionaire is honestly impressed by the fact that he can live on less
than his income, but his references to frugality are irritating.
They could only be convincing on the lips of a man poor
enough to be anxious about next week, a workman uncertain
about the continuance of his job, for instance, not a tramp who
does not worry, because he has not to worry, about the future.
The wealthy ought never to say a word about wealth.

New York, March, 1920.

All Americans want what they want without delay. Hence
their extraordinary decision in entering on a campaign in comparison with the dilly-dallying of Europeans. Hence also their
attention to ways and means, to data and methods. What are
our lean statistics compared with the gigantic tabulation of
almost everything likely to affect economic conditions which
goes on in New York and Washington? The descendants of the
frontiersmen—who could not afford to waste even a gesture—
insist on learning all that can be learned about the road they
are preparing to tread. An unexpected result of this tendency is
a timidity—as soon as information seems incomplete—which I
did not think possible in American business-men. Mr. B. scans
each sentence of our appeals as if a man's life were hanging on
every word. And he is obsessed by the fear of breaking post-
office regulations. But as soon as these same business-men feel
sure about their reconnoitring they see big and act boldly.

Why is it that this craving for clarity in planning is so often
defeated in apparently simple things? Why is the Grand Central
Subway a nightmare in comparison with the Saint-Lazare
Métro? A child of ten finds his way through the *Chaix* (the
French time-table), he cannot make a mistake. Adults in Amer-
ica do not go much beyond the Boston to New York schedule.

As soon as the trip involves changes they apply to the Information Office. Yet I have seen Information clerks or experienced hotel-porters in Denver hopelessly lost in their labyrinthic time-tables and unable to tell me how I should travel to Joplin, Mo. Street-marking is poor, even in cities like Philadelphia or Chicago. In Washington itself Pennsylvania Avenue inexplicably consists of two separate thoroughfares. Road-marking is inadequate everywhere. As for the house numbering, it is a joke which causes so much loss of time that the Washington statisticians ought to make a computation of it. But people do nothing about it beyond swearing. Strange anomalies in a nation which hates delay, demands minute organization and shows a genius for it.

Chicago, December, 1934.

I must have noted down ten times in these diaries that the spiritual climate of America compared to that of France is like a cheery Spring coming after a dull Winter. Even in times of depression America is the land of opportunity and—the poor immigrants were right—God's country. Chances for everything abound everywhere. My own personal activity is incessantly solicited in the United States, and I have infinitely more occasions to study human nature here than in Paris. My people at this distance seem to be, not in the least as the Chicago newspapers describe them, a set of unruly Latins, but a conclave of disenchanted old men.

Chicago, December, 1934.

Astonishing activity of the American newspapers. They have faults, but they are alive. Ours are like Orlando's mare which possessed every quality but unfortunately was dead. My dear *Journal des Débats* is unparalleled over here, only it might be edited by a symposium of Aristotles. Never a campaign or even the suggestion of one. The staff is a victim of the French fallacy that an idea correctly expressed is like an indestructible ether wave which must galvanize somebody somewhere. The waste of wisdom is enormous.

Americans are as keen on ideas as hawks on chickens. The handicap of Europeans arriving here is that they have no suspicion of that marvellous eagerness. But the American press knows how mercurial its readers are. An idea will be hammered in for months in the same newspaper. The knowledge of psychology involved always surprises me.

New York, October, 1933.

I saw the beginning of the hunting season in France, in the Aisne. The boundless plains were alive with coveys of partridges and neither man nor retriever knew where to look first. I find the same wealth of possibilities here, the day after landing. I find it every year, in fact, and that's what gave me, in 1919, the impression that New York was a city of kings.

This morning, after a visit to Miss C. at the Radio office, I went to Simon and Schuster's and afterwards to the office of the *Literary Digest*. The alertness, the rapidity and subtlety of comprehension, the immediate and inventive interest in any suggestion worth while evident in everybody with whom I talked recalled those sportsmen of mine in their rich hunting-grounds. Everything is welcomed with a smile but is seen to produce an immediate tension in the mind. An intelligent people? Strange that the question should still be asked. The presence of Americans vitalizes any European appreciative of a keen response.

The drawback of this keenness is its universality. Americans react to most things tensely. The result is a partly artificial— because contagious—intensity. Americans sound invariably confident because everybody about them is eager, and eagerness is the gesture of certainty. Never take a buoyant American's financial tip. He may be buoyant only because people in his circle are so. Buoyancy in America seems to be a pleasant condition to which everybody has a right. But this is a youthful view. Buoyancy is only the mimicry of optimism.

Washington, May, 1923.

American activity may well be a by-word. Ants and bees do not come near it. Even in this partly quiet Washington I see little scenes which make me dizzy. Mrs. L. returning from a shopping trip down town with her sister, this afternoon, no sooner opened the door of her car than the two ladies were bodily transferred to the throbbing car of the expectant husband. Full speed to a cocktail party, then to dinner at a faraway country-club, collecting a girl on the way. Then, *avec le dernier morceau dans le bec,* madly to an amusement park and to an evening of jollity. In between events people smoke or chew or sip, or eat nuts, or rock, or whistle, or suddenly rush to the telephone. They have to do something all the time but hardly anything is of any importance. Nobody seems to know how to dream. I often feel as if all I saw were a preparation for something which must soon begin but, in fact, never does begin. My American friends tumble into bed after six or seven hours of such good times but I never can: I have to rest first.

Paris (France), March, 1934.

Crowded Hours by Mrs. Longworth. Headachy book which recalls hectic experiences and which I had to give up every thirty pages to rest. Mrs. Longworth is remarkably intelligent, but her book is so full of things that there is no place in it for thoughts.

Los Angeles, November, 1930.

This city—like all Californian cities, excepting San Francisco—is full of people who have moved to it from elsewhere. Ask them questions, you will find how proud they are of being "native sons" of this or that. But this pride in their State or County is different from attachment. Moving is a joy in itself. An advertisement I have clipped speaks of "the happiness there is in newness in the home," a notion directly contrary to the attachment of Europeans to things which long habit has taught them to love. I personally cannot bear to see a piece of furniture displaced in my flat, and I dread presents of things which may seem like strangers in those rooms. My Trélon house is exactly as my aunt left it in 1914. But Americans cherish their *Wanderlust* and constantly look forward to changes. I hear them frequently using the words—hateful to them—"stale" or "in a rut." No sooner are they conscious of a lack of gusto than they run away from the place where they begin "to be vegetating."

They are not even afraid of moving their children up and down the country. Boys educated in the exclusive Church-schools in the east are seldom transferred to other schools, because of the waiting-list and of the impossibility, once gone, ever to return. But elsewhere I see a total indifference to changes of methods or atmosphere. I receive frequent letters from American friends, or from friends of those friends, concerning some school in France or Switzerland about which they have heard and to which they are more than anxious to send their children. Immediately, for the matter is urgent. Won't I enquire and advise them? Pretty often I am entreated to use my interest with the schoolmaster or with the Mother-Superior, as the least delay may be fatal. Not once have I seen those requests followed by any result. The correspondence is abruptly closed. A few months later I hear that the child never went to the school on which its whole future depended. Mrs. So-and-So is the person to blame. She was so sure about another Swiss school that the child went there, but that school was found to teach little else than calisthenics. Very disappointing! However, the child will be moved to a first-rate school at Bournemouth in September, so everything will be all right and it is useless to worry.

Chicago, November, 1935.

Mrs. R., in a circle of friends, is asked did she find it difficult to get adjusted to Gallic excitability after her marriage to that French officer. She is a calm-looking woman, over on a visit to her mother, and she evidently lives a quiet life in that house on the South Side, for this is the first time I have seen her, and I

see thousands of people. She answers in her staid manner that
French husbands, of course, are not like American husbands,
but she thinks French excitability is a myth. She has met many
American officers who told her that nothing surprised them so
much during the war as French coolness. Excitability is American. America endlessly provides chances of doing things over
which one can get excited. Paris, especially the quarter where
this lady lives, is provincial in comparison with Chicago.
"Only," she adds, "nobody there has breakdowns."

New York, December, 1935.

I have had dinner with my friends the Torrences in Morton
Street. As usual I have had difficulty in finding the street or
even in finding anybody abroad who could direct me to it. A
few coloured lights here and there make up all the gaiety of
Greenwich Village. Indeed, Morton and the neighbouring streets
might be in the most Quakerish part of Philadelphia. My evening with the Torrences has been infinitely restful. Both of them
say things worth discussing in their soft low voices. Not a sound
from the street, not a creak in the house, nothing but an impression of still deep life in those two existences, yet not a dull
moment.

The Torrences have always had wine on their table during
Prohibition, and peace on their faces during the depression.
Two years ago a mutual friend of ours asked Ridgely Torrence
about the crisis. "What crisis?" he said. This was no brag of
being wealthy, either.

I write this at 2 East Seventieth, where the same peace prevails. My hostess is a busy woman but her *life* is quiet. As a
matter of fact I know scores of homes in America (I have just
glanced through my address-book) where people insist on
living their lives. Little E. who was such an energetic débutante
got rid of all her excitability during that one year. Her apartment is as quiet as a convent. She sees only a few people and
lives entirely contented between her husband and her two children.

It is as easy to settle to retirement in New York as in Paris, and it is more enjoyable. For the ocean of American activity surges all round, and acts as a tonic. Why not admit also that it is pleasant to reflect that whenever solitude palls it can be enlivened in a moment by truly human companionship?

Atlanta, November, 1931.

A lady reporter called. Not brilliant but sensible and absolutely honest. We had the interview, then we had a talk. She, like all Americans, is full of one idea: HAPPINESS. America is one great collective straining towards that one thing. "Happy" is the word heard twenty times a day. People want happiness at all costs. They want it excitedly, feverishly, and rather blindly; they demand it loudly and positively.

I told the reporter that once, in Glasgow, my friend Phillimore, the Greek scholar, a recent Catholic, took me to a convent in town. The mistress of studies, a nun of about thirty-five, gave us tea. This lady possessed the usual charm, or more than the usual charm, of nuns: the marvellous blending of freedom with soul-discipline which religious orders know how to produce. She told us a story. She told it in a quiet *"parloir"* manner, but with an arch smile. The day before, the School Inspector—a melancholy and probably dyspeptic John Knox—, had called. He went through the class-rooms as usual. When his work was done the mistress of studies said to him: "We have a fresh cake, Mr. Inspector; let me make you a cup of tea that will make you feel happy." "We shouldn't feel happy, Sister," was the desolate answer.

America bears the Scotch imprint in many ways of which she is generally unconscious, but not the Calvinistic one. My Presbyterian friends are invariably more genial than my Episcopalian friends. No suspicion over here that happiness is not a right. No recollection of original sin, or of falling off, or of punishment; no thought of any valley of tears; none of the fundamental pessimistic Puritanism which André Siegfried, in spite of all I say to him, sees everywhere.

Washington, June, 1923.

How few among the people I meet read the spiritual authors or even the Portico moralists! I see Marcus Aurelius on a number of small tables apparently destined for "books one reads," but I am not quite convinced. Marcus Aurelius looks well on those little tables. Certain it is that most American people show little inclination towards the interior life. I am often at a loss to reconcile the evident pleasure they take in hearing about it with their ignorance of its indispensable conditions. They run after happiness and the race alone gives them contentment. Elsewhere a moralist would remember the *post equitem sedet atra cura* and imagine that they are running away from worries, but it is not so: Americans merely believe in the equation: activity = happiness and motion = activity.

Los Angeles, November, 1931.

This astonishing city is ten times more beautiful now than it was in 1919. New and yet poetic, undisguisedly pagan, yet happy, defiantly so. Newman thought that Nature was the edge of God's garment. Here I also seem to see all the time a veil of sunny muslin transfiguring everything, but what an effort it takes to imagine it as divine and not as the fringe of Lilith's garment!

St. Louis, October, 1932.

Were the authors of the Declaration of Independence well inspired in proposing the "*pursuit* of happiness" as a right similar to life and freedom?

What is happiness? According to philosophers it is the accomplishment of the highest act, the operation of reason, with the minimum effort. When potentiality makes room for constant actuality we have a "pure act" which is a well-known definition of God as well as a definition of supreme happiness.

Few people know this, of course, and those who do know it are far from always remembering it. The modern French have lately been taught by their Socialist economists to regard pros-

perity and happiness as synonymous, a fallacy which it is for
the high school sophomore even more than for the preacher to
dispel. But their fathers were happy in their art of making the
most of the slimmest chances, as the Italians are happy in their
cheerful resignation or the English in their quiet enjoyment of
themselves. The definition of happiness might vary under the
influence of innumerable contingencies. But to speak of the
pursuit of happiness is to include or suggest something feverish,
excited, and almost *ex hypothesi* futile. It is fortunate that the
average American never tries to analyze the phrase. To him it
means little else than legitimate activity with as much freedom
from pain as is possible to mankind, and he regards it as a given
notion which it is silly to look into too closely. "Feel well and do
something, anything, that you feel like doing" seems to be the
formula for happiness.

Does it work? Well, it may not produce the radiance I have
seen in certain religious houses, and it requires favourable conditions. But, by identifying contentment with activity Americans
have eliminated the danger inherent in the word pursuit. They
are, beyond all doubt, the happiest people I know. It is not a
mere phrase to say that they are happy as larks.

Same place, same date.

Americans are too deeply attached to life not to be violently
antagonistic to Death. They fight it scientifically in the most advanced laboratories in the world; they fight it out of charity in
the best-run and most Christian hospitals in existence, and they
fight it psychologically by ignoring it as much as they can. The
Latins will not be separated from their dead: they do not leave it
to outsiders to prepare them for their final journey, they watch
beside them for days, and, when the funeral is over, their thought
lingers with them. The horrid cemeteries of France or Italy are
full every Sunday of pathetically faithful visitors.

In America, on the contrary, the dead are quickly removed to
flowery funeral chapels and from these to elegant burial-parks
embellished with poetic names. The Freemasons Cemetery, out-

side San Francisco, is an enchanting spot, but I have never noticed that even its beauty attracted the relatives of the people lying there. Nothing in American literature recalls such a poem as Tennyson's *In Memoriam*.

A trip after a bereavement is frequent. Going into mourning is old-fashioned and will soon disappear altogether.

We Latins believe in immortality, or think we do, for I have known many people who only believed they believed in it. Do Americans? Who can tell? What I feel inclined to think is that Americans are so passionately devoted to life that the notion of death only makes them turn more nervously and feverishly to the enjoyment of life, what there is of it. Let the dead bury their dead is gospel truth to the ultra-modern.

Los Angeles, November, 1931.

Mrs. P. has written from Shanghai. Her letter was handed round at breakfast but was not commented upon as I expected it would be. It is a month to-day since the D.'s saw her to the boat. To my surprise they shed tears. Then, to my even greater surprise, they never mentioned her name again. Is it because they like her too much, or because they do not like her so very much after all? I can't believe that Galsworthy was summing up much experience when he wrote that "Americans are warm-mannered but cold-hearted." Like most of us he allowed a rhythm to dictate to him. What I think is that too much happens in America to give emotions a chance to last long.

New York, May, 1923.

Waiting for the Elevated, way up town, sat on a bench next to a woman and her little boy. They were French, she the wife of a *chef* at some hotel. We talked. They spent the summer at Tours and have only been back six weeks. In less than three months over there the little boy forgot all the English he knew. He does not feel like re-learning it. His heart is with his *Mémé* (grandmother) whom he could not bear to leave.

I gave a sidelong glance at the little fellow: the hot tears were welling from his eyes. He never said a word.

I, too, loved my grandmother like that. Sometimes the thought that I must lose her, "she must die," would roll over me like a terrible sea. I still remember the sensation, as of my heart capsizing within me. Grannies are not loved like that in America, I am afraid.

Cleveland, December, 1927.

Mrs. F. and her daughter. Christian Scientists. Distinguished, quiet, refined, kind as all Americans are. They told me about "Science." I offended them by asking to what extent they differed from Unitarians in their views concerning the divinity of Christ. They were not very definite. Christ was the great healer and could be called, to some extent, divine, but no, He was not God. Yet they admitted they would hate not to be called Christians. The technical meaning of the term visibly escaped them: the noun Christian has dwindled down to an adjective connoting little more than goodwill. Through all our conversation I was struck by their dread of suffering as Evil. But this is a characteristically American attitude. Even Catholics are not free from it; only the books they read, the doctrine endlessly recalled to them alarm their conscience about its fundamental paganism. It must be an immense difficulty to believe in the value, natural or supernatural, of suffering or sorrow in a country so brimful of life that life is everything or blocks out everything.

Chicago, December, 1935.

Jews hate suffering perhaps more than anybody else in America. But they can nurse a sorrow. Above all they do not banish the memory of their dead. In this, as in many other things, appears the something curiously European in them.

Richmond, November, 1934.

No country shows as much kindliness as America does. I used to think that the English rivalled them in this respect, but I have seen instances in which English kindness appeared suddenly limited by a "no more of that, enough has been done," which may be reasonable but which causes a vague dread. Yet, English families go on helping ne'er-do-wells in a way which is unparalleled in the rest of Europe.

I don't think American kindness has any limitations. C. D. Norton, the least gullible of men, could be tapped endlessly. R. J. Cuddihy sues people who have interfered with his business, and then pays the costs to which they are sentenced. Or he calls them to his office and berates them, but the moment he sees them scared he says everything will be all right and takes them out to lunch. Willy Ryan is just like him in this respect. John T. King, of New York and Bridgeport, astonished me many times by his unlimited generosity. Once, in Paris, he gave me twenty-five thousand francs for a Trélon widow with six children whom I had merely mentioned. A few days later, giving a huge tip to a taxi-driver he had employed during his visit, the man said that this would help him vastly to buy his own vehicle. Mr. King had imagined that the chauffeur owned his taxi. He immediately added enough for him to purchase it.

To say that this tenderness of heart is only a form of egotism, that Americans are so much in love with happiness that they cannot see anybody unhappy, is to say nothing or worse than nothing. Sceptics say exactly the same thing about the love of God, and terrible egotists who never do anything for anybody declare in perfect honesty that they are not selfish.

I am often vexed by the problem of evil. I know that if I allowed myself to dwell on the amount of individual suffering endured at any minute by millions of men or animals in the world, I should be in danger of going out of my mind. So I try to look away from it. To think of the tremendous amount of kindliness at work in America alone, at that same minute, makes the thought bearable. For I know that the fight between good and evil must go on, and the passion of Americans for sharing, for alleviating, certainly shows the divine action.

Washington, December, 1935.

My seventeenth visit to America is nearly over. As usual I
have met only nice, kind people. In fact, I have never met a
single American whom I should demur to call a good fellow.
There are roughish Americans galore, but they are not unkind.
Here, as elsewhere, a hurried passer-by may look away from
a beggar shivering in a doorway. But if the man has the least
chance of stating his plight, help will surely be given. No old
woman is ever allowed in America to carry a heavy parcel at a
railway station, as I have seen it often in Europe. I know that
such a thing can be done, as it can be left undone, from imitation. But sympathy is too often visible not to exist universally.
Only yesterday, at the station, I saw a woman watching with
some anxiety a little family who seemed rather lost in the vast
waiting-room: pretty soon she asked those poor people if she
could do anything.

The trolley-man will often forget to let you know when you
are near your stop in a strange town, but it will be his stupidity.
He jumps out too often to help women in to be really unkind.

What has created this Christian spirit among a hundred million men? Their religion, perhaps. Yet, they are not kind from
a religious motive. The coöperative tendency which must, from
the first, have gathered strength in sparsely-peopled plantations,
or, as long as there was a frontier, the dangers attending a
frontier life? No doubt. The spirit of give and take which, in
the United States, is not free from a tinge of Benthamism?
Surely. But the repugnance of the American for seeing another
in trouble is not selfish. In other nations this repugnance leads
people to turn aside from the other man's case, that is all. I
still hear in Paris, every now and then, a horrid old saying:
Chacun pour soi, Dieu pour tous, which preachers ought to
brand as blasphemous every Sunday. Americans would loathe it.

Paris, October, 1936.

Monsieur F. writes me that his wife is extremely nervous. He
feels she ought to do something to get herself out of imaginary

worries. He sensibly asks me if I can introduce her to some charitable group: they do not know of any.

As a matter of fact, Paris is full of such groups. Directories are published every year describing them. Yet an intelligent husband and wife who have lived here all their life do not know where to apply.

How often I have heard my American friends complain that charity is overorganized in the United States, that administrations invariably become bureaucratic, that is, as they say pretty harshly, materialistic, that quantity kills quality and campaigns never end in the spirit in which they were begun. It may all be true, as it is true of everything into which cool reason has to enter, and the kind-hearted Americans who have made powerful administrations necessary are not unlike the Trappist monks who have an office in Rome. But blessed be America for bringing to every door the chance of being charitable. The United States is the only country in which a rich man seldom dares to set a bad example by making a purely selfish will.

Los Angeles, November, 1929.

Americans are notoriously gregarious, one more trait which differentiates them from the English. I am surprised they do not seem to have re-invented the droll French proverb: *Plus on est de fous, plus on rit* (the more fools, the more fun,) for it belongs to them more than to any other nation. They are only happy in the company of their fellow-men. Ethnologists say that this aversion from solitude is the outcome of too much solitude in the early days, but the British can live in solitude without showing the same reaction.

Anybody can be company enough for an American: if it is not a duke let it be a tramp or a waitress: the attitude will be the same. Americans, more or less explicitly, have a high notion of human dignity. A man is a man whatever his background may be. Probably they show, in this, the spirit of Christianity better than any other people, and I wish they would not spoil the beautiful idea by associating it with the inferior adjective "democratic." I also wish they would not retain in their minds racial discriminations which are not natural to them and which they have to learn.

There is plenty of confidence in the American disposition: the atmosphere, physical as well as social, is too bracing to create complexes. But there is no *hauteur*: the word has had to be imported. I have never seen a single American actually browbeating another, even a servant, although Americans know how to expect and demand service. Yet, class feeling is far from having disappeared from the American mentality, but when it breaks out it is in childish anger rather than in a desire to show superiority. Indeed, the disputatious tone recreates equality.

The intercourse of Americans with one another is simple and honest, interspersed with innocent bragging which, at any moment, may make room for disarming sincerity, sometimes even for something which could be called humility if the word were not hateful to democratic ears. This attitude is so absolutely American that it can be modified in one instant if the conversation, instead of being carried on in American English, drops into any European language or in British English. At once the participants become conscious of the indignity currently called "knowing one's place." At once also the American is sure that the force which his habitual sincerity gives him has been threatened and he does not forgive the unpleasant sensation. There is little else that he does not forgive.

New York, December, 1927.

Americans love a good talker. Nobody gives eloquence such a chance, and it makes it the more unbelievable that the press of the United States, when summing up a speech, never even hints if it was a good speech or an indifferent one. It is only through oral report that I know of Senator Borah as an exceptionally good speaker. The newspapers merely tell me that the Idahoan said this, alleged that, or denounced the other.

An unfortunate consequence of the amiability with which an American circle will listen to even a drawing-room orator is that men (much more than women) fight for the floor and, when in possession, will not give it up. Our punishing word, *bavard*, does not exist in English ("tattler" expresses a different shade of meaning). An intemperate talker is only called a bore if, having nothing to say, he says it for hours. Otherwise there is no obloquy attached to the lack of social manners which transforms a party into endless orating on one hand and mute admiration on the other. Last month, in New York, Miss D. told her brother, as we left the house of the M.'s after luncheon: "O Jimmy! nobody could say a word, you talked the whole time."—"I certainly did," was the impenitent and, to tell the truth, triumphant answer.

Your bore begins to talk. You listen to him politely. He is a practised expert, and knowing that he has a long way to go he also knows how to husband his reserves. Slowly, steadily, taking full reposing breaths, he goes on, looking fixedly at you to be sure that your own eyes are not wandering, or to repress any intention on your part to interrupt his flow. A slight motion of his hand with a "Wait a minute," or a "No, but just listen," and you stand condemned to eternal listening. Frequently that kind of individual knows too little to suspect that you know more than he does, but in time the mere fact that he talks and you do not gives him a superiority over the little boy he is making of you. He never suspects that you are only acting the part of a gentleman, and if he expresses his opinion of you it will be that you are "a nice little man with not so very much to say."

Joplin, November, 1930.

Awful night at that good hotel. Four men in the room next to mine began to talk at nine o'clock and were still at it at two a.m. They were not riotous in any way, they drank their ginger ale straight and just talked, talked, talked long after there was nothing to say. I wrote a polite note which I slipped under their door. The voices dropped a little for a while, then the regular pitch was resumed and I knew that this was bound to be a sleepless night between two important lecture engagements. At half past three I called the night clerk and moved to another room. The chief talker opened his door and said he was awfully sorry. He was evidently sincere, and probably wondered honestly why I had not gone to sleep while he talked.

The California Club at Los Angeles has a cosy set of rooms, away from the bustle of the building, which a definite caution protects against all-night-talkers. In a Cincinnati hotel I also saw a notice suggesting to the guests to shut their door when they had company, a habit to which not a few Americans are hostile because, of course, the more fools the more fun. Curiously, the most irrepressible, the most truculent American men become extinct when they are in Europe. They say they want to go home because they want the home food, but what they really want is the home audience.

South Bend, December, 1933.

I saw an extraordinary thing last night. There were fourteen of us at dinner, fourteen at a big round table, and there were *not* seven conversations, or, I should say, dialogues, there was only one. Only one voice was heard at a time, and as there were no bores everybody had a chance. Only on one other occasion, since Mrs. Douglas Robinson used to plead so graciously for conversation at her house instead of hubbub, had I enjoyed a dinner-party so much. It was in Minnesota, at that dear little College, Northfield.

The habit of dialogues, soon rising to a scream, kills what is really meant by conversation and causes the loss of the most civilized pleasure men and women can enjoy. It is the more vexatious because the moment the women leave the men to their cognac and cigars, the conversation is apt to become excellent. Poor ladies, treated mostly to the echoes of the last Yale game, or the bridge tournament, or to the stupid man's wit, stories at second hand, clumsily retold! They bear the penalty of having been trained to expect too much private attention instead of insisting on general pleasure.

Sometimes too they are punished for a certain attitude of

superiority over the male which makes the shy man, or the resigned man. I have never forgotten the surprise of Mrs. W. in Washington when I said before her that her husband was one of the wittiest men I had met. You could not tell whether she was incredulous or hurt, hurt at me for saying about her married life something of which she had maliciously been left uninformed, or offended at her husband for displaying wit when he was not within sound of the whip.

New York, October, 1926.

I had a delightful experience at lunch. Laurence Veiller introduced me to the very nice Misses van Winkle and to another woman whose name only reached me indistinctly. I liked that lady at once. All she said came naturally and was delightfully original. I loved her voice and her English. I had to whisper Veiller to repeat to me the name I had missed. "Mrs. Sothern," he wrote on the menu. How glad I was to have discovered Julia Marlowe under that anonymity. Had I been told at once her arresting name, its fringe might have prevented me from really seeing the woman she is. I hope we shall be friends.

Commonness abounds in all parts of the world. But travellers frequently forget this and appear shocked at finding it in the foreign countries they visit. It is one of the strangest human anomalies: people go abroad deeply convinced of their national superiority, yet they resent other nations' shortcomings as if they had expected them to show nothing but continuous perfection.

Working men in America look more prosperous, better dressed, better groomed than elsewhere, and they know how to spend money. The consequence is that Europeans who see them for the first time mistake them for people of a better class and are shocked at their voices or their syntax, or at gestures which may betray a man's former status even long after he has attained to affluence. A decided final way of pushing off one's plate or one's glass at the end of luncheon can be a revelation.

So is a looseness of manners among men which may have been acquired in a camp but which is an unbounded surprise in a club-house. Whiskey too is a formidable destroyer of manners and when, as is frequently the case, it produces amorousness, the results are such as might convert even the most resolute anti-prohibitionists. I have seen pretty repulsive scenes the actors in which were, a few hours before, as grave as judges.

Many Europeans say: There is no distinction in America, even when people are obviously above coarseness. This, of course, is speaking without sufficient information, for really distinguished people are rare everywhere and can be unexpectedly discovered in the most unlikely places. But it is a fact that there is less in America than elsewhere of that capacity for not needing others which is felt at once in "distinguished people." The reason is that etymologically as well as in the nature of things distinction is akin to distance and connotes separation or what is called standoffishness.

Americans might, more easily than other people, show the indifference or the self-sufficiency which could be a good foundation for *hauteur,* because their country swarms with men and women, occasions for human intercourse are of constant occurrence, and excessive supply ought to result in a greatly diminished demand. Yet it is not so. An American is never indifferent to another human being; he is interested in him, wants to know details concerning him, and at any moment he is ready to enter into conversation with him. He is familiar, of course, sometimes familiar to sauciness, but his familiarity does not breed contempt. Contempt is rare in the United States and disdain can be said to be non-existent. It is only in older nations that familiarity denotes moral abandonment and justly deserves the compassion which is the sublimation of contempt.

The goodwill of the average American is unstinted and generous, it is so overflowing in its desire to assert itself that it produces appearances which elsewhere would not be consistent with manners, but this indifference to an artificial code exists in

the very young everywhere and I am confronted once more with
the fundamental youthfulness of America.

Courtesy is an American quality. I have been surprised to
find elaborate politeness in men who called me Cap or Governor. Negroes, I invariably notice it, show extraordinary capacity for pleasantness of address and surprise many times by an
innate graciousness (two porters eating their dinner in Cleveland had excellent table manners). Not infrequently the Red-
caps at the Grand Central speak better than the men whose
valises they carry. And it was delightful to listen to the conversation of those seven Negro singers to whom Mrs. Loomis
once gave tea at the Park Lane Hotel.

Baltimore, September, 1919.

People say there are no classes in America, but it is a mistake. The lower stratum consists of men who chew tobacco.
Above that is the class which chews gum. Higher up are the
Americans who do not chew, even gum, but who speak to you
of their wives as Mrs. So-and-So. At the top husbands and wives
speak of each other as "my husband" or "my wife," or as
Charlie and Kitty.

Only, the upper classes have been intelligent enough and
kind enough, or American enough, not to reveal to the chewing
classes that they are inferior. If socialism ever gets a footing in
the United States that revelation will come from Labor-leaders
who will remember the famous Marxian saying: "The workman
must be made conscious of his own misery which he does not
suspect." Then it will be good-bye to the universal good-fel-
lowship which is the foundation of American happiness.

Paris, August, 1936.

I have been trying to classify the notes I have accumulated
during almost twenty years about American psychology. I am
more and more convinced that André Siegfried is wrong in attaching so much importance to Puritanism. To me the phenomena seem capable of being explained, in nineteen cases out

of twenty by the reverse of Puritanism, by a simple hedonism, a search after pleasure, which the average American regards as eminently reasonable and which he wishes to make possible for everybody. The "pursuit of happiness" once more.

It is inevitable that this ever-recurring idea should dominate American notions concerning marriage. The whole world considers marriage as the fundamental condition of happiness. But whereas people in America are unshaken in their conviction that this is the principle on which they ought to build, they are astonishingly vague about what should be deduced from that principle. (The cinema, in this, mirrors the people accurately.) Nothing is so recognized in the United States as sex is, for love is a public affair, and the two sexes are incredibly conscious of each other. But sex is recognized as drink is, in a way that keeps it mysterious. There are sentimental plays as there are thousands of advertisements showing people in the enjoyment of some beverage; the deeper realities are not investigated.

Hence innumerable illusions about love as there are about happiness. What is striking, at first sight, is that such a one-sided statement as "Women are essential to happiness," should really sum up the American view. I know that most Americans are so unused to philosophizing that if they were told that "True love is essential to both sexes," ought to be substituted they would innocently say that the two sentences meant the same thing and hair-splitting is unnecessary in such simple affairs.

But it is a fact that women count for more than men in America. I once had a passing controversy, in *The New York Times*, with Count Keyserling concerning the reasons for this lopsidedness. I still believe, as I did then, that it is a mere bequest of the days, not long past, when women were scarce in America as they have since been, with the same consequences, in Australia. But whatever the cause may have been the consequences are still here.

Women are queens, and they know it, in the United States. When I write for a French review I say *"tous les hommes"* with-

out any fear of offending women. When I write in English I
have to say "all men and women," and it is lucky that I have
not to say "all women and men," for Americans say quite naturally "my mother and my father," which is never heard in
England. It is touching but ridiculous to see plainness expecting
all the refinements of chivalry with the superiority produced by
long habit. And I don't think that anything is gained by a
father giving the right of way to his thirteen-year-old daughter.
I have an American friend here in Paris who complains that
the French press seldom alludes to the French President's wife.
I reply that I am equally grieved in America never to read any
allusion to the husbands of ladies holding high official positions,
yet who must be admirably disinterested men and really fine
fellows.

Little brothers in America fetch and carry for their little
sisters, and early learn what Fulvia taught Cleopatra's Antony.
Little girls of twelve are visited by little beaux who bring them
presents and flattery. They soon learn that men have been created to support women. I am told that depression has eradicated
gold-digging and that nice American girls, like nice European
girls, think it more dignified to pay for their own pleasures. But
what I see, in my visits, still convinces me that our La Bruyère
was right in thinking that it is a misfortune to be in love without
having a good deal of money.

Husbands go on doing what they early learned to do. They
praise their wives to their faces till you feel uncomfortable at the
thought of what more praise may be coming. (Not in religious
families where the man is afraid Woman may loom behind
Wife.) They tell you how long they had to wait for their Rebekah
—no matter how Leah-like she may be—and how they chased
her for years around the United States. They speak of their
wives in their public speeches and, whether from love or from
terror, innumerable writer-husbands dedicate their books to
their wives. In most cases all this publicity arises from a sincere
feeling, even if it is caused by imitation, but I have seen, on
several occasions, that an exaggeration of it resulted in insin-

cerity: the man is only using forms of language, or bragging in an indirect way.

Surfeit may also come. I was surprised the first time an inscription over the mantelpiece of a well-known club-house told me that here was "a place where women cease to trouble." Also the natural tone in which my neighbour at the banquet of a famous humanitarian fraternity said to me "and no women, you know." Sometimes the surfeit is felt on the other side. A lady whom I highly respect had to go to South America for a rest "because she was courted to death."

Everybody gets tired of the love-making which goes on in public in America, in trains, in parks, in cars. A few years ago, in Washington, I saw a long queue of automobiles in each of which a couple were hugging in a way which the Paris police would certainly not have tolerated. Probably the Washington police after a time also interfered, for I have visited Washington many times since then and no such exhibition is at present to be seen. What will be long in disappearing is the boy following a girl from one end to the other of a jolting train: he may be young Galahad but he certainly looks like Fido. The girl hardly ever turns round to encourage him, he does not mind.

Love is evidently regarded in the United States as the *summum bonum* which needs no demonstration of its excellence: hence its publicity. A Frenchman may allude to a *béguin* (a superficial sentiment): if he is truly in love he is as silent about it as about a poetic or a religious mood. Even his most intimate friend hardly hears of it. In America, being in love is such a blessing that it has to be announced as glad tidings. I was asking news of an extremely nice girl in New York. The aunt who answered me capped a few details with the delighted declaration "and she is in love." I have not forgotten, either, the earnestness with which a Harvard student said to a friend of mine in my presence: "I think I am in love, Mrs. So-and-So." Nor the simplicity with which a young lady of Chicago, barely fifteen but looking like eighteen, told me in imperfect French that she would not go to the Sorbonne after finishing boarding-school *parce qu'il y a garçon que j'aime* (because there is boy I love).

I have heard widowed ladies discussing their possible re-marriage before children grown up enough to see all the im-plications of the conversation yet not old enough to have lost the sensitiveness which parents so often ignore. More unpleas-ant still was it to see another lady exchange endearments with a suitor in the car where her two observant boys were seated. Probably no American would have been shocked and this is one more case of the variability of morals with variations in location. Love in America means marriage, and marriage means conquest and triumph, which is not what it means in Europe where the old Catholic doctrine of matrimony in view of a family remains associated with the notion of duty.

So American women may seem to emulate their men in speak-ing proudly of their "best husband" but they know they are the privileged party in marriage. They are persuaded that their yea was a great favour to the man, so that tolerance long clings to their attitude. They do not immediately requite their man's devotion, and they expect more than they give. They make of man-kind the fun which in Europe is directed the other way. They are full of pride when they say "they never tried to make their man do what he did not want to do," a claim rich in implications. They take it for granted that a man should work a little more than is good for him, or they disbelieve his hints that he does; sometimes they titter when he complains. Finally inequality glaringly appears in the fact that a woman seldom helps her husband to get his divorce—a thing any gentlemanly husband is supposed to do for his wife—or seldom, after sepa-ration, praises his rare qualities as he generally praises hers.

All this is true, and will be recognized as true by most Amer-ican men and by not a few American women. Yet, when I allow, not my diaries, but my general impressions to speak, a different note is heard. I think highly of the American woman. Her attractiveness is universally admitted—although some people will make a distinction between her seduction and charm, adding that this is verified by the fact that charm which can subsist in old age seldom does so in America. In spite of this attractiveness she meets men halfway and spreads around her an atmosphere of comradeship. Foreigners who imagine that she is unduly encouraging quickly find out that she only appears to be so because she is sure of being discouraging the moment encouragement might be misinterpreted. She has had a training of which the visitor is unaware. The relations between the two sexes in America are an endless source of pleasure to initiated people who take them for what they are meant to give.

American women are pampered, of course. Even they complain of it. But just as the over-indulged American boy displayed wonderful fibre on the battlefields of France, the American woman surprises by her capacity to face a crisis. She can pass from the leisure of opulence to hard work at a single day's notice. She can be patient for years with a husband who, in the current phrase, waits too long "to make good." I have not seen a single American woman broken down by the depression. The American mother's devotion to her children is proverbial and could not be reconciled with fundamental selfishness.

More than by all the rest have I been struck by an all-important particular. There is nothing on which people harp so often as on the so-called "failure of marriage" in the United States. Statistics of course are made a great deal of. Now, these very statistics prove that marriage is *not* a failure in America. There are ten divorces out of sixty marriages. That means that fifty in every sixty American marriages are successful, for with the facility of divorce and the American belief in the dogma of married happiness at all costs, it is improbable that unhappy marriages should be borne with as they are pretty often in Europe. These figures are eloquent.

Another conclusion is that the American married woman cannot be the idol on a pedestal she is often represented as being. For durable happiness cannot be found apart from true love, and true love connotes not only sympathy but devotion and, even more than that, a certain amount of admiration which the American woman is not supposed to feel for her man. If so, the American woman can pass from a highly selective girl-hood to something very like old-fashioned wifehood and her part in life is what it should be.

New York, May, 1923.

"Alice, you're a good little Catholic. Tell me who are the Catholic Saints of America."

"The Catholic Saints? Why! Saint Rose!"

"South American! Try again."

"George Washington."

"Priceless! Try again."

"Mother Bourgeois."

"Canadian, and probably French originally. Real American Saints I want."

"Why! of course, the seven American martyrs."

"French, every one, my dear. You can't find American Saints because there aren't any. Wouldn't you like to be a Saint your-self?"

"Would I like to be a Saint? Yes, if . . . if Mother didn't mind."

"Why should your mother mind?"

"Because young Saints, sixteen or seventeen, like me, are so different from other young people. They leave their mother and father and walk out into the wilderness. I should not like to do that to Mother."

"Alice, you are wonderful! I see clearly that, were it not for your mother, America would have her Saint at last, over-night. Why are there no Saints in America?"

"Because Americans do not like doing the things which Saints do. They don't like praying all night, fasting, or doing penance for their sins, or especially for other people's sins. Once, in Orleans, I went with Josephine to see a cousin of hers, a Carmelite nun. We could not see her. She was on the other side of the grille and there was a thick black veil through which she could not be seen. Horrid! She sounded quite gay, though."

"Well, then, what do American people do to be religious?"

"Why! you know it. They go to mass on Sundays, and, if they can, other days; they eat fish on Fridays; they give up something in Lent; they say their Rosary; they help the Church and the poor. And so on. They do all that everybody should do."

"But, with the exception of the Rosary, do not Protestants do all you say?"

"Some do."

"Many do. What is the difference, then?"

"Oh! I see what you mean. Holy communion, of course. Protestants do not believe that Christ really is in the Blessed Sacrament. We do."

"Why do girls leave their mothers to join Carmelite convents?"

"For that. To pray day and night before the Blessed Sacrament. It makes them happier than anything. Yet, if I wanted to be a nun, I should not like to be a Carmelite nun. I should not like to join the Sacré-Cœur, either. Teaching must be boresome. I would be a nun in a hospital."

"But do not Protestant nurses do that too, with great devotion to their work?"

"Ah! but I'd receive communion every day. All nuns do."

"So do most Saints who are not in convents. Now you are getting near the definition of a Saint. A Saint is a person whose object in life is union with God. Many non-Catholic philosophers study the lives of Saints with interest and admiration. They generally call them Mystics."

"I know that. Mother says Mrs. Hugh Temple must be a Mystic, because she looks like an angel at mass."

New York, October, 1931.

I went last night to that debate on God at the Mecca Temple. Packed. It would not have been fuller if the posters had promised that, after the debate, the date of the end of the depression would be announced through the amplifier. I was exceedingly interested by what I felt was the atmosphere of the place. I could read on many faces that people had come rather to see the defeat of what they regarded as narrow theistic views than from a rational interest in the question. I am always surprised, in America, to see fundamental theological issues like the existence of God, or delicate questions involving the whole of Christianity, discussed in weeklies destined to be read by totally unprepared persons. The forum which concluded the debate demonstrated that a vast majority of the audience were vague about the import of many of the terms employed by the two so-called antagonists. Confusion being the rule, it is not surprising that scepticism should be the result.

On the other hand, the theistic champion was exceptionally illuminating and he made his Kantism unexpectedly attractive. At once I noticed a delighted surprise in the audience and I foresaw that their vote would be overwhelmingly on the side of the angels; as it was. I am certain that when undergraduates calmly state on a questionnaire that they do not believe in God, they mean a god restricted to the limits which primitive man assigned to his world. Naturally moderns accustomed to the scientific background of infinity in Time and Space rebel against a god too near man not to be like man, and frightening as soon as he ceases to be made friendly by propitiation. There is a tremendous amount of ignorance sitting in judgment over the most sublime idea in a gathering like last night's. The moment this ignorance is dispelled and it is pointed out, for instance, that the most up-to-date scientists believe in God, the attitude is modified. So, the adage which preachers often comment upon rather clumsily is verified: "A smattering of knowledge makes your atheist, deeper knowledge makes the believer."

Harvard, November, 1932.

Bliss Perry took me to the service in the University chapel. President Lowell, who sat almost opposite me, did look like the Pontifex Maximus. Not a priest, a pontiff. The service was eminently a collective affair, as religion was for a long time to Israel. Continual singing or reading made individual prayer— "where God-in-Man is one with Man-in-God"—almost an impossibility. The congregation were worshipping, not trying to reach union with God. People leave, after such a service, with a sense of duty accomplished, or of having strengthened a necessary social structure, but not with the warm tender feeling which devout Catholics—there are not millions—carry away from a low mass and communion. (C. D. sought that in his visits to Grace Church.)

Religion in the United States is not what most French people have been taught by hymn, sermon or devotional book to think it is, viz., the road to mystical union, largely through the Eucharist. This is saintliness, and saintliness is emphatically not an American attitude. Saints never walked in the streets as Americans do, erect, active, full of some human purpose, and trusting to their own energy to carry it out. As a matter of fact, it is never easy to explain to an American what saintliness is. His answers are disarming, both by their honesty and by their incomprehension. He immediately thinks of Gandhi, and Gandhi to him may be an admirable freak but he is a freak. Saints, in his view, are not exceptional, they are abnormal. American religion is simple and vague (which is the reason for its unexpected stability). It combines morals with a love for mankind and an invitation to coöperation or helpfulness which the American is always ready to accept. It is, at bottom, the religion of mankind with a veneer of Hebraism provided by Sunday schools and sustained by the enormous place given in the national life to preaching. The echoes of preaching fill the press.

The God of Americans is infinitely more remote than our God. If He came nearer He would interfere with the life of the individual. But He does not. He is not a jealous God. Americans hardly believe you when you tell them that human love is frequently sacrificed to divine love by predestined people. God is loving in a general and comfortable way and only enjoins what life in America makes almost imperative, viz., kindliness rewarded by the everlasting American achievement, happiness, or lack of suffering with an accompanying sensation that all is well, and that owing to inevitable progress all will improve and a millennium is sure to come.

This notion has evident advantages. It does not keep men from religion, as the burning language of mysticism frequently keeps unprepared Frenchmen from it. But is it religion? I am afraid it is rather moralism which would repel men like Bergson, or Unamuno, or Hindoos, or all fiery souls. My Episcopalian friends admit this. My Presbyterian friends feel it, for their lives are warmer than their doctrines. And have I not heard the astonishing statement that Unitarians have lately adopted a communion service?

New York, March, 1937.

I have just read over again these notes about American life. They all refer to some actual occurrence or observation, and so they are accurate in a way. But can notes made from a sprinkling of occurrences be a faithful picture of life? Can snapshots represent the world? To tell the truth, I wonder how anybody dares venture on the analysis of another race. People exclaim at my knowledge of America, and I know that I can frequently set right other foreign observers less fortunate than I have been. Yet, not a day passes without some impression contradicting the slowly accumulated total of my past impressions.

What I am sure of is that Americans are not wrong when they speak of themselves as the happiest people on earth. The warmth reflected from their contentment has many times saved me from the coldness of life. But their happiness is not the superior kind which the poet, the artist or the religionist enjoys. It is the happiness of innocent youth, the happiness born of unhampered, unperverted vitality. People who speak of it contemptuously are mostly weary sages.

IX

The contrast between my violently active life in America and my life in Paris need not be emphasized. In the United States I am a lecturer and a traveller. In Paris, since I retired from teaching, I am only a writer, constantly seeking that semi-solitude without which there is no pleasure in writing. It is true that visitors, mostly American or English, frequently ring my bell. It is also true that I cherish old French friends who all have rights on my time. Finally I daily receive a heavy mail which I seldom leave unanswered more than two or three days. But I can organize my life and be sure of doing certain things at certain hours, of being able to draw around my existence the protective curtain of uniformity.

The shadow of a cathedral like Notre-Dame adds not a little to that sensation of living in a world apart. Not that Notre-Dame is friendly, as a Romanesque church would be; it is too solemnly beautiful to allow familiarity and I retaliate by remaining sensitive to its obvious defects. But its grandeur casts a spell on the whole shy quarter where my house is hiding. I seldom receive a visitor without noticing that the sublimity of the bold silhouette or the emotion lurking in its ancient sculpture has reacted upon his mind and he is more ready for serious conversation than for indifferent chitchat. The past has a voice: Americans hear it in Santa Fe, New Orleans, Annapolis or Boston. The English are so familiar with its language that they speak it themselves.

I have published an enormous mass of material of which my books do not give an adequate idea, for most of it remains scattered in reviews. But I have written much more which I have never thought of publishing. A large portion of it has been destroyed at periods when I found it no longer corresponded with what I had gradually come to think or feel. But a vast amount still subsists. I knew, before I was ten years old, that my life would be spent in trying to capture elusive thoughts by writing them: the premonition has come true.

The writer's psychology makes him both an extrovert and an introvert. He is indefatigably attentive to what is going on around him, to the drama or the comedy of the world, to its changing appearances or to the reactions of his brother-observers. But, in buoyancy or in depression, he watches the effects of all he sees on his own soul. And oftener than is the case with average people he is conscious of an effort to give those reactions a beginning of expression. Experience soon shows him that nothing is so fugitive as mental registering which one had felt sure could be revived at a moment's notice. It cannot be. Hence the writer's diaries, marginal notes, or indications of rhythmical notation. In time a frightening mass of paper is accumulated, but through this apparent chaos run the main streams of the writer's psychology. No sooner does he endeavour to bring some order into this confusion than, under the diversity, he recognizes habitual moods of his own. In fact it is vital logic that separates those innumerable memoranda according to the sources from which they sprang. Thus are real books born. Like most literary men I have republished articles in book form. Some of those reprints are real books, *La Pensée Catholique en Angleterre,* for instance, or *From a Paris Balcony,* because their various chapters were intended to form a homogeneous total planned before they were written. Others, like *Figures de Moines,* are only volumes. Real books are mostly born in the subconscious way I have mentioned above.

Readers, in America and England, have seemed so particularly interested in my most successful book, *The Art of Thinking,* that I may not seem egotistical in choosing it as an example of that unsuspected creation. During my 'prentice years and long after, I was as attentive, while writing an essay, to the working of my mind as to the essay itself. Many articles were concluded or dismissed abruptly because my own interest in the handling of them was flagging. I did not, in those days, feel my responsibility towards the reader as I was to feel it later. My attitude was experimental: a good article was one which I had taken pleasure in writing, because it had given free play to my mental faculties; a bad article was one which had required more labour than I had counted on expending upon it. Even to-day I cannot help classifying my lectures according to the same rule. Good or bad, it was my custom never to send the article to the printer without recording how it had set my mind working. I accumulated those notes during at least fifteen years without even thinking of organizing them. When I finally did so, during the war, I was surprised to see that the subdivisions of my notes were, pretty clearly defined, the chapters of a book. I was even more surprised to find that those chapters, born of a huge dossier marked "Art of Writing" refused to be so entitled. What they wanted to be called was "An Art of Thinking" that is to say, an art of pleasurably setting the mind in motion.

I still felt so far from imagining that I should add nothing more to those notes that I avoided looking at them again. Expression has the habit of striving towards finality, that is to say of sterilizing the productive vein, and I hated the possibility of having to write "Finis" on what it is obviously impossible to exhaust. So, I went on adding memoranda to the dossier without even taking the risk of limiting their possibilities by inserting them into the likeliest chapter. It was not till 1924 that, having to give a course of lectures at the house of Mrs. Grenville Emmet, in New York, I bethought myself of my still virgin notes and outlined four lectures on The Art of Thinking.

As I prepared those lectures, constantly visualizing, of course, my future audience, I noticed that many of the observations I should have to expound orally referred to technicalities concerning style, or the art of writing, which would be of no interest to laymen. So they had to be left out. But as I began to weed them out I also noticed that most of them could easily be stripped of their technical character because they merely referred to thinking while writing. Leave out useless references to authorship and only an Art of Thinking would subsist.

I gave the four lectures—corresponding to the four parts of what ultimately became my book—not only in New York, but in many other American cities. I rebuilt them scores of times to bring them to the absolute simplicity of design which I said above I always endeavour to attain in preparing a lecture. Gradually they mirrored, as it was inevitable they would do, the living milieu which unwittingly collaborated with me in their composition. Many people have said to me that as they read *The Art of Thinking* they felt as if the writer were seated next to them and was actually speaking to them. I believe that to give that impression is only a form of politeness, as no reader wants a book which obviously is not intended for him. But this attitude is easier for a writer who is also a lecturer.

Some critics have blamed me for not discussing thought-theories expounded by other writers. The platform dissuaded me from adopting such a professorial attitude. Other critics evidently felt inclined to believe that if one writes for the reader one must also be writing for the horrible thing called the Market. But this is a mistake. While publishers and booksellers are keenly aware of that entity—the Market—the public is not. It recognizes what has been honestly intended for its benefit, and labels the rest not as market-stuff, but, in a general way, as something it dislikes, whether it is pretence or smart-aleckism. The reader is seldom taken in by greed in disguise. As for me I had been too long accustomed to a restricted audience to imagine one a hundred times larger. Yet, I felt sure *The Art of Thinking* would be a success. A few friends who read it told me that many people would be disappointed rather than pleased with the simplicity of my style. Perspicuity, they felt sure, was only a recommendation with the highly educated. The average reader would pass unnoticed original remarks because there had been no effort to decorate them with glittering expression. I was not convinced by this pessimism. I thought the public far superior to what many publishers imagine it is. Thousands of

letters drawing attention to the very things supposed to be lost
in the even tenor of my pages have shown me that I was right.

The book was finished in seven months though it was written
under difficulties and I often prayed for a quiet retreat. I outline my material so carefully that, if there is only time for a
hundred words I can sit down and be content with just writing
those hundred words. (The chapters on Religion in *What We
Live By* were written at sea, between Boston and the Azores,
on that fascinating Fabre boat, the *Providence* all muslin cur-
tains and oriental exotics. We had bad weather most of the
way, but the moment we did not rock too violently, I wrote.
The first land we were to see was the island of Flores. I could
not banish from my thoughts the poor nigger of the *Narcissus,*
in Joseph Conrad's novel. His fellow seamen, full of a well-
known superstition, knew that he would die as soon as the
Narcissus came in sight of land and that land was Flores. The
art of the novelist made that passage of his book an obsession.
I was glad when the sombre volcanic island disappeared under
the horizon and my chapters were finished, and we could look
forward to arrival in sunny colourful Lisbon.)

The Art of Thinking was ready for publication when, on
October 25th, 1927, I sailed for my yearly visit to America.

What with writing and lecturing, especially since my course
at Williamstown, I was far from being unknown in America in
1927. On the other hand I had a well-founded certainty that
many groups who had heard me lecture on *The Art of Thinking*
were looking forward to the publication of the book. So, I felt
tolerably sure that I could find a publisher without any of the
usual difficulties. Yet, after many satisfactory experiences in
book-publishing I had recently had a disappointing one. Twenty-
two American publishers refused my *The Brontë Sisters* which
in its French garb had had a first-rate press both in London and
New York, which Andrew Lang praises warmly in his *History
of English Literature,* and which had been admirably translated

into English by Louise Morgan Sill. Most publishers, it is true, would not even look at the manuscript. I still remember my interview, in Knopf's office, with a dear little girl, very serious and full of her responsibilities. She listened to me with the patience and kindness of a father confessor, then, suddenly, made up her little mind and said she was afraid Mrs. Knopf would not consider that book. I could not help laughing and the little girl wondered should she be offended.

Shortly after, being in London, I offered the book to the Constables who had published my *Paul Bourget*. Here the manuscript was examined, but only by the wet thumb of a stuttering partner. The examination—interrupted by telephoning, tobacco-plugging, and pipe-lighting—lasted about ten minutes, after which, the last page having been turned by the wet thumb, an unfavourable decision came. The next morning my friend, Miss Gray, took the MS. to Jonathan Cape who, by noon, accepted it. Whereupon one of the twenty-two New Yorkers who had refused the book cabled his eager acceptance of it. It has been a continuous success ever since. Such experiences leave one in grave doubts about publishing infallibility, and I record them to reassure young authors whom failure might drive to unwholesome diffidence.

The Art of Thinking, too, was turned down first by the Harpers because "there was no market for such a book." Harcourt Brace refused it, or, rather did not take it, next, but under conditions which the publishers never could elucidate to their satisfaction. In fact the MS. was returned without any explanations to my Harper friends. Hearing of this bad beginning my dear Mrs. Douglas Robinson took the MS. herself to Scribner's where she had a great pull. However, there, too, the book was rejected, but the junior partner who reluctantly gave the manuscript back to me said he was not sure "they were not making a big, big, mistake." My time getting short I telephoned two young publishers I slightly knew offering to sell the rights to them for three thousand dollars. Luckily they did not possess three thousand dollars. Five or six days before sailing, remembering that, while I was writing the book, Mr. Latham, of Macmillan had expressed interest in its publication, I called him up and he was most cordial. But he was leaving town and wished me to go down to him at once. Forgetting that you can walk down Fifth Avenue much faster than you can drive I took a taxi hoping to be able to hand in my MS. to Mr. Latham before he left. But he was gone when I arrived and I was received by a tall languid young man, evidently of some importance at the office. This young man beckoned me to a chair next to the revolving doors and when I hinted my preference for an office, if he had one, he frowned with displeasure but led the way to an office a little lower, I think, than the hall. I asked the young gentleman if he happened to know who I was. No, he was sorry, he did not. I had, a few days before, prepared two brief statements one concerning what I thought was my literary position in America, the other summing up my book. The young gentleman glanced at both, looking every now and then at my collar and probably coupling clericalness with foreignness in an unpromising association. Within forty-eight hours my book was back with a note saying that "although not devoid of merit, it did not seem to warrant an offer."

The day before I sailed, acting on the advice of Mr. Mitchell Kennerley, I took my two statements and my MS. to Messrs. Simon and Schuster. Both were out and I was received by Mr. Clifton Fadiman to whom I handed my statements. As he read the first Mr. Fadiman asked me, in excellent French, if I was not the author of that book on the Brontës which he liked. After reading the summary of *The Art of Thinking*, he said: "Why! this looks like a prize-book. I am sure we shall take this book."

This was a few days before Christmas and I was back in Paris by the New Year. In March, while visiting my friends, the Clews, on the Riviera, I received a note from Mr. Fadiman hinting that the office of Simon and Schuster were divided on the subject of my book. Much later I heard that Mr. Schuster did not then believe there was much chance for an *Art of Thinking* and, in spite of Mr. Fadiman's expostulations, had, week after week, put off examination of my MS. In the Spring, the Literary Supplement of the *New York Herald Tribune* published a seven-column review of my Brontë book admirably written by G. B. Stern. Mr. Fadiman reproachfully took this review to Mr. Schuster who, at once, read my manuscript and, at once, liked it as he can like a book, or anything, with the enthusiasm of his warm nature. A few weeks later Mr. Richard Simon came over to Paris and we discussed the usual details concerning publication. Mr. Simon told me that, by that time, his whole office, down to the humblest clerk, were already sure that the book would be an extraordinary success and were feverishly looking forward to its publication. I remembered that the London typist who had copied it from my longhand MS. showed the same eager interest in its future.

The Art of Thinking came out in New York on October 28th, 1928. I was on the ocean, and the book had been out four days when I landed. It was no immediate success and the critics were slower than usual in adverting to it. The first review published was the work of a serious critic in St. Louis who signed himself Fra Robertus. It was extremely favourable and I was glad to infer from certain sure signs that the critic had read the book carefully all through. No sooner was this review published than the sales increased.

A few days later I called at the friendly office of the *Saturday Review*. It was nearly five o'clock and only one girl was there to receive me. She said at once that she could show me, already set up, an important review of *The Art of Thinking* which was to come out in their next issue.

"Do you know who wrote it?"

"Oh! yes, it is signed. Professor Dewey wrote it."

I felt crestfallen. There was no man in America whose judgment I could respect so much as I did Professor Dewey's. But I had done all I could to make *The Art of Thinking* as unprofessional as such a book could be made and I was afraid that a professorial review must be decidedly professional. The young lady reassured me.

"The review is not what you think," she said as she took it out of a drawer.

In fact this review by Professor Dewey was the most simply human impression of a man who had entered at once into the spirit of the book, had found pleasure apparently in every page, and wanted everybody to share his enjoyment of it. Yet, one felt that these three or four hundred smiling words were charged with the weight belonging to any statement from such a writer. I had to go twice over the review to make sure that there was nothing to be read between the lines of an apparently complete endorsement.

A few days before, giving a short course at the University of Illinois, I had received a telegram from my publishers stating that "quickly mounting sales would make my presence in America longer than I had planned to make it." The book had suddenly shown the signs of life which publishers express in picturesque language. But Professor Dewey's opinion was invaluable, for it impressed critics as much as readers, and I soon found his review quoted in the most unexpected quarters. Only a few diehards were brave enough to find fault with my book for not being dull or for being different from *The Art of Thought* of Professor Graham Wallas.

I went back to my rue Chanoinesse and its apparent tranquillity, but constant cables from Simon and Schuster as well as innumerable clippings made the year which followed the most eventful in my literary life.

I never could have obtained the mass of information I have gradually accumulated about America if *The Art of Thinking* had not been circulated among such a variety of readers. Even now, almost ten years after its first publication, I still hear from people, young or old, who have only just discovered it or who, not unwisely, promised themselves to read it when it would no longer be a popular success. It is irritating at times to be tied to one book as I am to *The Art of Thinking*; it is also unfair to some other books of mine; but that is the ransom one has to pay for success in its most obvious aspects.

Hundreds of the letters I received from every part of the United States were entirely sincere and raised for me the veil covering many interior lives unsuspected of all. The impression which that vast correspondence has left is that conceited Europe knows nothing of America and conceited New York knows but little of the vague West it complacently looks down upon. Publishers, editors or theatre managers who base their knowledge of America on the success of inferior productions which they imagine the public likes may be wide of the mark: people, no doubt, can be deceived about beauty, as they can about equity, but they crave beauty as honestly as they crave justice and it is no fault of theirs if they are given the wrong education.

I shall never be able to write even an article or to give a lecture without a consciousness that in my audience must be several of those people whose admixture of simplicity and criticalness is the triumph of the real culture I admired in their letters. The thought makes one extremely modest. Once, lecturing in Albuquerque and noticing how much sensitiveness I felt in an audience consisting largely of delicate people, I was suddenly struck by the remembrance that many of the letters I received were dated from sanitaria. Nuns wrote me, too, from their convents, as well as scores of young people in colleges. Had it not been for that correspondence I should never have suspected, either, how much idealism can be latent in the not very articulate business-man of America. Like all Americans he works for success but, when success having come he notices that it is not so satisfying as he had imagined, he evolves a philosophy. Of this, people who despise his philanthropy, because they have unconsciously been jealous of his success, can have no suspicion. On the whole, readers of *The Art of Thinking* whose impressions have come to me have confirmed my belief that in no

country, however intellectual, has an idea such a chance of becoming an ideal as it has in the United States.

It is impossible for an author to realize that thousands of
people feel they can rely upon him for advice, or even—a formidable thought—for example, without simultaneously becoming conscious of his responsibility. The conclusion that he ought
to be ready at all times to give of his best to people who write
to him as if he himself had written not merely for them but *to*
them is forced upon his mind. I have no doubt that all successful literary men and women in America must have had experiences of this kind, even those whose medium is fiction or poetry.
They complain, sometimes, that they have no influence over the
national life, that their countrymen do not mind imagining them
all pent up in Greenwich Village, and that their work seems
as foreign to the people who, however, buy it, as if it were a
mathematical theory of the Cosmos. They point out the contrast
with France where a Dumas *fils*, after Balzac, or an Anatole
France, after Dumas, can be the guides of the national conscience, and where nine out of ten of the political leaders have
written books. But they do not know that even the greatest
French writers, in spite of that apparent influence, have hardly
any contact with individual readers and that when they do receive letters these come mostly from solicitors or from *détra-
quées* women. Purely literary influence mostly increases the
literary vanity; the honest appeal of the American reader—
even the frequent correspondent who confides to you that he
would like to write—reacts on one's conscience and ultimately
on one's productivity.

For as it induces humility and develops a sense of responsibility it also increases tenfold the joy which a writer finds in
his work, while his facility is proportionately strengthened.
Such a gain means infinitely more than petty satisfactions and
ought to be requited. Success which is not turned into a greater
capacity for service is as despicable as selfish wealth. The
haughty or crusty or cynical writer may adopt the cant of the

day about the rights of the little fellow, but in truth he is feeling a contempt for that same little fellow whom he regards as intellectually inferior, and secretly cherishes aristocratic aloofness.

Such an attitude, of course, is short-sighted as selfishness invariably is. Anybody who has worked wholeheartedly for a cause must have noticed that—to quote the French moralist, Joubert, once more—there is invariably more light in a soul as kindness makes it warmer. It is so especially in America. Give Americans the impression that you are willing to be one of them, and anxious to do your bit for the community, if the least distinction is attached to your way of doing it you will be encouraged, helped and feasted with all the alacrity belonging to a youthful country.

My own native France early taught me the lesson that clarity of thought is the condition of all true thinking; England, later on, showed me that fearlessness in clear thinking can be consistent with a religious faith more precious to one than anything purely intellectual; but America has spread over the last phase of my life the warm glow which makes one indifferent to the passage of years. I have often wondered what my life would have been without my introduction to that new world. I never do so without blessing the Providence which, in 1919, sent me to the United States on what I thought was the most uncongenial errand ever forced upon me.

Under this train of thought—inevitable in the concluding chapter of such a book as the present one—runs another of a more general character, for it is in no wise inherent in a literary career, even if a literary career can hardly fail to produce it. All men are born with a sense of the beautiful in human actions—it is a cruel blasphemy to speak of common children— and many of us unmistakably hear the call to the higher level, with a longing really to BE what the world only wishes to appear. Some—more numerous than is generally imagined— are even conscious of a superior vocation, of that attraction towards religion, art, charity, or the solution of the nobler riddles which requires a soul-absorbing courage. With many this spiritual dawn is enough, they are satisfied with the consciousness of fine possibilities and their day never really begins. Others do begin, but soon turn away from their furrow. Life is full of wasted careers. Even history, although dealing with men and women who have accomplished something, is a record of abortive ambitions. Wishes have not grown up to be real volitions, or success, coming too early, has been mistaken for fulfilment. In every case it appears that the victim of the failure has not been enough of what the Bible calls a Man of Desire, a *Vir Desiderii*, he has only wished to want. Some men who do persevere and may show indomitable courage to the end expend their superb reserves fruitlessly because they have been exaggeratedly ambitious and have not rightly estimated their possibilities. A sense of proportion, or the modesty born of it, is rare. Yet, as Musset says in his rhyme, a man should drink out of his own glass, however small the glass may be. If he does so, he will be rewarded by confidence—entirely unlike Romantic truculence—and every particle of his labour will tell. If he does not he will exhaust himself in acting a part in which he himself never does really believe.

Almost synonymous with the recommendation to be only oneself is the life-saving admonition to be one's best self. But there is a categorical imperative in the words: DO YOUR BEST. They may sound at first as if they were the tired advice of idealism to disheartening passivity. But they are no such thing. Indeed, what is echoed in them is the voice of God Himself, everlastingly heard in our conscience. Hence their remarkable capacity for being either an imperious order or an encouragement.

They amount to this: "Do what you know you have been created to do the best and the most happily." We never make a mistake about the pleasure attending the exercise of the noblest in us. We all remember occasions when the advice we gave either to ourselves or to a friend answered to the Kantian injunction to make our individual actions the embodiment of a general rule. We know that those instances have left the memory of something both easy and wonderful. We are surprised that gregarious imitativeness or wandering attention should often cause us to forego such a simple way of enjoying the fulness of our possibilities. For even when we lapse to the level of ordinariness we are not deceived about the falling-off and, not infrequently, we show our consciousness of it by a shrug or by a cynical smile. Indeed our very existence seems to be conditioned by obedience to the most human of divine commands.

So, the lesson of a life worth while can be summed up in the three guiding principles: Know yourself—Be yourself—Be your best self. My latest books, especially *What We Live By,* allude to these on almost every page. Is it necessary to admit that my life has been far from exemplifying them? How often I must have caused surprise and disappointment to readers of works which they know, nevertheless, were written honestly! All that a moralist can do is to confess his weaknesses, humbly rejoicing that they did not succeed in obscuring his inner light.

All of us are given to the almost habitual celebration of brief interior services the liturgy for which is provided by bits we may remember from our reading of the Scriptures or of the noblest poetry. Several times a day since boyhood I have been visited by such rhythms attuned to my needs of the moment. The two talismanic Latin hymns to the Holy Ghost, as well as stray verses from the Penitential Psalms which I knew by heart before I was ten, invariably sing themselves in my spiritual chantry. Sometimes too these verses from the epitaph which the French writer, Veuillot, produced out of the depths of his faith and humility:

> "*Je fus pécheur et sur la route
> J'ai chancelé souvent;*

Mais, grâce à Dieu, vainqueur du doute,
Je suis mort ferme et pénitent."

"I sinned, and often on the road
I faltered, strayed aside,
But thanks to God my faith abode,
And penitent I died."

INDEX OF NAMES

395

A NOTE ABOUT THE AUTHOR

ABBÉ ERNEST DIMNET *was born at Trélon in northern France on July 9, 1866. He took a degree in English at Paris after which he began teaching English literature at Lille. From 1902 to 1923, he taught English literature at the Collège Stanislas in Paris, and paid his first visit to the United States in 1908 as the guest of the late George Harvey. His first book to appear in America was* The Brontë Sisters *which was followed by* The Art of Thinking, What We Live By, *and* My Old World, *the first volume of his autobiography which he completes in* My New World. *Abbé Dimnet lives in Paris, in a seventeenth century house near Nôtre Dame, and now gives most of his time to writing, though he still makes an annual pilgrimage to the United States, his fountain of youth.*